JEWISH STUDIES

教育部人文社会科学重点研究基地

山东大学犹太教与跨宗教研究中心

U0885715

第18辑

犹太研究

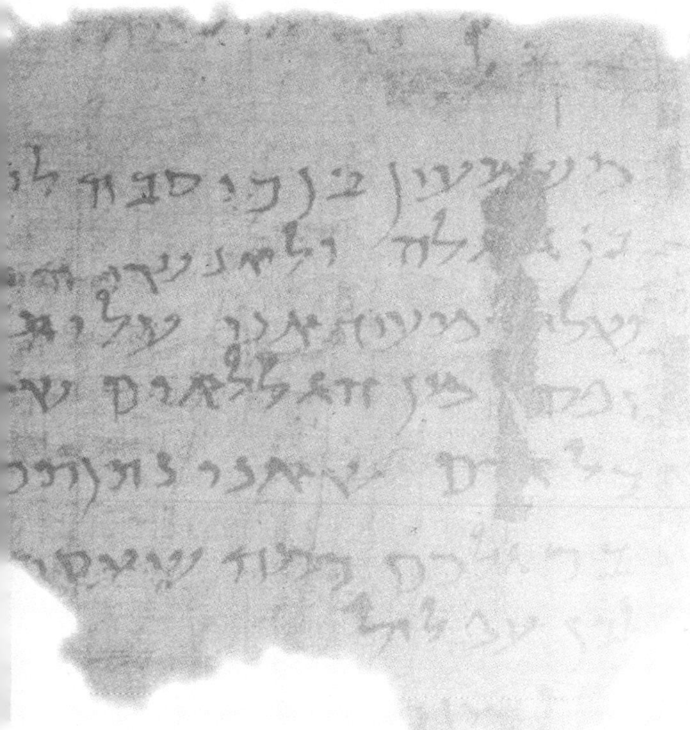

主编
傅有德
副主编
陈家富
董修元

山东大学出版社

图书在版编目(CIP)数据

犹太研究.第18辑/傅有德主编.—济南:山东大学出版社,2021.11
ISBN 978-7-5607-6963-9

Ⅰ.①犹… Ⅱ.①傅… Ⅲ.①犹太教—宗教哲学—研究②犹太人—研究 Ⅳ.①B985②K18

中国版本图书馆CIP数据核字(2021)第240473号

责任编辑 李 璐
封面设计 牛 钧 王秋忆

出版发行 山东大学出版社
社 址 山东省济南市山大南路20号
邮政编码 250100
发行热线 (0531)88363008
经 销 新华书店
印 刷 济南华林彩印有限公司
规 格 787毫米×1092毫米 1/16
16.25印张 308千字
版 次 2021年11月第1版
印 次 2021年11月第1次印刷
定 价 49.00元

版权所有 侵权必究

《犹太研究》编委会

主　编　傅有德（山东大学）

副主编　陈家富（山东大学）　董修元（山东大学）

编　委　（按姓氏拼音顺序排列）

傅晓微（四川外国语大学）　李炽昌（山东大学）

刘洪一（深圳大学）　刘平（复旦大学）

潘光（上海社会科学院）　王志军（黑龙江大学）

谢品然（中原大学）　徐新（南京大学）

游斌（中央民族大学）　张倩红（郑州大学）

赵敦华（北京大学）　钟志清（中国社会科学院）

卓新平（中国社会科学院）

Marc Brettler (Brandeis University)

Jay Harris (Harvard University)

Steven Katz (Boston University)

Josef Stern (Chicago University)

Zhang Ping (Tel Aviv University)

Jewish Studies Editorial Board

Chief Editor: FU Youde (Shandong University)

Associate Chief Editors: Keith CHAN ka-fu (Shandong University)
DONG Xiuyuan (Shandong University)

Board Members:

FU Xiaowei (Sichuan International Studies University)
Archie Lee (Shandong University)
LIU Hongyi (Shenzhen University)
LIU Ping (Fudan University)
PAN Guang (Shanghai Academy of Social Sciences)
WANG Zhijun (Heilongjiang University)
Philip P. Chia (Chung Yuan Christian University)
XU Xin (Nanjing University)
YOU Bin (Minzu University of China)
ZHANG Qianhong (Zhengzhou University)
ZHAO Dunhua (Peking University)
ZHONG Zhiqing (Chinese Academy of Social Sciences)
ZHUO Xinping (Chinese Academy of Social Sciences)
Marc Brettler (Brandeis University)
Jay Harris (Harvard University)
Steven Katz (Boston University)
Josef Stern (Chicago University)
ZHANG Ping (Tel Aviv University)

目录

A.文学、历史与读者

B.思想、历史与社会

A

文学、历史与读者

文学、历史与读者:希伯来《圣经》研究的进路(前言)

黄薇　李炽昌*

与《旧约》或《塔纳赫》这样的术语相比,希伯来《圣经》这一术语更受现代圣经学者的青睐。原因在于,比起前两者所带有的基督教与犹太教色彩,后者以该文本主要使用的古代语言来界定概念,更加符合现代学术追求的中立态度。而对希伯来《圣经》文献性质的定义,在很大程度上与解读该文本的诠释方法密不可分。采用神学的诠释方法,该文献就可以被定义为基督教经典或犹太教经典;采用文学批评的方法,该文献就是一部古代文学作品;采用历史批判的方法,该文献就是史料。不过,在现代圣经学者眼中,这三种对于希伯来《圣经》文献性质的定义并不是相互排斥的,因此,也没有任何一种诠释方法是绝对的。应当说,任何一种诠释方法实际上都是处境化的,都取决于读者对文献性质的接受,以及他们的社会文化定位。

本辑共收录研究文章 14 篇,以希伯来《圣经》文本研究为主。当中既包括较为宏观的思想观念研究,也有细致的文本分析。总结来看,文章多采用历史的视角,它们关注一些共同的核心议题,就是希伯来《圣经》中大多数书卷所面对的生存现实:失去应许之地的危机、圣殿被毁、北国以色列(公元前 722 年)与南国犹大(公元前 597 年)的最终陷落所导致的著名的“巴比伦之囚”(公元前 586 年)。毫无疑问,在众多《圣经》书卷中都可以看到,作者为以色列和犹大的失败报以哀叹,用泪水表达他们的绝望。《耶利米书》和《哀歌》中所表达的悲伤之情便是两个最经典的例子。被掳他国失去故土的经历促使上帝的子民进一步反思罪恶、惩罚和苦难等主题,这既是希伯来《圣经》的主要特征,也是后来犹太教和基督教主要的思考及关注重点,后代读者在历史长河中仍然还会不断遭受苦难,并且通过反思他们的苦难经验,在最为沮丧的情况下找到前进之勇气与力量。然而,确信会得到宽恕和接纳、获得救赎的观念也占据了中心舞台,但除了信仰及观念上的支持外,历史上实际的回归、复兴、重建构成了硬币的另一面。《圣经》中更多

* 黄薇,上海大学文学院历史系讲师;李炽昌,山东大学犹太教与跨宗教研究中心教授。

的篇幅和段落明确阐述了这些有关复兴和重建的主题。

与回归和重建主题密切相关的，是对于自我身份的追求，这既包括自我与他人的关系，也包括本族神与其他神的关系。例如，田海华的文章便探讨了《摩西五经》中上帝与诸神的问题，也就是耶和华上帝与其他神的关系问题；亨德尔与黄薇的文章都探讨了自我与他者的议题，考察古代以色列与其他群体的关系，既有观念上的也有历史上的；姜振帅的文章通过分析回归复兴的历史背景，指出《圣经》后期编者对早期西奈山传统的再利用。

所有解读《圣经》的文章，无论是关注解读某些个别章节，还是整体上解读《圣经》正典，几乎都需要或明确或隐含地采用某种阅读与诠释方法。希望读者能够在本辑文章中看到当代释经方法的应用。在本-兹维的文章中我们将会关注诠释过程中的读者。布伦纳-伊丹的文章从现代读者视角出发，对《路得记》做出与传统理解完全不同的新诠释。而亨德尔采用了一种比较人类学的方法，对照解读《圣经》和中国神话经典《山海经》。黄薇与田海华的文章都采用了学术界在过去一个世纪最为常见的历史批判方法，并从文化记忆的角度分别处理了先祖材料和五经传统。在姜振帅的文章中，可以看到传统-历史方法的运用，讨论的是《圣经》中的西奈山与锡安山两个圣山传统之间的内在关系。孙玥结合古代西亚的文献背景，针对《以西结书》中对于推罗王的描述进行再诠释。就诠释史而言，哲学的方法同样占据了很重要的地位，特别是犹太哲学家迈蒙尼德，张缨的文章主要处理的便是迈蒙尼德所代表的圣经传统。与之类似，曹坚的文章采用了历史的视角，对中世纪的犹太历史文献进行归纳整理，以此来描述中世纪犹太人对于历史的认知。

埃胡德·本-兹维的文章以《希伯来〈圣经〉的一些思维习惯：对不同历史形态的犹太教之影响》为题，展开对希伯来《圣经》思维习惯的讨论。他指出，无论是犹太教还是基督教的读者，在年复一年阅读经文的过程中，由于社会地位、文化背景以及知识视野上的差异，他们阅读经文的方式也会千差万别。近十年来的学术研究特别关注在跨越时间和空间维度下《圣经》文本的接受史。当然，就希伯来《圣经》而言，历史上不同形式的犹太教都将此文本作为最根本的正典文本。尽管无法在一篇文章中穷尽所有的诠释方法并展开分析，不过，本-兹维关注的是希伯来《圣经》所要传达的思维习惯，或者说，是对后世犹太教的形成发挥重要作用的思想前身。

希伯来《圣经》中的大多数书卷都是对过去的塑造，读者通过阅读进而共享书卷中对于过去的记忆。当然，这些记忆中的过去并不是完整及全面的，记忆会因读者的处境不同而关注某些特定时期、特殊事件及重要人物。本-兹维的文章首先指明，第一种思维习惯就是对于历史溯源之想象和记忆。对犹太人而言，最

重要的时间、人物和事件就是走出埃及事件和后续在旷野漂泊不定的生活回忆，这当中最具核心意义的事件是以色列在西奈山获得《妥拉》传统，该事件最终以在旷野建造会幕达到叙事高潮，会幕可以被看作耶路撒冷圣殿的模型。在这个记忆中，还有一个最重要的主题就是耶和华的应许。旷野生活中的以色列总会行差踏错，违背耶和华的诫命，因而常常受到耶和华的惩罚，导致灾难降临。但是，耶和华的应许却是永恒的，在惩罚以后耶和华最终会赦免以色列。希伯来《圣经》所塑造的过去，就是这样以螺旋式的形态循环发展的。并且，以色列在旷野中背叛耶和华的命令，以及耶和华的宽恕，最终产生了对于未来的一种想象，即以色列不会再背叛耶和华的话语、违背耶和华的教导。旷野时代的生活也将耶和华塑造成以色列的王，其承载着一般王权观念的特征，包括是位军事将才，是立法者、礼仪中心的建立者，对其臣民恩威并施。最重要的是，这为希伯来《圣经》的读者建立起一个最根本的观念:以色列的王不是摩西，甚至不是人类，而是耶和华。这成为希伯来《圣经》对于以色列历史的元叙事，是历史上每一个当下时刻的犹太群体跨越时空对于过往的根本记忆。

当犹太群体面对灾难的时候，通过回忆(或重现)过去曾经发生过的灾难来理解分析当下的情境是本-兹维文章所探讨的第二种思维习惯。每年的逾越节晚宴是必不可少的对于灾难事件的纪念。耶路撒冷圣殿遭到毁坏，是在希伯来《圣经》中起到重要作用的灾难事件。在对于灾难的记忆中，古代以色列要为自己所遭受的灾难负责，他们违背耶和华的教导，因此耶和华要将灾难降到他们头上。可以说，希伯来《圣经》具备很强的教化意义，一方面要求其读者能够遵循上帝的教导，另一方面也警告他们违背上帝旨意的后果很悲惨。因此，摩西作为传达耶和华教导的以色列民众的中介，是一位必不可少的宗师，以色列民众需要摩西式的继任者继续作他们的宗师，这就是犹太教传统的“拉比”，他们成为以色列律法一代又一代的守护者。耶和华的教导和律法正是希伯来《圣经》的核心文本——《妥拉》，是以色列群体的记忆核心。第三种思维习惯是《妥拉》的多义性和开放性，这种思维习惯并不追求单一的、明确的声音，或者形式上的逻辑一致性，而是将《妥拉》的智慧理解为各种互补声音的整合。另一方面，这种思维习惯围绕《妥拉》的核心地位展开，因而促使社会和文化资源集中到对《妥拉》文本的抄写、阅读、朗诵及解释上。相较于被毁的圣殿，经文反而是超越时空的智慧。因为它们不仅与所描绘的世界有关，而且与所有时代都有关，即《诗篇》第 78 章第 6 节所言的“将要生的后代子孙”。这样的思维习惯要求读者严格遵守《妥拉》(律法/教训)，而这正是对耶和华教导的遵守，并且，遵守《妥拉》并非出于获取个人利益的考量，而要将其作为神圣的诫命。最后一种思维习惯是对希望的坚守。事实上，这种思维习惯与前面提到的对于灾难的记忆是相辅相成的。对过去所遭受灾难的记忆与对未来的希望分不开。记得在埃及受到奴役,才会记得从为奴之家被释放的经验,才会重视《妥拉》的意义;记得耶路撒冷圣殿被毁,遭到流放,才会记得终有一天将会回归,并将其看作第二次走出埃及。先知文学记得以色列犯罪,耶和华因此才会以流放的形式来惩罚以色列。所有这些对过往苦难的记忆也都伴随着对乌托邦式未来的希望。耶和华的应许是永恒不变的,是终将实现的。

布伦纳-伊丹的文章《作为外来劳工的路得与族外婚政治》从当代读者视角,提出了与《路得记》传统解读完全不同的新颖诠释。当前全球普遍存在从次发达地区向较发达地区输入劳工的现象,外来劳工出于各种原因选择跨出国境、承担风险,往往从事处于社会底层的低报酬工作,以改善他们的生活。当代犹太人占多数的以色列社会,在文化上是高度封闭的,外来劳工融入当地社会,面临宗教、语言等一系列文化因素带来的障碍。正是受到以色列现实社会处境的启发,布伦纳-伊丹重新解读了《路得记》,因为与现代以色列社会中的单亲女性外来劳工类似,路得是从其他语言文化区(摩押)来到古代以色列社会的一位女性。在《路得记》中,路得在丈夫死后向她的婆婆拿俄米表示效忠,她到田间辛勤劳动,听从拿俄米关于投靠波阿斯的计划。因为她们都明白,外来女性若想要融入当地社会,只能通过婚姻并生养子嗣来实现。当波阿斯表明将迎娶路得的时候,经文将路得与另外三位族长故事中的外邦女子相提并论,即拉结、利亚和他玛,这意味着路得最终融入"以色列家"。然而,布伦纳-伊丹进一步指出,拉结、利亚和他玛三人都称不上楷模,拉结与利亚因嫉妒争吵斗争,导致她们的儿子也是如此,至于他玛,最后犹大也并未与之结婚。这说明外邦女子即便积极接受当地文化,恐怕仍然很难被完全接受。并且,路得在故事最后一个叙事场景中,即在给儿子取名的场景中彻底消失(《路得记》4:14—17)。因此,路得的故事是一个来自社会底层、没有财产的外邦女子的故事,与其说路得最终融入了当地社会,不如说当地社会吞并了路得。她的困境,与今天以色列和其他地方的外来女工的困境是可以类比的。将这两个案例相互对照,对其进行跨文本阅读,能够帮助我们增加对两者的理解。

罗纳德·亨德尔的文章《〈圣经〉与〈山海经〉中的巨人族:一种比较人类学研究》尝试借用巴西人类学家爱德华多·维未洛斯·德·卡斯特罗(Eduardo Viveiros de Castro)的"视角人类学"(perspectival anthropology),对自我与他者间的关系及表现进行一种跨文化比较。通过对照,能够更充分地认识每种文化的一些独有特征,及其共有的实践活动。亨德尔相信,所有视角,无论古今,都可能开启一场相互尊重且具有启发和批评意义的对话。

亨德尔的研究关注了两个文本对巨人族的记载:一个是希伯来《圣经》,另一

个是中国古代典籍，于公元前 4—前 1 世纪写成的《山海经》。《山海经》描述了一个神秘的想象世界中的山川景观，包括历述东南西北中群山风貌的《山经》和罗列四海方国的《海经》，同时也是一部记录旅行见闻的寓言集，展现出光怪陆离的异人怪物。那些想象中的远方世界是非我族类的蛮族之地，这一图景正是对中心文明世界与边缘野蛮世界的区隔。在对这些异域他者的想象中，北方和南方居住着若干巨人族，比如博父国、大人国。文中描写居住在那些国度的人都很高大，“其为人大”（《海外北经》《海外东经》）；在东海之外的大荒之中，“有大人之国，有大人之市”（《大荒东经》）；东北海之外，也有“大人之国”（《大荒北经》）；“南方有赣巨人”（《海内经》）。在《山海经》的这些记录中，部分巨人族具有一些文明行为，例如某些巨人族以黍为食物，某些巨人族制造船只等。应当说，《山海经》中的巨人族对人类世界是不具备威胁性的，是勤劳的，但同时也是滑稽可笑的。若仔细阅读南方赣巨人的记载，“南方有赣巨人，人面长臂，黑身有毛，反踵，见人笑亦笑，唇蔽其面，因即逃也”（《海内经》），亨德尔指出，这当中具有明确的视角特征。在中心文明世界的视角中，赣巨人好像猿猴，他们见人笑也跟着笑，长唇能够遮住面部，这突出了巨人族滑稽可笑的一面。然而，人们见到他们也想要逃走，这又说明文明人惧怕巨人族。反过来，在巨人眼中，文明人也是可笑的。在这种镜像视角中，双方都将对方看作异域怪物。《山海经》的这种反思性显示出一种本土人类学，尽管自我与他者在身体、地域及文化程度上有所不同，但双方存在认知与情感上的相似性。而这种对比又似乎暗示文本写作背后所具有的帝国结构，文明人与异族人和平共存在一个有序的、以中心—边缘为文化结构的等级空间中。东周末期的战国时代，社会动荡，中原各诸侯国扩张兼并，一些其他民族受到中原文化的影响，各诸侯国不断面临对异质多样文化的融合，这也成为这个时代的文化逻辑。巨人族作为文化融合的混血儿，并非需要被彻底消灭来为文明让路，他们可以与文明人合法共存，居住在神话空间，位于“天下”的边缘之地，从而封闭在更大的秩序中。《山海经》因此成为一部提供有关遥远异域之地文化信息的作品。

再看希伯来《圣经》的记载，在以色列人到来之前，巨人族就生活在迦南地。以色列人第一次遇到巨人族发生在摩西进入迦南之前，摩西打发探子窥探迦南地，探子回来禀报摩西，称住在那里的人强壮、身量高大，并称他们是亚衲族人，是伟人的后裔，“他们看我们如同蚱蜢一样”（《民数记》13:27—28、30—33）。此处同样存在一个视角的观察，以色列人通过巨人族的眼睛反观自身。只不过与《山海经》不同的是，这里的巨人族不是滑稽可笑的，而是具有威胁性的。在以色列人的想象中，希伯伦的巨人可以轻易打败他们。实际上，希伯来《圣经》使用了若干名称来指称迦南的巨人，例如此处的“伟人”（נְפִילִים）、“亚衲族人”（בְּנֵי עֲנָק），此外还有“利乏音人”(רְפָאִים)、“亚摩利人”(אֱמֹרִי)等。根据《创世记》所记,在大洪水以前,“伟人”是神的儿子们和人的女子们所生的后代,都是上古英武有名的人(《创世记》6:4)。这种半神半人的形象可能与美索不达米亚神话中英武有名的国王吉尔伽美什很相似,根据赫梯语版本,吉尔伽美什有 5 米高。

之后,摩西强调耶和华会灭绝这些巨人,将亚衲族人制伏在以色列人面前(《申命记》9:1—3)。《阿摩司书》也描绘了一段类似的图景,耶和华将除灭那些高大如香柏树一样的亚摩利人(《阿摩司书》2:9—10)。这些文本力图说明以色列将征服迦南,获得应许之地,实现出埃及的救赎和耶和华对以色列人祖先的应许。然而,真正击败亚衲族人的是摩西的继承者约书亚所带领的军队,战争结束后,还有一些幸存下来的亚衲族人留在迦萨、迦特和亚实突(《约书亚记》11:21—22),他们就成为后来大卫王击败的非利士人。《撒母耳记下》第 21 章第 15—22 节记载大卫的军兵杀死了四个伟人的儿子,其中一个是迦特人歌利亚。不过,在《撒母耳记上》第 17 章的记载中,是大卫杀死了非利士人的武士迦特人歌利亚,并且经文描写歌利亚身高六肘零一虎口,即 3 米左右。在大卫的视角中,歌利亚虽然高大,却是未受割礼的野蛮之徒,大卫将歌利亚比作狮子和熊(《撒母耳记上》17:43)。约书亚击败亚衲族人后,大卫为以色列杀死了最后一位巨人歌利亚,实现了耶和华必灭绝迦南的巨人的说法,从此开启了大卫王朝。在以色列人的自我建构中,巨人族属于过去的时代,他们的命运就是被击败。

与《山海经》对巨人族的记载对照来看,华夏民族占据世界的中心,巨人族则居住在遥远的边缘地区。这种中心与边缘的空间关系是由帝国秩序决定的,其中的文化逻辑将巨人族定义为滑稽可笑的异邦民众,他们在空间框架中位于边缘。然而,在希伯来《圣经》中,巨人族原本就居住在世界中心,以色列人反而是作为边缘民族来到历史舞台上的。在希伯来《圣经》的文化逻辑中,以色列的兴起才是历史转折点,巨人族只在以色列到来之前短暂地居住于世界中心,他们注定是要被灭绝的,这样巨人族在时间框架中位于边缘。

另外,中国和以色列还拥有一个共同特征,即在两者的文化遗产中,都存在巨石遗迹,其代表对于巨人族留存在地貌上的一种记忆。在中国东北地区,特别是在辽东半岛发现了许多大约公元前 2 千纪的巨大石棚墓葬。朝鲜半岛也有许多巨大石棚遗迹。在以色列北部及约旦河西岸,也保留下来一批大约源自公元前 3 千纪,即青铜时代早期的巨石遗迹。对于铁器时代的人而言,这些巨石遗迹极有可能被认为是古代巨人留下的。

通过这样的对照,每一种文化都具有对陌生世界的某种类型的想象。在这些想象背后,是政治和宗教的观念在起作用,中国是天命观,以色列是被拣选的立约的人民。两者对于巨人族的不同想象是各自文化自我构建的方式。视角人类学也能够阐明现代思想。现代人往往对巨人族的存在抱有怀疑,这正是韦伯所谓理性主义进程对于"世界的祛魅"。而这一进程在古代中国和古代以色列都曾有过先例。对于《山海经》所记载的异邦怪物,汉代史家司马迁在《史记》中表示"余不敢言"。这表明,史家追求的是一个没有神话,可观察、可经验、可验证的对于异邦的认识。类似地,对于《圣经》中巨人族的记载,公元 1 世纪亚历山大的斐洛认为不能将其按字面意义去理解,摩西是想要表达这些人身材异常高大。后世犹太教和基督教的许多传统释经者都沿用斐洛的理性方式去解释经文。尽管在现实世界我们再没能看到巨人族的存在,但是存在于古代经典文本中的巨人族丰富了我们的文化地图和谱系。

黄薇的文章《〈创世记〉先祖叙事中的文化记忆》同样关注了以色列自我身份认同与他者群体的关系问题。该文以《创世记》中的先祖叙事部分为研究对象,通过对从亚伯拉罕开始的家族故事进行分析,来考察以色列群体的形成。先祖叙事对"以色列"自我身份的构建,与其对以色列周边群体的描述是分不开的。换句话说,先祖叙事在时间和空间两个维度上,构建出以色列与其周边群体的社会地缘关系。同时,先祖叙事对以色列共同体的定义也成为后来以色列民族的集体记忆。

尽管圣经学者曾经尝试通过先祖叙事还原历史上的先祖时代,然而现有史料表明,要还原历史上的亚伯拉罕、以撒和雅各的事迹是不可能的。这并不意味着先祖叙事的记载都是毫无历史根据的臆想。这三代先祖的故事,包括对以色列周边群体的记录,实际上在一定程度上反映出铁器时代以色列民族形成时期黎凡特地区的社会组织和地缘政治格局。《创世记》先祖叙事中存在南北两个传统——代表南国犹大的亚伯拉罕传统、代表北国以色列的雅各传统,其在以色列民族形成发展过程中被整合在一起,成为共有的文化记忆。

亨德尔及黄薇的两篇文章揭示出《创世记》中两个相对独立却又密切相关的叙事体系。通常认为《创世记》第 1—11 章是对远古时代的神话记述,第 12—50 章是对先祖时代的历史记载。当然,这两个文学叙事体系有各自独特的文本来源、中心议题和视角。但是,这两部叙事作品一并被放置在《创世记》这一书卷中,它们共同关注的是对以色列身份的寻找,他们的身份要以存在于遥远过去的群体、生活在边境或居住在他们中间的群体为参照。并且,这种对于自我和他人的视角是互动形成且不断转化的。

田海华的文章《五经中的上帝与诸神》同样处理了以色列宗教史发展过程中有关上帝与诸神的观念,特别关注了《摩西五经》(《妥拉》)的祭司典与申命典中西奈启示对于以色列宗教的意义)。该文以传统的来源批判为理论基础,以四底本说为展开讨论的基本架构,分别考察了耶典、神典、申命典与祭司典中有关上帝和诸神的一系列观念，指出四底本对上帝的特点和属性持有不同观点，上帝与其他神祇的关系也有所不同。

从文化记忆层面来看，耶典模仿并转化了亚述帝国的思想观念，反转当下的政治力量，使得雅威成为所有民族的原初神。神典则将雅威崇拜局限在以色列民族中，同时默认其他民族神祇的存在。申命典强调雅威崇拜的中央化，取缔地方性圣殿，禁止其他形式的偶像崇拜。作为最晚成书的祭司典，其认定除雅威之外，没有别的外邦神祇，没有神的使者，没有天象，由此走向一神论的宗教新时代。

对于西奈山的记忆，申命典以摩西之口重申雅威与以色列之间的立约关系，祭司典将西奈山上的神圣显现化为上帝的"荣光"，以一种革新的历史记忆教导以色列人遵从圣洁的宗教愿景。正是在祭司典与申命典作者笔下，一神论成为以色列宗教的显著特征。

姜振帅的文章《圣山的兴起：希伯来〈圣经〉中的锡安山与西奈山历史传统》探讨了希伯来《圣经》书写中两处非常重要的山脉及其所象征的两个传统。这两座山分别与两位英雄即摩西、大卫密切相关，西奈山传统和锡安山传统后来发展成摩西律法传统和弥赛亚锡安传统。这两个主题一起构成了旧约《圣经》的核心部分，值得进行更广泛和更深入的探讨，并且也极大地影响了对希伯来《圣经》的诠释。

姜振帅的文章主要对这两个传统的关系及发展做出了解释。西奈山是以色列获得耶和华启示的地方，也是摩西从耶和华那里获得律法的地方。西奈山传统与出埃及叙事关系密切，发生于以色列的旷野生活时期。锡安山则与耶路撒冷的圣殿联系在一起。从希伯来《圣经》叙事的时间线来看，锡安山传统晚于西奈山传统。然而，两者之间的关系实际上更为复杂。就其观念来看，锡安山传统更强调耶路撒冷及其圣殿的重要性，或者说锡安山对于耶路撒冷这座城市而言是非常重要的。耶和华居住在锡安山，并且在锡安山上，耶和华守护着耶路撒冷圣城及其民众。锡安山与耶路撒冷关系密切，说明该传统源自晚期犹大地区的语境。

再看西奈山传统。只有在《摩西五经》文本中，西奈山传统才与耶和华赐予律法的事件联系在一起，西奈山是以色列与耶和华立约的地方，在《摩西五经》以外的经文中，西奈山与律法、立约这些重要事件的关系并不明确。甚至在波斯早期的祭司典文献中，西奈并不是山，只是旷野的代名词。这些文本证据说明可能有一个很古老的、独立存在的西奈山传统，耶和华曾在此地显现，但西奈山并未同律法、立约这些事件联系起来。随着以色列宗教的发展，西奈山传统才与耶和华的律法、旷野生活，甚至出埃及叙事联系在一起。

对耶路撒冷及其圣殿的重视是建构锡安神学的关键,耶和华在锡安山圣殿守护着耶路撒冷的城墙及其居民。然而,新巴比伦帝国在公元前 6 世纪,对耶路撒冷及其圣殿的毁灭给锡安山传统带来严峻挑战。因此,从以色列宗教史发展的角度来看,锡安山传统需要变革以应对挑战。在前流放时期的观念中,锡安山是耶和华的居所,自流放时期开始,鉴于新的历史环境,回到锡安山甚至回归的观念都与以色列走出埃及的历史叙事联系起来,对流放后回归的盼望代表以色列再一次走出埃及,锡安山与耶和华的关系也更为密切。这种观念的转变在对《以赛亚书》《耶利米书》,以及祭司典和申命典的文本分析中都可以观察到。由于耶路撒冷及其圣殿被毁,最终在巴比伦之囚晚期和波斯早期,西奈山传统整合了耶和华与以色列的立约传统,成为与锡安山传统并行的另一个传统,呈现在目前的希伯来《圣经》书写中。

本书另外还有一篇侧重希伯来《圣经》文本和历史的文章《边界和秩序:〈以西结书〉28:11—19 中关于推罗王的神谕》。其作者孙玥注意到,两个文学意象——“基路伯”和“宇宙山”对理解关于推罗王的神谕有重要意义,就此展开分析。其中“基路伯”用来描述推罗王,孙玥根据历代释经学家对“基路伯”的考证,结合古代西亚的图像学证据,提出“基路伯”作为推罗王的形象,代表边界的守卫者,职责是分清人神界限,维护上帝作为唯一统治者的王权身份。“宇宙山”就是“上帝的圣山”,根据古代西亚构造的世界图景,这里是世界的中心,代表上帝所维系的宇宙秩序。《以西结书》利用这两个意象说明人神界限和宇宙秩序的重要性。

张缨的文章《〈迷途指津〉的双焦点之一:初探迈蒙尼德的“开端论”》讨论的是迈蒙尼德对《圣经》文本的犹太解读,迈蒙尼德在《迷途指津》中的解经基于犹太教信仰,并且采用了更为哲学化的方法。《迷途指津》是一部针对希伯来《圣经》的解经著作,对犹太教信仰进行了理性化塑造,并将希伯来《圣经》中隐藏的知识揭示出来。迈蒙尼德在对创世开端进行解读的时候,借用了希腊哲学家柏拉图、亚里士多德使用的哲学概念,在本体论基础上探讨世界的起源问题。该文指出《迷途指津》还将“开端”指向“律法的开端”,指出与上帝创世一样,上帝启示摩西赐予他律法也是出于上帝的“目的和意志”,而“律法总是倾向于顺应自然”,是自然构成了律法的尺度。这也就是迈蒙尼德所说的“开端论等于自然科学”。

曹坚的文章《中世纪犹太人的历史书写与认知活动》以历史视角审视中世纪犹太人的历史书写活动。文中列举大量代表人物及其作品,还包括对宗教仪规和敬拜仪式的梳理,并尝试通过分析这些历史著作来探讨中世纪犹太人对于历史的认知。文章指出,中世纪犹太人在数百年里经历了影响世界格局的重大历史事件，例如十字军东征，穆斯林势力在军事上成功战胜了基督教会等。与此同时，中世纪犹太人所面临的历史处境也迫使他们反省自身的民族认同、历史处境和未来发展，从而产生新的历史认知和历史书写动机，构建了中世纪犹太人的历史认知世界。

Some Habits of Thought Reflected in and Communicated by the Hebrew Bible That Played Important Roles in Various Forms of Historical Judaisms

Ehud Ben Zvi*

Abstract: This essay explores four underlying habits of thought that were communicated across many of these books of the Hebrew Bible and the collection itself, or an earlier close forerunner of it, and which eventually played important roles in the later development of multiple historical manifestations of Judaism. Following an introduction, the essay focuses first on the habit of imagining and remembering a foundational past and its implications. Then, it explores the habit of remembering calamity and its relation to "chosen trauma," didactic approaches and the related habit of thinking of Mosaic / Torah teachers. The third habit of mind that it investigates is that of thinking in terms of and about divine teachings / Torah and some of its multiple implications, including the related habit of thinking of Mosaic / Torah teachers. The essay then discusses the habit of being hopeful. As a whole, the essay conveys some of the ways how readings or awareness of the Hebrew Bible have contributed to the shaping of key socially shared habits of thought and mind among diverse historical communities that existed across multiple times and geographical (and social) spaces.

Key Words: Hebrew Bible, Habits of Thought, Judaism, Remembering

---

* Ehud Ben Zvi, Professor, History and Classics, University of Alberta.

Ⅰ. Introduction

The Hebrew Bible (hereafter, HB) is a collection of books composed and edited over centuries. ① Moreover, it was brought together as a collection via a long process over centuries which included the development of several sub-collections (e.g., the Pentateuch) that were included as such in the HB.② All these books were meant to be read directly by literati and some included explicit references about the character of those able to understand them well.③ At the same time, many of the books played important roles in Jewish liturgy / liturgies, already in the Second Temple period, and since then to the present.④ Needless to say, liturgical settings contribute to the shaping of the pragmatic meaning of a text, emphasizing some aspects and de-emphasizing others.⑤ This is particularly true when a text or portion of a book was read alongside and in integrated ways with portions of other books, biblical or not. Moreover, there is a long tradition of publicly reading books or selected portions thereof

---

① There is also plenty of evidence that many of these books existed in multiple textual versions.

② The date and process by which the eventual "canon" of the HB emerged has been the topic of much debate in recent years. It may well be that the collection that became the HB originated, likely in the main, in what was earlier an authoritative collection of a particular late Second Temple Jewish group / s. See, Timothy H. Lim, "An Indicative Definition of the Canon," in *When Texts Are Canonized*, eds. T. H. Lim and Kengo Akiyama (Providence, RI: Brown Judaic Studies, 2017), 1-24; John J. Collins, "Before the Canon: Scriptures in Second Temple Judaism," in *Old Testament Interpretation: Past, Present and Future. Essays in Honor of Gene Tucker*, eds. James L. Mays, David L. Petersen and Kent H. Richards (Nashville, TN: Abingdon Press, 1995), 225-241; and bibliography. Cf. the summary essay by Marc Z. Brettler, "The Canonization of the Bible," in *The Jewish Study Bible*, eds. Adele Berlin and Marc Zvi Brettler 2nd edition (Oxford / New York: Oxford University Press, 2014), 2153-2158.

③ See, e.g., "Those who are wise understand these things [i. e., the contents of the book of Hosea]; those who are discerning know them" (Hos 14:10a). Of course, to state that these books were meant to be read by qualified readers able to understand them implies that those who are not wise, or discerning are unable to.

④ See, e.g., Avigdor Shinan, "The Bible in the Synagogue," in *The Jewish Study Bible*, 2049-2057; Ruth Langer, "The Bible in the Liturgy," in *The Jewish Study Bible*, 2057-2067; Michael Fishbane, *Haftarot. A Commentary* (Philadelphia: JPS, 2002).

⑤ See, e.g., Michael Fishbane, *Haftarot. A Commentary*, passim.

and their meaning explained to those in attendance.① Altogether, this means that a long history of commentary accompanied the texts of the HB, from the inception to the present.

Readers (including, but not restricted to Christians and Jews) read these books century after century in vastly different ways, depending on their social location, culture, the world of knowledge they had, and the textual collection within which they included them such as Tanakh or the various Christian Bibles each of them with their own sets of books and their internal classification of them. ②

In addition, Jews and Christians have read these books through history as a crucial but integral part of their own various "libraries" and especially in the context of their collections of culturally / religiously authoritative texts, and thus have encountered different "things" when reading these books. Much

---

① See, e.g., Neh. 8:1-12; 2 Chr. 17:7-9; cf. Deut. 31:9-13; Josh. 8:34-35. Multiple social and ideological factors contributed to this outcome. See Ehud Ben Zvi, *Social Memory among the Literati of Yehud* (BZAW, 509; Berlin: De Gruyter 2019), passim.

② Cf., for instance, the Protestant Bible with the Catholic or Orthodox Christian Bibles. For a helpful comparative "table of contents" of the HB, the Protestant Old Testament, the Catholic Old Testament and (most of the) Orthodox Churches Old Testament see Marc Zvi Brettler, "The Canonization of the Bible," p. 2155. There are significant differences not only between the HB and Christian Old Testaments, but also among the tables of contents of the Old Testaments of the mentioned Christian books.The Tanakh itself, even within the Masoretic tradition, has not shown a uniform order of books when it comes to the Latter Prophets (Isaiah-Malachi) and the Writings. Differences in order implied and communicated differences of interpretation. A Tanakh with Chronicles as the first rather than the last book in the Writings is different from one in which this is not the case. Similarly, whether the Latter Prophets should begin with Isaiah, followed by Jeremiah and then Ezekiel (as in the current "traditional" order or with Jeremiah, followed by Ezekiel and only then Isaiah, see b. B. Batra 14b and Maimonides *Mishneh Torah* [Laws of the Torah Scroll, ch. 7, Halakha 15]) establishes a difference in terms of the readers' general understanding of the books. This is clear from the explanation for the Jeremiah-Ezekiel-Isaiah order in b. Batra 14b ("The Gemara further asks: Consider: Isaiah preceded Jeremiah and Ezekiel; let the book of Isaiah precede the books of those other prophets. The Gemara answers: Since the book of Kings ends with the destruction of the Temple, and the book of Jeremiah deals entirely with prophecies of the destruction, and the book of Ezekiel begins with the destruction of the Temple but ends with consolation and the rebuilding of the Temple, and Isaiah deals entirely with consolation, as most of his prophecies refer to the redemption, we juxtapose destruction to destruction and consolation to consolation. This accounts for the order: Jeremiah, Ezekiel, and Isaiah.") (explanatory ET translation of the section according to the William Davidson Talmud, an English version of Adin Steinsaltz's Talmud, freely available at https://www.sefaria.org / Bava_Batra.14b.10? lang=bi).

research has been devoted in recent decades to these various readings. In fact, the history of "reception" of biblical texts over time and space has been among the most vibrant fields of studies for academic scholars of these texts. ①

The HB, which is referred to as *Tanakh* or *Miqra* within Judaic mental libraries, ② has undoubtedly been a foundational text for all historical forms of Judaism, across time and geographic space, and of course, it was read in a large variety of ways in the last two millennia. It is impossible to discuss these multiple readings and the worlds that they evoked in an essay. ③

Thus, in what follows I will only focus on underlying habits of thought that were communicated across many of the books of the HB and the collection itself, or an earlier close forerunner of it, and which eventually played important roles in the later development of multiple historical manifestations of Judaism. To be sure, there are more habits of thought and mind. In fact, there are even more that could be considered and discussed here, but, needless

---

① An important outcome of this enhanced interest on these matters is the ongoing publication of the *Encyclopaedia of the Bible and Its Reception* by De Gruyter.

② It should be mentioned that the Bible of Beta-Israel, i.e., the Ethiopian Jews, is neither referred to as *Tanakh* nor as *Miqra*, but *Orit*; moreover, its "table of contents" differs from the usual HB in significant ways. In addition, its language is Ge'ez. Recently an academic program ("תופסי האורית") has been launched at Tel Aviv University to further studies of the *Orit*.

③ A good starting point for many of these readings is found in the essays section in Adele Berlin and Marc Zvi Brettler, eds. *The Jewish Study Bible*, esp. 1833-1977, 2049-2106, 2159-2165, 2208-2214. Those interested in the modern period, may consult Yaacov Shavit and Mordechai Eran, *The Hebrew Bible Reborn from Holy Scripture to the Book of Books. A History of Biblical Culture and the Battles over the Bible in Modern Judaism* (Studia Judaica, 38, Berlin: De Gruyter, 2007); for those interested in the engagement of (mainly) Orthodox Jews with contemporary research, or as phrased in the volume mentioned below, "the belief in the sanctity of the Torah and the consequent obligation to observe the commandments... and the intellectual obligation to impartial analysis, which is also a religious imperative," see Tova Ganzel, Yehudah Brandes, and Chayuta Deutsch, eds. *The Believer and the Modern Study of the Bible* (Boston: Academic Studies Press, 2019), available online at https://library.oapen.org/handle/20.500.12657/25322. Likewise see the summary of contemporary understandings of such a central concept as "torah from heavens," among a quite similar group of contemporary Jewish thinkers at https://www.thetorah.com/article/current-approaches. (This summary does not include, "cultural," humanistic, and similar contemporary Jewish groups.) For women-centered, Jewish readings of the Hebrew Bible see Tamara Cohn Eskenazi and Andrea L. Weiss, eds. *The Torah: A Women's Commentary* (New York: Women of Reform Judaism, URJ Press, 2008), and Elyse Goldstein, ed. *The Women's Torah Commentary: New Insights from Women Rabbis on the 54 Weekly Torah Portion* (Woodstock, VT: Jewish Lights Publishing, 2000).

to say, writing, even if briefly, about the various historical manifestations of the four habits selected here over circa two millennia of history would yield an encyclopedic work. Even the sayings in / of Qohelet reached an end, and to the amount of writing to be included in a journal article there is certainly an end.[1] Thus, in what follows I will discuss only these four important and influential habits of thoughts and mind.[2]

Ⅱ. The habit of imagining and remembering a foundational past and some of its implications

Leaving aside the explicit injunctions to remember e.g. particular days and events, godly teachings, that the Israelites were slaves in Egypt or Miriam's skin-disease (e.g., Exod. 13:3; 20:8; Deut 15:15; 16:12; 24:9, 22; Josh. 1:13), even the most cursory reading of the HB reveals that most of its books are past-shaping books, that is, books that shape images of the past and thus the memory of the past shared by the readers (see, e.g., Genesis-2 Kings, 1-2 Chronicles, Isaiah-Malachi, Ruth, Esther, Ezra-Nehemiah, Daniel, and notice that many Psalms, many Proverbs, Qohelet, are associated with personages of old). But it also reveals that the past to be remembered is not one which is evenly distributed. Not all periods, let alone events or personages, were to be remembered. In other words, the habit is one of remembering mainly particular times, circumstances, and characters.

One may argue that the most important set of times, characters and events are those associated with the Exodus from Egypt and the subsequent

① I am here alluding to "Of making many books there is no end" (Qoh. 12:12).

② There is a very large corpus of works dealing with "habit," with a similar term in social studies, namely "habitus," and with teaching (critical) habits of thought in the realm of Education Studies. Readers interested may consult e.g., Nick Crossley, "Habit and Habitus," *Body and Society* 19 (2013): 136-161 and cited bibliography. Scholars trained in a particular discipline, tend to share some "habits of thought" and unsurprisingly, scholars who advance "interdisciplinarity" often challenge these habits of thought. Notice the title of Myra H. Stober, *Interdisciplinary Conversations: Challenging Habits of Thought* (Stanford: Stanford University Press, 2011, 2020). From a cognitive, social-psychological approach to the concept of "habit of thought" see, e.g., Richard E. Nisbett, Kaiping Peng, Incheol Choi and Ara Norenzayan, "Culture and Systems of Thought: Holistic Versus Analytic Cognition," *Psychological Review* 108 (2001): 291-310.

period in the desert at whose center stand the related foundational, often remembered events of receiving divine teachings (Torah), and along with them, the progression of instructions and activities leading up to and culminating in the building of the tabernacle.

Readers of the HB construed, of course, the tabernacle as transitory and as the forerunner of the Jerusalemite temple (i.e., from within the perspective communicated by the HB as a whole, "the Temple"). Thus, a link is established not only between the former and the latter but also between the main human characters, namely Moses and David,[①] alongside YHWH and Israel as a collective group.

In terms of spaces, when the readers of the HB recall the Moses era, they encounter a liminal landscape, namely the wilderness. Such a space keeps evoking and activating both their imagination and their imaginary. This is the place in which, inter alia, (a) the Israelites, via Moses, receive YHWH's teachings (see below), (b) the Israelites are under the best possible leadership, (c) YHWH's promise of the land to the ancestors is reaffirmed to them, (d) the tabernacle is built and the camp around it shapes an image of a well-organized Israel at whose center is YHWH, which in a later and different iteration appears as an utopian image in Ezekiel, (e) YHWH directly feeds them and provides them with water, and like the humans in Eden, they need not to toil for food, (f) the Israelites may enjoy the safety provided by the mighty acts of YHWH who brought them out of Egypt, and are the only generation of Israelites who were eye-witnesses to that act of divine salvation. But the same wilderness is also the place in which the Israelites, who received all these benefits and lived in what might have been considered a kind of Edenic

① David's son, Solomon is the king who carried out the building of the temple, following the instruction of his father and the divine instructions communicated to both Moses and David. David, himself, was forbidden to build the Temple because he "shed much blood and have waged great wars" (see 1 Chr. 22:8; 28:3). Solomon is characterized as a man of peace and well-being and no wars were associated with him.

period, [①] responded to all these divine gifts with rebellion after rebellion against their K / king / deity / benefactor and the latter's human representatives.[②] The combination of divine action and human response turns the wilderness into a space in which utopian and dystopian features interweave time and again.

Moreover, although it helps those remembering the period to explore the motif of human inability to dwell and live in utopian spaces, it also communicates that although Israel's rebellions caused one generation to die without reaching the land, Israel survived and took over the promised land. Moreover, as Moses already knew, Israel will end up losing that land — as a consequence of their rebellions against their K / king / deity; see below — but not the divine promise; YHWH will still return them from the Exile (a point made in Deut 30:1-6, and repeated time and again in prophetic literature).

The theme (of the permanence of) the promise — along with the hope it conveys, and the related motif of the (permanent) willingness of YHWH to forgive the misdeeds of Israel — even if, at times or often, after the deity enacted punishment — shape a strong sense of an underlying element of permanence within a basically helically or cyclically construed past. Calamities may happen and are somewhat expected, but there is no risk of annihilation, and the divine promises stand fast (alongside Torah and hope, see below).

Since these promises are to a large extent associated with the three patriarchs (Abraham, Isaac and Jacob) within the world of memory and ideology conjured by the HB (see e.g., Exod. 3:5-7; Deut. 4:37; 7:8; 9:27; 2 Kgs. 13:23; Jer. 33:26; Mic. 7:20), their stories were also allocated a great deal of social mindshare. For comparable reasons, David was allocated substantial mindshare, and the four of them were construed as types through

---

① Notice also that some "autobiographical" memories of YHWH (Hos. 2:16-17; 9:10; 11:1-4; 12:9-10; 13:4-5) construe the period in which YHWH was with Israel in the wilderness as "happy times," much better than those that followed in the land, despite the fact that the latter is explicitly imagined as YHWH's land (see Hos. 9:3; cf. "YHWH's kingdom" in reference to Israel / Judah in 1 Chr. 17:14).

② On the importance and implications of this seemingly strange response, from a different perspective, see e.g., Adriane Leveen, *Memory and Tradition in the Book of Numbers* (New York: Cambridge University Press, 2008). See also, e.g., Ps. 78; 106. On the motif of the wilderness / desert, see also M. de Roche, "Jeremiah 2:2-3 and Israel's Love for God during the Wilderness Wanderings," *CBQ* 45 (1983): 364-376.

which to imagine Israel.[1]

The combined weight of memories of Israel's rebellions and of unprecedent divine gifts in the wilderness and the character of the latter as an anteroom that serves as a space, place and environment leading to the promised land resulted eventually in the generation of memories about a future, utopian wilderness, in which YHWH transforms existing Israel into one unable to rebel against YHWH and disobey YHWH's teachings again (see, e.g., Deut. 30:6; Hos. 2:16-25; see below), and thus, bringing the repeating cycle of rebellion and forgiveness to an end, before YHWH ends Exile.

This association of wilderness's memories and images with overcoming Exile in the utopian future carries much rhetorical power because it elicits and engages those associated with the first wilderness period, which are recalled time and again in the HB (in addition to Exodus-Deuteronomy, see, e.g., Ezek. 20:5-17; cf. Ps. 105-106, a pair of psalms that although distinct from one another, comment and inform each other).

The wilderness period also conjures an image of YHWH as their foundational king, who integrates multiple common ideological features associated with foundational kingship, including being a (a) powerful warrior / deliverer with no peer, (b) lawgiver who establishes wise laws for the people, (c) king who commands the establishment of the cultic center of the people and its ordinances, and (d) ruler who instills obedience, awe, and fear among the subjects. Significantly, the HB readers are supposed to keep in mind that this foundational king is not a human, even not a human of the highest quality

---

[1] On the transfer of the image and promise of David to all Israel, see e.g. Isa. 55:3-5. This transfer went hand in hand with the processes of (partial) "kingization" of Israel within the discourse of the literati responsible for most of the books that ended up in the HB (see e.g., the concept of a covenant between the deity and the people, in which the traditional role of the king is performed by the people; cf. characterization of the Davidic Manasseh in Chronicles [see 2 Chr. 33] and the manner in which he was identified with pre-exilic, exilic and post-exilic / future Israel or that of David as a person whose sin (see Bathsheba-Uriah affair) made him liable for divine execution (see 2 Sam. 12: 1-14), although he was punished and harshly humiliated, but he was allowed by YHWH to survive and eventually organized the future building of the temple, all of which parallel the basic memory narrative about Israel conveyed by the HB. This process of (partial) kingization went along with one of (partial) priestization of Israel (see, e.g., Exod. 19:6; Isa. 61:6) and both constructed an ideological / imagined Israel marked by a strong level of horizontal cohesion.

(such as Moses) really fulfil this role.

In strong contrast, David, the most central and most memorable human king of Israel within the world of memory of these readers, is construed in multiple ways. Since he is a site of memory integrating so many images, he ends up being an extremely complex figure, with multiple highs and lows, and evoking images of grievous sin and of elevated piety. Further, his son and successor, who is characterized as the paradigmatic example of a wise man, is also imagined as one who nonetheless fails, especially when old age reached him. Human frailties thus apply to human kings. In any case, their dynasty failed Israel and led to the calamity of the destruction of the Jerusalemite temple / the Temple and the E / exile of the people. The events associated with the latter (and some key godly figures related to them, e.g., Jeremiah, Ezekiel, Isaiah) represent the other key section of the past evoked time and again through the HB.

Another central point of this imagined foundational past of the Israelites that comes upon often in the HB involved turning upside down a common motif in ancient West Asia. In the HB the key narrative is not about a deity searching for and eventually selecting a proper human king, but rather about a monarchic deity who selects a people to be ruled, judged and protected by that deity. It is one about a king-god selecting his subjects, and not necessarily due to the latter's qualities (cf., for instance, Isa 1:2-3; see also Exod 33:6 and esp. Exod 34:9, and notice that the text may be understood "... let the Lord go with us, *because* this is a stiff-necked people..," see already Ramban's commentary on the verse). At the same time, since Israel received YHWH's wise teachings (i.e., Torah), which provided Israel with lasting (godly) wisdom (cf. Deut. 4:6-8), even if often within the world portrayed by the HB, it (/ she?) rejected it.

Allocating much social mindshare to this past contributed much to the presence of this remembered past in the present of Jewish communities over time and space. It also contributed much to an ideological construction that brings to the forefront the pastness of their presence.① These communities and their members saw themselves, inter alia, as living in the desert / wilderness,②holding to divine promises, enjoying Torah but often failing to (fully) follow it, asking for divine forgiveness, in need of Mosaic teachers and construing and remembering mental temples and their worship (see, e.g., the emphasis on the temple in the Mishna, a foundational work written after the destruction of the second temple). Their main meta-narratives about the past provided them not only with a present past, but also structured, to an extent, their ideological constructions of their (various and different) presents over centuries.

Ⅲ. The habit of remembering calamity and its relation to "chosen trauma," didactic approaches and the related habit of thinking of Mosaic / Torah teachers

Contemporary scholars often explore the social roles of recalling and "reliving" past social traumas. The clear focus on recalling and explaining the destruction of the temple play a prominent role in the HB. The narrative from Deuteronomy to 2 Kings is teleological and, despite occasional and necessary detours, it moves towards the destruction of the Temple and Exile. Not only does this calamity figure prominently in this collection of books, but implicitly or explicitly is central to the collection of prophetic books, and to texts such as Lamentations and some Psalms. Even Moses is imagined as being aware of the calamity to come (see, e.g., Deut. 30:1-5; 32:19-25, and the pragmatic meaning of it (e.g., Deut. 28:15-68; 29:13-27; 30:17-19; 31:19-22) and in Chronicles, David, at one of, if not the highest moment of his reign, is

① I am closely following Jacob Neusner's phrase, explicitly and intentionally. See Jacob Neusner, *The Presence of the Past, The Pastness of the Present. History, Time, and Paradigm in Rabbinic Judaism* (Bethsheda, MD: CDL Press, 1996), even if my focus here does not necessarily overlap that of Neusner's cited work.

② This may not necessarily be the case among some groups of contemporary Jewish Israelis. On the HB among Jews in the State of Israel and their culture / s in general, see Uriel Simon, "The Bible in Israeli Life," in *The Jewish Study Bible*, 2071-2081.

imagined as having knowledge of the E / exile to come.①

From the perspective of recent scholarship, it seems that the HB communicates a habit of mind to recall and re-configure a "chosen trauma."② There is, however, a major difference. Contemporary groups recalling and vicariously revisiting regularly their "chosen trauma" strongly tend to imagine themselves as (innocent) victims, and as (past) powerless agents. Reading the HB shaped, in the main, an image of ancient Israel as neither a group of innocent victims nor a powerless one.③ In fact, it construed an image of ancient Israel as agents of their own calamity, for having disobeyed YHWH's teachings.

To be sure, there is a strong didactic point to this rather unusual approach to the "chosen trauma." The point, of course is to socialize the readers to follow the divine teachings and warn them (like Moses did) of the consequences of failing to do that. This required imagining and remembering Moses as a necessary human intermediary and teacher of YHWH's teachings to the people. Since Moses was the foundational prophet, he was conceived as a unique character, but this habit of mind expressed and instilled by the HB requires thinking and imagining Mosaic successors of Moses, i.e., teachers in each generation. These teachers of the divine teachings / Torah become necessary for the welfare of the people; they serve within the logic shaped by this habit of mind, they serve as "guardians of Israel."

---

① See Ehud Ben Zvi, "Who Knew What? The Construction of the Monarchic Past in Chronicles and Implications for the Intellectual Setting of Chronicles," in *Judah and the Judeans in the Fourth Century B.C.E.O.*, eds. Lipschits, G. N. Knoppers and R. Albertz (Winona Lake: Eisenbrauns, 2007), 349-360 (esp. 349-354).

② The concept of "chosen trauma" was developed by Vamik D. Volkan, see, e.g., Vamik D. Volkan, "Transgenerational Transmissions and Chosen Traumas: An Aspect of Large-Group Identity," *Group Analysis* 34 (2001): 79-97, esp. 87-95 and bibliography.

③ The Holocaust has led many Jewish circles to question this habit of mind. But even in their opposition to it, they indicate the long-term influence of this habit of mind. Moreover, challenges to it were often involved in the construction of processes for overcoming, by human hands, the state of powerlessness.

Ⅳ. The habit of thinking in terms of and about divine teachings / Torah and some of its multiple implications, including the related habit of thinking of Mosaic / Torah teachers

Few would doubt that the concept of Torah / YHWH's teachings is central to the HB as a collection. ① Within the world of the HB, Israel and the Israelites are taught the wise teachings of the wisest possible personage in their conceptual world, i.e., YHWH. Although the latter is also remembered, inter

① There are multiple concepts of (divine) Torah in the HB. References to the YHWH's Torah carried both a meaning of "godly instruction" but also of written corpora, namely the Pentateuch, as instantiated in one or multiple versions. As Honigman and I wrote elsewhere, "the large social, ideological, symbolic, and mnemonic power of the concept of Torah in the literati's world was grounded precisely in its ability to engage more than one meaning and the associated "generative" ambiguity or even multivalence that this created," (Sylvie Honigman and Ehud Ben Zvi, "The Spread of the Ideological Concept of a (Jerusalem-Centred) Tōrâ-centred Israel beyond Yehud: Observations and Implications," *HeBAI* 9 [2021]: 370-397 [371]). The present discussion refers to the concept of Torah in the HB as a collection and above all within the ideological world that it construes. A good attestation of this concept is to be found in a group of relatively late Psalms such as Ps. 19; 119. On these matters and on Psalm 119, see Kent Aaron Reynolds, *Torah as Teacher: The Exemplary Torah Student in Psalm 119* (Leiden / Boston: Brill, 2010) and bibliography; and esp. for an insightful study of similarities and dissimilarities between this understanding of Torah and traditional Chinese concepts, Zhenshuai Jiang, "A Comparative Study of the Concepts of Torah in the Hebrew Bible and Li in *Zuozhuan*," *Journal of Chinese Philosophy* 45/3-4 (2018): 175-189. Cf. Konrad Schmid, "The Genesis of Normativity in Biblical Law," in *Concepts of Law in the Sciences, Legal Studies, and Theology*, eds. Michael Welker and Gregor Etzelmüller (Tübingen: Mohr Siebeck, 2013), 119-135. I would like to mention in this context that, contrary to a long tradition of interpretation, I doubt that even e.g., the cultic or social regulations, and prescriptions such as the command to obey the Shabbat really (or fully) qualify as "law." At the most, within this context these are discrete bits or sets of bits of "ideal" (or "utopian") regulations, and within the intellectual discourses reflected in the HB, "commandments" that all together and interacting with one another at multiple levels served to explore and construct a discourse about which particular social, cultural, interpersonal, cultic and sexual behaviors might be conducive to, or consistent with the establishment of what the ancient readers thought that an ideal society should be. Of course, later, not just "commandments," but even the Pentateuchal stories were used in rabbinic texts to advance halacha (see, e.g., Jane L. Kanarek, *Biblical Narrative and the Formation of Rabbinic Law* [New York: Cambridge Univ. Press, 2014]). That said, I am not sure that law is a good English translation of the Hebrew term halacha either, despite its widespread use. For a comparable issue of translation, see Lena Salaymeh, "Decolonial Translation: Destabilizing Coloniality in Secular Translations of Islamic Law," *Journal of Islamic Ethics* 5 (2021): 1-28.

alia, as a warrior, and as a king, his most substantial attribute implicitly and explicitly is being a teacher (see e.g., Ps. 78:1; 119:12, 33-36, 64), and the ultimate source of the most important teachings of Israel.

Within the world of the HB, these teachings make the "simple" wise, the heart rejoice, and engender and communicate love (e.g., Ps. 19; 119: passim). Following these teachings leads, within that discourse, to wisdom, well-being, and joy (cf. Deut. 4:5-8; Ps. 1:2; 19:7; 94:12; 119). But conversely, defying them leads to calamity. Not only are the Israelites supposed to learn these teaching constantly, but in some constructions of the utopian future, these teaching will eventually become innate and embodied in the future Israelites (see Jer. 31:33; cf. Ps. 40:8), while pious men of the past were imagined as studying these teachings day and night (see Josh 1:8; Ps. 1:2). To some extent, already at this level here, there is a strong tendency towards a convergence between wisdom and Torah.①

The centrality of such a Torah in the HB draws attention to readers expectations about Torah that become habits of mind. For instance, the teacher of this Torah, i.e., YHWH, speaks in multiple dictions and expresses seemingly contradictory positions, depending on the literary world in which YHWH's sayings are reported. Since all of these are associated with the same character and, from the perspective of the community core site of memory, namely YHWH, the latter becomes multivocal and polyvalent, and conversely multivocality and polyvalence become "divine." The same holds for godly human characters (e.g., Moses), and within a world of thought in which pious humans are supposed to strive to approximate the divine image (*imago dei*), these pious characters as well as the literati reading and writing these books are supposed to strive for an inherent, internal multivocality. In other words, the habit of mind mentioned here is not one conducive towards univocal, clear-cut voices, or (formal) logical consistency, but one towards of fluidity and

① Cf. Sirach, but see Anja Klein, "Half Way between Psalm 119 and Ben Sira: Wisdom and Torah in Psalm 19," in *Wisdom and Torah: The Reception of Torah in the Wisdom Literature of the Second Temple Period*, eds. Bernd Schipper and D. Andrew Teeter (Leiden: Brill, 2013), 119-136.

fuzziness.①

Since all that multivocality is embodied in and thus integrated in the same character / site of memory (e.g., YHWH, Moses) and thus the different perspectives are construed not as dissonant, but as interrelated, integrated, and complementary. Torah / wisdom thus is construed as a complementary array of voices (and sets of voices) informing each other, without any of them being identified alone as Torah.

This approach is extended to narratives. Thus, for instance, the Israel that left Egypt could be imagined and remembered as so populous that the Egyptians — one of the "ethnies" with the largest population in the ancient world — were outnumbered (see Exod. 1:9; cf. Exod. 1:7) and there are said to be as many as the stars in heaven (Deut. 1:10; 10:22; 28:62); yet at the same time as the least populous of ethnie (in the entire world (Deut. 7:7), depending on the context and the didactic (and ideological) message that the relevant text was meant to communicate.②

To be sure, the mentioned, integrative openness to multiple voices has limits too. Anything that would be patently inconsistent with the basic ideological tenets of the group (e.g., positions that YHWH is not "the God" or that YHWH's Temple should not be in Jerusalem or that the authoritative texts of the community carry no authority) was out-of-limits.

Another important habit of mind developed by the centrality of Torah is the communal focus on (wise / divine / authoritative) written texts. Inevitably, this focus increased the social and cultural capital of those able to directly read them and teach, according to their understanding, them to others. But there is more. The material character of texts written in papyrus stands in sharp contrast with that of non-textual monuments, including and particularly relevant to our case, the Jerusalemite temple. Papyri are fragile, but they can be copied, reproduced, hidden from enemies, etc. In that sense, papyri (and later parchment) texts can continue to exist under any

① I discussed these matters elsewhere, see, e.g., Ehud Ben Zvi, *Social Memory among the Literati of Yehud* (Berlin: De Gruyter 2019), passim.

② Examples like these can easily be multiplied and are attested in all literary genres and across book collections; see, e.g., 2 Chr. 14: 2, 4 and contrast with 2 Chr. 15:17; 17:6; 20:33.

circumstances and remain "functional." A temple is none of the above. It can be destroyed, polluted, and so on. Only temples that exist in texts in fragile material and in the minds of those reading them (like Ezekiel's temple, and the tabernacle, etc.) are conceptualized as impervious to the vicissitudes of history.[①] This also explains the elevation of Torah and the conceptualization of the temple as sacred because it is grounded in and conforms to Torah and not the other way around.

Another habit of mind that emerges from the focus on Torah is one in which the latter, YHWH's wishes and YHWH's wisdom and thus Israel's deal and are both atemporal or better transtemporal since they are relevant not only to the world portrayed in the book but to "all times" (as wisdom generally is), but also at times contingent on the circumstances in which the people live. Thus, what seems a clear rule that Levites assume their responsibilities when they are 30 years old (Num. 4:3), is shown to have only a temporally related validity (see 1 Chr. 23:24-27), because the Jerusalemite temple is not the Tabernacle.[②] Similarly, the rules for the first Passover do not necessarily apply

---

① Cf. Hanna Liss, "'Describe the Temple to the House of Israel': Preliminary Remarks on the Temple Vision in the Book of Ezekiel and the Question of Fictionality in Priestly Literatures," in *Utopia and Dystopia in Prophetic Literature*, ed. Ehud Ben Zvi (PFES 92; Helsinki: Finnish Exegetical Society / Göttingen: Vandenhoeck & Ruprecht, 2006), 122-143.

② Remembering the establishment of the tabernacle, the central place in the liminal, temporary space of the desert recalls and necessitates a memory about the establishment of the permanent central place in the land. Thus, the stories of the tabernacle lead and are linked within the memoryscape shaped by the HB to those of the establishment of the Jerusalemite temple, its permanent successor. That said, the fixed temple and the mobile tabernacle cannot but be different in terms of physical structure, even if imagined physical structures. This observation only emphasizes that the linkage between the two is grounded on the divine rites and regulations governing the temple, and the identity of the proper priests (i.e., the sons of Aaron). But they also suggest that these rites and regulations are that are associated with Moses, under whose initiative the tabernacle was established, require those of David / Solomon, under whose initiative the Jerusalemite temple was set up. Within this frame Moses and David / Solomon become complementary foundational leaders, and so are the regulations that they instituted for the proper function of the cultic center. See 1 Chr. 28:11-19 (esp. v 19), 2 Chr. 8:14; 23:18. See, e.g., Simon J. De Vries, "Moses and David as Cult Founders in Chronicles," *JBL* 107 (1988): 619-639; William Riley, *King and Cultus in Chronicles. Worship and the Reinterpretation of History* (JSOT Sup 160; Sheffield: JSOT Press, 1993), 61-63. Of course, it is the job the Mosaic teaching voices of later times to keep it functioning properly, and if / when required they may also, within this logic, add complementary regulations.

to others. At the same time, even when the rule is imagined as not applicable anymore given the changed circumstances, the memory of the previous rule remains important, and part of Torah / wisdom.

Another important habit of mind communicated by the HB is associated with following Torah, along with the understanding that following Torah means following YHWH, namely to construct following Torah as a categorical imperative that is not dependent on contingent circumstances or potential rewards. Despite the fact that Torah is generally associated in the world portrayed in the HB with joy, and well-being, reading the HB conjured multiple cases that balance this portrayal and advance the important concept that people should not follow Torah (only) for the sake of fostering their own well-being, but as a divine, categorial commandment. Thus, for instance, as a consequence of their piety — which for the readers of the HB was understood as following YHWH and hence Torah — most of the prophets of YHWH were killed by Jezebel (1 Kgs. 18:4), the true prophet Uriah was killed by order of his Davidic king (Jer. 30:20-23), Jeremiah was sent to prison (Jer. 32-33; 37:11-16) and cast into a pit with no water (Jer. 30:4-5) and widely ridiculed, Hanani the seer and others associated with him were imprisoned and likely tortured (2 Chr. 16:7-10), and Zechariah was killed by his Davidic king (2 Chr. 24:20-22). Moreover, although Uriah behaves much more accordingly to YHWH's teachings than David, it is the former, not the latter that ends up being killed. Further, Josiah, one of the few good Davidic kings in later memory① purges the land and temple; and seals a covenant before YHWH to follow the deity's teachings (see 2 Kgs. 22:3-23:27; cf. 2 Chr. 34:8-35:20a), while knowing all too well that the temple will be destroyed and the land polluted after his death. ② Qohelet explores at length the observed lack of consistency between proper behavior and reward, but the exploration leads to the basic operative and conceptual statement that "the end of the matter: all

① See, e.g., "except for David and Hezekiah and Josiah, all of them [i.e., the Davidic kings of Israel] were great sinners" (Sir. 49:4; NRSV).

② This viewpoint is conveyed both by Kings and Chronicles as after reporting his death, the narrative moves quickly from his death to the dramatic end of the kingdom of Judah and the fall of YHWH's temple in Jerusalem.

has been heard; fear god, and observe his commandments; for that is the whole duty of everyone" (Qoh. 12:13).[1] This approach is clearly attested in later texts; see e.g., "he [Antigonos, a man of Socho and disciple of Simon, the Righteous] used to say: do not be like servants who serve the master in the expectation of receiving a reward, but be like servants who serve the master without the expectation of receiving a reward, and let the fear of Heaven be upon you" (m. Avot 1.3). "Heavenly" teachings may be conceptualized as necessary for the upkeeping of the entire world, but not necessarily for the personal welfare of individuals, except for the sense of the joy they may feel because they are "fulfilling their duties" as ordained by their heavenly teachings.[2]

Ⅴ. The habit of being hopeful

The habit of remembering calamity mentioned above goes together with the habit of being hopeful. The social reproduction of a community requires not only calamities and traumas to remember, but also hope for the future. Since I have expanded on these and related matters of utopian thinking and utopias in the texts that eventually ended up in the HB,[3] I will only summarize some crucial points here. That said, this essay could not properly conclude without a reference to the habit of being hopeful.

Past calamities are remembered, for didactic reasons, and essentially for

---

① For the present purposes I leave aside the statement in Qoh. 12:14 that requires a separate discussion that bears not direct relevance to the matters at stake here.

② Of course, this approach facilitated the development of memories of persecution and martyrdom, which were already shaped and evoked in some texts within the HB (e.g., 1 Kgs. 18:4; Jer. 26:20-23; 2 Chr. 24:20-22), became far more attested and important in later texts and liturgies (see, e.g., 2 Macc 7; b Ber. 61b; "The Ten Martyrs" or *Eleh Ezkerah* [אלה אזכרה] in the *musaf* service for Yom Kippur, etc.).

③ I expanded on these matters in Ehud Ben Zvi, "Reading and Constructing Utopias: Utopia /s and / in the Collection of Authoritative Texts / Textual Readings of Late Persian Period Yehud," *Studies in Religion / Sciences Religieuses* 42 (2013): 463-476, available at https://journals.sagepub.com/doi/pdf/10.1177/0008429813488344; and "Utopias, Multiple Utopias, and Why Utopias at All? The Social Roles of Utopian Visions in Prophetic Books within Their Historical Context," in *Utopia and Dystopia in Prophetic Literature*, ed. E. Ben Zvi (PFES, 92; Helsinki / Göttingen: Finnish Exegetical Society / Vandenhoeck & Ruprecht, 2006), 55-85.

the sake of social reproduction. That said, social reproduction always requires hope. Thus, it is not a surprise that in the HB memories of calamities are often associated with hope-creating images. The memory of slavery in Egypt leads to the memory of the Exodus, and the divine gift of Torah. The memory of the calamity of the destruction of temple, city and exile leads to the memory of the "return" and in some texts to that of a second Exodus (e.g., Isaiah, Ezra-Nehemiah). In prophetic literature memories of the extremely sinful behavior of Israel / Judah that justified YHWH's punishment in the form of destruction and exile were always associated with memories of YHWH's announcements of hope and even utopian futures that were communicated to Israel / Judah by pious prophets precisely when the latter behaved at its worst. Similarly, the wilderness motif brings up memories of (seemingly) incomprehensibly sinful behavior with memories of utopian futures. Memories of the past and of the fulfilment of divine announcements of doom to Israel / Judah served to socialize people to imagine and remember a future in which the divine announcements concerning future will be fulfilled.

Finally, a seemingly unexpected habit of thought followed this emphasis on hope for the future and on calamity in the past. Some periods and locations are allocated much textual space in the HB and in the memory-scape it evoked, others are rarely considered worth remembering. Thus, for instance, the stories of "falling" into Exile and about the events associated with returning from it are very much worth remembering in the HB, but life in Exile itself is not. The mainly sinful monarchic past is worth remembering, but the present of the literati who wrote these books is not much, because their hope and their memories of a glorious future are, of course, in the future of the readers.

Likewise, while the characters in the books written by the literati are memorable, the actual authors of the books are not; they do not belong to that memorable period. The text, its main characters (e.g., Moses, David, etc.) and the memories that the text evokes are central, but the human agents shaping and transmitting them are imagined as secondary to them. The former were construed as permanent and transtemporal, the latter were temporal, and evanescent. Along with this conceptual process stands the idea that the great people of the past stood and will always stand well above those of the present. Prophets after Moses can only be Mosaic, no king can be David, and so on (cf.

the later rabbinic, and still strongly influential in many Judaic circles, concept of "generational decline."① While the habit of thought shaped by the HB construed indeed a narrative of descent from the heights of the foundational period, it also shaped a complementary one about a great ascent leading to a great utopian future. This future is, of course, imagined in multiple, complementary ways, just as the imagined, remembered past and its main characters (see above).

No article can cover the full impact of the HB on the various communities of Jews over time and space, nor among their respective systems of Judaic thought or observance. ② Even if one were to focus on habits of thought and mind, there are many more that can be considered. Those discussed here serve as a minor lamp helping the visitors to illuminate, even if partially and with only a flickering, a very large, immensely diverse, ever shifting and much alive "neighborhood."

---

① Cf. b. Šabb. 112b ("Rabbi Zeira said that Rava bar Zimuna said: If the early generations are characterized as sons of angels, we are the sons of men. And if the early generations are characterized as the sons of men, we are akin to donkeys. And I do not mean that we are akin to either the donkey of Rabbi hanina ben Dosa or the donkey of Rabbi Pinhas ben Yair, who were both extraordinarily intelligent donkeys; rather, we are akin to other typical donkeys," (English translation and interpretation according to the William Davidson Talmud).

② One should add also that the impact of the HB was filtered through and interacted with the impact of the other authoritative works (e.g., Talmud, Mishna) that existed in the relevant, mental core "libraries" held by each of the said communities. To approach these matters, even if briefly, constitutes an encyclopedic endeavour.

希伯来《圣经》的一些思维习惯:对不同历史形态的犹太教之影响

埃胡德·本-兹维

【摘要】本文探讨了希伯来《圣经》本身及其诸多书卷所传达出的四种潜在的思维习惯,该思维习惯在后世犹太教各种历史形态的变迁中发挥了重要作用,这是本文的研究重点。在导言之后,本文首先关注根源历史及其意义的想象和记忆的思维习惯。随后,本文探讨了对灾难的记忆,以及该记忆与"被拣选的创伤"之间的关系,还包括摩西传统/托拉宗师之思维习惯与教导方法。本文关注的第三种思维习惯涉及神圣教义/托拉思想的多重含义。本文最后讨论的是抱有希望的思维习惯。总而言之,本文想要说明的问题是,在不同时代和地域(及社会)空间中,对希伯来《圣经》的不同阅读方式或认知如何塑造关键的、社会共享的思想和思维习惯。

【关键词】希伯来《圣经》;思维习惯;犹太教;记忆

Ruth as a Foreign Worker and the Politics of Exogamy

Athalya Brenner-Idan*

Abstract: The book of Ruth can and has been read as an optimistic, idyllic story of integration, of polemic against exogamy and xenophobia (see Ezra and Nehemiah), as a story of love, as a story of duty and ḥesed, of traditional Jewish conversion. Such readings and others are possible, certainly. What marks such interpretations is the common denominator of viewing the story as a comedy, the birth of a son being interpreted as a happy ending. But a happy ending for whom? Ultimately, so it appears, foreigners may be accepted into the target community: less so if they are of the underprivileged classes and women; and full integration, even in the case of Ruth, is in fact impossible. The variables of class, occupation and femaleness usually override those of foreignness and personal excellence — then and now.

Key Words: The Book of Ruth, Exogamy, Foreign Worker, Gender

Temporary, hopeful migration of workers from underprivileged locations to more developed locations sometimes results in the workers' settling in the host location and a permanent or semi-permanent abandonment of the source community. A cluster of cultural issues — economic, religious, linguistic, and more — either contributes to the integration of the foreign worker in the host culture / location or hinders it. In this essay I shall examine some of such foreign workers' issues in modern Israel in light of the Ruth narrative while, simultaneously, rereading the Ruth narrative in light of those foreign workers' situation.

* Athalya Brenner-Idan, Professor Emerita, Biblical Studies University of Amsterdam.

Modern Israel imports workers, chiefly from Eastern Europe and the far east (for the purpose of the present paper, I shall not look at Israel's employment of Arab workers from the occupied territories). The importation of foreign workers is dictated by the country's fluctuating needs and human resource shortages and is subject to relatively stringent rules and quotas. Foreign workers sign a contract of employment. They generally do menial jobs, are often underpaid and badly treated by their employers. Presumably, however, they would fare even less well in their source communities economically; this is their prime motivation for coming and for staying for a while. Fifty-six foreign workers died in Israel in 1996, according to a report in the newspaper Ha'aretz from the end of August 1997, in spite of their legally enforced access to health and social care.

Foreign work in modern Israel is decidedly gendered. In sociological analyses, any line of employment whose practitioners are over fifty percent females is feminized, and vice versa. To follow this broad definition, the gendering of foreign workers is as follows. The majority of male workers will do construction and agriculture, a minority basic health care for the physically handicapped and other services. The majority of female workers do care work for the young, elderly or disabled, a minority agricultural work and other services. Female foreign workers are much in demand. Their stereotyped image is: young, positive, modest, trustworthy, industrious. Male workers have a stereotyped image of troublemakers and drunks.

There is no question of widespread integration of migrant foreign workers into Israeli society: the work permit is valid for a fixed and short period; cultural and religious differences are too great; there are language barriers; Israeli society is, by and large, snobbish and insular, suspicious of strangers and xenophobic; personal isolation and workers' group dynamics, not to mention specific living arrangements, contribute to their isolation. And yet, for financial gain and perhaps for other motives, foreign workers keep on coming back to Israel. And yet again, against all odds, some integration occurs in the form of cross-cultural marriages (although not all workers are single upon arrival). In Israel of the 1990s and beyond, such unions will be less problematic if the local spouse is a woman, ostensibly because any offspring of this union will still be considered Jewish according to orthodox halakhah;

however, both combinations are known to have happened. And, remarkably, more unions of local man-foreign woman worker are registered.

It is possible, perhaps illuminating, to read Ruth's story against this background. Some similarities between her situation and that of single, female foreign workers in modern Israel are apparent — although dissimilarities obtain as well they will not be discussed here. In the following discussion, I'm heavily indebted to Jack Sasson's commentary, whose results I view from this specific angle.①

Ruth comes from another culture, another language, another place. She is a *zārāh* (Heb. foreign, "other", not belonging to the community or family) woman (see Prov. 1-9). It is customary to idealize Ruth's decision of following Naomi to the strange land into a decision primarily motivated by her love for her mother-in-law, thus filling an obvious gap in the text: this is how I have read it, too. Point One of the present cross-cultural, cross-everything reading: Ruth might have had less of a free choice than we fondly imagine, as is the case with many a foreign worker nowadays.

Sasson points out in his commentary that Ruth binds herself to Naomi by verbal contract (1: 16-17). The concept of "love" (Heb. ḥesed) that is applicable here, as in the slave's love for his master in Exod. 21:2-6 [5], is a legal rather than an emotional concept: it indicates intent as well as consent. Point Two: Ruth initiates a contract implying that she has to work for Naomi, she has to take care of the older woman — see ch. 2 — as is true of many contracted female foreign workers. Questions concerning Naomi's inability or ability to fend for herself are thus made redundant: she has somebody contracted to do it for her.

The only one to notice Ruth at the end of ch. 1, the homecoming scene, is the narrator. Neither Naomi nor the Bethlehem women acknowledge her existence. Point Three: foreign workers are largely invisible to the dominant culture, in spite of the important work they perform.

Ruth decides to glean in Boaz's field. It can be argued that she thus

① J.M. Sasson, *Ruth: A New Translation with a Philological Commentary and a Formalist-Folklorist Interpretation* (Baltimore: The Johns Hopkins University Press, 1979); The Biblical Seminar, 10; Sheffield: JSOT Press, 2nd edn.

becomes a lowly agricultural worker. The laws, or customs, or utopian demand to make gleaning of agricultural produce accessible to the poor are codified in Lev. 19:9-10 and 23:22, Deut. 24:19 (see also Talmud Bavli, Pe'ah and Gittin). One could argue that Ruth is not an agricultural worker, since she is not employed by Boaz and does not receive wages for her activities. However, from her implied viewpoint, she is self-employed; does work in the field for her livelihood; does support Naomi by it. In that Hebrew Bible world, wages were probably in kind anyway. And, as will be seen, she does aspire to become a contractually recognized worker of Boaz's economic family (next point). Point Four: most foreign workers work as menial laborers; their livelihood depends to a large extent on seasonal changes and market demands.

Ruth is noticeably industrious. Point Five: a foreigner's — a foreign worker's — way to becoming visible is to try harder.

Boaz notices Ruth in his field, awards her some privileges but refuses to grant her a more solid footing among his local workers (ch. 2). Point Six: hard work is noticed; so is devotion. However, these are not enough for a female foreign worker if she seeks integration into the host society.

Naomi recommends that Ruth create a situation of seduction (3:1-4). Ruth apparently knows that seduction alone will not mean integration and asks Boaz directly to marry her (3:9). Irrespective of what precisely happens on the *goren* (Heb. "threshing floor") — did they? did they not? — Ruth is well aware of Point Seven: integration into the host community, if at all possible, can be achieved primarily and perhaps only by marriage. Having a "mentor" is not sufficient. And of Point Eight, of which Boaz is also aware (3:14): a foreign (working) woman should be especially mindful of her reputation; she has an image to protect as well as an image (the *zārāh*) to shun. And if she wants to be accepted by the host community, a foreigner — particularly such a female worker — ought to maintain a stereotype of apparent modesty and reticence. Hence, Ruth is silent and invisible through the negotiations in ch. 4 (vv. 1-10).

When Boaz declares his intention to marry Ruth she is compared to Rachel, Leah and Tamar (4:11-12); these verses are usually read as a special blessing conferred on a foreigner, thus concluding her integration into Judahite society. This can undoubtedly be so read. The mention of those female forerunners has a sting, however — and perhaps also a veiled sub-textual threat or warning. Those female figures constructed "the house of Israel", true; all three entered exogamous marriages or sexual relations with "our" men Jacob and Judah; all three produced children, future leaders and heirs. However, none is portrayed as an exemplary figure. The Leah and Rachel of the obvious intertext, Genesis 29-30, bicker and compete and their sons imitate their behavioral patterns. Tamar (Gen. 38) stretches sexual norms beyond the utmost limits. If the world of the Hebrew Bible, if the world-vision of the Ruth Scroll is of a world inhabited by just desserts and earned rewards, then Rachel's early death, Leah's death before Jacob, and Tamar's non-marriage to Judah are relevant asides on their behavior. It is futile to ask why no other ancestress is mentioned in this string of "foreign women". Nevertheless, a suspicion of ambivalence can and should be retained. Point Nine: can foreignness (Moabite in this case) and class (menial worker) be overcome, even when the foreigner conforms to a positive stereotype and embraces the local culture?

Much has been written about Ruth's disappearance from the last narrative scene of "her" story, the child's name-giving scene (4:14-17), in the text that bears her name. It seems unwarranted that, immediately upon fulfilling her duty as set out in the 'blessing' by bearing a male child, immediately upon following in Rachel and Leah and Tamar's footsteps, Ruth is rewarded by becoming as invisible as she is at the end of ch. 1. Several explanations for her disappearance from the final stage of the narrative have been offered. One solution is the traditional viewing of Naomi as the baby's caretaker or adoptive mother. Another is the understanding of the word bēn (Heb. "son"; v. 17: "a bēn is born unto Naomi") as 'child, offspring' rather than the straight forward "son", as if Naomi is not the male child's mother, but "simply" ancesteress, a figure in his blended family tree. Yet another explanation is to view the story's ending as a final fusion into one finale of the pretextually separate Naomi and Ruth stories.[1] Yet, another possibility is to draw one more analogy to the plight of female foreign workers in Israel and beyond today. Point

[1] A. Brenner, "Naomi and Ruth," in *A Feminist Companion to Ruth*, ed. A. Brenner (Sheffield: Sheffield Academic Press, 1993), 70-84.

Ten: a female foreigner can perhaps be integrated into Judahite, or Israelite, or Israeli, or another, society through marriage and motherhood — if and when the additional issue of class does not occur. Cultural, religious, linguistic, ethnic and similar variables can be overridden: this is the basis for royal political marriages and even nowadays for achieving citizenship status, for instance. Therefore, it seems that stereotypes of foreign femaleness can be either negative or positive or in between. But ultimately the factor of class, of social background and wealth or its lack and the resultant personal status involved, is the decisive determinant. Hence, finally, Ruth might be a prime example of this reality: a low-class foreign woman, a worker without property, will become invisible in the host community. She will be absorbed rather than integrated. Her prospects, however virtuous she is, are less than promising.

The book of Ruth can be read and has been read as an optimistic, idyllic story of integration, of polemic against exogamy and xenophobia (see Ezra and Nehemiah), as a story of love, as a story of duty and ḥesed. It has also been read as a story of traditional Jewish conversion. These readings and others are possible, certainly. What marks them is the common denominator of viewing the story as a comedy, the birth of a son being interpreted as a happy ending. But a happy ending for whom? Is it a happy ending for the foreigner, for the menial working woman Ruth? Read against the reality of foreign female work today, the story may seem much less celebratory. The realpolitik of economics, law, and labour supply and demand, supports the necessity to treat the foreigner reasonably well. However, custom mitigates the possibility of the foreigner crossing cultural boundaries into integration in the host culture. Foreigners may be accepted: less so if they are of the underprivileged classes and women; and full integration, even in the case of Ruth, an exemplary female character in many ways, is in fact impossible. The variables of class, occupation and femaleness usually override those of foreignness and personal excellence — then and now.

Postscript: Some further thoughts

This analysis of the Ruth story as the story of a labor worker was first

published about twenty years ago,[1] and I've returned to it as a possible interpretation of the Scroll's heroine motivation for her linking herself with Naomi several times.

Ruth's motivation is neither fully disclosed by the story's "real" narrator (outside the story, the one who composed it) nor by the implied narrator (inside the story, the implied narrator who tells us the story in the text itself). And while the woman neighbors assure Naomi that Ruth's motivation is "love" for her (4:15), this is one possible interpretation of her behaviour: it comes to us, as text consumers, from a third source, not put into the mouth of Ruth herself. Therefore, as often in reading biblical narratives or in listening to or visualizing them, even when the narrators (external and / or internal) seem to align themselves with a certain figure, a space may remain for more than one interpretation.

As stated above (p. 26), most commentators tend to valorize Ruth and her motives, in keeping with ideologies of social inclusion or the literary genre of comedy, or a successful origin story. Indeed, Ruth's behavior in chapters 1-3— her declared fealty to Naomi, her industrious work in the field, her obedience to Naomi's plan concerning Boaz — is presented as completely voluntary. Hence, it is easy to understand as motivated by her feelings for Naomi. And yet, since Ruth is so active throughout chs. 1-3, it is difficult to understand why she consistently chooses an inferior position to that of the other characters in the story by relying on emotional factors alone.

"Voluntary" behavior has many shades. It may be altruistic and unselfish; it may also be self-interested. Or a combination of the two — depending on the case and social circumstances.

Indeed, in terms of the story Ruth is socially inferior: a woman, a foreigner, a widow, and landless. Modesty behooves her in her new social environment if her goal is integration. Nevertheless, the question remains: why does she choose to leave her own land and go to the Unknown, then work so hard? She acts like a fugitive, or a refugee!

Here the analogy to modern-day work immigrants springs forcefully to

① Original version in A. Brenner ed. *A Feminist Companion to Ruth and Esther* (Sheffield: Sheffield Academic Press, 1999), 158-162.

mind. In our global world, migrants cross borders and risk their lives for many reasons: because of violence and military and political prosecution of race, color, religion and more, as well as natural catastrophes like draught, earthquakes, floods and hunger. Such a refuge seeking is hardly "voluntary", in many senses. But people also choose to migrate in order to improve their lot in life, or to help their families back home, at least for a fixed period.

Israel is a young country that is being relentlessly developed, but is aging fast, not least because of the high life expectancy. Its work force suffers permanent shortages of construction and agricultural workers on the one hand, and domestic care workers on the other hand. These are menial jobs, at the bottom of the social and financial scale, that Israeli citizens — even Israeli Arabs — tend to refuse. As a result, Israel allows a legal quota of foreigners, females and males, divided into categories, that can receive a working visa linked to a local employer for a fixed period of time. Thereafter the worker has to leave the country, unless s/he marries an Israeli citizen and thus becomes an immigrant and gains permanent residency or even citizenship.①

How are such foreign workers treated in Israeli society? Here we have to separate judicial regulations and social attitudes. Salaries, benefits and other employment conditions are mostly strictly controlled by the State, even enforced — but so are terms of sojourn, including expulsion from the country beyond the employment period. Socially, the picture is more complicated. Israeli society, especially Jewish society with Jews in the majority, is highly insular. Class, race, language, customs, gender and financial status are heavy markers. But a special hindrance to the integration of foreigners is that of identity. Israel, as a State, has not decided yet whether it is a democratic State operating equally for all its inhabitants; or a Jewish Homeland, in which Jews hold favored positions in many areas of Law and praxis. This is partly explained by the trauma of antisemitism which explains why every person born Jewish is immediately admitted into citizenship, unless a criminal. At the same time, it makes life for the foreign laborers in our midst, mostly Christians, unequal and unstable. The situation is of course exacerbated for laborers at the

① Like in other countries, there are many illegal refugees and work immigrants in Israel, especially in some urban areas. This article doesn't ignore their plight but also doesn't deal with that directly.

bottom of the pecking social order, and for women in particular, in spite of the essential jobs they do. And yet, as already noted, the foreign workers keep coming and are often unwilling to depart, citing the even worse conditions in their original communities.

So let's examine anew Ruth's declaration to Naomi (1:16-17).

> Do not urge me to leave you, to turn back and not follow you. For wherever you go, I will go; wherever you lodge, I will lodge; your people shall be my people, and your God my God. Where you die, I will die, and there I will be buried. Thus, and more may the LORD do to me if anything but death parts me from you. (JPSS)

Viewed in the light of female foreign workers, Ruth's declaration is a choice. She chooses to leave her own country. She chooses to join another community. She chooses to change her religion. She chooses for a permanent solution for herself, not a time-limited one. And she chooses to care for Naomi, the elder woman.

I personally know of several Israelis, especially elderly, whose foreign care givers remained with them, serving them with devotion and love, until their death, then left to go back to their own country, or tried to stay with another employer, in most of the cases illegally. I also know of cases of eventual marriage, especially of female foreign workers with Israeli men. The case of Ruth is so similar to that of reading both "texts" cross-textually (to borrow a term from Archie C.C. Lee) against each other — the Ruth Scroll against the foreign workers' situation — that it may enhance our understanding of both.

I've interpreted Ruth specifically against the Israeli context because this is the context which I know best. But you, every one of you, can compare this with your own context; and see how much you can gain, for the then and for now, and for biblical scholarship.

作为外来劳工的路得与族外婚政治

阿塔雅·布伦纳-伊丹

【摘要】《路得记》通常会被解读成一个乐观的、具有田园诗意的、关于外族融入以色列民的故事，是对族外婚和排外主义（见《以斯拉记》与《尼希米记》）的论战，同时也是一个关于爱的故事，关于责任与慈爱的故事，代表对犹太教传统价值的皈依。当然，这样的解读或者其他的解读都可以是合理的。这类解读的共同点是把这个故事看作是一部喜剧，最后儿子的出生被理解为一个合家欢的结尾。然而，对谁来说这是一个合家欢的结局？看起来最终异邦人似乎会被目标群体接纳。但是，假如这些异邦人属于贫困阶层或是女性，就不会那么容易。而要获得完全接纳，甚至在路得的故事中，事实上也是不可能的。阶级、职业、性别，这些变量往往比异邦的独特性、个人特性有更重要的决定性作用——过去如此，现在依然如此。

【关键词】《路得记》；族外婚；外来劳工；性别

Giants in the Bible and the *Shanhaijing*: A Study in Comparative Anthropology

Ronald Hendel*

Abstract: A study of the perspectives on giants in the Bible and the *Shanhaijing*. The two perspectives are organized by different hierarchies of space and time and distinctive ideologies, but similarly privilege the observer — Chinese or Israelite — in the order of things. Both perspectives are arguably shaped by a shared ecological feature: megalithic structures in the landscape that serve as a visual reminder of the presence of giants in the periphery or the past.

Key Words: Giants, Bible, *Shanhaijing*, Center-Periphery

The ancient Classic (or Guideways) of Mountains and Seas (*Shanhaijing*, ca. 4th-1st cents. BCE) includes a cautionary note in the prologue to its second section: "Things possessing anomalous forms are those born with divine natures. Whether they are long-lived or short, only the sage can understand their ways" (6.1a).[1] Despite this limitation, I wish to explore the ways of some of the anomalous creatures in the *Shanhaijing* and the Hebrew Bible as an exercise in what Eduardo Viveiros de Castro calls "perspectival anthropology,"[2] that is, a comparison of the relations and representations of self and others across cultures. Such comparison also

---

* Ronald Hendel, Professor, University of California, Berkeley.

① Trans. Richard Strassberg, *A Chinese Bestiary: Strange Creatures from the Guideways Through Mountains and Seas* (Berkeley: University of California Press, 2002), 30.

② Eduardo Viveiros de Castro, *The Relative Native: Essays on Indigenous Conceptual Worlds* (Chicago: Hau, 2015), 55-74.

necessarily includes the researcher's perspective as a mediating and equivocal term. Castro writes:

> Doing anthropology means comparing anthropologies, nothing more —but nothing less. Comparison is not just our primary analytic tool. It is also our raw material and our ultimate grounding, because what we compare are always and necessarily, in one form or another, comparisons.①

By comparing comparisons, we perceive more richly some of the distinctive features of each culture in conjunction with their shared practices. Comparison always entails a blend of similarity and difference, such that the comparanda — in this case, giants and humans — can expose different constellations of local anthropology. In this sense all our perspectives — ancient and modern — may enter a dialogue of respectful illumination and critique.

I hope to show that the perspectives on giants in the *Bible* and the *Shanhaijing* are organized by two different hierarchies: (1) a spatial order arranged around a cosmic center in the *Shanhaijing*, which implicitly supports an ideology of imperial expansion and rule, and (2) a temporal order arranged around the genealogical principle in the Hebrew Bible, which implicitly supports the ideology of a peripheral latecomer in its cultural sphere. Each hierarchy serves to privilege the observer — Chinese or Israelite — in the order of things, either as its spatial center or its temporal turning point. These two perspectives also shape different affective responses to the giants in distinctive mixtures of wonder and fear. While the giants are conceived differently in the two book — particularly with respect to space, time, and affect — both perspectives are arguably shaped by a shared ecological circumstance. The presence of megalithic structures in the landscape seems to be a visual reminder, in both cultures, of the presence of giants in the periphery or the past.

Giants in the *Shanhaijing*

The *Shanhaijing* presents a mythic geography of the world, proceeding from the mountains of central China — organized into the center and the four

① Eduardo Viveiros de Castro, *The Relative Native: Essays on Indigenous Conceptual Worlds*, 56.

cardinal directions — to the surrounding seas and the lands within and beyond them.[1] This is an imagined landscape, which only loosely corresponds to physical geography (e.g., there are no encircling seas around central China). The book is an itinerary of strange creatures, some of which have healing or other propitious properties, and local gods and spirits. After leaving the mountains of central China, the local creatures include strange humans with one or more bizarre features, such as the Pendant-Ears People, the One-Eyes People, the Long-Arms People, the Long-Thighs People, the People Without Calves, and the Feathered People. As Richard Strassberg observes, the *Shanhaijing* is a mythic travelogue and bestiary, in which "fact and fantasy combined... to distribute a diverse population of strange creatures throughout a vast, sacred geography where they dwell in the eternal present of mythological time."[2] Over five hundred anomalous creatures populate this cosmic geography.

This panorama illustrates a binary opposition of civilized people and barbarians. As Anne Birrell comments, this duality "followed the notion that non-Chinese people and foreign lands were symbolically and literally separated from the sacred heartland by four surrounding seas, divided into inner and outer, which formed a sort of cordon sanitaire between civilization and barbarism."[3] The peoples of foreign lands are "others" both with respect to geography and physiognomy — they are distant from the center and have strange bodies.

Among these exotic creatures are several groups of giants, mostly to the north and east, who are described with a blend of wonder and amusement:

> The Land of Bofu [in the north] lies east of the Land of the People Who Hold Up Their Ears. They are giants. In their right hand they hold

① See Trans. Richard Strassberg, *A Chinese Bestiary: Strange Creatures from the Guideways Through Mountains and Seas*; Rémi Mathieu, *Étude sur la mythologie et l'ethnologie de la Chine ancienne: Traduction annotée du Shanhai jing* (2 vols.; Paris: Collège de France, 1983); Riccardo Fracasso, "The Shanhaijing: A Bibliography by Subject," *Cina* 23 (1991): 81-104; Anne Birrell, *The Classic of Mountains and Seas: Translated with an Introduction and Notes* (New York: Penguin, 1999).

② Trans. Richard Strassberg, *A Chinese Bestiary: Strange Creatures from the Guideways Through Mountains and Seas*, 10.

③ Anne Birrell, *The Classic of Mountains and Seas: Translated with an Introduction and Notes*, XVII.

a green snake, and in their left hand they hold a yellow snake. (8.3a)[①]

The Land of Giants lies to the north [beyond the seas]. Its people are very big. They sit down and scrape away to make boats. (9.1a)[②]

Beyond the East Sea in the Great Wilderness... is the Land of Giants. There is the market of Giants. Its name is the Hall of the Giants. One of these Giants sits back on his heels up on the Hall. He is pulling on both of his ears. (14.2)[③]

There are people here [beyond the northeast sea] named the Giants, and here is the Land of Giants. They have Li as their family name. They are millet-eaters. (17.2a)[④]

In the southern region [within the south sea] there are the Giants of Gan. They have a human face, long forearms, and a black body. They are hairy and their heels are back-to-front. When they see humans, they laugh so much that their lips cover their whole face. This is how other people make their escape from the giants. (18.5b)[⑤]

Several of these groups of giants practice arts of civilization — they carve wooden boats, shop at a big market, and eat millet, a civilized food.[⑥] These traits mark the giants as at least partially civilized "others." As Birrell observes, "millet-eaters among foreign peoples classify them as 'one of us,' but not quite." The giants also seem unthreatening. They are pictured as

---

① Anne Birrell, *The Classic of Mountains and Seas: Translated with an Introduction and Notes*, 123; Trans. Richard Strassberg, *A Chinese Bestiary: Strange Creatures from the Guideways Through Mountains and Seas*, 180.

② Anne Birrell, *The Classic of Mountains and Seas: Translated with an Introduction and Notes*, 127; Rémi Mathieu, *Étude sur la mythologie et l'ethnologie de la Chine ancienne: Traduction annotée du Shanhaijing*, 1. 429-430.

③ Anne Birrell, *The Classic of Mountains and Seas: Translated with an Introduction and Notes*, 159; Rémi Mathieu, *Étude sur la mythologie et l'ethnologie de la Chine ancienne: Traduction annotée du Shanhaijing*, 1. 526-527.

④ Anne Birrell, *The Classic of Mountains and Seas: Translated with an Introduction and Notes*, 183; Rémi Mathieu, *Étude sur la mythologie et l'ethnologie de la Chine ancienne: Traduction annotée du Shanhaijing*, 1. 601.

⑤ Anne Birrell, *The Classic of Mountains and Seas: Translated with an Introduction and Notes*, 193; Rémi Mathieu, *Étude sur la mythologie et l'ethnologie de la Chine ancienne: Traduction annotée du Shanhaijing*, 1. 635.

⑥ Anne Birrell, *The Classic of Mountains and Seas: Translated with an Introduction and Notes*, XX.

sitting down, some to carve boats and another to pull on his ears while resting on the market roof. They are, by turns, industrious and amusing. The southern giants are even comical. They look like monkeys, and when they see humans, they laugh uproariously.

The last instance — the Giants of Gan — has a distinctly perspectival quality, showing how the humans and giants perceive and respond to each other. To human eyes, the giants look like huge simians, perhaps "an anthropomorphic vision of an orangutan."[1] The giants' distended lips when they laugh accentuate their comical bodies and mask the giants' eyes, which is "how other people make their escape from the giants." This comment, while comical, implies that the humans fear the giants. They are exotic but potentially dangerous creatures. To the giants' eyes, it is humans who are exotic and comical, provoking uproarious laughter. In this mirrored perspective, each see the other as strange creatures, objects of wonder. This reflexivity shows a native anthropology in which the Self and Other are alike in their perceptions and affects, even as their bodies, locales, and degrees of civilization differ. This comparison seems at home in an imperial structure, in which civilized humans (i.e., Chinese) and foreigners subsist together in an ordered spatial hierarchy. The giants and the humans have their respective places in the cosmic imperium, with each kind practicing its ways in peace.

This picture of spatial hierarchy between center and periphery, in which humans, gods, and hybrids dwell, arguably reflects and supports the political ideology of the book's era of composition. As Strassberg argues, "The proliferation of the hybrid during the latter part of the Zhou dynasty can... be seen to embody a certain kind of cultural logic particular to the age... [and] mirrors the pluralistic nature of the feudal state... [E]ach major state was faced with reconciling the increasing quality of 'strangeness' to itself as it expanded and annexed culturally different appendages."[2] By this cultural logic, the hybrids "legitimately dwell in the environment alongside humankind and simply represent another, overlapping order with its own principles."[3] The

① Rémi Mathieu, *Étude sur la mythologie et l'ethnologie de la Chine ancienne: Traduction annotée du Shanhaijing*, 635 n. 4.

② Trans. Richard Strassberg, *A Chinese Bestiary: Strange Creatures from the Guideways Through Mountains and Seas*, 45.

③ Trans. Richard Strassberg, *A Chinese Bestiary: Strange Creatures from the Guideways Through Mountains and Seas*, 44.

hybrids are not monsters, who must be exterminated to make way for civilization. They dwell in their own mythical space, enclosed within the larger order.

In the *Shanhaijing*, the anomalous forms and strange natures of the giants are securely located in the distant periphery of the Kingdom of Heaven. This perspectival anthropology persisted for millennia. As Strassberg observes, "The Guideways continued to be a major source of... cultural information about distant foreign lands up until the late nineteenth century," ① as illustrated in Fig. 1.

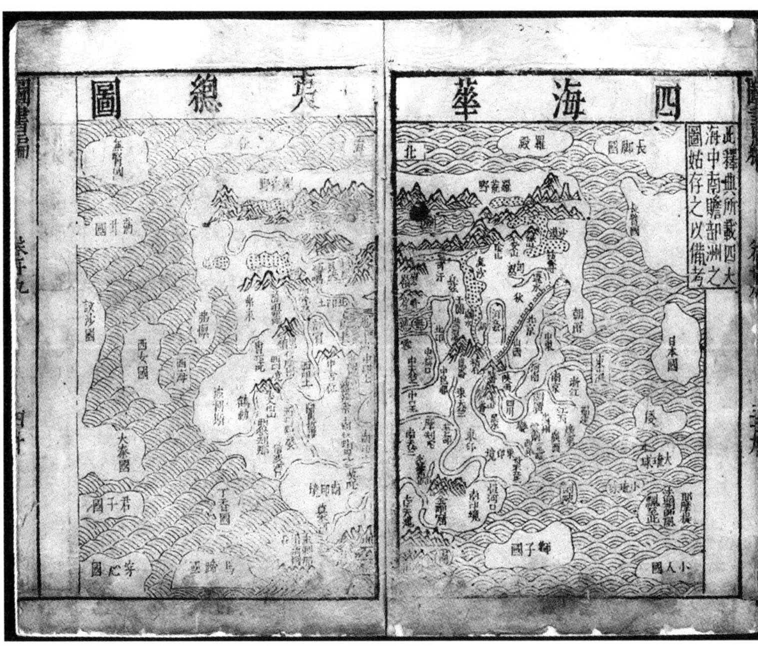

Fig. 1. Complete Map of the Four Seas, China, and the Barbarians (Sihai huayi zongtu), 1532.

Note: Several of the hybrid peoples from the *Shanhaijing* are listed in the regions within and beyond the surrounding seas, including the Long-Arms People and the Long-Thighs People (upper right) and the People Without Calves (upper left).

Source: Zhang Huang's Tushu bian (1613), Harvard-Yenching Library.

① Trans. Richard Strassberg, *A Chinese Bestiary: Strange Creatures from the Guideways Through Mountains and Seas*, 35.

Giants in the Hebrew Bible

According to the testimony of the Hebrew Bible, giants lived in the land of Canaan prior to the Israelite conquest. [1] The Israelites first encounter these giants when Moses appoints scouts to explore the region of Hebron prior to their entry into Canaan. On the scouts' return to the Israelite encampment, they report to Moses:

> "We came to the land that you sent us, and indeed it is flowing with milk and honey, and this [huge grape cluster] is its fruit. However, the people who live in the land are strong, and the cities are fortified and very great, and indeed we saw there the children of Anak." ...Caleb quieted the people before Moses and said, "Let us go up immediately and possess it, for we are able to prevail over it." But the people who went up with him said, "We are not able to go up against the people, for it is stronger than us... There we saw the Nephilim — the children of Anak are from the Nephilim — and we seemed in our eyes like grasshoppers, and so we seemed in their eyes." (Numbers 13:27-28, 30-31, 33)

This report (from the J source) ends with a striking perspectival note. To the Israelites, their puny size in the presence of the giants makes them seem like insects in comparison: "we seemed in our eyes like grasshoppers, and so we seemed in their eyes." They see themselves from the giants' perspective. But, unlike the Giants of Gan in the *Shanhaijing*, this perspectival encounter creates not comedy but terror. The scouts see that the giants would destroy them in battle with as little effort as humans would crush a grasshopper. The giants of Hebron, in this case of perspectival encounter, are wholly fearsome and dangerous. This is, of course, an imagined perspective — the Israelites see themselves through the giants' eyes, but we are not told what the giants themselves perceive. The Israelites are the agents in this scene ("we seemed...

---

[1] Ronald Hendel, "The Landscape of Memory: Giants and the Conquest of Canaan," in *Collective Identity and Collective Memory: Deuteronomy and the Deuteronomistic History in Their Context*, eds. Johannes U. Ro and Diana Edelman, BZAW 534 (Berlin: De Gruyter, 2021), 263-288.

we seemed"), and the giants the objects of terror.

The giants of Canaan go by several ethnonyms in the *Bible* — here Nephilim and children of Anak, and elsewhere Rephaim, Amorites, and other terms. The ethnonym Nephilim recalls the story in Genesis of their origins in the era before the flood:

> The Nephilim were on the earth in those days — and also afterwards — when the Sons of God went into the daughters of humans, and they bore children for them. These were the warriors of old, the men of renown. (Genesis 6:4)

The Nephilim are the hybrid offspring of male gods and female humans, and they become mighty warriors — although we are not told the details of their famous exploits. Their giant size — also not mentioned in Genesis — seems to come from their hybrid, semi-divine origins. This concept is shared with the Mesopotamian warrior-king Gilgamesh, who was two-thirds divine and one-third human, and was, according to the Hittite version, eleven cubits tall (16.5 ft. or 5 m).①

In Deuteronomy, Moses emphasizes the fearsome size of the giants, echoing the scouts' report: "It is a people greater and taller than us, with great cities fortified up to heaven, and indeed we saw there the children of the Anakim" (Deuteronomy 1:28). Moses expands on his description of the giants in his exhortation to Israel about the upcoming conquest:

> Hear O Israel, you are going to cross the Jordan today to go in and dispossess nations greater and mightier than you, with great cities fortified up to heaven, a people great and tall, the children of the Anakim, whom you know. And you have heard it said, "Who can stand before the children of Anak?" But know today that Yahweh, your God, he is going to cross before you as a devouring flame. And he will destroy them and subdue them before you, and you will dispossess them and destroy them quickly, as Yahweh has promised you. (Deuteronomy 9:1-3)

---

① Andrew R. George, *The Babylonian Gilgamesh Epic: Introduction, Critical Edition and Cuneiform Texts* (2 vols.; Oxford: Oxford University Press, 2003), 1. 447.

Moses emphasizes that Yahweh will vanquish the giants — "he will destroy them and subdue them" — after which the Israelites finish the job — "you will dispossess them and destroy them." Yahweh's destruction of the giants is the prelude to the Israelite conquest and settlement, which completes the redemptive drama of the Exodus and fulfills his promises to the ancestors.

The book of Amos draws a similar picture of Yahweh's destruction of the giants of Canaan (calling them Amorites):

> It was I who destroyed the Amorite before them,
> whose height is like the height of cedars,
> and whose strength is like oaks.
> And I destroyed his fruit above,
> and his roots below.
> It was I who brought you up from the land of Egypt,
> and I led you in the desert for forty years
> to inherit the land of the Amorite. (Amos 2:9-10)

The giants' height is compared to the height of cedars (the tallest known tree) and their strength to oak trees (the strongest tree). The tree metaphor is developed further when Yahweh states that he destroyed them utterly, from "his fruit above" to "his roots below." Even the strongest and tallest are utterly vanquished by Yahweh. In this perspectival poetry, the giants are huge and mighty in the natural landscape, but are insignificant compared to Yahweh. From God's perspective, the giants are mere grasshoppers.

According to these texts, Yahweh destroys the giants so that Israel can inherit the promised land. In Deuteronomy and Joshua, there is a double causality, such that the Israelites also destroy them. This destruction is carried out by Joshua's army:

> At that time Joshua came and cut off the Anakim from the hill country, from Hebron, from Debir, from Anab, and from all the hill country of Judah and from all the hill country of Israel, with their cities. Joshua eradicated them. No Anakim remained in the land of the children of Israel; only in Gaza, Gath, and Ashdod did they remain. (Joshua 11:21-22)

As this passage relates, a few giants survived the conquest. They survive in Israel in cities that will later become Philistine-Gaza, Gath, and Ashdod. The last of these giants are eventually destroyed by David and his men. According to 2 Samuel 21: 15-22, David's men kill four huge warriors "descended from the Raphah" (a biform of Rephaim), including one named Goliath of Gath. The defeat of this giant is retold in 1 Samuel 17, where it is David who kills Goliath. Goliath is a mighty warrior and tall — six cubits and a span (9.75 ft., 3 m; 1 Samuel 17:4)[①]— but David defeats him easily with his shepherd's sling.

The encounter between David and Goliath also has a perspectival touch. Although Goliath is a huge warrior wearing heavy armor, David, a young shepherd, views Goliath as a strange and uncivilized foreigner, comparable to a wild animal. As David says to King Saul:

> Your servant was a shepherd for his father's sheep, and when a lion or a bear would come and take a sheep from the flock, I would go out after it and kill it and rescue it from its mouth. And if it rose against me, I would seize it by the beard and strike it and kill it. Just as your servant killed the lion and the bear, so this uncircumcised Philistine will be like one of them. (1 Samuel 17:34-36)

Although this mighty warrior instills fear in Saul and the other Israelites, to David he is but an uncircumcised foreigner, comparable to the lions and bears that used to menace David's flock. The giant Philistine is but a wild beast.

Goliath mimics David's perspective when he asks, "Am I a dog, that you come to me with sticks?" (1 Samuel 17:43). This mockery is ironic, since David easily defeats Goliath with his sling and stone, as one would a dog or beast. David's victory over Goliath signals his ascent to kingship, which transforms his status as shepherd into the royal shepherd of Israel. His defeat of this last giant in Israel is a sequel to the conquest of the giants of Canaan by Yahweh and the Joshua generation.

In these stories of biblical giants, there is an implication that their existence is limited to the past. Yahweh and the Israelites destroy them so that

① 4QSam[a] and the LXX have a smaller height, four cubits and a span. It is not clear which number is original.

Israel may inherit the promised land. The giants' end is Israel's beginning. This theme is recapitulated in the story of David's rise, which yields the Davidic monarchy. In each case, the destruction of the giants is a necessary preliminary to the proper order of things. The giants belong to a past era, and their fate is their destruction. This temporal pastness of the giants seems to be encoded in several of their ethnonyms. They are Nephilim, literally the "fallen ones." The giants of Transjordan are the Rephaim, which also refers to shadowy spirits of the dead. Other ethnonyms include Emim, literally "terrors," and the Zamaummim, literally "whisperers." These mighty peoples were giants, but now they sleep in the dust. As Julius Wellhausen observed, the ethnonym Amorite also has a quality of past time: "While the Canaanites still live in the land in the present of the biblical narrator... the Amorites... belong only to the past, they have been exterminated."① The mighty giants are now only a memory.

The pastness of the giants is a feature of Israel's self-fashioning as a chosen people dwelling in a promised land. The place of the giants in their local anthropology can be elucidated in comparison with the anthropology of giants in the *Shanhaijing*. For the latter, the people of China are the indigenous inhabitants in the cosmic center — the Middle Kingdom — and the giants — anomalous hybrids-dwell in the periphery. The center and periphery are linked spatially and conceptually within the imperial order of the cosmos. This cultural logic makes the giants objects of wonder — and even comedy — in their exotic domains. In the Hebrew Bible, the giants are the indigenous people in the cosmic center, and it is Israel who are a peripheral people, arriving on the scene of history long after the dispersion of the nations (see the Table of Nations and the Tower of Babel in Genesis 10-11).

In the cultural logic of the Hebrew Bible, other people came first in the genealogy, and Israel's rise is a turning point of history. In the meantime, the cosmic center — the land of Israel — is occupied by dangerous "others" — giants — until the time of Israel's conquest and settlement. The indigenous giants are liminal, both with respect to their anomalous physiognomy and their

① Julius Wellhausen, *Die Composition des Hexateuchs und der historischen Bücher des Alten Testaments* (3rd ed.; Berlin: Reimer, 1899), 343.

existence in the pre-Israelite era. In a sense, they are a temporal place-holder — a people doomed to die — until the time when the rightful dwellers in the cosmic center arrive.

Tab. 1 indicates some contrasts in the human-giant relations in the Bible and the *Shanhaijing*. For Israel the giants are peripheral in time, while in China they are peripheral in space.

Tab. 1 Contrasts in the Human-Giant Relations in the Bible and the *Shanhaijing*

	periphery	center
space	giants	Chinese
time	giants	Israelites

In both cultures, the giants are foreign and hybrid "others," dwelling on the far side of the central order of things. For Israel, this set of contrasts marks the Israelites as the rightful possessors of the land, fulfilling their destiny as the chosen people and liberating the land from frightening creatures. For China, the rightful possession of the land is not in question, since the civilized Chinese are the land's original inhabitants, perpetually dwelling in the cosmic center. In the *Shanhaijing* the perspectival anthropology is rooted in the spatial hierarchy of empire, whereas for Israel the perspective is temporal, embedded in genealogical time. The indigenous giants, in this sense, guard the temporal boundary of Israelite identity.

The Landscape of Memory: Megaliths in China and Israel

The *Shanhaijing* attributes the creation of the landscape to the great god Yu, who filled in the surface of the earth after the flood and "mark[ed] the divisions and boundaries under the sky and on earth" (5.54a).① Within this landscape is a feature that may be related to the anthropology of giants in China and Israel. This is arguably a shared feature of the two cultures, in

① Anne Birrell, *The Classic of Mountains and Seas: Translated with an Introduction and Notes*, 103; Rémi Mathieu, *Étude sur la mythologie et l'ethnologie de la Chine ancienne: Traduction annotée du Shanhaijing*, 1. 372.

which the giants are signified in the landscape. In both cases, massive stone structures seem to mark the existence of giants.

In traditional Chinese scholarship, the giants of the *Shanhaijing* are often identified with foreign peoples of northeast China (Dongbei) or Korea. As Strassberg observes, the passages about giants tend to "refer to the north or east, leading to speculation that ancient mythology located such a giant people somewhere between China and the Korean Peninsula."① It may not be coincidence that the landscape in this area is marked by a profusion of dolmens, huge stone structures built in the Bronze Age (ca. 2000-200 BCE) as burial chambers. These dolmens are found throughout northeast China and Korea. Fig. 2 presents a dolmen in Shipengshan. Sarah Nelson writes:

> The Chinese term is *shipeng*, stone huts, which indicates both their size and their construction with four upright stone slabs topped by a much larger capstone. Dolmens are most numerous in the Liaodong peninsula, where they tend to be large and well made, with polished stones rather than the raw slabs that characterize Korean dolmens. One dolmen near Yingkou, for example, was large enough to have been reused as a building. The interior is 2.8 by 2.6 m while the cover slab is 8.6 by 5.7 m. Dolmens are known as far north as Jilin province.②

The dolmen fields are densest in the Korean peninsula, where some 50,000 have been recorded. As Jangsuk Kim comments, "Dolmens were conspicuous monuments that were both physically and symbolically imprinted on the landscape."③

---

① Trans. Richard Strassberg, *A Chinese Bestiary: Strange Creatures from the Guideways Through Mountains and Seas*, 207; Rémi Mathieu (*Étude sur la mythologie et l'ethnologie de la Chine ancienne: Traduction annotée du Shanhai jing* , 1. 429 n. 8) notes that the Han state conquered and colonized northwest Korea (Gojoseon) in the late second century BCE.

② Sarah Milledge Nelson, "Introduction," in *The Archaeology of Northeast China: Beyond the Great Wall*, ed. Nelson (London: Routledge, 1995), 16. See further Bai Yun Xiang, "Megalithic Monuments in the Northeast Area and Eastern Coast of China," in *Meeting on Megalithic Culture: Comparing Prehistoric Ruins of the East and Europe* (Nara, Japan: ACCU, 2003), 41-53 (www.nara.accu.or.jp/img/report/Internationalconference/i2002.pdf).

③ Jangsuk Kim, "From Labour Control to Surplus Appropriation: Landscape Changes in the Neolithization of Southwestern Korea," *Journal of World Prehistory* 27 (2014): 270.

Fig. 2. Dolmen in Shipengshan 石棚山石棚, near Yingkou, Liaodong Peninsula, China. Note: The capstone is 8.6 m (28.2 ft.) long and 5.7 m (18.7 ft.) wide.

The connection between the landscape of megalithic structures in northeast China and Korea and the locale of the giants of the *Shanhaijing* is comparable to the link between megalithic structures in Israel and Transjordan and the locale of giants in the Bible. The dense dolmen fields in northern Israel and Transjordan, built during the Early Bronze age of the Levant (third millennium BCE), corresponds to the regions of Bashan, Ammon, and Moab, the territory of the Transjordanian Rephaim, Emim, and Zamzummim. The Bedouin call these stone structures "houses of the ghouls" (biyūt el ghūl). As Paul Karge and others have argued, these megalithic structures were likely viewed by Iron Age peoples as the remains of ancient giants.① Other huge stone structures in Israel — particularly the ruins of Middle Bronze Age cyclopean walls (ca. 2000-1550 BCE) in sites such as Hebron and Gath — were likely also instrumental to the biblical memory of giants in the land.

Fig. 3 is a photo of two dolmens near Amman, Jordan. One of the

① Paul Karge, *Rephaim: Die vorgeschichtliche Kultur Palästinas und Phöniziens. Archäeologische und religionsgeschichtliche Studien* (Paderborn: Schöningh, 1917), 612-613.

dolmens is roughly the size of the bed of Og, one of the last of the Rephaim, which could be seen in biblical times at Rabbat-Ammon:

> For only Og, king of Bashan, was left of the remnant of the Rephaim. Behold his bed — an iron bed — is it not in Rabbat of the children of Ammon? Nine cubits is its length and four cubits its width, according to the common cubit. (Deuteronomy 3:11)

The bed of this "remnant of the Rephaim" measures some 13.5 feet long and 6 feet wide. The capstone of the dolmen on the right (below) in Amman measures 12 feet long and 6 feet wide. It was razed during the expansion of Amman in the 1950's, but it — or a dolmen like it — was likely regarded as a giant's bed in biblical times.[1]

Fig. 3. Dolmens near Amman, Jordan.

Note: The capstone of the foreground dolmen is 8 ft. (2.4 m) square. The capstone of dolmen on the right is 12 ft. (3.7 m) long and 6 ft. (1.8 m) wide.

Source: Photo by A. M. Mantell, 1910, courtesy of the Palestine Exploration Fund (PEF-P-4048).

---

① The description of Og's bed as "iron" is a difficulty; one would expect stone or flint; see Ronald Hendel, "The Landscape of Memory: Giants and the Conquest of Canaan," 280.

Elsewhere, dolmens are often identified as giants' beds or tombs, for example German: *Riesenbetten*, *Hünenbettten*, or *Riesengräber*; Dutch: *hunebedden*; Swedish: *Jättegrafvar*; and Italian (Sardinia): *Tombe dei Giganti*. In this respect, the dolmens are memory-stones, the works of giants.

In his study of the "legendary topography" (topographie légendaire) of the Holy Land, Maurice Halbwachs remarks that the landscape's "visible facts are the symbols of invisible truths."① Megaliths in China and the Levant, to premodern eyes, arguably signified the past existence of giants. Their works were striking features of the landscape. These stone structures point to mighty figures and forces of the past and present. Compared to them, the people may have seemed in their own eyes like grasshoppers, evoking emotions of wonder and fear.

Conclusions

Mary Douglas emphasizes on anomalies in the task of cross-cultural comparison: "By focusing on how anomalous beings may be treated in different systems of classification, we make a frontal attack on the question of how thought, words and the real world are related."② This task has global and particularistic aspects: we gain insight into how people across time and space connect up thought, word, and reality, and how particular peoples do this in local contexts. Anomalous creatures — for instance, pigs and giants in the Hebrew Bible — can be real or fictive, and their status is dependent on the background classification scheme. For instance, pigs are unclean within the class of land animals because they do not chew their cud (Leviticus 11:7), while giants are anomalous because they are hybrids of humans and gods (Genesis 6:4). In the *Shanhaijing*, giants and other exotic creatures are anomalous hybrids, "born with divine natures" and difficult to understand (6.1a).

By comparing the comparisons between humans and hybrids in these

① Maurice Halbwachs, *On Collective Memory*, ed. Lewis A. Coser (Chicago: University of Chicago Press, 1992), 204.

② Mary Douglas, *Implicit Meanings*: *Essays in Anthropology* (London: Routledge & Kegan Paul, 1975), 282.

two cultures, we learn about each culture's "typology of the strange."[①] The political and religious ideologies behind these typologies are also illuminated: the imperial Mandate of Heaven in China and the temporally belated chosen people in Israel. The different perspectives on giants point to the importance of hybrid forms in each culture's self-fashioning.

This type of perspectival anthropology also illuminates modern constellations of thought. We moderns tend to be skeptical of the existence of giants for a variety of reasons, including what Weber called the rationalizing process of "the disenchantment (*Entzauberung*) of the world."[②] This process has analogues and precedents in ancient China and Israel. The founder of Chinese historiography, Sima Qian, wrote in his *Shiji* (ca. 100 BCE): "As for the strange beings illustrated in the 'Basic Annals of Yü' and in the *Shanhaijing*, I do not dare speak about them." [③] As Nicola Di Cosmo comments, "This passage constitutes the most direct evidence of the historian's quest for a non-mythological, observable, and empirically testable knowledge of foreign lands."[④] On the biblical side, the allegorist Philo of Alexandria (1st cent. CE) maintained that the concept of giants in the Bible is meant non-literally: "He [Moses] uses this name analogically, when he wishes to indicate excessive size of body."[⑤] Philo rationalizes the giants by redefining the terms, an exegetical move adopted by many interpreters in Jewish and Christian traditions.

Chinese interpreters also appealed to figurative language in order to maintain the veracity of the *Shanhaijing*'s hybrid creatures. As Strassberg observes, the scholar Bi Yuan (1730-1797) "argued that the book was not at all concerned with discussing the strange, for if the language were understood

---

① See Trans. Richard Strassberg, *A Chinese Bestiary: Strange Creatures from the Guideways Through Mountains and Seas*, 43.

② H. H. Gerth and C. Wright Mills, eds. *From Max Weber: Essays in Sociology* (New York: Oxford University Press, 1958), 139-140.

③ Trans. Nicola Di Cosmo, *Ancient China and Its Enemies: The Rise of Nomadic Power in East Asian History* (Cambridge: Cambridge University Press, 2004), 292.

④ Trans. Nicola Di Cosmo, *Ancient China and Its Enemies: The Rise of Nomadic Power in East Asian History*, 292.

⑤ Philo, *Questions and Answers on Genesis*, ed. and trans. Ralph Marcus (LCL 380; Cambridge: Harvard University Press, 1953), 60-61.

figuratively, even the most fantastic descriptions could be seen to refer to actual creatures or foreign peoples."① The category of the figural allows the classic text to preserve its truthful representation of reality.

In 1869 Theodor Noldeke took a step that these interpreters could not, describing the giants as fictional creatures of folklore: the giants "were for the Hebrews about the same as the Hunen for our people and the Joten for the Scandinavians."② This perception of the biblical giants as fictive rests on a comparison with other giants, whose nature is shaped by the background category of folklore. This category, constructed in the mid-nineteenth century, has, as Dan Ben Amos observes, "a triad of attributes — traditionalism, irrationality, and rurality."③ For the modern scholar, giants are what other people believe, primarily peasants and premoderns. In the Folk-Studies Movement in China of the 1920's and 30's, scholars brought this perspective to bear on the *Shanhaijing*.④ Here too, the conceptual and affective responses to anomalous creatures are determined by the local classificatory system.

For us moderns, the status of giants remains perspectival, but when we see them in our classic texts, they no longer look back at us. In a sense, our understanding of how thought, words, and worlds relate still includes their hybridity, marking a difference with others in space and time. The giants animate our cultural maps and genealogies, even as they no longer exist in the landscapes of the real world.

① Trans. Richard Strassberg, *A Chinese Bestiary: Strange Creatures from the Guideways Through Mountains and Seas*, 25.

② Theodor Nöldeke, *Untersuchungen zur Kritik des alten Testaments* (Kiel: Schwers, 1869), 161; see also Theodor H. Gaster, *Myth, Legend, and Custom in the Old Testament* (2 vols.; New York: Harper & Row, 1969), 1. 311-312.

③ Dan Ben Amos, "The Idea of Folklore: An Essay," in *Folklore Concepts: Histories and Critiques* (Bloomington: Indiana University Press, 2020), 1.

④ Trans. Richard Strassberg, *A Chinese Bestiary: Strange Creatures from the Guideways Through Mountains and Seas*, 27-28.

《圣经》与《山海经》中的巨人族:一种比较人类学的研究

罗纳德·亨德尔

【摘要】本文是对《圣经》与《山海经》中有关巨人族记叙的视角研究。这两个视角,以不同时空等级及独特的意识形态建构而成,当然,作为观察者的中国人和以色列人,可以从其建构的秩序中获得(显出)其特权。可以说,这两个视角皆被共同生态环境特征塑造:巨石结构在他们的视觉上提醒他们,巨人族存在于文化边缘或是遥远的过去。

【关键词】巨人族;《圣经》;《山海经》;中心—边缘

JEWISH STUDIES
犹太研究
第18辑

The Rise of Holy Mountains: Historical Traditions of Zion and Sinai in the Hebrew Bible*

JIANG Zhenshuai**

Abstract: The traditions of the holy mountains, which refer primarily to Mount Zion and Mount Sinai, are presented prominently in the biblical writings. The tradition of Mount Sinai has long been conceived as the starting point for discussion of the chronological relationship between Mount Zion and Mount Sinai. However, with the discovery of new archeological data and new insights into the compositional history of the Torah over the last several decades, there have been increasing voices arguing that the relationship between the traditions of Mount Zion and Mount Sinai probably has a more complex history than what has been perceived. Thus, the historical interactions of the two mountains have to be reconsidered. This article will contextualize the historical development of the traditions of the holy mountains against the background of the historical experiences of the Jerusalem temple in the Babylonian exilic and early Persian periods. It will argue that the interactions of the traditions of Zion and Sinai eventually led to a historical transformation from the traditions of the former to those of the latter.

* This article is a part of a research project of the Humanities and Social Sciences Foundation of the Ministry of Education of China (The Interrelations between Legal and Prophetic Traditions in the Hebrew Bible; Project No. 20YJC730002).

** Jiang Zhenshuai, Associate Researcher, Center for Judaic and Inter-Religious Studies, Shandong University.

Key Words: Ancient Israelite Religion, Hebrew Bible, Mount Zion, Mount Sinai, Jerusalem Temple

Ⅰ. Introduction to Traditions of Holy Mountains in Ancient Israel

The traditions of the holy mountains in the ancient Israelite religion refer primarily to Mount Zion and Mount Sinai. In biblical writings, Mount Zion and Mount Sinai are constructed rhetorically as two important natural places at the geographical level, and as sacred places on the symbolic level.① Mount Sinai is constructed not only as a place where the Israelites receive YHWH's revelation, but also as the place where Moses, as the leader of the Israelites, receives the law and make a covenant with YHWH. It eventually becomes a place with religious significance, wherein the identity of Israelites is defined by an association with the covenant of YHWH.② Mount Sinai's broader narrative context is that of the Israelites wandering in the Sinai wilderness, and is thus closely connected with the Exodus narrative. The tradition of Mount Zion, on the other hand, is closely linked with the city of Jerusalem and the Jerusalem temple.③ Compared to the term "Sinai," the term "Zion," however, is primarily presented outside of the Torah.

From the perspective of the biblical narrative, the tradition of Mount Sinai

---

① Jon D. Levenson, *Sinai and Zion: An Entry into the Jewish Bible* (San Francisco: Harper & Row, 1987); George J. Brooke, "Moving Mountains: From Sinai to Jerusalem," in *The Significance of Sinai: Traditions about Divine Revelation in Judaism and Christianity*, eds. George J. Brooke et al. (Leiden and Boston: Brill, 2008), 73-89; Konrad Schmid, *A Historical Theology of the Hebrew Bible*, trans. Peter Altmann (Grand Rapids, MI: Eerdmans, 2019), 412-424; Andreas Bedenbender, "Warum am Horeb? Zur Lokalisierung von Gottesoffenbarungen in der Hebräischen Bibel," *BK* 66 (2011): 219-223.

② Graham I. Davies, "Mount Sinai," in *The Anchor Bible Dictionary* Ⅵ, ed. David N. Freedman (New York: Doubleday, 1992), 47-49; Stefan Timm, "Sinai," in *Theologische Realenzyklopädie* ⅩⅩⅪ, ed. Gerhard Müller (Berlin: De Gruyter, 2000), 283-285; Christoph Dohmen, *Exodus 19-40* (Freiburg: Herder, 2004), 52-57.

③ Martin Metzger, "Zion: Gottes Berg, Gottes Wohnung, Gottes Stadt," in *Laetare Jerusalem: Festschrift zum 100 jährigen Ankommen der Benediktinermönche auf dem Jerusalmer Zionsberg*, ed. Nikodemus C. Schnabel (Münster: Aschendorff, 2006), 41-63; Eckart Otto, "צִיּוֹן ṣijjôn," in *Theologisches Wörterbuch zum Alten Testament* Ⅵ, eds. G. Johannes Botterweck et al. (Stuttgart: Kohlhammer, 1989), 994-1028; W. Harold Mare, "Zion," in *The Anchor Bible Dictionary* Ⅵ, 1096-1097.

appears much earlier than that of Mount Zion. From a historical perspective, however, the issue is more complicated. While there is still a possibility that the tradition of Mount Sinai is an ancient tradition in Israelite history, it is becoming increasingly plausible that the Sinai tradition in its present form, i.e., associated with the revelation of YHWH, is a later construct. Traditional perceptions of the relationship between the traditions of Sinai and Zion need to be reconsidered.① This article will first discuss how the tradition of Mount Zion, with its religious significance, originated in the late Judean context, and then analyze the historical process of transformation from the tradition of Mount Zion to that of Mount Sinai in the exilic and the postexilic periods. Lastly, it will point out that the interactions of the traditions of Mount Zion and Mount Sinai were mainly shaped by the fall of the Jerusalem temple in the Babylonian Exile.

Ⅱ. The Rise of the Tradition of Mount Zion in the Late Judean Context

The term "Zion" in the biblical narrative has multiple meanings. It was generally associated with Mount Zion and the city of Jerusalem. Most of the texts referring to the Zion tradition appear in the prophetic writings such as Isaiah and in The Book of Psalms. The earlier traditions of Mount Zion are presented in Isa. 1, 8; Ps. 46, 48, 76, 84, 87. The basic features of the early tradition of Mount Zion should thus be deduced from these texts.②

Isa. 8 is generally considered to be the core text of Isa. 1-12 and, as such, is an important window into understanding the beginning of the composition of The Book of Isaiah in the 8th century BCE.③ There is a statement about the

---

① See, e.g., Konrad Schmid, *A Historical Theology of the Hebrew Bible*, 412-424.

② Corinna Körting, *Zion in den Psalmen* (Tübingen: Mohr Siebeck, 2006); Ulrich Berges, "Die Zionstheologie des Buches Jesaja," *EsBib* 58 (2000): 167-198; Ronald E. Clements, "Zion as Symbol and Political Reality: A Central Isaianic Quest," in *Studies in the Book of Isaiah*, eds. Jacques Van Ruiten and Marc Vervenne (Leuven: Peters, 1997), 3-17.

③ Reinhard G. Kratz, *The Prophets of Israel*, trans. Anselm C. Hagedorn and Nathan MacDonald (Winona Lake: Eisenbrauns, 2015), 40-45; Konrad Schmid, "The Origins of the Book of Isaiah," in *Sibyls, Scriptures, and Scrolls: John Collins at Seventy*, eds. Joel Baden, Hindy Najman, and Eibert Tigchelaar (Leiden: Brill, 2017), 1166-1185; Uwe Becker, *Jesaja — von der Botschaft zum Buch* (Göttingen: Vandenhoeck & Ruprecht, 1997).

close connection between YHWH and Zion in Isa. 8: 18. Here, Zion is understood as a dwelling place for YHWH. This notion demonstrates the typical traditional perception of the relationship between YHWH and Mount Zion: YHWH resides on Mount Zion and from there YHWH protects the city of Jerusalem and its citizens.①

The tradition of Mount Zion as the "holy mountain" can be found in Ps. 48 (e.g., Ps. 48:2 [Eng. 48:1]).② Psalm 48 also states the significance of the relationships between Mount Zion and the city of Jerusalem.③ Psalm 48 presents Mount Zion as a place belonging to YHWH, who "has shown himself a sure defense" (Ps. 48:4 [Eng. 48:3]). In this appraisal of Mount Zion Jerusalem is understood as being protected from YHWH who resides on it. With the notion of Mount Zion as the residential place of YHWH, Ps. 48 therefore also includes a typical traditional idea of Mount Zion: YHWH is portrayed as ruling from Mount Zion, and the appearance of YHWH on Mount Zion ensures the stability and security of the city of Jerusalem and the state of Judah. The notion of YHWH living on Mount Zion further strengthens the concept of an invulnerable Jerusalem.

In the broad cultural context of the ancient Near East, the concepts of holy mountains such as Zion are not exceptional.④ The notion of Zion as a divine residential place stems from a similar cultural background. The entire formation of the Zion theology, which portrays Mount Zion as being capable of protecting Jerusalem and the temple with the presence of the divine power,

① Konrad Schmid, "Zion bei Jesaja," in *Zion: Symbol des Lebens in Judentum und Christentum*, eds. Tanja Pilger and Markus Witte (Leipzig: Evangelische Verlagsanstalt, 2013), 9-23.

② All translations of biblical texts are from the NRSV.

③ Corinna Körting, *Zion in den Psalmen*, 165-177.

④ Richard Clifford, *The Cosmic Mountain in Canaan and the Old Testament* (Cambridge MA.: Harvard University Press, 1972); Klaus Koch, "Ḫazzi-Ṣafôn-Kasion: Die Geschichte eines Berges und seiner Gottheiten," in *Religionsgeschichtliche Beziehungen zwischen Kleinaisien, Nordsyrien und dem Alten Testament, Internationales Symposion Hamburg 17-21. März 1990*, eds. Bernd Janowski et al. (Freiburg: Universitätsverlag; Göttingen: Vandenhoeck & Ruprecht, 1993), 171-223; Johannes Renz, "'Jahwe ist der Gott der ganzen Erde': Der Beitrag der außerkannonischen althebräischen Texte zur Rekonstruktion der vorexilischen Religions-und Theologiegeschichte Palästinas," in *Israel zwischen den Mächten: Festschrift für Stefan Timm zum 65. Geburtstag*, eds. Friedhelm Hartenstein and Michael Pietsch (Münster: Ugarit-Verlag, 2009), 289-377.

was probably significantly influenced by the Neo-Assyrian force's unsuccessful invasion of the city of Jerusalem in the late 8th century BCE. This invasion and the subsequent retreat of the Neo-Assyrians can be arguably conceived as a critical turning point for the formation of the Zion theology.①

In the late 8th century BCE, the force led by the Neo-Assyrian king Sennacherib attacked Jerusalem after conquering the northern kingdom of Israel. The invasion of Jerusalem, however, was unaccomplished; Sennacherib abandoned the invasion and his force retreated. The Neo-Assyrians' surprising and unexpected departure from their siege of Jerusalem is arguably attributable to the Judean king Hezekiah's promise of a hefty tribute tax to the Neo-Assyrian Empire (see, e.g., 2 Kgs. 18:13-16). It is important to note that the same historical event is also reflected in Isa. 36-39 and Ps. 46 and 48, each with its own particular theological adaptations and interpretations.② According to Isa. 36-39, for example, the Neo-Assyrians' retreat from Jerusalem is mainly due to YHWH's protection of Jerusalem from atop Mount Zion (e.g., Isa. 37:22, 32).③ It is probably also in this historical context that the notion of Zion reflected in Ps. 46 and Ps. 48 was formed, presenting the city of Jerusalem and the Jerusalem temple as being invulnerable. The rise of Zion theology should therefore be attributed to the late Judean context, presenting a stable mountain and an indestructible city with the protection of YHWH on Mount Zion.④

① Eckart Otto, *Das antike Jerusalem: Archäologie und Geschichte* (Munich: Beck, 2008); Thomas Römer, *The Invention of God*, trans. Raymond Geuss (Cambridge MA.: Harvard University Press, 2015), 182-187; Ronald E. Clements, *Isaiah and the Deliverance of Jerusalem: A Study of the Interpretation of Prophecy in the Old Testament* (Sheffield: JSOT, 1980), 84-86; Jan C. Gertz et al., eds. *T&T Clark Handbook of the Old Testament: An Introduction to the Literature, Religion and History of the Old Testament* (London: T&T Clark, 2012), 416.

② Raymond F. Person, "Ⅱ Kings 18-20 and Isaiah 36-39: A Text Critical Case Study in the Redaction History of the Book of Isaiah," *ZAW* 111 (1999): 373-379.

③ Christopher R. Seitz, *Zion's Final Destiny: The Development of the Book of Isaiah; A Reassessment of Isaiah 36-39* (Minneapolis: Fortress Press, 1991), 228.

④ Herman Spiekermann, "Stadtgott und Gottesstadt: Beobachtungen im Alten Orient und im Alten Testament," *Bib* 73 (1992): 1-31; Matthias Köckert, "Wie kam das Gesetz an den Sinai?" in *Vergegenwärtigung des Alten Testaments: Beiträge zur biblischen Hermeneutik: Festschrift für Rudolf Smend*, ed. Christoph Bultmann (Göttingen: Vandenhoeck & Ruprecht, 2002), 13-27.

Ⅲ. Historical Transformation from Mount Zion to Mount Sinai

A. The Development of the Tradition of Mount Sinai

In the history of the development of the ancient Israelite religion, Mount Sinai is also a significant and prominent spatial image that embodies a strong sense of holiness. The biblical Mount Sinai is embedded in the present grand narrative from Exodus to Numbers, which consist of the traditions of the Sinai wilderness, lawgiving, and divine revelation.[1]

The possible original independence of the tradition of Mount Sinai from its narrative context has already been observed since the 19th century. It has taken a complicated redactional process before the tradition of Mount Sinai incorporated into the present Exodus narrative. According to Julius Wellhausen, its earliest form has probably already acquired some divine components. It was perhaps only at a later stage that it has gradually become closely related to the themes of YHWH's lawgiving at Sinai and the wandering of the Israelites in the wilderness.[2] In the middle of the last century, Gerhard von Rad also looked into the relationship between the Sinai tradition and the Exodus tradition. He argued that they are two independent traditions that were integrated on the compositional level only at a later stage.[3]

Whether or not Mount Sinai was originally an independent theme embedded within the Exodus narrative, as a tradition it has long been considered to constitute the beginning of the history of the Israelites who received the revelation from YHWH at Sinai. In this sense, Mount Sinai was a place where the Israelites and their relationship to YHWH was defined. The perception of Mount Sinai as a place of YHWH's revelation has, accordingly, long been considered as constituting the background of the discussion about the

---

① Wolfgang Oswald, *Israel am Gottesberg: Eine Untersuchung zur Literargeschichte der vorderen Sinaiperikope Ex 19-24 und deren historischem Hintergrund* (Freiburg: Universitätsverlag; Göttingen: Vandenhoeck & Ruprecht, 1998); Manfred Görg, "Der Sinai. '(der Berg) des Erzgebietes'?" *BN* 54 (1990): 12-18.

② Julius Wellhausen, *Prolegomena zur Geschichte Israels* (Berlin: Reimer, 1886), 358-360.

③ For a review of the discussion of Gerhard von Rad on Sinai tradition, see, e.g., Herbert B. Huffmon, "The Exodus, Sinai and the Credo," *CBQ* 27 (1965): 101-113.

relationship between Mount Sinai and Mount Zion, indicating that the tradition of Mount Sinai is much older than the tradition of Mount Zion.

In the last several decades, however, interpretations of the relationship between Sinai and Zion have become increasingly diverse and complex.① The new understanding of the interaction between Mount Sinai and Mount Zion is, first, based on the reevaluation of the texts outside the Torah regarding the tradition of Mount Sinai. Compared to the Torah, in which there are numerous texts referring to the tradition of Mount Sinai, texts outside the Torah containing such references are few. Furthermore, these texts show the relatively different features of Mount Sinai from those portrayed in the Torah. For instance, although the text in Ps. 106:19 refers clearly to Mount Sinai, it does not mention lawgiving by YHWH. It is also noteworthy that while Jug. 5:4-5, Hab. 3:3 and Ps. 68:9 (Eng. 68:8) — which are also considered important texts referring to the Sinai tradition — mention the "Mount of God" with or without referring to Sinai, there are no specific statements about the spatial relationship between YHWH and Sinai.② These texts probably demonstrate more ancient traditions about Mount Sinai in the Israelite culture, in which Mount Sinai was understood only as a place where YHWH appeared, but did not yet involve the traditions of lawgiving, covenant establishment, or wandering in the wilderness. It is only in the later texts that there is a combination of the traditions of Mount Sinai and lawgiving. The predominant example is from Neh. 9, which refers to Mount Sinai and the tradition of lawgiving together (e.g., Neh. 9:13-14). Furthermore, it is important to note that the Priestly texts, which are generally considered to be from the early Persian period, only mention Sinai as the wilderness — rather than as the mountain — in the Priestly Sinai pericope.③

Second, the new interpretations of the interaction between Sinai and Zion

---

① For an overview, see Konrad Schmid, *A Historical Theology of the Hebrew Bible*, 412-424.

② Martin Leuenberger, "Jhwhs Herkunft aus dem Süden: Archäologische Befunde — biblische Überlieferungen — historische Korrelationen," *ZAW* 122 (2010): 1-19.

③ Konrad Schmid, "Der Sinai und die Priesterschrift," in "*Gerechtigkeit und Recht üben*" (*Gen 18,19*): *Studien zur altorientalischen und biblischen Rechtsgeschichte*, *zur Religionsgeschichte Israels und zur Religionssoziologie*: *Festschrift für Eckart Otto*, eds. Reinhard Achenbach and Martin Arneth (Wiesbaden: Harrassowitz, 2009), 114-127.

are significantly influenced by the reconstruction of the intellectual history of ancient Israel since the mid-1970s. This reconstruction is particularly concerned with the concept of the "covenant". As one of the important themes referring to the relationship between YHWH and the Israelites, the concept of the covenant is generally associated with Mount Sinai, that is, YHWH establishes the covenant with the Israelites through Moses at Sinai. However, given the increasing emphasis on the influence of Neo-Assyrian culture on the history of ancient Israel, the concept of the covenant has gradually come to be recognized as having been influenced by the model of the vassal treaty established between the Neo-Assyrian power and its vassal states.[1] The reevaluation of the concept of the covenant is primarily motivated by Neo-Assyrian documents such as *Esarhaddon's Succession Treaty*. The similarities between the Neo-Assyrian vassal treaty and the covenant established between YHWH and the Israelites support the idea that the origination of the notion of the covenant in the biblical narratives should not have been earlier than the 8th century BCE.[2] Therefore, the historical relationships among the covenant and the Exodus tradition, the historical development of the tradition of Mount Sinai, and the narrative background of the latter need to be reconstructed.

Lastly, the new understanding of the development of the tradition of Mount Sinai and its narrative function accompanies new insights into the composition of the Torah. There is a growing emphasis on the exilic profile of the Torah, emphasizing that the formation of the Torah should be understood according to the historical event of the Babylonian exile.[3] The exilic features presented in the Torah are increasingly interpreted in historical terms against the background of the late Babylonian and early Persian periods. The embedding of the tradition of Mount Sinai within the Exodus tradition is thus

---

① The significant influence of Assyrian culture on the biblical covenants is emphasized by Lothar Perlitt, *Bundestheologie im Alten Testament* (Neukirchen-Vluyn: Neukirchener Verlag, 1969); see also, Eckart Otto, *Das Deuteronomium: Politische Theologie und Rechtsreform in Juda und Assyrien* (Berlin: De Gruyter, 1999).

② Bernard M. Levinson and Jeffrey Stackert, "Between the Covenant Code and Esarhaddon's Succession Treaty: Deuteronomy 13 and the Composition of Deuteronomy," *JAJ* (2012): 123-140.

③ Jean-Louis Ska, *Introduction to Reading the Pentateuch*, trans. Sr. Pascale Dominique (Winona Lake: Eisenbrauns, 2006), 217-229.

gradually placed in the exilic and postexilic periods.

Given the above considerations, it is obvious that the tradition of Mount Sinai may have been ancient and independent. It was probably originally formed as tradition in which YHWH appeared as the God of the Israelites, but without the traditions of the establishment of the covenant, the lawgiving, or the wanderings in the wilderness. It is only after a long historical development of the tradition that Mount Sinai has become a mountain of divine revelation.

B. From Mount Zion to Mount Sinai

The reinterpretation of the Sinai tradition must be associated with an understanding of the historical development of the Zion theology. While the survival of Jerusalem and the temple influenced the formation of the Zion theology, the destruction of Jerusalem and the fall of the temple caused by the Neo-Babylonian Empire challenged the traditional notion of Mount Zion and urged a transformation of its religious attributions. As discussed, the traditional understanding of Mount Zion emphasizes that Mount Zion assures the stability and indestructibility of the city of Jerusalem. However, the fall of Jerusalem and the Jerusalem temple, led by Nebuchadnezzar in the 6th century BCE, makes the transformation of the traditional Zion theology necessary.[①]

The alternative to the preexilic notion of Zion as the divine residential place and protectorate of Jerusalem is presented in Isa. 40-66, which is traditionally divided into Isa. 40-55 and Isa. 56-66 as two independent units.[②] There are increasing debates about the specific relationship between Isa. 40-55 and 56-66 on the compositional level; however, Isa. 40-55 can still be considered to be from the exilic period while Isa. 56-66 can be dated to the Hellenistic period, on the basis of the different historical backgrounds

① Konrad Schmid, "The Canon and the Cult: The Emergence of Book Religion in Ancient Israel and the Gradual Sublimation of the Temple Cult," *JBL* 131 (2012): 289-305.

② Andrea Spans, *Die Stadtfrau Zion im Zentrum der Welt: Exegese und Theologie von Jes 60-62* (Göttingen: V & R Unipress, 2015); Antti Laato, "Understanding Zion Theology in the Book of Isaiah," in *Studies in Isaiah: History, Theology and Reception*, eds. Tommy Wasserman, Greger Andersson, and David Willgren (London: Bloomsbury T & T Clark, 2017), 22-46.

and religious thoughts they demonstrate.① The transformation of the preexilic notion of Zion can be found in Isa. 40, in which exile is an important topic. Zion, in Isa. 40, is equated with the city of Jerusalem, and is presented as a different concept from that in the preexilic period: it is apparently no longer impregnable but has been abandoned by YHWH (Isa. 40:1-11). This notion of the weak and abandoned Zion should be understood in the context of the loss of Jerusalem and the temple in the 6th century BCE. Still, the Zion of Isa. 40 is understood as an important space for the Israelites. There is a strong expectation of the return to Zion, which may be perceived as corresponding to the theme of the Israelite exodus, strengthening the relationship between Mount Zion and YHWH in a hopeful voice.

In addition to the Isaiah tradition, Jer. 6 reappropriates the preexilic notion of Mount Zion with the Babylonian exile as its narrative background. In Jer. 6, similarly to Isa. 40, the connotation of Zion is extended to include the whole city of Jerusalem. Zion is no longer constructed as a place of divine residence and manifestation, but has rather become turbulent and vulnerable. This perception becomes clearer when Jer. 6 is compared with Ps. 48, which presents the typical preexilic notion of Zion. There are significant adaptations and repatriations of Ps. 48's notion of Zion by Jer. 6 in the exilic context.② In the historical context of the loss of Jerusalem and the fall of the temple, the connotation of Mount Zion is extended beyond the mountain itself to the whole city of Jerusalem. By contrast, Mount Zion is no longer a place for protecting Jerusalem in the exlic period, which has become turbulent and vulnerable.

It is probably in this historical context of the development of Zion theology that a historical transformation emerged from the tradition of Mount Zion to that of Mount Sinai on both the symbolic and cultural levels. The transformation of the tradition of Mount Zion to that of Sinai is prominently presented in the Sinai pericope from Exod. 19 through Num. 10. Mount Sinai is

① Uwe Becker, "Das Jesajabuch als Jesajas Buch: Zu neuesten Entwicklungen in der Prophetenforschung," *TRev* 104 (2008): 3-14; Hugo G. M. Williamson, *The Book Called Isaiah: Deutero-Isaiah's Role in Composition and Redaction* (Oxford: Clarendon, 1994).

② Konrad Schmid, "The Canon and the Cult: The Emergence of Book Religion in Ancient Israel and the Gradual Sublimation of the Temple Cult," 302-303.

especially associated with the concept of the covenant established between YHWH and the Israelites. This is presented in Exod. 19-24 and 32-34. In the Sinai pericope, the concept of the covenant no longer takes Jerusalem and the temple as the basis for its development. The place where the covenant is established between YHWH and the Israelites is, rather, transformed from Jerusalem to remote Mount Sinai, which is also difficult to be located precisely.①

The transformation from Zion to Sinai can also be found in the Priestly texts, while the concept of Sinai in the Priestly texts essentially refers to the wilderness rather than the mountain.② In the Priestly texts originating from the exilic and the postexilic periods, the center of the worship cult is no longer linked with the Jerusalem temple, but is dramatically transferred to the wilderness of Sinai, where it is rendered as the space for the Israelite wanderings. Furthermore, according to the Priestly texts, the tabernacle constructed in the wilderness of Sinai was understood to be the place where YHWH could appear.③ The residential place of YHWH is also understood as a dwelling among the Israelites.

An alternative to the preexilic notion of Zion as the residential place of YHWH protecting Jerusalem and the temple thus accompanies the rise of the theological appropriation of the Sinai tradition. In this sense, it is not a development from the tradition of Sinai to a tradition of Zion; rather, it is a transformation from the tradition of Zion to that of Sinai. It is ultimately from Mount Sinai that the covenant is established between YHWH and the Israelites. Mount Sinai acquires the nature of holiness when combined with the tradition of the covenant. The rise of the Sinai tradition in its present form in the Torah thus corresponds with the alternative to the traditional Zion theology, which has to be intellectually reappropriated because of the fall of Jerusalem and the loss of the temple.

① Konrad Schmid, *The Old Testament: A Literary History*, trans. Linda M. Maloney (Minneapolis: Fortress Press, 2011), 140-141.

② Konrad Schmid, "Der Sinai und die Priesterschrift," 114-127.

③ Mark George, *Israel's Tabernacle as Social Space* (Atlanta: Society of Biblical Literature, 2009).

Ⅳ. The Separation and Integration of Sinai, Zion, and the Jerusalem Temple

Whether in the preexilic or the postexilic period, the interactions between traditions of Mount Zion and Mount Sinai are connected directly with the fall and rise of the Jerusalem temple.[1] The traditions of Mount Zion and Mount Sinai were adapted or reinterpreted around the Jerusalem temple's historical experiences. Specifically, the transformation from Zion to Sinai in the exilic and postexilic periods is primarily based on the reorientation of the concept of the Jerusalem temple. This transformation is primarily indicated in the Priestly texts and the Deuteronomistic texts.

Although the origination of the Deuteronomistic texts can be dated to the late Judean period, the systematic formation of the Deuteronomistic texts as a whole is dated to the exilic and postexilic periods.[2] The Deuteronomistic tradition gives its own particular interpretation of the fall of Jerusalem and the loss of the temple. The Deuteronomistic idea that originated in the preexilic period primarily concerns the centralization of the cult and the purification of the worship. The Deuteronomistic texts in the exilic period, however, have to interpret the contemporaneous situation of the fall of the Jerusalem temple. On one hand, the notion of the covenant established in the Deuteronomistic tradition is based on the conditional propositions that the Israelites should obey the instructions of YHWH. On the other hand, the place where the covenant is definitely established is Mount Sinai, which is rendered by the Deuteronomistic

---

① Martin Metzger, "Zion: Gottes Berg, Gottes Wohnung, Gottes Stadt," 41-63; Michael Tilly, *Jerusalem-Nabel der Welt: Überlieferung und Funktionen von Heiligtumstraditionen im antiken Judentum* (Stuttgart: Kohlhammer, 2002); Herman Spiekermann, "Stadtgott und Gottesstadt: Beobachtungen im Alten Orient und im Alten Testament," 1-31.

② Thomas Römer, *The So-Called Deuteronomistic History: A Sociological Historical and Literary Introduction* (London: T &T Clark, 2005); Thomas Römer, "From Deuteronomistic History to Nebiim and Torah," in *Making the Biblical Text: Textual Studies in the Hebrew and Greek Bible*, ed. Innocent Himbaza (Fribourg / Göttingen: Academic Press / Vandenhoeck & Ruprecht, 2015), 1-18.

tradition as the Horeb (e. g., Horeb; Deut. 5-11).[①] The concept of the covenant in the Sinai pericope was initially influenced by the preexilic Deuteronomistic understanding of the covenant, which was then appropriated into the postexilic period. According to the basic Deuteronomistic ideas, the total obedience of the Israelites to the instructions of YHWH is the assurance of the wellness of the Israelites. The basic Deuteronomistic ideas are still concerned with the reestablishment of the Davidic kingdom. The Sinai events in the Deuteronomistic ideas thus became the fundamental basis for the development of ancient Israel with the expectation of the restoration of Jerusalem.

As with the Deuteronomistic texts, the Priestly texts also demonstrate historical reflections about the fall of Jerusalem and the temple. However, the Priestly texts present different reactions from the Deuteronomistic tradition. Particularly, the Priestly texts indicate an alternative view of the notion of the covenant established between YHWH and the Israelites. By contrast with the Deuteronomistic tradition associating the covenant with the law at Sinai, the Priestly version of the Sinai pericope does not emphasize the covenant in the wilderness of Sinai.[②] Further, the Priestly texts highlight the unconditional covenant for the Israelites as a whole, and there is an absence of the Israelites' obedience to the law as the assurance of their relationship with YHWH. The Priestly texts' view of the covenant is primarily indicated by the narrative of the covenant established by YHWH to Noah (Gen. 9) and Abraham (Gen. 17).[③] Furthermore, while the Priestly texts were probably influenced by the notion of the cultic centralization advanced by the Deuteronomistic ideas, the tabernacle is constructed as the important cultic space according to the Priestly texts.

Therefore, the Priestly texts and the Deuteronomistic texts show different understandings and reactions to the fall of Jerusalem and the loss of the

---

① The Deuteronomistic tradition probably rendered Mount Sinai as Horeb because of the particular relationship with Edom, from which the ancient Sinai tradition likely originated. See Lothar Perlitt, "Sinai und Horeb," in *Beiträge zur alttestamentlichen Theologie: Festschrift für Walter Zimmerli* (Göttingen: Vandenhoeck, 1977), 302-322.

② Konrad Schmid, "Der Sinai und die Priesterschrift," 114-127.

③ For the establishment of the covenant in the Priestly texts, see Konrad Schmid, *A Historical Theology of the Hebrew Bible*, 152-154.

temple. Both the Priestly and the Deuteronomistic texts demonstrate the historical transformation from Zion to Sinai, although the Priestly texts render Sinai mainly as the wilderness rather than the mountain. The Priestly and the Deuteronomistic texts, however, give different interpretations of the relationships among Zion, Sinai, and the Jerusalem temple. The Deuteronomistic tradition emphasizes that the definite covenant was established at Sinai. For the Priestly texts, however, the relationship between YHWH and the Israelites has already been assured by the covenants established with Noah and Abraham. Moreover, while the Deuteronomistic tradition still considers Jerusalem the center for the restoration of the Davidic dynasty, the Priestly texts present the tabernacle constructed in the wilderness of Sinai was for the appearance of YHWH. The alteration of the preexilic theology of the Jerusalem temple thus significantly influenced the historical encounters between the traditions of Zion and Sinai.

V. Conclusions

The discussions above show a historical transformation from the traditions of Mount Zion to those of Mount Sinai in the exilic and postexilic periods. Mount Zion, in the preexilic period, was conceived of as a divine residential place from which YHWH protected the city of Jerusalem. The formation of the Zion theology was motivated by Jerusalem's survival of the Neo-Assyrian invasion in the late 8th century BCE. After the fall of Jerusalem and the loss of the temple in the early years of the 6th century BCE, the traditional Zion theology underwent a fundamental alteration. The historical encounter between the traditions of Mount Zion and Mount Sinai has started during the exilic period. While the Sinai tradition is originally an independent ancient Israelite tradition, it is in the context of the transformation from the traditions of Zion to those of Sinai that Mount Sinai has started to become an important place for the formation of the relationship between YHWH and the Israelites.

In the historical transformation from Mount Zion to Mount Sinai, the Priestly texts and the Deuteronomistic texts show a different understanding of the relationship between Sinai and Zion. While the Deuteronomistic tradition perceives the conditional covenant established at Mount Sinai as important to the Israelites, with the expectation of the restoration of the Davidic dynasty, the Priestly texts construct Sinai as the wilderness in which YHWH lives among the Israelites and the covenant was understood to have already been established before the Sinai pericope. On the whole, from a historical view, it could be argued that there is a transformation from the traditions of Mount Zion to Mount Sinai with the reinterpretations of the relationship between YHWH and Israelites in the late Babylonian exilic and early Persian periods.

圣山的兴起：希伯来《圣经》中的锡安山与西奈山的历史传统

姜振帅

【摘要】在古以色列宗教历史发展过程中，圣山传统作为重要的文化因素，在希伯来《圣经》的相关书写中起着重要作用，集中表现在对锡安山与西奈山传统的建构上。长期以来，学界通常以西奈山传统作为圣山传统研究的出发点，认为其是在古以色列历史早期形成并相对独立于锡安传统的传统，但随着最近几十年关于古以色列的考古学的发展以及对《妥拉》研究的进一步深入，西奈传统与锡安传统的历史发展和建构过程表现出了越来越复杂的特点，而两者之间的互动关系也由此需要重新理解与讨论。本文以希伯来《圣经》中锡安山传统与西奈山传统的发展为中心，探讨在古以色列宗教历史发展中，圣山传统的建构与形成过程如何表现出与圣殿传统的多层次互动，指出在巴比伦流放时期以及波斯帝国统治时期，古以色列的圣山传统产生了从锡安山传统到西奈山传统的历史转化。

【关键词】古以色列宗教；希伯来《圣经》；锡安山；西奈山；耶路撒冷圣殿

《创世记》先祖叙事中的文化记忆

黄薇*

【摘要】现代圣经学者通常认为,《创世记》先祖叙事反映的是后期以色列民族的自我定义,而非对以色列民族起源的如实记录。本文首先对学术史进行简要回顾,从而指出先祖叙事表面上是古老的家族故事,实际上是能够凝聚以色列民族的集体文化记忆。其次,本文将结合先祖叙事文本和西亚的历史背景,考察以色列对于其近邻族群的记忆图景,及其自我身份认同的构成。

【关键词】先祖叙事;以色列;文化记忆;《创世记》

从亚伯拉罕开始,《创世记》写作进入"先祖历史"阶段,讲述了三代先祖的家族故事。《创世记》第12—36章通常被称作先祖叙事,有时也被称作族长叙事。《创世记》后面的部分,也就是第37—50章,记载的则是约瑟故事,约瑟是故事的主角,故事涉及先祖雅各流散在埃及的最后几年,还包括对他的过世、埋葬以及遗嘱的记载。[①]从先祖叙事到约瑟故事,再到出埃及叙事[②],之后时代成为主流传统的祭司典,将这些故事中非祭司典的叙事串联起来,可形成一套整体的、具有

* 黄薇,上海大学文学院历史系讲师。

① 冯拉德(Gerhard von Rad)指出这里的编纂过程很值得注意,雅各逝世成为约瑟故事结尾的一部分(《创世记》49),《创世记》第37—50章可以理解为先祖叙事的尾声,参见:Gerhard von Rad, *Genesis*, trans. John H. Marks (Philadelphia: Westminster, 1972)。

② 就以色列民族的起源问题而言,先祖叙事和出埃及叙事分别代表两种不同的解释传统,参见:Konrad Schmid, "The So-Called Yahwist and the Literary Gap between Genesis and Exodus," in *A Farewell to the Yahwist? The Composition of the Pentateuch in Recent European Interpretation*, eds. Thomas B. Dozeman and K. Schmid (Atlanta: Society of Biblical Literature, 2006), 29-50。

连续性的对以色列历史的描述，同时也促成了五经的整体性。[①]

先祖叙事很显然是具有政治意义的，其将从亚伯拉罕开始的家族故事与以色列群体的形成过程联系起来。特别是到了《创世记》第 32 章第 28 节，雅各改名为以色列，之后的世代都可以称为以色列的子孙。当然，除了构建一个以“以色列”为名的共同体之外，先祖叙事也关心以色列周边的其他群体。在《创世记》第 17 章第 5 节中，亚伯兰改名为亚伯拉罕，并且经文解释这个名字的意思就是“多国之父”。此外，亚伯拉罕的侄子罗得是亚扪人和摩押人的始祖（《创世记》19:30—38）；亚伯拉罕的儿子以实玛利生了十二族长（《创世记》7:20），是以实玛利人的祖先；以东和西珥是雅各的孪生兄长以扫的领地（《创世记》32:3）。这里提到的亚扪、摩押、以实玛利、以东以及西珥都与以色列群体存在一定关系。实际上，《创世记》的先祖叙事在时间和空间维度上，反映出以色列与其周边其他群体的社会地缘关系。先祖叙事是对以色列与其周边其他群体间关系的记录，此关系图景通过对历史的编排，代表了《圣经》编写者对过去的认可，反映了他们对当下复杂世界的理解。

简而言之，先祖叙事探讨了以色列民族的形成问题，也对以色列在世界上的位置做出一种解释，或者可以说，先祖叙事构建了以色列的群体边界，以及作为一个民族的认同感和集体身份。这种以亲缘关系来定义以色列共同体的方式，促使认同先祖叙事的群体在主观上相信他们源自共同祖先，也同时使得先祖叙事成为以色列民族的集体记忆。

一、历史批判视野下的先祖叙事

回顾希伯来《圣经》研究的学术史，20 世纪初，当贡克尔(H. Gunkel)对先祖叙事进行解读的时候，学界曾展开有关史学与诗学之间差异问题的讨论。在贡克尔看来，先祖叙事始终带有诗意的调子，而非史编。因此，从文体角度出发，他将先祖叙事看作传奇故事，指出先祖叙事在本质上是诗学而非史学。也就是说，其叙事目的不是以真实发生的历史事件来指导后人，而是以传奇故事去感动后

① 有关先祖叙事、约瑟故事以及摩西故事之间的联系，可参见：Jan Christian Gertz, “Transition between Genesis and Exodus,” in *A Farewell to the Yahwist? The Composition of the Pentateuch in Recent European Interpretation*, 73-87; Jan Christian Gertz, “Abraham, Mose und der Exodus: Beobachtungen zur Redaktionsgeschichte von Gen 15,” in *Abschied vom Jahwisten: Die Komposition des Hexateuch in der jüngsten Diskussion*, eds. Jan Christian Gertz, K. Schmid and M. Witte (Berlin: De Gruyter, 2002), 63-81。

人、启发后人,使后来的读者从这些古老的传奇故事中获得某种价值认同及审美感知。[①]贡克尔当然是在一定程度上承继着前人的学术传统。18世纪的圣经学者,也是启蒙先驱德维特(W. M. L. de Wette)在谈到《旧约》的时候,明确指出《旧约》不是历史,是诗学。[②] 21世纪,当代圣经学者罗纳德·亨德尔(Ronald Hendel)对先祖叙事进行研究的时候,仍然沿用"诗学"概念来描述先祖叙事。在亨德尔那里,先祖叙事的"诗学"意味着一种文学表达,亨德尔进一步提出了"社会体制"与"文学艺术"在先祖叙事中达到和谐,换句话说,他认为先祖叙事是由一系列政治文学话语构成的。[③]

从纵向时间的维度观察先祖叙事研究,可以发现当代圣经学者与前代学者间的联系与区别。在史学与诗学的讨论中,亨德尔与德维特都认为先祖叙事是诗学而不是史学,也就是说,先祖叙事不是历史,不是对真实发生事件的记载。然而,从最终的研究结果来看,当代先祖叙事研究走上与前代研究完全不同的道路。

考虑到德维特(1780—1849)所处的时代,当时的欧洲知识界学术环境中弥漫着科学史学的氛围[④],与其同时代的著名德意志史学家有尼布尔(Barthold Georg Niebuhr,1776—1831)、兰克(Leopold von Ranke,1795—1886)等,他们都是科学史学的代表人物。简单地说,科学史学主张以科学的态度对待历史,强调对史料的运用,只有确证史料的真实性,才能确保史实的真实性。或许是为了回应这种对待史料的态度,作为圣经研究先驱的德维特,否认《旧约》作为史料的可靠性,他强调先祖叙事不能用来重建先祖时代的历史,先祖叙事的重要性不在于其历史真实性,叙事中找不到"事实",最富成果的研究应当从诗学维度出发,探讨先祖叙事的意义。最有价值的应当是对亚伯拉罕信仰的讨论,亚伯拉罕是宗教信仰上一种最高的理想化先祖形象。[⑤]德维特认为,研究先祖叙事最好的方法应当是文学的方法,而非史学的方法。在先祖叙事中,德维特看到的是一个民

---

① H. Gunkel, *Genesis*, trans. M. E. Biddle (Macon: Mercer University Press, 1997), Ⅺ.

② W. M. L. de Wette, *Beiträge zur Einleitung in das Alte Testament* (Halle: Schimmelpfennig, 1806 / 1807).

③ Ronald Hendel, "Politics and Poetics in the Ancestral Narratives," in *The Politics of the Ancestors: Exegetical and Historical Perspectives on Genesis 12-36*, eds. Mark G. Brett and Jakob Wöhrle (Tübingen: Mohr Siebeck, 2018), 11-34.

④ 或称客观主义史学,参见:张广智 Zhang Guangzhi,《西方史学史》[A History of Western Historiography](第四版)[Fourth Edition](上海[Shanghai]:复旦大学出版社 [Fudan University Press], 2018),256-266;王晴佳 Q. Edward Wang,李隆国 Li Longguo,《外国史学史》[A History of Historiography Around the World](北京[Beijing]:北京大学出版社 [Beijing University Press],2017),219—228。

⑤ W. M. L. de Wette, *Beiträge zur Einleitung in das Alte Testament*, 2:103.

族对其基本信仰的表达，而非对历史事实的还原。

不过，到威尔豪森(Julius Wellhausen)与底本假说时代，对先祖叙事的研究开始发生变化。虽然威尔豪森没有对先祖叙事进行专门研究，但是他将《创世记》第1—11章与《创世记》第12—50章区分开来，前一部分是对宇宙起源的描述，不存在任何意义上的历史背景，后一部分的叙事则更接近历史。后来贡克尔通过对口头传统的研究探讨先祖叙事的传统构成。①贡克尔一方面呼应德维特，认同先祖叙事绝非兰克定义下的史料；另一方面，他认为流行于民间的诗歌和传奇故事会对某些历史事件的掌故有所引用。德维特与贡克尔都以文学的视角看待先祖叙事，但两者的不同之处在于：贡克尔还关注先祖叙事对于历史处境下受众的确切意义。虽然传奇故事属于口头传统，但后世将口头传统记载下来，使其固定成为书写记录得到传承，这意味着贡克尔比德维特更注重文本形成的历史层次，同时也比德维特更注重文本的历史性。至于口头传统的历史处境如何，由于可靠史料的缺乏或许没有还原的可能，然而，现存文本的历史形成过程，则是威尔豪森及之后持有历史批判视角的圣经学者致力于讨论的问题。这种历史批判视角在先祖叙事研究上的表现②，便是对先祖叙事所包含的政治特征的关注。

先祖叙事的政治性并非一个全新的议题。暂且不论先祖叙事是否具有历史意义上的可靠性③，其叙事内核是古老的家族故事，叙事主线特别关注子嗣绵延、家族继承、不同家族间的亲疏关系等问题，故事中的主要人物是后来的以色列民族的祖先，还包括以色列周边族群的祖先。通过讲述以色列家族三代先祖的经历，先祖叙事说明了以色列民族的诞生、国家的形成，而所有这些都建立在

---

① 贡克尔对《创世记》的研究出版于1910年，其英译本出版于1997年(见前文注释)：H. Gunkel, *Genesis* (Göttingen: Vandenhoeck & Ruprecht, 1910)。有关贡克尔的学术史研究，参见：E. S. Gerstenberger, "Albert Eichhorn and Hermann Gunkel: The Emergence of a History of Religion School," in *The Nineteenth Century*, Vol. 3. 1 of *Hebrew Bible-Old Testament: The History of Its Interpretation*, ed. M. Sæbø (Göttingen: Vandenhoeck & Ruprecht, 2013), 454-471。

② 受到贡克尔的影响，后来学界从历史视角出发的进一步研究，参见：T. L. Thompson, *The Historicity of the Patriarchal Narratives: The Quest for the Historical Abraham* (Berlin: De Gruyter, 1974); J. Van Seters, *Abraham in History and Tradition* (New Haven: Yale University Press, 1975)。

③ 奥布莱特试图考察历史上的先祖，他结合考古材料展开研究，认为从历史观点上看，先祖叙事具备可靠性，是关于后来的以色列民族的前史。尽管他的观点在一定程度上也受到现代学者的否定，但是先祖叙事反映出的游牧部落的生活方式，能够对应考古材料反映的铁器时代巴勒斯坦地区居民的生活状况，参见：W. F. Albright, *From the Stone Age to Christianity: Monotheism and the Historical Process* (Baltimore: The John Hopkins, 1940), 179-189。

对家族和祖先起源的记忆上。[①] 20 世纪对先祖叙事的大多数研究都处在底本假说的框架下,认为先祖叙事中最早的底本是耶典,通常被断代为公元前 10 世纪,也就是王国时代开始的时候。[②]此外,四底本(耶典、神典、祭司典、申命典)在先祖叙事中的构成也成为学者研究的重点。[③]然而,在过去几十年间,有关五经文本形成的研究发生了巨大变化,对四底本成书年代的讨论也变得相当分化[④],越来越多的学者甚至彻底抛弃了底本假说。[⑤]汤普森(T. L. Thompson)对文本来源研究的分析很有启发意义,他指出四底本或更多的有关文本来源的讨论,实际上反而脱离了先祖叙事的历史处境,不同文本来源所代表的传统最终得以被整合起来,是因为这些传统对以色列而言具有重要意义。[⑥]

因此,比起讨论有哪些底本构成先祖叙事,以及这些底本的来源及形成过程,更有意义的研究是关心叙事本身得以构成的历史处境。可以说,先祖叙事源自小规模形成的独立传统,其中最主要的是较为完整的亚伯拉罕叙事和雅各叙事,到较晚的时代,这些独立的文学单元才被整合到一起成为先祖叙事。[⑦]而先祖叙事作为一个整体,代表的是对以色列先祖时代历史的文化记忆。[⑧]称先祖叙事是政治性的,在于这是集体形塑自我的一种方式,是构想政治共同体的一种模式。先祖叙事成为《创世记》书卷的一部分文本,可能经历了从王国时代至波斯晚期漫长的多层次编撰过程,展示出时空中多面历史的融合,最引人注目的可能

---

① 韦斯特曼(C. Westermann)指出先祖叙事讲述的是构成人类社会群体最基本的单位:家庭。参见:C. Westermann, *Genesis 12-36: A Commentary*, trans. John J. Scullion (S. J. Minneapolis: Augsburg, 1985), 23。

② G. von Rad, "The Form Critical Problem of the Hexateuch," in *The Problem of the Hexateuch and Other Essays* (Edinburgh: Oliver & Boyd Ltd., 1984), 1-78.

③ C. Westermann, *Genesis 12-36: A Commentary*, 570-578.

④ 例如范赛特斯(J. Van Seters)将耶典断代于巴比伦流放晚期,参见:J. Van Seters, "Dating the Yahwist's History: Principles and Perspectives," *Biblica* 96.1 (2015): 1-25。有关耶典研究的学术史综述,参见:Jean Louis Ska, "The Yahwist, a Hero with a Thousand Faces A Chapter in the History of Modern Exegesis," in *Abschied vom Jahwisten: Die Komposition des Hexateuch in der jüngsten Diskussion*, eds. Jan Christian Gertz, K. Schmid and M. Witte (Berlin: De Gruyter, 2002), 1-23。

⑤ 有关五经的新研究参见:J. C. Gertz, et al., eds. *The Formation of the Pentateuch: Bridging the Academic Cultures of Europe, Israel, and North America* (Tübingen: Mohr Siebeck, 2016)。

⑥ T. L. Thompson, *The Historicity of the Patriarchal Narratives: The Quest for the Historical Abraham*, 326.

⑦ Konrad Schmid, "The So-Called Yahwish and the Literary Gap between Genesis and Exodus," 29; Rolf Rendtorff, *The Problem of the Process of Transmission in the Pentateuch*, trans. J. J. Scullion (Sheffield: JSOT Press, 1990).

⑧ 从文化记忆的角度对先祖叙事进行研究的代表性著作,参见:Ronald Hendel, *Remembering Abraham: Culture, Memory, and History in the Hebrew Bible* (New York: Oxford University Press, 2005)。

是当中所蕴含的以色列与其周边邻国间的族群关系图景。

总而言之，自 18 世纪现代圣经研究展开以来，在先祖叙事研究的第一阶段，该叙事作为史料的可靠性首先被否认，学者强调要从诗学的层面探讨先祖叙事带给读者的价值与意义。第二阶段的研究建立在第一阶段研究的基础之上，认同叙事不具备史料可靠性，但是这一阶段的研究更重视文本背后的历史，特别是通过结合考古材料，尝试探讨以色列民族的历史处境，文本的历史性受到关注。到了第三阶段，先祖叙事的研究倾向于从文化记忆的角度分析文本的叙事功能，特别是该叙事在构造民族共同体上的重要价值。接下来，本文将对先祖叙事所构造的文化记忆展开分析。[①]

二、以色列与其近邻族群的关系图景

正如罗纳德·亨德尔所言，对《创世记》先祖叙事的研究不是为了证明或是证伪，这不是一个在历史与虚构之间简单地去判别真假的研究，先祖叙事融合了历史记忆、传统民间故事、文化上的自我认同，还包括出色的文学叙事手法。[②]谈及先祖所处的历史时代，就目前学界的证据来看，仍然很难达成共识。尽管没有足够证据去讨论历史上的亚伯拉罕、以撒、雅各这些人物，但是由他们所代表的传统是真实存在的，并且由《创世记》写作整合为一体，成为以色列民族自我身份认同的一个根深蒂固的传统。

以色列是西亚地区的一个民族，同时，在自我意识中，以色列在整个西亚文化环境里有自身独特性。希伯来《圣经》描绘的以色列及其历史，正是以色列民族对其身份的自我构造，将自我与古代西亚的其他族群区别开来。以色列的身份认同又与其对自身历史的反思分不开，是通过走出埃及、在西奈受到启示、旷野生活，再到作为一个统一的民族最终获得应许之地实现的。[③]类似地，先祖叙事作为一种对过去的编排和认可，为以色列群体的外部关系和内部关系划定界限。

① 在希伯来《圣经》其他书卷，如先知作品和历史文献中，同样存在以色列民族对自我身份的建构问题，相关研究可参考埃胡德·本-兹维(Ehud Ben Zvi)近年来的作品：Diana Edelman and Ehud Ben Zvi, eds. *Imagining the Other and Constructing Israelite in the Early Second Temple Period* (London: Bloomsbury T &T Clark, 2014); Ehud Ben Zvi, *Social Memory among the Literati of Yehud* (Berlin: De Gruyter, 2019)。国内学界的研究成果参见：游斌 You Bin,《圣书与圣民：古代以色列的历史记忆与族群构建》[Holy Book and Holy People: Historical Memory and Ethnic Construction in Ancient Israel](北京[Beijing]:宗教文化出版社[Religious Culture Press],2011)。

② Ronald Hendel, *Remembering Abraham: Culture, Memory, and History in the Hebrew Bible*, 46.

③ Ronald Hendel, *Remembering Abraham: Culture, Memory, and History in the Hebrew Bible*, 3.

凭借有关先祖的故事,以色列将自己与周边近邻族群区分开来,建立并维护他们在血缘、地域以及宗教文化等诸多方面的异同。

在亚伯拉罕、以撒、雅各三代先祖的叙事中,文本通过族谱记载表达了以色列与其周边族群的关系。亚伯拉罕有两个兄弟——拿鹤与哈兰。哈兰生罗得(《创世记》11:27),摩押和亚扪人的始祖是罗得与他两个女儿所生的儿子(《创世记》19:30—38)。从族谱上看,雅各(以色列)与亚扪、摩押同辈,只不过后两者在族谱上并不属于亚伯拉罕这一支,也就与以色列区别开来。在地理上,亚扪与摩押位于约旦河东。总体而言,有关亚扪与摩押的记忆总是负面的,以色列与这些邻居常常产生争执。扫罗曾经打败亚扪和摩押(《撒母耳记上》14:47),大卫也曾制服过亚扪和摩押(《撒母耳记下》8:11—12)。巴比伦王尼布甲尼撒攻破耶路撒冷之前,亚扪和摩押也都曾来攻击犹大(《列王纪下》24:2)。《申命记》要求亚扪人和摩押人永不可入耶和华的会(《申命记》23:3)。

希伯来《圣经》中另一个常常与亚扪、摩押一起被提及的族群是亚兰,三者往往都是以色列的敌人(《士师记》10:6;《撒母耳记下》8:12),亚兰也多次与以色列争战(《列王纪上》20:1—29;《列王纪下》6:8)。但在先祖叙事中,以色列与亚兰的关系却更为正面。与雅各的情况类似,亚伯拉罕的另一个兄弟拿鹤生了 12 个儿子,其中一个儿子基母利是亚兰的父亲(《创世记》22:20—24)。亚兰与亚伯拉罕一支的血缘关系更密切。首先,亚伯拉罕原本住在迦勒底的吾珥,要迁到迦南应许之地,途径哈兰就住下了(《创世记》11:31),亚伯拉罕的父亲他拉在哈兰过世(《创世记》11:32),哈兰是亚兰人拉班所在之处(《创世记》27:43),拉班是彼土利的儿子(《创世记》28:5),拉班所在之处也被称作巴旦亚兰(《创世记》28:5),字面意思是亚兰平原。其次,亚伯拉罕的儿子以撒娶了利百加,利百加是拿鹤的儿子彼土利之女(《创世记》24:15),而以撒的儿子雅各娶了利亚和拉结,她们是利百加的哥哥拉班的两个女儿(《创世记》24:29—30,29:16)。《创世记》在提到彼土利与拉班的时候,称他们为"亚兰人"(《创世记》25:20,31:20、24)。此外,《申命记》提到普通的古代以色列人要将初熟的收成带到圣所献给上帝,作为仪式的一部分,要在祭司面前说出这样一句话:"我祖原是一个将亡的亚兰人,下到埃及寄居。"(《申命记》26:5)《申命记》对祖先身份的认同与先祖叙事在这里有所呼应。

在有关继承权的问题上,先祖叙事中出现了对继承权的两次争夺:一次发生在以实玛利与以撒之间,另一次发生在以撒的两个儿子以扫和雅各之间。两次均以小儿子获得继承权而告终。这或许同以色列在古代西亚文化中的地位有关,以色列就是古代西亚大家庭中的"小儿子",其最终获得了继承权。这里的"继承权"指的是在古代西亚文化中,以色列自身的独特性。先祖叙事中的以实玛利作为亚伯拉罕的长子,是撒拉使女埃及人夏甲所生(《创世记》25:12),虽然没能获得亚伯

拉罕的继承权,但以实玛利也得到如同雅各一样的祝福,他的 12 个儿子作了十二族的族长(《创世记》25:16)。以实玛利的子孙住在他众兄弟的东边,直到埃及前,在亚述的道上(《创世记》25:18)。而以扫就是以东,以东就是以扫(《创世记》36:1、8、9、19、43),以扫是西珥山里以东人的始祖(《创世记》36:9),位于死海以南。以扫娶迦南的女子,即赫人的女儿为妻(《创世记》26:34),在他失去长子继承权后,他便往以实玛利那里去,还娶了以实玛利的女儿为妻(《创世记》28:9)。《申命记》要求以色列不可憎恶以东人,因为他是你的弟兄(《申命记》23:7)。波斯晚期/希腊化早期的犹大文士对以东的记忆则更为复杂。[①]

另外,还有一段简短的家谱式记录提到亚伯拉罕与基土拉所生的后代,并且亚伯拉罕趁着自己还在世的时候,打发他们离开以撒,往东方去(《创世记》25:1—6),这显然是要强调以撒继承权的正统性,避免这里突然出现的后代会产生继承权问题。基土拉的儿子中有一个名叫米甸,米甸的 5 个儿子也被记录下来(《创世记》25:2、4)。对于基土拉及其所生的后代,希伯来《圣经》再没有给出更多信息。不过,《创世记》后来提到将雅各之子约瑟卖给埃及人的是米甸的商人(《创世记》37:28、36),其也被称作米甸的以实玛利人(《创世记》37:25);[②]而摩西为躲避法老,也曾到米甸居住(《出埃及记》2:15)。米甸位于以色列以南,位于去往埃及方向的地域。

根据以上对《创世记》先祖叙事的考察,能够获得以色列与其近邻族群(或者政治实体)关系的观念图景。三代先祖族谱见图 1。以色列与迦南人、赫人、亚摩利人和非利士人同住在一片土地上;但是他们与亚兰人(以撒、雅各之妻),与南部沙漠地区的部落(以扫,即以东)有亲缘关系;与亚扪和摩押的亲缘关系较远,且以色列人蔑视亚扪与摩押;与阿拉伯部族(基土拉的后代)、以实玛利人也有亲缘关系。

---

① 埃胡德·本-兹维 Ehud Ben Zvi,《以东:波斯晚期和希腊化早期犹大文士的复杂记忆场》[Edom as a Complex Site of Memory among the Literati of Late Persian / Early Hellenistic Judah: Some Observations],于《圣经文学研究》[Journal for the Study of Biblical Literature],2020 第 1 期[2020, Issue 1],1—33。

② 根据《士师记》第 8 章第 24 节,米甸人就是以实玛利人。不过大多数现代圣经学者认为这里存在两个底本,提及米甸人的是神典,提及以实玛利人的是耶典。对于米甸人与以实玛利人的讨论,参见:Ernst A. Knauf, "Midianites and Ishmaelites," in *Midian, Moab and Edom: The History and Archaeology of Late Bronze and Iron Age Jordan and North-West Arabia*, eds. John F. A. Sawyer and David J. A. Clines (Sheffield: JSOT Press,1983), 147-162;有关文本构成的分析,参见:Donald B. Redford, *A Study of the Biblical Story of Joseph (Genesis 37-50)* (Leiden: Brill, 1970)。

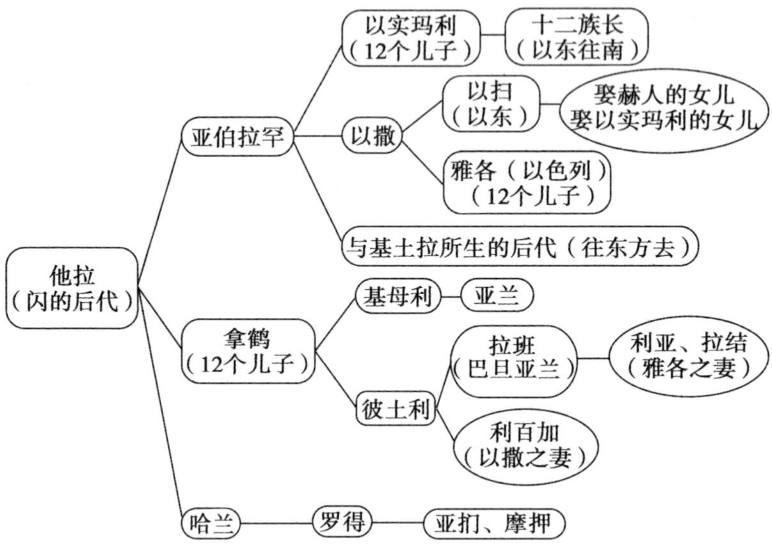

图 1　三代先祖族谱

然而,为何以色列对周边族群的态度各不相同？或者说,如何理解先祖叙事在观念上构造的族群边界？先祖叙事中有关以色列与其周边族群的记忆是如何形成的？这需要在古代西亚地区更广的历史背景下展开讨论,由此才能进一步理解以色列民族有关先祖记忆的构成。

三、作为共同体的"以色列"

青铜时代晚期至铁器时代的过渡时期,公元前 13—前 12 世纪至公元前 11—前 10 世纪,被埃及人称作"海上民族"的移民来到地中海东岸,定居在巴勒斯坦沿海地区,他们被认为是《圣经》中的非利士人。原本在青铜时代曾达到辉煌阶段的赫梯与埃及此时均出现衰退趋势,这两个强大的政权对巴勒斯坦地区的控制随之转弱。从考古证据上看,青铜时代晚期巴勒斯坦地区的城市规模的确逐渐萎缩。然而在这一时期,小规模农业定居点出现在巴勒斯坦的山区地带。这成为有关以色列民族起源,或是国家起源最重要的讨论基础。①差不多同一时期,约旦河东出

① W. G. Dever, *Who Were the Early Israelites and Where Did They Come From?* (Grand Rapids: Eerdmans, 2003); R. D. Miller Ⅱ, *Chieftains of the Highland Clans: A History of Israel in the Twelfth and Eleventh Centuries B. C.* (Grand Rapids: Eedmans, 2005).

现其他新兴政体。[①]公元前 9 世纪,阿拉伯部族向黎凡特地区迁移。[②]直到公元前 8 世纪,位于约旦河东的亚扪、摩押和以东,在社会组织、文化以及地缘政治上都与同时期的以色列、犹大王国相近[③],这些小规模地区国家既是邻居也是对手,在亚述帝国向黎凡特扩张之际,它们便有可能成为盟友。

与上述新兴地区国家不同的是,公元前 11—前 10 世纪的亚兰已经掌控了大部分叙利亚地区,并向上美索不达米亚地区渗透甚至入侵,这也可能成为引起亚述重拾军事征服向西扩张的动因之一。亚述历史文献记载:提格拉特帕拉沙尔三世(公元前 745—前 727 年在位),也就是《圣经》中的提革拉毗列色,登上王位之后,亚述帝国的军事扩张开始逐步走向顶峰。经过一系列战役,亚述的西征战略最终获得重大成功,大约在公元前 732 年,亚兰战败,被并入亚述帝国版图。[④]北国以色列王国在公元前 722 年或前 720 年败于亚述人之手。可以说,对公元前 8 世纪地中海东岸的地区国家而言,亚述帝国入侵成为当时政治环境中最大的威胁。

在希伯来《圣经》的记载中,北国以色列的形象几乎总是负面的。申命史派的南国立场尤其明显,北国国王的所作所为都是耶和华眼中为恶的事,因而才会导致最终败给亚述。不过另一方面,考古信息及其他文献史料表明,无论是政治、经济、人口数量,还是军事实力,历史上的北国以色列才是较强大的,犹大王国各方面实力远逊色于以色列王国。[⑤]公元前 8 世纪前半叶的以色列王国,是当时地区性国家中具有一定影响力的政治实体。结合《圣经》史书的信息,在亚兰—大马士革国王的领导下,黎凡特南部地区成立了一个包括以色列在内的反亚述同盟,犹大王国因拒绝加入该同盟,遭到亚兰王与以色列王的攻击(《列王纪下》15:37,16:5)。犹大向亚述王提革拉毗列色请求支援并向亚述纳贡,亚述王于是去攻打大马士革,并杀死了亚兰王(《列王纪下》16:7—9),反亚述同盟瓦解,亚述也基本完成对该地区的军事征服,亚述王撒缦以色五世(公元前 727—前

---

① 结合最新考古材料的研究表明,摩押地区早期政体出现于公元前 11—前 10 世纪,参见:Israel Finkelstein and Oded Lipschits, "The Genesis of Moab: A Proposal," *Levant* 43.2 (2011): 139-152。

② 阿拉伯部族在公元前 9 世纪的活动保留在新亚述文献的记载中,参见:J. Retsö, *The Arabs in Antiquity: Their History from the Assyrians to the Umayyads* (London: Routledge Curzon, 2003), 126-128。

③ Bruce Routledge, "Transjordan in the Eighth Century BCE," in *Archaeology and History of Eighth-Century Judah*, eds. Zev I. Farber and Jacob L. Wright (Atlanta: Society of Biblical Literature), 139-159.

④ K. Lawson Younger Jr., "Assyria's Expansion West of the Euphrates," in *Archaeology and History of Eighth-Century Judah*, 17-34.

⑤ Israel Finkelstein, *The Forgotten Kingdom: The Archaeology and History of Northern Israel* (Atlanta: Society of Biblical Literature, 2013).

722 年在位)在公元前 722 年征服了撒玛利亚。[①]而犹大通过向亚述帝国纳贡保有以耶路撒冷为中心的王国。直到公元前 587 年,耶路撒冷与圣殿毁于巴比伦王尼布甲尼撒二世之手,犹大人被流放,巴比伦之囚成为以色列民族的核心创伤记忆。

回到亚伯拉罕、以撒、雅各三代的先祖叙事上,叙事者的历史地理视角,在一定程度上映射出公元前 9—前 8 世纪以色列、犹大王国与其近邻族群间的关系。就叙事本身的文学形态而言,考虑到古代以色列的文化与书写发展,先祖叙事不可能早于公元前 9—前 8 世纪出现。[②]尽管通过现有史料并不能够还原历史上的亚伯拉罕、以撒和雅各,但是先祖叙事中的确存在南北两个传统:亚伯拉罕的故事围绕希伯仑、幔利,以撒在别是巴、基拉耳,其都属于南国犹大;雅各的故事主要发生在犹大山地,包括伯特利、示剑。雅各和拉班的故事,作为雅各叙事的核心部分,呼应了公元前 9—前 8 世纪以色列同亚兰—大马士革之间的政治关系[③];并且,雅各改名为以色列,所有这些表明,雅各叙事属于北国传统。

三代先祖以亚伯拉罕为第一代,雅各为第三代,源自南国的亚伯拉罕传统似乎最早。然而,实际上的情况可能恰恰相反。正如上文所述,历史上的以色列王国是两个希伯来王国中实力最强的,北国以色列的出现也比南国犹大更早,南国犹大要在 1—2 个世纪后,即公元前 9 世纪晚期才开始有所发展。[④]因此,代表北国以色列的雅各故事才更有可能包含最古老的传统。[⑤]而让代表南国传统的亚伯拉罕成为雅各的祖父,说明先祖叙事以南国立场,将南北传统整合起来。亚伯拉罕四处迁居正是这种后期编撰的产物。[⑥]整体来看,希伯来《圣经》的叙事视角

---

① Gilad Itach, "The Kingdom of Israel in the Eighth Century: From a Regional Power to Assyrian Provinces," in *Archaeology and History of Eighth-Century Judah*, 57-77.

② Christopher Rollston, *Writing and Literacy in the World of Ancient Israel* (Atlanta: Society of Biblical Literature, 2010).

③ Ronald Hendel, "Historical Context," in *The Book of Genesis: Composition, Reception, and Interpretation*, eds. C.A. Evans, et al. (Leiden: Brill, 2012), 58; Omer Sergi, "Jacob and the Aramaean Identity of Ancient Israel between the Judges and the Prophets," in *The Politics of the Ancestors: Exegetical and Historical Perspectives on Genesis 12-36*, eds. Mark G. Brett and Jakob Wöhrle (Tübingen: Mohr Siebeck, 2018), 285.

④ Israel Finkelstein, "The Rise of Jerusalem and Judah: The Missing Link," *Levant* 33 (2001): 105-115.

⑤ Israel Finkelstein and Thomas Römer, "Comments on the Historical Background of the Abraham Narrative: Between 'Realia' and 'Exegetica'," *Hebrew Bible and Ancient Israel* 3 (2014): 7.

⑥ Ernst Axel Knauf, "Towards and Archaeology of the Hexateuch," in *Abschied vom Jahwisten: Die Komposition des Hexateuch in der jüngsten Diskussion*, eds. Jan Christian Gertz, K. Schmid and M. Witte (Berlin: De Gruyter, 2002), 280.

一贯以南国为中心，强调南国犹大对于北国以色列的主导地位。当然，将北国以色列放在从属地位，只能发生在北国灭亡之后，犹大因此成为希伯来民族古老传统唯一的继承者。因此说明先祖叙事必定是更晚时代的产物，铁器时代北国以色列的记忆成为后来世代建构身份认同的基础，南国也认可自己为以色列的子孙，在经历灭国、流放、回归这些核心记忆之后，到波斯时期以耶路撒冷为中心的犹大知识阶层构想出整合南北传统的共同记忆。[①]

① 有关犹大知识阶层对以色列社会记忆的建构研究，参见：Ehud Ben Zvi, *Social Memory Among the Literati of Yehud* (Berlin: De Gruyter, 2019)。

Cultural Memory of the Patriarchal Narratives in Genesis

HUANG Wei

Abstract: In modern biblical scholarship, the patriarchal narratives in Genesis are usually viewed as the self-definition of Israelite nation in later period rather than a factual record of the origins of the Israelite nation. Firstly, this paper provides a brief review of the history of scholarship. By doing so, one may find that the patriarchal narratives on the surface are ancient family stories, yet the narratives are in fact consolidating the collective cultural memory of the Israelite nation. Secondly, the paper will examine the cultural memory of ancient Israelites on its neighboring communities against the narratives and the historical background of West Asia. Besides, the composition of this cultural memory is also discussed in this paper.

Key Words: Patriarchal Narratives, Israel, Cultural Memory, Genesis

五经中的上帝与诸神[*]

田海华[**]

【摘要】本文以传统的来源批判为理论基础，以五经中四个不同的来源为文本考察的中心，探讨其中的上帝与诸神，呈现当中的宗教发展历史，力图再现古代以色列的宗教图景。这四个来源分别是耶典、神典、申命典与祭司典，它们反映了四种平行且不相称的对过去的理解，以及对上帝的建构。本文重点分析了申命典与祭司典中的西奈启示，指出它们在五经宗教史中的意义。五经中的宗教史是复杂而多元的画卷，它们并非单向演进，而是多头并进。通过对文化记忆中上帝的不断改写，以色列人告别多神论的过往，开启一神论的新时代。

【关键词】五经；来源批判；上帝；诸神；宗教史

作为《圣经》的首五卷书，五经中的宗教奠定了以色列宗教史的基础。从文本著述与编修的历史来看，五经中的源流，可谓杂而多端，而且历经漫长的编修之后，五经中的宗教传统层层叠叠，这在四经（前四卷书）中表现得尤为显著。在《以色列史绪论》中，德国圣经学者威尔豪森（Julius Wellhausen, 1844—1918）追问：律法是否构成古代以色列史的起点？在回答这一追问的过程中，他在前人研究的基础上建构了来源批判（source criticism）理论，认为五经主要有四个来源。换言之，五经是由 JEDP 四个来源合并而成的，它们分别代表不同的作者与传统。① 这四个来源，其著述的形成，贯穿了由所罗门王到波斯时代的历史，论及

* 本文为国家社科基金项目“五经中的宗教、记忆与传统研究”（19BZJ003）的阶段性成果。

** 田海华，四川大学道教与宗教文化研究所教授。

① Julius Wellhausen, *Prolegomena to the History of Israel*, trans. J. Sutherland Black and Allan Menzies, with a preface by William Robertson Smith (Cambridge: Cambridge University Press, 2013), 1-13. 该著德文版初版于 1878 年，名为《以色列史》(*Geschichte Israels*)，1883 年再版时，改名为《以色列史绪论》(*Prolegomena zur Geschichte Israels*)。1885 年，依据德文再版译出的英文版出版。这些来源是基于对五经文本的假设而建构的，故又被称为文本假设(documentary hypothesis)。

由世界创造到摩西死亡的主题。其中的来源 J,通常又被称为“耶典”(Jehovist,英语学界名之为 Yahwist),缘于其圣号为耶和华(又称雅威),即德语中的 Jehovah,其可追溯至公元前 10 世纪末的联合王朝时代,著述于南国的犹大;来源 E 被称为“神典”(Elohist),神名用的是高高在上的 Elohim,神典可被归于王朝分裂时代的作品,体现了公元前 8 世纪的北国传统,但是它比较零碎;来源 D (Deuteronomist)又称为“申命典”,源于公元前 7 世纪末的约书亚王宗教改革时代,《申命记》是其主体部分,反复强调以色列人的违逆和道德因果报应;最后形成的来源 P,又被称为“祭司典”(Priestly writings),被视为巴比伦被掳之后的作品,祭司典强调秩序与圣洁,参与了整个五经的编修,在由第一个创造故事到《申命记》文末的增补中,都可看到祭司典作者的著述印记,而耶典和神典部分主要集中在《创世记》里。

一个世纪以来,这一批判理论尽管受到一些犹太教与基督教学者的抵制,但是,在过去的几十年里,它依然得到圣经学者的广泛接受与支持,并在争论中不断得到修正。[①] 作为历史批判的重要方法论之一,来源批判的要旨在于“通过将五经之著述与发展的历史理解为一种合成的文本,从而确立古代以色列宗教史演化的依据”[②]。来源批判主导了 20 世纪五经研究的主流话语。可以说,“20 世纪每一个历史批判学者,直接或间接地,都在认可他(威尔豪森)的文本假设论,而且,著述于这一世纪的任何一种《旧约》批判导论,都说明了这一理论的卓越性,它被视为解决五经形成之复杂问题的一种恰当答案,同时也是重构古代以色列宗教发展史的一个坚实基础”[③]。在这些不同来源中,古代以色列人表达了对

---

① Mark S. Smith, *The Memoirs of God: History, Memory, and the Experience of the Divine in Ancient Israel* (Minneapolis: Fortress Press, 2004), 9. 在欧洲学界的教科书或学术出版物中,文本假设论已被稳固地确立,且拥有更多的读者。参见:Thomas C. Römer, “The Elusive Yahwist: A Short History of Research,” in *A Farewell to the Yahwist? The Composition of the Pentateuch in Recent European Interpretation*, eds. Thomas B. Dozeman and Konrad Schmid (Atlanta: Society of Biblical Literature, 2006), 9。关于五经的著述与来源,北美、欧洲与以色列学界对文本假设论有不同的立场和倾向,不过,欧洲学界对此有更多的讨论和修正,尤其是对祭司典来源从未言弃,并将耶典与神典归为非祭司典。参见:Konrad Schmid, “Has European Scholarship Abandoned the Documentary Hypothesis? Some Reminders on Its History and Remarks on Its Current Status,” in *Pentateuch: International Perspectives on Current Research*, eds. Thomas B. Dozeman, Konrad Schmid and Baruch J. Schwartz (Tübingen: Mohr Siebeck, 2011), 17-30。

② Thomas L. Thompson, *Early History of the Israelite People: From the Written & Archaeological Sources* (Leiden: Brill, 2000), 2.

③ Pauline A. Viviano, “Source Criticism,” in *To Each Its Own Meaning: An Introduction to Biblical Criticisms and Their Application*, eds. Steven L. Mckenzie and Stephen R. Haynes (Louisville: Westminster / John Knox Press, 1999), 41.

上帝(God)的不同观念,描绘了上帝同其他神祇(gods)之关系,呈现了以色列宗教史的不同阶段和文化景观,成为“一神论起源的另类记忆”①。《圣经》之上帝观的形成,是从特定的传统中逐渐建构出来的。有关上帝的叙述话语,经历了漫长的发展过程,其观念在变动的社会与历史场景中不断得到修正,属于一种“集体发明”②。本文依据传统的来源批判理论,以五经中四个不同的来源为文本基础,结合当今欧美学界的研究成果,尝试分析和讨论其中的宗教史,力图再现古代以色列的宗教图景。

一、耶典中的上帝与诸神

耶典中的上帝雅威,是四圣字母 YHWH(יהוה)与“我主”(*ʼădōnāy*)的元音合成的音译。当前,欧美学者惯用的译名是“雅威”(Yahweh)。③ 关于雅威的起源,基于对乌加里特文本(Ugaritic texts)的研究,史密斯(Mark S. Smith)认为,以色列人最初崇拜的是迦南主神艾勒(El),而非雅威。雅威起初是个来自南部山地的风暴之神,是神勇的武士,像巴力(Baal)那样。在历史过程中,雅威融合

---

① Ronald Hendel, “God and the Gods in the Tetrateuch,” in *The Origins of Yahwism*, eds. Jürgen van Oorschot and Markus Witte (Berlin: De Gruyter, 2017), 238.

② Thomas Römer, *The Invention of God*, trans. Raymond Geuss (Cambridge: Harvard University Press, 2015), 4.

③ 希伯来经文最初是以辅音写成的。根据拉比释经集《密释纳》(*Mishna*),唯有在赎罪日(Yom Kippur)当天,犹太教高级祭司方可进入圣殿中的至圣所读出四圣字母的的正确发音。而依据撒马利亚传统,高级祭司会将正确读音秘传给后继者。久而久之,正确的读音失传。中世纪的马索拉学者发明了希伯来《圣经》的注音系统,并区分了读与写。他们规定文本中的四圣字母要读作*ʼădōnāy*,意为“我主”。13 世纪多明我会的修士马里(Raimundus Mari)将四圣字母译为 Yeh(o)wah,即耶和华。这一译名后被广泛用于各种《圣经》译本中。不过,在基督教时代,早期教父克莱门特(Clement of Alexandria)将《出埃及记》第 3 章第 14 节中的四圣字母称为 Iaoue,奥利金(Origen)在对《诗篇》的评注中讨论了圣名,将四圣字母对应 Yahweh。9 世纪君士坦丁堡牧首佛提奥斯(Photios)证明圣名为 Yabe 或 Yahweh。Yahweh 的发音,相当于词根“是”(*h-y-h*, to be)的动词阳性第三人称单数的使动式的发音。参见:Thomas Römer, *The Invention of God*, 25-32。本文在论述和引用《圣经》文本时,如非特别说明,经文出自和合本,且沿用“雅威”这一译名。

了艾勒与巴力神的特征，发展成为以色列人的民族神。[①] 其间，雅威曾经与迦南诸神一起受到崇拜，比如艾尔、巴力与亚舍拉(Asherah)等。[②] 在君王制时代，雅威成为耶路撒冷圣殿中的最高神，因为在至圣所中，基路伯之下的雅威之约柜即是其临在的象征(《列王纪上》8:6)。此后，随着北国以色列与南国犹大的建立，雅威作为一个民族神，已经成为这两国及其王室的最高神。根据考古发现，在铁器时代，雅威已经成为以色列和犹大的主神，他出现在印章、印鉴和著述文献中，但是雅威信仰植根于迦南宗教中，它同迦南宗教之间有紧密的连续性。[③] 在多神论的处境里，雅威如何被整合进以色列当地的崇拜形式中？这一问题不仅涉及以色列人文化身份的核心，同时触及《圣经》宗教的本质。在耶典里，上帝雅威在荆棘丛中的神圣显现(theophany)，最为惊心动魄：

> 雅威的使者从荆棘里火焰中向摩西显现。摩西观看，不料，荆棘被火烧着，却没有烧毁。摩西说："我要过去看这大异象，这荆棘为何没有烧坏呢？"(《出埃及记》3:2—3)[④]

在此，"荆棘"(סנה)与"西奈"(סיני)构成双关语。雅威的形象与火相关。类似的经文有《出埃及记》第19章第18节："西奈全山冒烟，因为雅威在火中降于山上，山的烟气上腾，如烧窑一般，遍山大大地震动。"雅威的名是如何启示于以色列人的？或者说，古代以色列人是如何认识雅威的？根据耶典的宗教史，雅威崇拜是古老而悠久的。在《创世记》第4章第26节中，求告雅威之名要推源到亚

① Mark S. Smith, *The Origins of Biblical Monotheism: Israel's Polytheistic Background and the Ugaritic Texts* (New York: Oxford University Press, 2001), 142-148. 另参见：Daniel E. Fleming, "Yahweh among the Baals: Yahweh and the Storm Gods," in *Mighty Baal: Essays in Honor of Mark S. Smith*, eds. Stephen C. Russell and Esther J. Hamori (Leiden: Brill, 2020), 160-174。关于雅威的原初特征，主要有五种学术观点。参见：Mark S. Smith, "YHWH's Original Character: Questions about an Unknown God," in *The Origins of Yahwism*, eds. Jürgen van Oorschot and Markus Witte (Berlin: De Gruyter, 2017), 37-43。米廷格(T. N. D. Mettinger)认为，雅威也吸收了迦南死神莫特(Mot)的特征，参见：T. N. D. Mettinger, "The Elusive Essence: YHWH, El and Baal and the Distinctiveness of Israelite Faith," in *Die Hebräische Bibel und ihre zweifache Nachgeschichte*, eds. Blum Erhard, Christian Macholz and Ekkehard W. Stegemann (Neukirchen-Vluyn: Neukirchener Verlag, 1990), 412。

② Mark S. Smith, *The Early History of God: Yahweh and the Other Deities in Ancient Israel* (Grand Rapids: Eerdmans, 2002), 7.

③ Amihai Mazar, "The Divided Monarchy: Comments on Some Archaeological Issue," in *The Quest for the Historical Israel*, ed. Brian B. Schmidt (Atlanta: SBL, 2007), 175.

④ 在讨论五经的编修时，有些学者将该段经文视为耶典的作品。参见：Joel S. Baden, *J, E, and the Redaction of the Pentateuch* (Tübingen: Mohr Siebeck, 2009), 269-270, 尤其是注释20。

当的孙子以挪士："那时候，人开始求告雅威的名。"[①]这说明雅威崇拜已经成为原初人类的首要宗教。[②] 其实，早在该隐与亚伯的时代，他们就向雅威献祭(《创世记》4:3—4)。及至挪亚时代，挪亚指出"雅威是闪的上帝"(《创世记》9:26)，意指雅威是所有闪族人的上帝。美索不达米亚首位伟大的君王宁录，"在雅威面前是个英勇的猎户"(《创世记》10:9)。而且，雅威的使者向埃及人夏甲传递其后裔繁多的应许(《创世记》16:11)，其就是以实玛利的后裔，也是游牧的阿拉伯部族。此外，巴比伦的建造者(《创世记》11:1—9)、埃及法老(《创世记》12:17)、索多玛和蛾摩拉的居民(《创世记》19)，都受制于雅威之公义的裁决。显然，雅威是权威的。作为世界的创造者，雅威是伊甸园叙述中的上帝。

耶典的宗教史将雅威崇拜限定在特定谱系里，使之同族长发生直接关联。雅威应许亚伯拉罕："地上万族都要因你得福。"(《创世记》12:3)亚伯拉罕三次求告雅威的名字，两次是在伯特利和艾之间的仪式场所(《创世记》12:8，13:4)，一次是在别是巴(《创世记》21:33)。以撒后来也在别是巴筑坛，求告雅威的名(《创世记》26:25)。在耶典中，世界创造后的三代人以挪士最早求告雅威的名，经亚伯拉罕与以撒之后，雅威在西奈山面向摩西的神圣启示成为巅峰之作(《出埃及记》33:12，34:9)，尤其是《出埃及记》第 33 章第 19 节与第 34 章第5 节这两节经文都论及"求告雅威的名"。[③] 摩西求雅威与之同行，求雅威显出荣耀。雅威告诉摩西："我要显我一切的恩慈，在你面前经过，宣告我的名。"(《出埃及记》33:19)在这里，"宣告我的名"既是对"求告雅威之名"的回应，也是其文学表达的变形。雅威再次向摩西显现，将自己的本质启示于摩西：

> 雅威在云中降临，和摩西一同站在那里，宣告雅威的名。雅威在他面前宣告说："雅威，雅威，是有怜悯、有恩典的上帝，不轻易发怒，并有丰盛的慈爱和诚实，为千万人存留慈爱，赦免罪孽、过犯和罪恶，万不以有罪的为无罪，必追讨他的罪，自父及子，直到三四代。"(《出埃及记》34:5—7)

在此，雅威宣告了他的名，并显示了这个名的深层意义，成为耶典宗教史上

---

① Adele Berlin and Marc Zvi Brettler, eds. *The Jewish Study Bible* (New York: Oxford University Press, 2004), 20.中文和合本、思高本、新译本等在翻译这句话时，加入"才"一字，使句意含混。现代中文译本译为"那时候，人开始求告'耶和华'的名"。而吕振中译本更是直截了当："这人(以挪士)是最先呼求永恒主之名的。"

② Ronald Hendel, "God and the Gods in the Tetrateuch," 249.

③ 关于这段经文的分析，参见：Joel Baden, *J, E, and Redaction of the Pentateuch*, 166-172, 270; Joel S. Baden, *The Composition of the Pentateuch: Renewing the Documentary Hypothesis* (New Haven: Yale University Press, 2012), 78。

至关重要的时刻,开启了新的篇章。上帝是"怜悯"的,有"慈爱"的。"怜悯"和"慈爱"的希伯来文与"母腹"(*reḥem*)相关,多用于与上帝相关的属性上。《出埃及记》第33章第19节与第34章第5—7节这两处经文,以重复教义声明的形式,"宣告了神圣之爱丰富的、无尽的与坚定不移的本质。这种神圣的慈爱唤起了来自母腹的意象,即上帝对以色列具有强大的母爱"①。当雅威向摩西宣告他的荣耀之名时,"求告雅威之名"这一格式带出了全新维度。它并不关注雅威身体上的临在,而是扩大和阐发了荣耀之名的伦理属性。② 如此,上帝的启示是基于他自身本质的一种道德意义,其特性是仁爱、怜悯、公义和宽恕。在耶典中,虽然没有西奈律法的颁布③,却有耶和华之公义、恩典与真理的辩证属性。在这一神圣显现中,我们看到"求告雅威之名"的深层含义。雅威的这一自我启示,为宣告雅威之名的漫长宗教史画上句号。

在耶典的宗教史中,"其他神祇"是从属于雅威的神圣存在。这些神祇包括传递雅威之信息的天使(מלאכים)、《创世记》第6章第1—4节中的神子(בני האלהים)等。关于神子,在《申命记》第32章的摩西之歌中,神子也可以是其他民族的神祇(《申命记》32:8)。④ 因此,耶典的作者具有"国际视野",期待将雅威作为宇宙的创造者以及历史的上帝进行崇拜。

二、神典中的上帝与诸神

神典与耶典有密切关联,二者的界限有时含混不清,甚至难以区分,但是神典作为一个单独的来源,在叙述风格、主题与语言上,依旧有迹可循,有自己的特点。⑤ 相较而言,神典对本土宗教有更为细致的描述。神典强调预言,神典的上帝常常出现在人们的愿景或梦境里,言说上帝的奇迹、异事与大能。在《创世记》

① Carol Meyers, *Exodus* (Cambridge: Cambridge University Press, 2005), 123.另参见:Phyllis Trible, *God and the Rhetoric of Sexuality* (Philadelphia: Fortress, 1978), 31-59。

② Ronald Hendel, "God and the Gods in the Tetrateuch," 252.

③ Joel S. Baden, *The Composition of the Pentateuch: Renewing the Documentary Hypothesis*, 76-78.

④ 根据七十士译本和死海古卷,这段经文译为:"至高者(עליון)将地业赐给列邦,将世人分开,就照神子的数目,立定万民的疆界。"这里的"神子"是指El的众子,雅威是其子之一。另参见:《申命记》第4章第19节以及《诗篇》第82章。

⑤ Joel S. Baden, *The Composition of the Pentateuch: Renewing the Documentary Hypothesis*, 104-128.

里，神典的传统与雅各—约瑟之叙述的关系尤为密切。[①] 雅各在别是巴给他父亲以撒的上帝(אלהים)献祭后，上帝向他神圣显现：

> 夜间，上帝(אלהים)在异象中对以色列说："雅各！雅各！"他说："我在这里。"上帝说："我是上帝，就是你父亲的上帝。你下埃及去不要害怕，因为我必使你在那里成为大族。我要和你同下埃及去，也必定带你上来，约瑟必给你送终。"(《创世记》46：2—4)

在此，上帝应许雅各以个人的出埃及记。这一应许涉及雅各由埃及地回归，并葬在他的先祖之地，叶落归根。同时，它预言了约瑟在埃及得势。这种回溯于父家宗教传统的表述结构，也出现在摩西的神圣显现中。在神典里，燃烧的荆棘丛中的启示，通常与耶典中西奈山上的启示形成对比。在何烈山，上帝在燃烧的荆棘丛中向摩西启示：

> 上帝(אלהים)就从荆棘里呼叫说："摩西！摩西！"他说："我在这里。"上帝说："不要近前来，当把脚上的鞋脱下来，因为你所站之地是圣地。"又说："我是你父亲的上帝(אלהים)，是亚伯拉罕的上帝，以撒的上帝，雅各的上帝。"摩西蒙上脸，因为怕看上帝。(《出埃及记》3：4—6)[②]

在此，上帝自我认同为"你父亲的上帝"，与《创世记》第 46 章中对雅各的自我认同一样。《创世记》里族长的上帝，成为摩西之父的上帝，同时也成为摩西的上帝。[③] 通过这样的连接与过渡，由亚伯拉罕至摩西的宗教史就被建构起来。在古代以色列，一个个体的身份通常是由其所在父系族谱中的地位界定，而他的宗教身份是由他同父系族谱之关系界定，因此，他的神就是父家的神。[④] 在希伯来《圣经》里，当下常常通过与过去的关联而被建构，而过去是被记忆、被呈现的过去，建构的目的在于服务当下。在对摩西的神圣启示中，摩西与先前的族长发生了关联，成为以色列民族新的被拣选的族长与引领者，成为以色列宗教史中人神之间的重要中介。上帝在《出埃及记》第 3 章第 3—6 节中对摩西的启示，同

---

① Antony F. Campbell and Mark A. O'brien, *Sources of the Pentateuch: Texts, Introductions, Annotations* (Minneapolis: Fortress Press, 1992), 161.

② 在讨论五经的编修时，巴登(Joel S. Baden)认为《出埃及记》第 3 章第 4 节的上半句为耶典，下半句为神典。参见：Joel S. Baden, *J, E, and the Redaction of the Pentateuch*, 269-270。施密德(Konrad Schmid)认为《出埃及记》第 3 章第 4—6 节是个统一的著述。参见：Konrad Schmid, *Genesis and the Moses Story: Israel's Dual Origins in the Hebrew Bible*, trans. James D. Nogalski (Winona Lake: Eisenbrauns, 2010), 172-181。

③ Konrad Schmid, *Genesis and the Moses Story: Israel's Dual Origins in the Hebrew Bible*, 172-173.

④ Ronald Hendel, "God and the Gods in the Tetrateuch," 241.

《创世记》中对雅各和亚伯拉罕的启示形成共鸣，深化了新启示的内容，建构了神典叙述中宗教史的进程。上帝向摩西提示过去的宗教史，激活对过去的记忆。以色列的宗教史由此而得到更新。①

其实，在神典的宗教史中，《创世记》第 35 章第 1—7 节体现了较早时期以色列宗教的更新。其中，上帝(אלהים)要雅各住在伯特利，筑一座坛给上帝，就是雅各逃避以扫时遇到的上帝(《创世记》28:10—22)。② 于是，雅各要求他的家人除掉外邦的神，从而洁净自己。他的家人将外邦人的神像和耳环交给雅各，他将它们葬在示剑的橡树下。示剑是一个宗教圣地，是外邦人神像所藏之地。这个神圣启示，主要属于神典，它承认外邦神的存在。它传递出古代以色列人对外邦神像的某种宽容，甚至敬意。③ 雅各筑坛的伯特利(בית-אל)，意为"上帝之家"，或"神的殿"(《创世记》28:17—19)。④ 在神典的记忆里，对雅各的家族而言，在伯特利对上帝崇拜的更新，意味着由多神崇拜向一神崇拜(monolatry)的转化。但是，对以色列人崇拜外邦神的苛刻谴责，神典亦有记载。在上述宗教仪式里，外邦人的神像与耳环一同被埋葬，与神典之宗教史的金牛犊故事形成呼应。在《出埃及记》第 32 章第 2 节中，亚伦对以色列百姓说："你们去摘下你们妻子、儿女耳上的金环，拿来给我。"亚伦将其用于金牛犊的铸造，并称这是带领以色列人出埃及的神，是"你们的神"(אלהיך)，以此谴责以色列民的败坏。因为在进入与上帝的约之后，拜外邦的神是危险的，它打破了神圣的边界，会引致暴怒与死亡(《出埃及记》32:12)。⑤ 神典的作者将金牛犊视为外邦的神，谴责偶像崇拜的北国以色列。通过这样的谴责，神典将以色列的上帝与外邦的神祇区别开来。⑥ 这是神典宗教史演化的重要一步。

---

① Ronald Hendel, "God and the Gods in the Tetrateuch," 244.

② 《创世记》第 35 章第 1—7 节曾三次提到伯特利的神圣显现。不过，它保留了艾勒(אל)的神名。参见：Aren M. Wilson-Wright, "Bethel and the Persistence of El: Evidence for the Survival of El as an Independent Deity in the Jacob Cycle and 1 Kings 12:25-30," *Journal of Biblical Literature* 138(2019): 711-714。这两段经文都属于神典，具有统一性，参见：Joel S. Baden, *The Composition of the Pentateuch: Renewing the Documentary Hypothesis*, 238-241。

③ Ronald Hendel, "Cultural Memory," in *Reading Genesis: Ten Methods*, ed. Ronald Hendel (New York: Cambridge University Press, 2010), 33-38.

④ 作为重要的宗教圣祠，伯特利体现了古代以色列人的集体身份与宗教命运。参见：Ronald Hendel, "Cultural Memory," 34.

⑤ "以色列啊，这是领你出埃及地的神。"(《出埃及记》32:4、8)"你们的神"用的是复数形式，是对耶罗波安在伯特利和但筑坛建殿拜金牛犊的回应(《列王纪上》12:28)。它们都反映了北国的仪式传统。参见：Mark R. Smith, *The Memoirs of God: History, Memory, and the Experience of the Divine in Ancient Israel*, 34-35。

⑥ Ronald Hendel, "God and the Gods in the Tetrateuch," 248.

在神典的宗教演化历史中，上帝与其他诸神之间的关系，可以被描述为具有文化连续性的特征。神典中对外邦神的认可，说明以色列的宗教在铁器时代同周遭民族的宗教是相容的。[①] 可以说，崇拜金牛犊事件是雅各故事中对最早同外邦神相分离的一种逆转，而埋葬的金耳环在伯特利和但的仪式中回归(《列王纪上》12:29)。雅各承认外邦神的存在，并给出一个体面的埋葬，也就是说，神典曾经认可外邦诸神的存在，只是警告不可侍奉他们。但是，外邦的神是危险的。比如，出自公元前 9 世纪中叶摩押王室的米沙石碑给出了典型的例子。它描述了摩押的民族神基抹在历史中是大有能力的，并认可以色列的神雅威。[②] 神典中的神学表明，每个民族都有自己的民族神，都具有相较于其他民族的切实的宗教与社会身份。这一点与耶典中雅威崇拜在早期世代中广为流传有所不同。因此，《创世记》第 35 章第 1—7 节中与外邦神的仪式分离，具有深层的神学与政治意义。这一分离体现了以色列与其他民族之间的界限。而且，因这一分离而制定的律例，宣告以色列的文化身份，使以色列成为不同于其地缘家族的一个民族。在地理与宗教上，以色列的民族与宗教身份已不同于过往。[③] 这是北国以色列在宗教与政治建构中同新亚述帝国进行抗辩的一种反映和结果。

三、申命典中的上帝与诸神

申命典主要集中于“第二律法”《申命记》中，强调对律法的遵从以及对雅威的爱与崇拜。这同公元前 622 年或前 621 年约西亚的宗教改革相关。在那一年，“律法书”在圣殿的废墟中被发现，约西亚宣称其为圣书，将之归于摩西，赋予其权威，要求全地的民众都遵从这律法(《列王纪下》22:8)。这开启了希伯来宗教历史上的伟大革新，其意识形态是要实现宗教崇拜的中心化，即将所有的宗教崇拜活动集中于耶路撒冷且只崇拜雅威。这一改革所呈现的意识形态，同样反映在《约书亚记》至《列王纪下》的书卷中。相较于五经其他书卷，早在 1805 年，德国著名圣经学者德维特(Wilhelm Martin Leberecht de Wette)认为，《申命记》另有作者，是一个单独的来源，不同于五经其他书卷，其所表达的宗教观念亦有

① Ronald Hendel, “God and the Gods in the Tetrateuch,” 261.

② 摩押与以色列的冲突就是基抹(כמש)与雅威(יהוה)之间的冲突。亨德尔(Ronald Hendel)将第 17 节的内容译述为：雅威是基抹的附庸，米沙将雅威捉住并放在基抹面前。参见：Ronald Hendel, “God and the Gods in the Tetrateuch,” 261，注释 55。

③ Ronald Hendel, “God and the Gods in the Tetrateuch,” 261.

所不同。[①] 他发现《申命记》是五经中唯一强调崇拜场所中央化的书卷。就《申命记》的文本结构而言,冯拉德(Gerhard von Rad)认为:"《申命记》遵循了一种传统仪式的范式,它或许是一种礼仪节期的礼拜仪式。"[②]在这个礼仪场景里,《申命记》反复训谕人们要维护雅威的圣所,不可悖逆上帝雅威,宣扬在耶路撒冷进行对雅威的崇拜,抵制迦南的神祇。

在申命典的宗教史中,"以色列啊!你要听"(ראלשי מעש),又简称为"舍玛"(מעש,意为"听"),它高度概括了对雅威的一神崇拜:

> 以色列啊!你要听,雅威我们的上帝是独一的(אחד)主。你要尽心、尽性、尽力爱雅威你的上帝。(《申命记》6:4—6)

这里"独一的",是指数量上的"一",指明对雅威的一神崇拜,并未在本质上否定其他神祇的存在。因为以色列的上帝雅威是"忌邪的"(《申命记》4:24,5:9),即在崇拜雅威的仪式场所,禁止供奉其他神祇。十诫之"在我面前(על־פנה),不可有别的神"(《申命记》5:7),也清楚表达了这种宗教实践。此诫的字面意思是:不可将其他神放置在我面前。[③] 换言之,在崇拜雅威的场所,不可同时崇拜别的神。在这里,耶和华以第一人称的语气,要求他的子民做出排他性的抉择,从而建构他们的宗教身份,正如柯林斯(John J. Collins)指出的,《申命记》中的"宗教,尤其是对雅威的一神崇拜仪式,是正在形成的民族身份的核心要素"[④]。仅选择雅威作为崇拜对象,而远离其他民族的神,有助于以色列人从周遭民族中分离出来。

关于雅威崇拜的中央化,《申命记》第12章做了进一步阐释:

---

① Henning Graf Reventlow, *History of Biblical Interpretation*, Vol. 4 (Atlanta: Society of Biblical Literature, 2010), 232-233.

② Gerhard von Rad, *Deuteronomy*, trans. Dorothea Barton (London: SCM Press, 1976), 12.

③ Dale Patric, "The First Commandment in the Structure of the Pentateuch," *Vetus Testamentum* 45 (1995): 107.《出埃及记》第20章第3节也有相同的表达,但是学者认为《申命记》中的十诫是原初的,而《出埃及记》中的十诫则是编修者加插的结果。参见:Joseph Blenkinsopp, *The Pentateuch: An Introduction to the First Five Books of the Bible* (New York: Doubleday, 1992), 207-208; Cornelis Houtman, *Exodus* Vol.3 (Leuven: Peeters, 2001), 10-11; John van Seters, "Pentateuch: Genisis, Exodus, Leviticus, Numbers, Deuteronomy," in *The Hebrew Bible Today: An Introduction to Critical Issues*, eds. Steven Mckenzie and Patrick Graham (Kentucky: Westminster John Knox Press, 1998), 48。

④ John J. Collins, *The Invention of Judaism: Torah and Jewish Identity from Deuteronomy to Paul* (Oakland: University of California Press, 2017), 39. 尼尔森(Eduard Nielsen)认为:这具有耶路撒冷之圣殿传统的印记,而且同具有以色列北国传统的申命学派运动相关。参见:Eduard Nielsen, *The Ten Commandments in New Perspective: A Traditio-historical Approach*, trans. David J. Bourke (London: SCM Press, 1968), 98。

> 那时要将我所吩咐你们的燔祭、平安祭，十分取一之物，和手中的举祭，并向雅威许愿献的一切美祭，都奉到雅威你们的上帝所选择要立为他名的居所(כקש)。你们和儿女、仆婢，并住在你们城里无份无业的利未人，都要在雅威你们的上帝面前欢乐。你要谨慎，不可在你所看中的各处献燔祭。唯独雅威从你那一支派中所选择的地方(מקם)，你就要在那里献燔祭，行我一切所吩咐你的。(《申命记》12:11—14)

结合上下语境，经文反复强调以色列民众献祭的地方是雅威从支派中选择的，也是雅威立名的居所。雅威选择的这个地方，非耶路撒冷莫属，而被拣选的支派是南国犹大。[①] 对犹大的拣选，也出现在《诗篇》第 78 章中。雅威拣选犹大支派，在他喜爱的锡安山建造他的圣所(《诗篇》78:68—69)。这样的拣选传统体现了申命学派的观念。[②] 在《申命记》中，雅威的选择同样具有排他性，即禁止敬拜雅威的其他圣所存在。敬拜的唯一地点，就是中央圣所耶路撒冷。因此，《申命记》第 16 章第 16 节规定："你一切的男丁，要在除酵节、七七节、住棚节，一年三次，在雅威你上帝所选择的地方(מקם)朝见他，却不可空手朝见。"[③]

同时，《申命记》明令禁止偶像崇拜。在申命典作者看来，偶像崇拜是对雅威的悖逆和亵渎，因此，在立约语境中颁布的申命典律法，反复强调偶像崇拜的恶果。《申命记》限定了偶像崇拜的范围，包括上天、下地和地底下水中的百物(《申命记》5:8)。具体而言，以色列人要尽心尽性爱雅威，他们若拜金牛犊，雅威要发烈怒，镌刻着十诫的约版就要在以色列民面前被摔碎，牛犊被焚烧，且磨成灰(《申命记》9:15—21)[④]；若侍奉先祖素不相识的别神，也就是周遭列国的神，就要被击杀(《申命记》13)；拜日月星辰等天象，就要被石头打死(《申命记》17:3—5)；不可随从异邦的恶俗，包括占卜、巫术与交鬼等(《申命记》18:9—14)。违逆雅威诫

---

① Andrew D. H. Mayes, *Deuteronomy* (Grand Rapids: Eerdmans, 1981), 227.另参见：Thomas Römer, *The Invention of God*, 205。《申命记》第 16 章反复提及"雅威所选择要立为他名的居所"(《申命记》16:2、6、11)。

② 李炽昌 Archie Lee,《重述过去:〈诗篇〉78 与〈诗经〉的跨文本阅读》[The Recitation of the Past: A Cross-Textual Reading of Psalm 78 and Other Odes]，徐雪梅 Xu Xuemei 译，收录于《跨文本阅读:〈希伯来圣经〉诠释》[Cross-Textual Reading of the Hebrew *Bible*]，李炽昌 Archie Lee 编，(上海[Shanghai]: 上海三联书店[SDX Joint Publishing Company]，2015)，65。

③ Shimon Gesundheit, *Three Times a Year: Study on Festival Legislation in the Pentateuch* (Tübingen: Mohr Siebeck, 2012), 158-162.

④ 金牛犊事件也出现在《出埃及记》第 32 章第 1—20 节中，但是《申命记》的记述与之不同，摩西并未俯伏在雅威面前为民恳求，因为在《申命记》里摩西重述过去，重塑对过去的记忆，成为以色列之过去的诠释者。参见:Joel S. Baden, "Deuteronomy Reads the Pentateuch," *Biblical Interpretation* 28(2020): 10-14。

命的必受咒诅和重祸,而忠诚于雅威的必受祝福(《申命记》27—28)。在申命典的意识形态里,雅威是生死祸福的来源,选择雅威,就是选择生命:

> 我今日(היום)呼天唤地向你作见证,我将生死、祸福陈明在你面前,所以你要拣选生命,使你和你的后裔都得存活。且爱雅威你的上帝,听从他的话,专靠他,因为他是你的生命。你的日子长久也在乎他。这样,你就可以在雅威向你列祖亚伯拉罕、以撒、雅各起誓应许所赐的地上居住。(《申命记》30:19—20)[①]

因此,通过立约关系的建立、雅威崇拜仪式的中央化以及对各类偶像崇拜实践的拒斥,申命典的作者突出以色列人对雅威的选择,以及与之相关的宗教道德的因果报应观念。

四、祭司典中的上帝与诸神

在经历被掳的历史事件之后,祭司典对犹大与以色列的宗教传统进行了新的诠释。对于现代的《圣经》诠释者而言,祭司典来源中的上帝概念显得既熟悉又陌生。一方面,这个上帝的概念类似于犹太教、基督教与伊斯兰教传统中的上帝,是个超验的、抽象的、非神人同形同性的上帝,也是个无所不知且全能的上帝。正是这个上帝,其通过话语创造了宇宙,创造了治理全地的人类,制定了各种有关仪式与献祭的律例。但另一方面,相较于耶典与神典中的上帝概念,这个上帝显得很陌生,因为在祭司典中没有天使,没有神子(Sons of God),也没有外邦的神,简言之,唯有上帝。[②] 罗默(Thomas Römer)认为:《利未记》第16章可能是祭司典最初的文本,是在赎罪日的仪式中吟诵的,它强调高级祭司要定期洁净圣所与会众,坚持雅威的子民与其他民族之间的严格分离,主张一种包容的一神论(inclusive monotheism),在万民及其各自的神祇中,力图界定以色列与雅

① “今日”是《申命记》中的一个关键词,频繁出现(《申命记》26:16—19,27:9—10,28:13—14,29:10—15,30:1—20)。“今日”是指被掳或被掳后时期,而非摩西时代。耶和华“今日”同以色列立约,要他们遵从他的诫命、律例、典章。如果以色列人诚心忏悔并忠于耶和华,耶和华便应许他们在被掳回归后拥有自己的土地与家园,因此,立约与否意味着在生与死之间做选择。参见:Richard D. Nelson, *Deuteronomy: A Commentary* (Louisville: Westminster John Knox Press, 2002), 77。

② Ronald Hendel, “God and the Gods in the Tetrateuch,” 256.《利未记》第16章的主要特征就是强调祭司与百姓有切实的祛除过往罪愆的需要。参见:Calum Carmichael, *Illuminating Leviticus: A Study of Its Laws and Institutions in the Light of Biblical Narratives* (Baltimore: John Hopkins University Press, 2006), 38。

威的居所与角色。[①] 祭司典作者对王室历史兴趣不大,但极为强调雅威崇拜礼仪的有序化与圣洁化。

在某种程度上,祭司典的文本消灭了其他神祇存在的可能性,呈现去神圣化的过程,类似于韦伯的理性"除魅"。[②]《圣经》的别处多次提到其他神祇的各种变体。比如,古代以色列人供拜的日月星辰,它们属于"天上的万象",是上帝的万军,有时是"神子"的同义语。但在《创世记》第 1 章里,日月只是上帝造出的两个大光(《创世记》1:16),是宇宙这一机器上的部件,没有位格。此外,上帝创造出(ברא)大鱼或海怪(《创世记》1:21)。上帝作为 ברא 的主语,造出了两样特殊的生物,即海怪与人。[③] 但是,这里的大鱼或海怪与人一样,并不构成上帝的对手,不像在被掳后文献中表现的那样威胁到上帝的创造,最终被上帝在末世时代击败。而且,在《创世记》第 1 章第 27 节中,上帝以自己的形象创造了人,并命令他们治理全地,清空了其他神祇存在的空间。因此,祭司典的上帝选择将人作为与之建立关系的共同体。[④] 在古代亚述的观念里,君王在身体上与神相像,君王就是神在世上的形象,拥有像神那样的神圣权威。而在祭司典的创造叙述里,人与上帝相像,人被赋权(empower)。

在祭司典的叙事中,由于人和动物以暴力染污了地面,上帝决定发动大洪水开启新纪元。随即上帝开始与人立约,并由此建构了祭司典中上帝与人立约的宗教史。各种各样的约,界定了人当遵从的规则和律例,限定了人神关系的边界,从而维护公义的宇宙秩序。上帝与他的子民在律法意义上建构的关系,沿袭了遍及古代近东世界对于秩序的传统观念,这一秩序将公义的概念象征化。对祭司典作者而言,毁灭与放逐并不意味着犹大与以色列历史的终结,这样的观念主要体现在祭司典的立约神学中。其中,无条件的挪亚之约(《创世记》9)与亚伯拉罕之约(《创世记》17),确保世界的延续以及上帝对以色列持续的亲近。[⑤] 伴随立约的是一系列神圣应许与仪式实践。而且,每次立约都由上帝的启示发起。在立约过程中,上帝的名渐次显示。施密德认为,在《创世记》第 1 章至《出埃及记》第 6 章,祭司典以希伯来通用术语 Elohim(אלהים)指涉上帝。正如《创世记》

---

① Thomas Römer, *The Invention of God*, 225.

② Max Weber 马克斯·韦伯,《学术与政治》[Science and Politics],冯克利 Feng Keli 译,(北京[Beijing]:商务印书馆[The Commercial Press],2018),17。

③ Ronald Hendel, "God and the Gods in the Tetrateuch," 257.

④ Ronald Hendel, "God and the Gods in the Tetrateuch," 257.

⑤ Konrad Schmid, *Is There Theology in the Hebrew Bible?*, trans. Peter Altmann (Winona Lake: Eisenbrauns, 2015), 88-90.

第1章里，上帝的名是 Elohim，充满威严，统治着他所创造的整个世界。[①] 在语法上，这个词是个强化的复数。不过，在《创世记》第17章中，上帝向亚伯拉罕启示了一个新的名字：

> 耶和华向他（亚伯拉罕）显现（ראה），对他说："我是全能的上帝（דיש אל），你当在我面前作完全人，我就与你立约，使你的后裔极其繁多。"（《创世记》17：1—2）

这个新名是"全能的上帝"（El Shaddai），而且这是耶和华的圣名第一次出现在祭司典里。El Shaddai 最初可能是至高神 El 的名字，他居于山地。[②] 在祭司典里，上帝是多名的，他隐匿而神秘，显得深不可测。族长亚伯拉罕的上帝被称为"全能的上帝"，或是 El Elyon（《创世记》14：19），其常被译为"至高的上帝"。以撒的上帝是 El Olam（《创世记》21：33），译为"永生上帝"。但是，上帝终极之名最终显示于摩西。当上帝向以色列人更新所立之约时，他说：

> 上帝（אל）晓谕摩西说："我是雅威。我从前向亚伯拉罕、以撒、雅各显现为全能的上帝（דיש אל）；至于我名耶和华，他们未曾知道（ידע）。"（《出埃及记》6：2—3）

上帝的这一启示，可以追溯至《创世记》第17章中上帝给亚伯拉罕的应许。那时，上帝显现，并应许赐给以色列土地。而在《出埃及记》中，上帝向摩西启示他的名，要让以色列人知道雅威就是他们的上帝。[③] 因此，这个将族长与摩西连接在一起的启示是渐进的启示，它符合祭司典的神学。首次将《创世记》与摩西的故事结合在一起的，是祭司典的作者。[④] 上帝对于其名的最终启示，促使其在西奈山的旷野由天而降，居于其百姓中间。雅威的荣光充满会幕（《出埃及记》40：34），象征上帝的神圣临在。在祭司典关于上帝的观念里，这种神圣的临在是非

---

① Konrad Schmid, *Is There Theology in the Hebrew Bible ?*, 91.

② 在雅威的圣名启示于摩西之前，El Shaddai 是祭司典更喜欢用的上帝之名，Shaddai 已经出现在公元前10世纪的文本中，比如《创世记》第49章第25节与《民数记》第24章4节等。传统上，El Shaddai 被译为"全能的上帝"，沿袭了七十士译本和武加大译本的用法。参见：John Day, *Yahweh and the Gods and Goddesses* (London: Sheffield Academic Press, 2002), 32。

③ 罗默认为，祭司典叙述中的雅威启示经历了三个阶段：第一，在世界起源和洪水故事里，雅威将自己启示于所有人为 Elohim，这个术语可被译为一位神、诸神或上帝；第二，雅威启示于亚伯拉罕及其后裔为 El Shaddai；第三，上帝向摩西启示为 Yhwh。参见：Thomas Römer, *The Invention of God*, 225-226。

④ 施密德认为，《创世记》与《出埃及记》是关于以色列起源的两种独立的叙述，祭司典作者连接并调和了二者，创制出以色列起源的一种新历史。参见：Konrad Schmid, *Genesis and the Moses Story: Israel's Dual Origins in the Hebrew Bible*, 241-248。这一假设若是正确的，那么，它标志着对希伯来《圣经》最为重要的文学与历史的综合。参见：Konrad Schmid, *Is There Theology in the Hebrew Bible ?*, 88。

物质的火焰般的聚集,上帝的神圣性远离人的肉体所具有的性与死亡的身体特征。[①] 会幕就是上帝在地上的居所。[②] 它是一个流动的神圣空间,进入圣所献祭的祭司与一般会众,在身体上先要保持洁净和完整,带入的祭品必须符合相应的等级和洁净的品质。[③] 性与死亡同神圣是不相容的。在《利未记》与《民数记》中,有诸多有关圣洁的律法,它们都规定了上帝与以色列人近距离接近的危险性。[④]

在祭司典的圣洁法典(《利未记》17—26)中,以色列人进入会幕的神圣空间,必须遵守洁净的律例和仪式。上帝晓谕摩西的律法,严控人的不洁对神圣空间的侵蚀,认为人不洁的身体会污染会幕,从而引致死亡与灾难。在道格拉斯(Mary Douglas)看来,《利未记》中的"身体"是一个宇宙符号。[⑤] 她指出:"身体即祭坛,祭坛即身体。"[⑥]污染祭坛就是污染以色列人的身体。如此,以色列会众的身体被视为对祭坛的类比,处于神圣律法的约束之下,不洁净的食物不可吃,保护圣所洁净的规则同样适用于献祭者。唯有祭司可以就近祭坛,但也必须遵守相关的洁净定例,不然要担罪而死。比如,祭司亚伦和他儿子进入会幕,或是

---

① 《利未记》第 13—15 章与《民数记》第 12 章第 12 节指明性和死亡与上帝的神圣性格格不入,是不洁的。因为,雅威超验的身体不具有性,也不会死亡。史密斯(Mark S. Smith)认为:在祭司典里,上帝的身体是超自然的、宇宙化的"神秘"存在。《出埃及记》第 40 章第 34—35 节中临于会幕中的上帝的荣光(כבוד),并非有形的身体,而是神圣临在的灿烂光辉。在祭司典的观念里,kābôd 不是神的身体。参见:Mark S. Smith, "The Three Bodies of God in the Hebrew Bible," *Journal of Biblical Literature* 134 (2015): 487-488。

② 包肯索普(Joseph Blenkinsopp)将圣所会幕的建造(《出埃及记》39—40)同第一个创造故事进行对比,认为在祭司典的仪式律法(cultic laws)中,旷野圣所的建造是六日创造的完成。因此,《利未记》中在西奈山颁布的仪式律法是在圣所完成之后进行的。圣所在旷野生活中起主导作用,影响社会、政治与宗教的各个方面。在国家覆亡之后,这是祭司阶层的目标所在。参见:Joseph Blenkinsopp, *The Pentateuch: An Introduction to the First Five Books of the Bible* (New York: Doubleday, 1992), 217-219。

③ Saul M. Olyan, *Rites and Rank: Hierarchy in Biblical Representations of Cult* (Princeton: Princeton University Press, 2000), 54-61.

④ 神圣与凡俗之间有明确界限,因为它们不同质。Mircea Eliade, *The Sacred and the Profane: The Nature of Religion*, trans. Willard R. Trask (New York: Harcourt, 1987), 20.祭司典的律法与训谕,包括《出埃及记》第 25—31 章和第 35—40 章、《利未记》第 1—27 章以及《民数记》第 1—10 章。参见:Mark S. Smith, *The Memoirs of God: History, Memory, and the Experience of the Divine in Ancient Israel*, 10。

⑤ Mary Douglas 玛丽·道格拉斯,《作为文学的〈利未记〉》[Leviticus as Literrature],唐启翠 Tang Qicui、徐蓓丽 Xu Beili、唐铎 Tang Duo 译,(北京[Beijing]:社科文献出版社[Social Sciences Academic Press],2018),13。伊利亚德(Mircea Eliade)也表达了类似观念。他指出人的身体和宇宙有对应关系,认为"宗教人的居所是一个小宇宙,他的身体也是一个小宇宙"。参见:Mircea Eliade, *The Sacred and the Profane: The Nature of Religion*, 172。

⑥ 玛丽·道格拉斯,《作为文学的〈利未记〉》,124。

就近祭坛供职，不可露出下体(《出埃及记》28:43)，不可饮酒(《利未记》10:9)，不可蓬头散发、撕裂衣服和走出会幕(《利未记》10:6—7)，必须洗手洗脚(《出埃及记》30:20—21)。对身体的控制和严格的洁净要求，使祭司必须保持神圣的仪式状态，否则，会被上帝充满危险的圣洁击杀。但是，人的不洁是自然的，也是必要的，它是可朽之身体的条件，是人的属性，但这同上帝的神圣临在不相容。因此，这就构成一个悖论：上帝选择居于他的百姓中间，但是上帝的神圣性对百姓是危险的。① 在其他神祇缺席的情况下，上帝的社群就是他的百姓，但是他在其中的临在是有代价的。祭司典奠定了祭司的神圣权威，以及雅威与其百姓之间紧密依存的危险关系，为圣经一神论的演进铺设道路。

五、结语

耶典、神典、申命典与祭司典的宗教史，呈现了四种平行且不相称的过去的宗教图景。每一种宗教图景都描述了族长的上帝将自己显现为摩西与以色列之上帝的历史，但是正如亨德尔指出的，每一种都有不同的叙述情节，对雅威的特点与属性持有不同的观念，并将雅威置于同其他神祇不同的关系中。它们形成对文化记忆的不同建构。② 在耶典的宗教史里，以色列人对其他神祇和民族的焦虑是显著的，耶典将耶和华的崇拜广而扩散到早期人类世代中，让所有早期民族都崇拜他，包括宁录、巴比伦与亚述的首位君王、巴比伦的缔造者，这可能受到各种文化冲突与焦虑的驱动，可能是对新亚述帝国政治处境的回应。③ 在文化记忆的层面上，耶典的宗教史模仿并转化了亚述帝国的意识形态，使雅威成为所有民族的原初神，因此，它是一种混杂的叙述话语，目的是要反转当下的政治力量。神典将雅威崇拜只限于以色列人，同时，认可其他民族其他神祇的存在。申命典的宗教史，在立约的语境里，强调雅威崇拜的中央化，取缔地方性神坛，禁止偶像崇拜。祭司典的宗教史有所不同。祭司典是在巴比伦被掳期间著述的，除了雅威之外，没有外邦神，没有天使，也没有天象，海怪成为上帝创造的一部分，但似乎没有冲突到需要上帝去征服(《创世记》1:21)。亨德尔指出："在帝国为主

① Ronald Hendel, "God and the Gods in the Tetrateuch," 259.

② Ronald Hendel, "God and the Gods in the Tetrateuch," 260.

③ Ronald Hendel, "God and the Gods in the Tetrateuch," 262. 新亚述帝国的影响对以色列一神论的兴起可能是一种激励。因此，史密斯认为以色列曾居于帝国的阴影之下，它现在要表达明确的一神论。这同它在历史上要同其邻邦区分开来的自身经验与传统是一致的。以色列的一神论是在其面对帝国而缺乏权力的处境中产生的，这是一种抗衡帝国的形式。参见：Mark R. Smith, *The Memoirs of God: History, Memory, and the Experience of the Divine in Ancient Israel*, 120。

导,而且在失去土地、君王与国家的处境里,这可能是集体盼望与生存的策略。"[①]以上四种不同的宗教观,对过去及其与当下的关联提出了不同的理解。

关于西奈启示,申命典与祭司典有不同的解读,它们呈现了对上帝的不同理解,再现了对上帝的不同记忆。具体而言,《申命记》第4章对上帝在西奈山的降临提供了一种"新的回忆"[②]。其中,唯有摩西上山面见上帝,但上帝没有身形,只有声音传出,这就是各种律例和训谕,是极尽语重心长的谆谆教导。祭司典对西奈启示的再现,伴随雷暴、闪电与烟雾(《出埃及记》24:18—21),还有旷野的圣所,诸如此类的神圣显现在祭司典里被特征化为上帝启示的"荣光"。而且,上帝是圣洁的,因此,以色列百姓也要圣洁(《利未记》20:26)。祭司典对西奈山之上帝的记忆,正如史密斯所称:"不是将西奈事件看成历史,而是看成以色列革新的集体记忆,旨在教导以色列人遵从一种宗教愿景:以色列当要圣洁,因为,上帝是圣洁的。"[③]对于祭司典而言,西奈启示是至关重要的神圣时刻。伴随着对西奈记忆的改写,以色列的过去被重新建构,以色列的起源与身份被重新塑造。在以色列的文化记忆里,耶典与神典的宗教再现,在突出雅威宗教上是具有创新意义的。申命典中立约关系的建立,以及雅威崇拜的中央化,同样具有积极的宗教改革意义。不过,相较而言,祭司典的宗教创新最为显著,因为它倡导一神论。历经被掳的洗礼,深受波斯宗教的影响,及至希腊化时代,在祭司典与申命典作者的努力下,一神论愈来愈成为以色列宗教的显著标志,并赋予犹太教身份特征,使其成为适合散居者的流动宗教。[④] 整个以色列宗教的观念与历史,跌宕起伏,甚为曲折,因社会生活的处境、类型与形式而异。[⑤] 同样,五经中的宗教史亦是复杂而多元的,并非单向演进,而是不对等的多头并进。总之,通过对文化记忆中上帝的不断改写与重构,以色列人告别多神论的过往,开启一神论的宗教新时代。

---

① Ronald Hendel, "God and the Gods in the Tetrateuch," 263-264.

② Mark S. Smith, *The Memoirs of God: History, Memory, and the Experience of the Divine in Ancient Israel*, 144.

③ Mark S. Smith, *The Memoirs of God: History, Memory, and the Experience of the Divine in Ancient Israel*, 145.

④ Thomas Römer, *The Invention of God*, 230-239.

⑤ 值得留意的是,古代以色列人对上帝与诸神的概念,以及诸神祇在时空中的多种显现与超验方式的认识,均不同于现代人。在他们眼里,两个或多个神名可以无区别,而一位神可以有不同的名,他们通常会在唯名论与唯实论之间摇摆不定。参见:Ronald Hendel, "Gods in Translation and Location," in *Mighty Ball: Essays in Honor of Mark S. Smith*, eds. Stephen C. Russell and Esther J. Hamori (Leiden: Brill, 2020), 133-134。

God and the Gods in the Pentateuch

TIAN Haihua

Abstract: Based on the theory of traditional source criticism and centered on the textual examination of the four different sources in the Pentateuch, this thesis discusses God and the gods therein to present the religious development and religious landscape of ancient Israel. These four sources are the Yahwist, Elohist, Deuteronomist, and Priestly writings, which represent four parallel yet incommensurate understandings of the past and of God. The thesis lays special emphasis on the analysis of the Sinai revelation in the Deuteronomic and Priestly writings and argues for their significance in the religious history of the Pentateuch. The complex and diverse religious history in the Pentateuch is not a single evolution, but multi-pronged development. Through rewriting and reconstructing God in their cultural memory, the Israelites bid farewell to their polytheist past and embark on the new era of monotheism.

Key Words: Pentateuch, Source Criticism, God, Gods, History of Religion

边界和秩序:《以西结书》28:11—19 中关于推罗王的神谕

孙玥 *

【摘要】本文通过对《以西结书》第 28 章第 11—19 节关于推罗王神谕中“基路伯”和“宇宙山”两个形象的分析,得出代表推罗的基路伯作为王权和伊甸园的守卫者,其职责与土地的丰产、人类的生命、上帝的祝福、世界的秩序和安全息息相关。如果推罗王——基路伯——不能明确地知道人和神的界限,僭越上帝权力,那么不但自身会受到惩罚,世界秩序也会遭到破坏。宇宙山是世界的中心,上帝的统治权便是维系宇宙秩序的唯一有效因素。和谐的宇宙秩序不但为世界带来丰产的景象,而且还带来了公平正义的审判。

【关键词】:《以西结书》;推罗王;基路伯;宇宙山

一、导言

《以西结书》第 28 章是雅威针对推罗王的神谕,可分为两个部分:第一部分是第 28 章第 1—10 节,第二部分是第 28 章第 11—19 节。第一部分清晰地描述了推罗王“居心自比神”的高傲和自大,虽然他比但以理更有智慧,但是其狂傲也终使其落得个被外邦人击杀、下坑的结果。而第二部分之所以比第一部分得到历代读者更多关注,主要是因为推罗王身份和文本的复杂性。

德尔图良(160—225)是第一位将推罗王看作撒旦的教父,他认为,上帝让后来成为撒旦的天使按照他的善行做好事,但天使的自由选择却使他堕落,成为上帝的对立面。[①] 奥利金(185—251)将推罗王和《以赛亚书》第 14 章第 12—15 节中的明亮之星都指称为堕落天使撒旦,他认为这两段经文(《以西结书》28:11—

* 孙玥,西北师范大学哲学学院讲师。

① Suk Peter Choi, “The Garden of Eden in Ezekiel 28,” unpublished dissertation, Trinity Evangelical Divinity School, downloaded from ProQuest, 2005, 1.

19 和《以赛亚书》14:12—15)都传递了同一个主题,即魔鬼从高处坠入低处。[①] 教父神学对推罗王身份的判定主要依据的是基督教神学中罪的概念,而推罗王的高傲自大正是其被上帝惩罚的罪源。

推罗王还常常被认为是《创世记》第 2—3 章中的亚当。首先是因为《以西结书》第 28 章第 14 节经文文本的争议性,马索拉抄本中推罗王是"扩展(翅膀)遮掩的基路伯"(את-כרוב ממשח הסוכך),文中用第二人称单数阴性代词"את"来指代推罗王,而非第二人称单数阳性代词"אתה"。加之,七十士译本将את翻译作介词"和",并取消了基路伯在马索拉抄本中的属性"展翅遮掩",基路伯便成了伴随推罗王在圣山上的神物("我将你安置在基路伯旁上帝的圣山上"),而非推罗王本身。[②] 回顾《创世记》第 3 章第 23—24 节,亚当、夏娃因食生命树之果,被上帝逐出伊甸园,基路伯就在伊甸园处守卫着生命树的道路。[③] 所以不少学者认为推罗王映射的形象就是当初被上帝驱逐出伊甸园的第一人亚当。[④] 其次,从历史背景看,推罗王的亚当身份似乎进一步加深了对流放时期圣殿、圣城和以色列民陷落的反思以及重建第二圣殿的愿景。根据祭典,"人是上帝的形象"(《创世记》1:26—28),人替上帝管理地上的一切。人类自身不仅成为与神圣相连的形式,上帝的神圣王权也能在地上得到实现。因此,作为上帝的形象,人类潜在地具有使自己变成偶像、僭越上帝权力的可能。这和雅威对推罗王的批判不谋而合。另外,除了出现在神谕中的伊甸园神话外,《以西结书》中记载了大量同《创世记》相关的主题,如第 36 章第 26—27 节和第 37 章第 1—14 节的"造人"过程,以及第 36 章中反复出现的"生养众多""变化""耕种""伊甸园"等创世词语。无非是说,一方面,人类的历史充满悖逆和反叛,就连神物基路伯都无法独善其身,这种反叛是源自世界之初的,因此上帝必须为人类明确职权、树立界限;另一方面,人类世界

① Suk Peter Choi, "The Garden of Eden in Ezekiel 28," 3。

② 此外,《马索拉抄本》的《以西结书》第 28 章第 16 节说"我玷污你(推罗王),赶你离开上帝的山。(展翅)遮掩的基路伯啊,我已将你除灭,从发光如火的宝石中",而《七十士子译本》再次将基路伯和推罗王分别对待,删减了基路伯的"展翅遮掩"属性,写道:"你(推罗王)在上帝的山上受了伤,基路伯将你从发光如火的宝石中送出。"

③ 巴尔(James Barr)认为被逐出伊甸园的不只是亚当,还有基路伯。《创世记》中守卫伊甸园的基路伯是复数(כרבים),而《以西结书》中代指推罗王的基路伯用的是单数(כרוב),所以《以西结书》中的基路伯其实就是《创世记》中守卫伊甸园的基路伯之一。其玩忽职守,最终因过失,被上帝驱逐。James Barr, "'Thou Art the Cherubim': Ezekiel 28.14 and the Post-Ezekiel Understanding of Genesis 2-3," in *Priests, Prophets and Scribes: Essays on the Formation and Heritage of Second Temple Judaism in Honour of Joseph Blenkinsopp*, eds. Eugene Ulrich et al. (Sheffield: JOST Press, 1992), 220.

④ 具体研究可参见:Hector M. Patmore, *Adam, Satan, and the King of Tyre: The Interpretation of Ezekiel 28:11-19 in Late Antiquity* (Leiden, Boston: Brill, 2021), 16-26。

秩序需要重建,即建立第二圣殿,这代表上帝唯一统治权的确立。

此外,很多圣经学者将推罗王同古代西亚的王及神话故事联系在一起,例如,蒲波(Marvin H. Pope)认为推罗王代表了神伊勒(El)[1];范斯特(J. van Seters)对比新巴比伦帝国时期(公元前 626—前 539 年)王诞生时的形象和加冕仪式与推罗王的形象,认为推罗王那种“无所不备、智慧充足、全然美丽”的特质(《以西结书》28:12)正是古代美索不达米亚王拥有统治王权时的样子。[2] 在古代西亚,王是人类与神圣交流的中介,常常被称作“祭司王”,意味着王可以拥有同神圣相当的力量。[3] 因此古代西亚王权统治者的高贵形象和与神祇并肩的地位,自然而然也就成为先知批判的对象。

综观《圣经》诠释史上针对推罗王身份的分析和判定,其主题离不开其因狂傲自大而犯下的罪。狂傲使得推罗王失去分寸,进而将自身等同于神,这无疑是一种偶像崇拜。这种自负的情绪不但模糊了人神间的界限,还扰乱了纯洁的祭祀体系[4]及其代表的有序世界,挑战了上帝的权威性。以上种种对于深陷流亡处境的以色列民来说都是危险的,他们既有可能因乱拜别神和王失去作为上帝子民的身份,也会因心智迷乱而无法回归上帝、反思灾难。所以“边界”和“秩序”是此神谕向我们传递出的最核心的两个信息。

为了传递这两个信息,《以西结书》第 28 章第 11—19 节运用了大量图像式象征,如各式宝石、宝石的光、基路伯、山、火等,而这些象征物在以色列、古代西

---

① Marvin H. Pope, *El in the Ugaritic Texts* (Leiden: Brill, 1955).

② J. van Seters, “The Creation of Man and the Creation of the King,” *ZAW* 101 (1989): 333-342.

③ 相关研究可参见:Peter Machinist, “Kingship and Divinity in Imperial Assyria,” in *Text, Artifact, and Images: Revealing Ancient Israelite Religion*, eds. Gary M. Beckman and Theodore J. Lewis (Providence: Brown Judaic Studies, 2006), 152-188。

④ 威尔森(R. R. Wilson)注意到《以西结书》第 28 章第 13 节中推罗王佩戴的宝石和《出埃及记》第 28 章第 17—20 节、第 39 章第 10—13 节中祭司的宝石很像,“发光如火的石头”也许指的是祭坛上用来焚祭的火炭,“上帝的圣山”也可用来指称圣殿,且《以西结书》第 28 章第 16 节明确提到推罗王亵渎(חלל)圣所。威尔森认为《以西结书》第 28 章第 11—19 节中祭司传统相关术语和表达代表对以色列祭祀体系和祭祀团体的批判。R. R. Wilson, “The Death of the King of Tyre: The Editorial History of Ezekiel 28,” in *Love and Death in the Ancient Near East: Essays in Honor of Marvin H. Pope*, eds. J. H. Marks and R. M. Good (Guilford: Four Quarters Publishing, 1987), 211-218. 祭祀体系的破坏一方面是流亡灾难造成的,面对破殿亡国的现实处境,以色列人不得不转向新的宗教生活体系;另一方面,宗教生活与外邦强权政治的交织,迫使原本纯洁的宗教生活成为政治的附庸品和工具。而推罗王身上暗含的祭祀和王权两种因素,正是这一现实的反映。纽瑟姆(Carol A. Newsom)甚至把“伊甸/亚当”和“圣殿/祭司”看作一组对应,认为“逐出伊甸园”和“流亡巴比伦”指的是同一件事。Carol A. Newsom, “A Maker of Metaphors: Ezekiel's Oracles against Tyre,” *Int* 38 (1984): 162. 犹太传统习惯将伊甸园看作上帝的殿,具体研究参见:Jon Levenson, *Creation and the Persistence of Evil: The Jewish Drama of Divine Omnipotence* (San Francisco: Harper & Row, 1998)。

亚都是被人熟知的。虽然表面上看，经文呈现的具体图像似乎是可以被刻画的，但是图像本身常常象征着一个远大于其具体含义的现实，并且这些具体的图像“根据当下语境或观察者的态度，其意义可以解释为从历史的、具体的事件到普遍的、永恒的世界秩序”[①]。所以图像释义法是用可见或可想象的形象表达一种抽象的含义，就像太阳与正义、树木与丰产等。但是越是容易被刻画的形象或标记，越容易发展成为宗教崇拜的对象，成为希伯来《圣经》官方神观所谴责的偶像崇拜。因此在用图像表达的比喻义分析经文时，重要的是观察图像是如何在反偶像崇拜的前提下传达象征意义，并帮助建立人与上帝关系的。本文将通过神谕中“基路伯”和“宇宙山”两个形象来分析以西结是如何通过它们来树立边界和重建秩序的。

二、基路伯:边界的守卫者

“基路伯”是施密特(Brian B. Schmidt)口中的“混合生物”(*Mischwesen*)[②]，同时拥有人和动物的外观特征[③]，通常被塑造成两足或四足的带翅膀生物。在希伯来《圣经》中，基路伯主要有四个显著功能:生命树的守卫者(《创世记》3:24);雅威战车(《撒母耳记下》22:11;《诗篇》18:11;《以西结书》1:5—20,10:1—22);雅威王座的一部分(《列王纪上》6:23—28,8:6—8);会幕和圣殿的装饰品(《出埃及记》26:1、31,36:8、35;《列王纪上》6:29、31—35;《以西结书》40:18、20,41:17—20、25)。费德曼(D. N. Freedman)和康纳(M. O'Connor)认为，“基路伯”一词的词根כרב(*krb*)不仅仅只出现在希伯来《圣经》中，阿卡德语里其对应同源词是 *karābu* 和 *kurību*。[④] *karābu* 是动词，意为“祈祷”“祝福”。*kāribu* 是 *karābu* 的分词形式，作为形容词 *kāribu* 表达的是“一个人进行特定的宗教活动”或“代表做出崇拜姿态的神祇”，因此在 *kāribu* 前常常会加有表达神祇身份

① Othmar Keel, *The Symbolism of the Biblical World: Ancient Near Eastern Iconography and the Book of Psalms*, trans. Timothy J. Hallett (Winona Lake: EISENBRAUNS), 9.

② Brian B. Schmidt, "The Aniconic Tradition on Reading Images and Viewing Texts," in *The Triumph of Elohim: From Yahwisms to Judaisms*, ed. Diana V. Edelman (Leuven: Peeters, 1995), 102.

③ 在古代近东，混合生物是很常见的，主要象征着神圣世界和人类世界的统治权，也做避邪之用。常见的一些动物外貌有鸟类(其翅膀象征保护)、公牛(典型的力量和丰产标志)、狮子(咆哮声代表武力和威胁)等。同时这些混合生物还被描述为充满智慧和技巧，而这些特征又会以人的样貌(人头)来展现，如 *lamassu*、牛人。

④ D. N. Freedman and M. O' Connor, "kerub," in *Theological Dictionary of the Old Testament*, Vol. 7, eds. G. Johannes Botterweck et al. (Grand Rapids: Willam B. Eerdmans Publishing Company, 1995), 308.

的限定词 *dingir* 使其成为一个神的名称^{d}*Kāribu*。[①] 伍德(Alice Wood)说"*kāribu* 可能只不过是一个描述性的词,修饰一个神(或一个神像),而不是一个指定一种神性存在的名词。事实上,从 *kāribu* 的一般使用情况看,它指的是任何以祈祷姿态塑造的雕像。"[②]*kurību* 代表的是"具有特定非人类特征的保护生物或守护神"[③],如狮子、*anzû* 鸟、*laḫmu* 怪兽[④]等,而这些保护神雕像常被建在房屋内或神殿门口,以做辟邪和保护生命之用。[⑤] 即使无法期待 *karābu* 和 *kurību* 与基路伯的功能完全契合,但是它们出现的场景的确能为我们理解推罗王—基路伯提供一个思路。

推罗王不仅是基路伯,还是"受膏者"和"扩展翅膀"(ממשח)的基路伯[⑥],而且

---

① *CAD* s.v. *kāribu*.

② Alice Wood, *Of Wings and Wheels: A Synthetic Study of the Biblical Cherubim* (Berlin: De Gruyter), 152.

③ *CAD* s.v.*kurību* .

④ *laḫmu* 怪兽的三个功能和特征为赤裸的英雄,作为河流的保护神主要掌管野生动物,以及用水滋养牲畜;作为辟邪之用,*laḫmu* 常与蛇联系在一起;*laḫmu* 有时还会与山羊、树枝的形象结合在一起,就像阿普卡鲁(*apkallu*)一样,拥有净化的功能。F. A. M. Wiggermann, *Mesopotamian Protective Spirits: The Ritual Texts* (Groningen: STYX & PP, 1992), 164-166.

⑤ 在《埃努玛·埃利什》(V 73—76)中,提亚马特造了 11 个怪兽(混合生物),这些怪兽最终都被做成了雕像,竖立在甜水阿普苏(*Apsû*)的大门口。新亚述帝国的仪式文献将其中之一的怪物乌尔蒂姆(^{d}*Urdimmu*)同马杜克及其伴侣萨帕泥图(*Ṣarpanītu*)联系在一起,仪式规定用雪松制作一个乌尔蒂姆雕像,挂在金和亚麻的环上,并配有一个Ṣarpanītu石头,上面刻着"你是马杜克,邪灵的驱逐者,赶走一切巫术",以此来治愈生病的人,为其带来新的生命。乌尔蒂姆作为房屋的守护者,时常被放置在大门处或屋内,代表其主人马杜克及萨帕泥图,以此通过神祇的力量来保护生命、带来健康。《埃努玛·埃利什》文本参见:W. G. Lambert, *Babylonian Creation Myths* (Winona Lake: Eisenbrauns, 2013), 100-103; 仪式文献参见:F. A. M. Wiggermann, *Mesopotamian Protective Spirits: The Ritual Texts* (Groningen: STYX&PP, 1992), 173-174。

⑥ ממשח只在《以西结书》第 14 章第 28 节中出现了一次,其阿卡德语的同源词是 *mašahu*,意为"丈量"。这里"丈量"表达的是基路伯翅膀扩展的状态。而另一个表达"受膏"的希伯来语是משח,"通常标志着权力的授予或地位的提升"。例如,《出埃及记》第 29 章第 29 节;《利未记》第 4 章第 3、5、16 节,第 6 章第 20 节;《诗篇》第 105 章第 15 节, 第 132 章第 10 节;《撒母耳记上》第 16 章第 13 节;《撒母耳记下》第 2 章第 4 节;《列王纪上》第 19 章第 16 节;《历代志上》第 16 章第 22 节。参见:Lydia Lee, "'You Were the (Divine) Cherub': A Potential Challenge to YHWH's Sole Divinity in Ezekiel 28.14," *JSOT* 41.1, (2016): 113, no. 69。另外,《创世记》第 28 章和第 35 章描述了伯特利(又被称作神的殿)的由来,雅各因梦到雅威以及同雅威说话后,便在一根石柱上浇(יצק)膏油(שמן)。很显然,浇奠膏油的行为和雅威的显现有关。西北闪米特伊玛(Emar)的祖克鲁(*zukru*)庆典上,祭司通过向作为神像的石柱上浇膏油而使其神圣化,进一步说明了"受膏"和神祇之间的关系。关于伊玛和以色列宗教实践之间对比的更详细讨论,参见:Daniel E. Fleming, "More Help Form Emar to Biblical Study," *BA* 58. 3 (1995): 143-146。

作为神圣存在又是雅威天庭的成员之一。[①] 蒂迈尔(Lena-Sofia Tiemeyer)说,天庭成员最主要的两个任务:一是,协助雅威在军事上采取行动,如"坐在基路伯上的万军之雅威"(יהוה צבאות ישב הכרבים)(《撒母耳记上》4:4),此处代表军队力量的称呼"万军"与基路伯结合在了一起;二是,为正义做审判,如《以西结书》第10章第2节"穿细麻衣的人从基路伯中间取火炭,撒在城上"。火代表雅威的愤怒,用火炭烧城代表雅威对耶路撒冷城罪行的审判。[②] 作为雅威天庭的成员,基路伯应以低姿态服从雅威的命令,它非但没有,反而"居心(לב)自比神"(《以西结书》28:2)。[③]

此外,基路伯的反叛的可能性还来自它的守护功能。基路伯的守护功能离不开其翅膀意象。《创世记》虽然没有明确提到基路伯是有翅膀的,但是《以西结书》第1章和第10章都提到了基路伯的翅膀,而且《撒母耳记下》第22章第11节和《诗篇》第18章第11节也说"雅威乘坐(רכב)基路伯飞行,在风的翅膀上显现",《诗篇》第104章第3节雅威"借着风的翅膀而行"。很显然,这里的基路伯是雅威带着翅膀的坐骑或天上战车,并伴随风一般的力量,体现着雅威权力和战斗力。[④] 但是并不是所有的翅膀意象都象征着保护,例如,拥有四个翅膀的魔鬼帕祖祖(Pazuzu),其翅膀所带来的只有恐惧、灾难和疾病。[⑤] 翅膀的功能是双面的,正如基路伯也会叛变一样。就像格林(Anthony Green)所说,混合生物在古代近东很常见,且它们通常会陪伴在诸神周围做辟邪之用或象征物,但是它们一

---

① 关于基路伯作为雅威天庭成员的研究,参见:Lena-Sofia Tiemeyer, "Zechariah's Spies and Ezekiel's Cherubim," in *Tradition in Transition: Haggao and Zechariah 1-8 in the Trajectory of Hebrew Theology*, eds. M. J. Boda and M. H. Floyd (New York: T &T Clark, 2008), 107-109。

② Lena-Sofia Tiemeyer, "Zechariah's Spies and Ezekiel's Cherubim," 107.

③ 哈滕斯坦(Friedhelm Hartenstein)提到一个值得注意的情况:在古代西亚,一些伴随在神祇身边的特殊生物会成为神祇特征的一部分。参见:Friedhelm Hartenstein, "Cherubim and Seraphim in the Bible and in the Light of Ancient Near Eastern Sources," in *Deuterocanonical and Cognate Literature, Yearbook* 2007. *Angel. The Concept of Celestial Beings-Origins, Development and Reception*, eds. Friedrich V. Reiter, Tobias Nicklas and Karin Schöpflin (Berlin: De Gruyter, 2007), 160。譬如古拉(Gula)的狗、埃阿(Ea)的羊-鱼、太阳神的牛人等。这更增加了这些神物"自诩"为神的资本。

④ 麦汀格还认为《诗篇》第104章第3节与《诗篇》第18章第11节描述的是同一种场景,"云彩车辇"和"基路伯"是相对应的。雅威的战车形象和风暴神巴力很像,因为巴力也被称作"云的驾驶者"(*rkbʿrpt*)。麦汀格坚持无论是坐在圣殿里王座上的雅威,还是驾着战车、伴随着风飞行和显现的雅威,本身并无差异,都只是历史连续性的表现,区别仅在于它们展现的方式不同,一个围绕着王座,一个围绕着战车。参见:Tryggve N.D. Mettinger, *The Dethronement of Sabaoth Studies in the Shem and Kabod Theologies*, trans. Frederick H. Cryer (Lund: CWK GLEERUP, 1982), 32-36。

⑤ Joel M. LeMon, *Yahweh's Winged Form in the Psalms: Exploring Congruent Iconography and Texts* (Göttingen: Academic Press, 2005), 50.

旦和所伴之神分开,便会败坏世界秩序、与神反目。[①] 推罗王—基路伯便是那无法确定自己身份,僭越上帝地位的反叛者。

同 *karābu* 和 *kurību* 一样,基路伯也出现在圣殿中。依据《列王纪上》第6章第23—28节,基路伯在被安置在内殿(דביר)中。哈滕斯坦(Friedhelm Hartenstein)认为,这段经文也许保留了早期传统,即基路伯属于内殿。在腓尼基和埃及传统中,内殿是圣殿最里面的圣所,作为放置代表神祇神像的王座房间。[②]麦汀格(Tryggve N. D. Mettinger)称,基路伯王座体现了"神圣的空无"(sacred emptiness)[③]。不同于其他宗教传统[④],基路伯王座上是没有神像的,但是这并不妨碍基路伯守护王座和约柜的形象(《出埃及记》20:25,37:9;《列王纪上》8:7)。在古代西亚,坐在王座上的不只是神祇,还有王。希伯来《圣经》中不乏容易使人误解王就是上帝的经文,如在赞美大卫王室时说,"上帝啊,你的宝座是永永远远的"(《诗篇》45:7)。哈洛(W. W. Hallo)认为,从美索不达米亚的史前时期到早王朝时期,最早崇拜的雕像代表的是死去的王室或他们的家族。到了阿卡德时期,也就是萨尔贡王时期,活着的王开始被神化。美索不达米亚既有被神化的王,也有为他们建立的、以供崇拜的殿宇。[⑤]因此推罗王像神祇一般坐在王座之上并不稀奇,尤其是《以西结书》第28章第13节还提到了各式宝石,其像极了装饰神像的材料。[⑥] 推罗王成了王座上的神,跨越了神与人的边界,"亵渎了圣地",守护者基路伯便也成了反叛的力量。

---

① 具体研究参见:Anthony Green, "Beneficent Spirits and Malevolent Demons: The Iconography of Good and Evil in Ancient Assyria and Babylonia," *Visible Religion* 3 (1984): 80-105。

② Friedhelm Hartenstein, "Cherubim and Seraphim in the Bible and in the Light of Ancient Near Eastern Sources," 158-159.

③ Tryggve N.D. Mettinger, *No Graven Image? Israelite Aniconism in Its Ancient Near East Context* (Stockholm: Alqvist & Wiksell, 1995), 19.

④ 综观西部闪米特其他地区,公元前12—前13世纪米吉多地区坐在两侧基路伯中间的人形像,公元前1000年左右腓尼基王阿希雷姆两侧的基路伯以及公元前6世纪黎巴嫩、塞浦路斯、西西里岛、撒丁岛等地区坐在基路伯王座上的神祇的像,都进一步说明了以色列空置王座的独特性。Mary Douglas, "The Cloud God and the Shadow Self," *Social Anthropology* 3 (1995): 87. 不过,不可否认的是无像的空置王座曾在腓尼基地区占据非常显著的地位,麦汀格甚至认为所罗门圣殿空置的基路伯王座是腓尼基工匠的作品。Tryggve N.D. Mettinger, *No Graven Image? Israelite Aniconism in Its Ancient Near East Context*, 113.

⑤ W. W. Hallo, "Texts, Statues and the Cult of the Divine King," in *Congress Volume Jerusalem*, ed. J. A. Emerton (Leiden / New York / Köln: Brill, 1986), 56-60.

⑥ 奥本海姆的《古代美索不达米亚:一个灭亡文明的肖像》一书中,其中有一小节的标题就叫作"神祇的照料和供养"。里面提到了大多数的像是用珍贵的木头和石头制成的,并会用珍贵的珠宝和金子装饰这些像。参见:A. Leo Oppenheim, *Ancient Mesopotamia: Portrait of a Dead Civilization* (Chicago: The University of Chicago Press, 1964), 183-198。

这里基路伯的职责到底是什么？在亚兰语和南部闪米特语里，词根 *krb* 还有“耕种”的意思。《以西结书》第 28 章第 14 节中推罗王被描述为在伊甸园中“扩展（翅膀）遮掩的（סכך）基路伯”，对比《创世记》第 3 章第 24 节，基路伯的主要任务是保护伊甸园中的生命树。围绕伊甸园主题，《以西结书》中出现了大量与创世相关的描述：

> 我必使人和畜牲在你上面加增，他们必生养众多。我要使你照旧有人居住，并要赐福与你比先前更多，你就知道我是耶和华。（《以西结书》36:11）
>
> 过路的人虽看为荒废之地，现今这荒废之地仍得耕种。他们必说：‘这先前为荒废之地，现在成如伊甸园；这荒废、凄凉、毁坏的城邑，现在坚固有人居住。’（《以西结书》36:34—35）

《以西结书》第 36 章第 34—35 节的“荒废之地”呼应了《创世记》第 2 章第 5 节“这地尚未有任何田野的灌木，田间的蔬菜之前也都没有发芽；也没有人耕种（עבד）土地”。而在伊甸园般的土地上，人和牲畜便会“生养众多”“比起初好”。所以伊甸园在《以西结书》中是丰产、富饶的象征，既表达着“耕种”的意思，又代表着上帝对人类的祝福。虽然没有经文表达过基路伯耕种土地，但是《以西结书》第 41 章第 18 节在描述殿内的装饰时说“墙上雕刻基路伯和棕树。基路伯和基路伯中间有一棵棕榈树，每基路伯有二脸”（《列王纪上》第 6 章第 29 节里基路伯和棕榈树、初开的花一同被雕刻在圣殿的墙上）。这个场景让人不禁联想到亚述王亚述那西尔帕二世（Assurnasirpal Ⅱ，公元前 883—前 859 年）时期尼姆拉德（Nimrūd）西北宫殿的神树浮雕（见图 1）：浮雕上两个带翅膀的鸟头生物，一手拎着桶状物，一手拿着松果，呈崇拜状，分别站立在一棵树状物两侧。波特（Barbara N. Porter）推测，浮雕中的树为枣树，而枣树在阿卡德语里素有“丰饶之树”（*iṣ mašrê*）、“富贵之树”（*iṣ rašê*）之称。[①] 带翅膀的鸟头生物，一方面代表对丰产之树的保护，另一方面它们的崇拜姿态以及手中的桶和松果，“比喻将富足和安全作为众神的礼物赐给王”[②]。这里王权统治和丰产、祝福是统一的。也就是说，作为伊甸园和王权的守护者，基路伯的职责与土地的丰产、人类的生命、上帝的祝福、世界的秩序和安全息息相关。但是即便树木的丰产是上帝给予的祝福，其也不能因此超越上帝的权力，将自己自比为神。《以西结书》第 31 章第 9—10 节进一步将伊甸园、丰产、狂傲联系起来，将王比作荣美的树

① Barbara N. Porter, “Sacred Trees, Date Palms, and the Royal Persona of Ashurnasirpal Ⅱ,” *JNES* 52.2 (1993): 134.

② Barbara N. Porter, “Sacred Trees, Date Palms, and the Royal Persona of Ashurnasirpal Ⅱ,” 137.

木,批判树木也会因为高大而心(לבב)骄气傲。同雅威对推罗王的惩罚一样,一切心骄气傲的结局都是下地府(《以西结书》28:8,31:14—18),由此再次强调了边界的重要性。

图 1　尼姆拉德西北宫殿的神树浮雕

资料来源:Barbara N. Porter, "Sacred Trees, Date Palms, and the Royal Persona of Ashurnasirpal II,"130.

那么《以西结书》又是怎样通过基路伯来建立雅威的唯一统治权的呢?首先可以肯定的是,《以西结书》第 1 章和第 28 章的基路伯存在一定的对应关系。巴尔说,《以西结书》第 28 章第 14 节中用阴性代词 את 代替阳性的情况是很少见的,希伯来《圣经》中一共有三次这样的情况,另外两次出现在《民数记》第 11 章第 15 节和《申命记》第 5 章第 24 节。[①] 但是《以西结书》第 1 章第 10—11 节却通过阴阳性代词的交替使用,在语法上和《以西结书》第 28 章形成了对应:

> 至于(他们)脸的形像:前面各有人的脸,(他们四个)右面各有狮子的脸,(她们四个)左面各有牛的脸,(她们四个)后面各有鹰的脸。(《以西结书》1:10)[②]
>
> 各展开上边的两个翅膀相接,各以下边的两个翅膀遮体。(《以西结书》1:11)

---

① James Barr, "'Thou Art the Cherubim': Ezekiel 28.14 and the Post-Ezekiel Understanding of Genesis 2-3," 215.

② 《以西结书》1:10。为了展示人称代词的阴阳性变化,在经文中我以加括号的方式将其标记出来。中文译文来自和合本《圣经》,添加的人称代词来自希伯来语与英文对照版《圣经》。

其次,《以西结》第1章和第10章写道:伴随雅威王座出现的是有四个脸面、四个翅膀,并带有轮子的活物形象,且轮子行走时,四方都能直行,灵/风(רוח)往哪里去,活物就往哪里去,活物的灵在轮中。第一,"四个脸面""四个翅膀"与灵/风的结合,代表了雅威对宇宙世界的管理能力。古代西亚的王常常被称作"四方之王",四方象征着世界的四个基点。[①] 再加上移动的轮子更强调了雅威统治大能的无处不在。艾希罗特(Walther Eichrodt)说,活物头上似苍穹(רקיע)的形象(《以西结书》1:22)是模仿了造物主用苍穹分水的情景(《创世记》1:6),而苍穹之上正是雅威登基成王的地方。因此代表世界四角的四个活物,象征雅威管理世界四方的能力,而四个活物就是雅威登基成王的地方。[②] 作为王座的守护者,这个活物与无法守其边界的基路伯形成了明显对比,活物是跟随雅威的灵而活动的。再次,《以西结书》第1章第13节中出现了代表雅威荣光的火炭形象,当推罗王—基路伯听话时,其便在发光如火的宝石中往来(《以西结书》28:14),当他行不义之事时,火变成了惩罚的工具(《以西结书》28:18)。

三、圣山:秩序之地

《以西结书》第28章第14节说雅威曾将推罗王——受膏的基路伯安置在"上帝的圣山"上。对于古代西亚人来说,山也被称作宇宙山(cosmic mountain),在世界/宇宙图景的构造上具有非常重要的地位:高山是天、地、阴间[③]交界的地方,与此同时,山位于地的中心,也是世界的中心。克利福德(Richard J. Clifford)是这样描述宇宙山的:"高山可以是众神的聚集地,是水源和丰产的源头,是自然力量冲突的战场,是天与地的交汇处,是发布有效法令的地方。"[④]

按照克利福德的定义,首先,高山是众神的聚集地。《以赛亚书》第14章第13节里明亮之星在从天山坠落之前曾幻想成为雅威的天庭成员,"坐在聚会的山上"。众神集聚本身就是一种秩序的体现,如马杜克在杀死提亚马特后,将其居所埃萨吉拉神庙建于巍峨之坛上,其中"礼仪悉备、规章既定、天地间众神分

① Wayne Horowitz, *Mesopotamian Cosmic Geography* (Winona Lake: Eisenbraus, 1998), 196-199.

② Walther Eichrodt, *Ezekiel: A Commentary* (Philadelphia: The Westminster Press, 1970), 57-58.

③ 苏美尔语 kur 除了用来表达"山"以外,还有"阴间"和"土地"的意思。虽然现有的材料不能说明为什么 kur 可以指"阴间",但是很显然山、地、阴间有不可分割的联系。参见:Wayne Horowitz, *Mesopotamian Cosmic Geography*, 272。

④ Richard J. Clifford, *The Cosmic Mountain in Canaan and the Old Testament* (Cambridge: Harvard University, 1972), 3.

配，各就其位”[①]。巍峨之坛代表着高山[②]，高山之上众神各就其位代表着马杜克的领导权。基路伯被安置在上帝的圣山上，就必须遵守上帝的秩序。但马杜克与提亚马特，以及其他神祇之间的斗争也体现了宇宙山是自然力量冲突的战场，因此反叛力量就显得不足为奇。

其次，宇宙山是水源和丰产的源头，这一点在《以西结书》第 28 章第 11—19 节中颇为明显，尤其是伊甸园和上帝圣山的结合。《创世记》第 2 章第 10—14 节讲述了从伊甸园流出的四道河流。《以西结书》第 47 章第 1—12 节用伊甸园主题描绘了第二圣殿的重建：从新殿的门槛和祭坛流出的水滋养着其所到之处的万物。第一，伊甸园四道水流的“四”就代表着一种世界图景，如前面提到的“四方之神”，还有《以赛亚书》第 11 章第 12 节提到“地极(כנף)的四方”[③]，《撒迦利亚书》第 1 章第 8 节用四匹马象征全地等。伊甸园水流的世界图景对应宇宙山的世界图景，体现的是雅威的统治范围。第二，《撒迦利亚书》借用活水从重建后的耶路撒冷流出来的景象宣告，“雅威必作全地的王，雅威必是独一无二的，他的名也是独一无二的”(14:9)。说明必须在承认雅威在宇宙的唯一统治权的前提下，随着雅威的祝福才能带来丰产、富足的水流，即雅威的统治权是丰产的保证。

最后，山是颁布有效法令的地方，有效法令指的是公平正义的审判。山与正义的关系主要跟太阳神沙玛什的世界图景有关。王那普-阿普拉-伊地那(Nabû-apla-iddina，公元前 888—前 855 年)的太阳石碑上，太阳神沙玛什和他的蛇形遮棚将天、地、阴间这三个部分紧密联系在一起。黎明时沙玛什打开天门，从东

---

① 饶宗颐 Rao Zongyi 编译，《近东开辟史诗》[Epic of the Exploration in Near East]，(沈阳[Shenyang]：辽宁教育出版社[Liaoning Education Press]，1998)，53。

② 古巴比伦有一种建筑被称作古庙塔，其苏美尔语为 ziqqurrat，意为“建造在一块高地上”。布罗斯(Father Eric Burrows)认为古塔庙反映了巴比伦的宇宙观，他称其为“神圣象征的现实主义”(hierocentric realism)，即将象征神圣的样子带到现实当中。古塔庙垂直地连接着天、地和阴间，水平地连接着土地，象征宇宙山作为宇宙中心连通三界。参见：Father Eric Burrows, “Some Cosmological Patterns in Babylonian Religion,” in *The Labyrinth*, ed. S. H. Cook (London: Society for Promoting Christian Knowledge, 1935), 45-46。在高耸神庙之中的王座便也成了“威严之座”，统治者坐在其上可俯瞰一切，象征井然有序的政治统治。参见：《埃努玛 · 埃利什》(Ⅵ 61—65)；W. G. Lambert, *Babylonian Creation Myths*, 112-115。

③ כנף除了有“地极”的意思外，还表示“翅膀”(《以西结书》第 1 章第 6、8、9、11、23、24、25 节，第 3 章第 13 节，第 10 章第 5、8、12、16、19、21 节，第 11 章第 22 节)。而翅膀意象既和王权统治有关，还有医治之能的意思，如《玛拉基书》第 3 章第 20 节说：“你们敬畏我名的人，必有公义的太阳出现，在它的光线(כנף)里有医治之能。”כנף在和合本中翻译成“光线”，但原文指的是翅膀。参见：李炽昌 Archie Lee，《国语〈和合本〉圣经：经典翻译抑或宗教传播》[Chinese Union Version Bible: Translation of Classics or Religion Propagation]，收录于《自上帝说汉语以来：〈和合本〉圣经九十年》，谢品然 Xie Pinran、曾庆豹 Zeng Qingbao 编，(香港[Hong Kong]：Verbum Press，2010)，71—89。

边的山脉升起,并在这一刻为地上实施公义的审判,晚上则会划船于阿普苏并通过阴间。[①]《诗篇》第 15 章第 1—2 节说:"雅威啊,谁能居于你的帐幕?谁能住在你的圣山,就是行为正直、做事公义、他心里说实话的人。"而《以西结书》第 28 章第 18 节中推罗王罪孽众多,贸易不公,亵渎了圣山处的圣所,雅威便对他进行了审判,使其变为地上的炉灰。

以上种种都说明上帝的圣山是世界的中心,而上帝的唯一统治权便是维系宇宙秩序的唯一有效因素。和谐的宇宙秩序不但为世界带来丰产的景象,而且还带来了公平正义的审判。

四、结语

以西结先知面对的以色列群体,经历了第一次流亡、圣殿被毁、第二次流亡的深重灾难,这其中的主要原因是:罪行深重的以色列民违背与雅威之间的约,敬拜他神,祭拜偶像,不按照所要求的祭祀生活方式敬拜。这种不洁的生活和崇拜方式不仅仅是具体地崇拜某一个神像,还包括内心产生的自负情绪和高傲姿态。自负情绪虽然是抽象的,但是抽象的自负情绪一方面包含不纯洁的动机,另一方面会渐渐演变成一种实际具体的崇拜行为。在面对破殿亡国的大灾难时,只有保持纯洁的心、与上帝合一的心,才能维护以色列民族的身份以及宗教,而非那种狂傲自大的心。《以西结书》第 28 章第 11—19 节中推罗王因自大而失了分寸,自诩为神。经文将推罗王比作受膏的基路伯。基路伯作为王权和伊甸园的守护者,随时要懂得分清人和神的界限,维护上帝——唯一统治者的王权身份,而非利用与上帝亲近的关系,僭越上帝的权力和地位,破坏宇宙秩序。经文还利用伊甸园和宇宙山意象来说明宇宙秩序的重要性,以及上帝拥有唯一的统治王权。

① 关于太阳神世界图景的研究,参见:孙玥 Sun Yue,《古代西亚太阳意象在〈希伯来圣经〉中的功能和意义》[The Function and Significance of the Sun Image in the Hebrew Bible in Ancient West Asian],于《世界宗教文化》[The World Religious Cultures],2020 第 3 期[2020, Issue 3],39—46。

Boundary and Order: Divine Oracles about the King of Tyre in Ezekiel 28:11-19

SUN Yue

Abstract: Through the analysis of the two images of "cherubim" and "cosmic mountain" in the oracle of the king of Tyre in Ezekiel 28:11-19, this paper argues that the roles of the cherubim representing Tyre as the guardians of the kingship and the Garden of Eden are related to the abundance of the land, the life of mankind, the blessing of God, and the order and security of the world. If the king of Tyre, symbolized as a cherub, did not clearly recognize the boundaries between man and God and overstepped God's authority, not only would he be punished, but the whole world order would also be destroyed. As the cosmic mountain is the center of the world, and the sole dominion of God over it is the only effective factor in maintaining the cosmic order. A harmonious cosmic order brings not only a fruitful world, but also a fair and just judgment.

Key Words: *The Book of Ezekiel*, King of Tyre, Cherubim, Cosmic Mountain

《迷途指津》的双焦点之一：初探迈蒙尼德的“开端论”*

张缨**

【摘要】在拉比传统中，与《创世记》第1章相连的“开端论”以及与《以西结书》第1章和第10章相连的“神车论”是禁止传授的关于上帝的秘密知识。在《迷途指津》里，迈蒙尼德多次指出，解释“开端论”与“神车论”中可以解释的内容是此书的首要目的。可以说，“开端论”与“神车论”构成了《迷途指津》的双焦点。与此同时，迈蒙尼德指出，“开端论”等于自然科学，“神车论”等于神的科学。这使得部分研究迈蒙尼德“开端论”的学者将注意力集中于“开端论”与自然科学的关系。通过梳理和解读 *ma ʻaseh bereshith* 在《迷途指津》各章的出现及其语境，本文意在论证，迈蒙尼德不仅如众所公认的那样，将“开端论”与“世界的开端”即创世相连，而且通过表明“法版上所写的就像所有‘开端的作品’一样”，将“开端论”与“律法的开端”即“西奈启示”相连。进而，通过将“开端的作品”与事物的自然本性之不易性相提并论，迈蒙尼德暗示，“开端论”与“从无中创世”这种神迹观点不相容。

【关键词】迈蒙尼德；《迷途指津》；“开端论”；世界的开端；律法的开端

* 本文是国家社科基金后期资助一般项目“自然与律法——迈蒙尼德《迷途指津》解读”(19FZXB033)的阶段性成果。

** 张缨，华东师范大学哲学系副教授。

小引:何为"开端论"

迈蒙尼德的《迷途指津》[①]是一部极为特别的解经著作,在"卷首引言"("绪论")里,他指明"此论章(*al-maqāla*; treatise)[②]的第一个目的(*ḡaraḍ*)是解释某些出现在预言书(books of prophecy)里的措辞的含义",这些词有些是"带有歧义的"(equivocal),有些是"衍生性的"(derivative),还有些是"模棱两可的"(amphibolous),也就是说,他要辨析预言书里那些多义词在不同语境下的词义。随后,迈蒙尼德说,本论章还有第二个目的:解释出现在先知作品(book of the prophets)里的极为灰色的各种寓言(卷首引言,5—6/5—6)。无论是"预言书"还是"先知作品",都属于犹太人的《圣经》,就此而言,《迷途指津》是一部解经著作。然而,《迷途指津》绝非一部寻常的解经著作。《迷途指津》对犹太教《圣经》的解释,带有作者独有的理论意图。这一独有的理论意图直到卷二 29 章才得到明确的揭示,迈蒙尼德在那里明确指出:"**本论章的首要目的**是解释开端论和神车论里可以得到解释的内容。"(卷二 29 章,319/346;另见卷三"导言",379/415)。那么什么是"开端论"和"神车论"?

在《迷途指津》的"卷首引言"里,迈蒙尼德说,他已经在《重述托拉》(*Mishneh Torah*)里提到"开端论"(*ma 'aseh bereshith*)和"神车论"(*ma 'aseh merkabah*)[③],在这里,他进一步表示,"开端论"就等于自然科学(natural

---

① 迈蒙尼德的《迷途指津》以犹太-阿拉伯语(Judeo-Arabic)撰写(按:犹太-阿拉伯语指以希伯来语字母标示的阿拉伯语),原名*Dalālatul al-hā'irīn*,学界更常用的是该书的希伯来语译名*Moreh Nevukhim*。本文的《迷途指津》引文依据中译本(傅有德 Fu Youde、郭鹏 Guo Peng、张志平 Zhang Zhiping 译,济南[Jinan]:山东大学出版社[Shandong University Press],2007/1998)以及 Shlomo Pines 英译本(*The Guide of the Perplexed*, trans. Shlomo Pines, Chicago, London: University of Chicago Press, 1963)。下引《迷途指津》,随文注明引文卷次、章节及中译本页码(在"/"前)和 Pines 译本页码(在"/"后)。《迷途指津》引文中加下划线的部分表示其原文为希伯来语,正文或引文里加粗的字体是笔者所加的重点。

② 在施特劳斯(Leo Strauss)看来,使用 maqāla 一词表明迈蒙尼德的《迷途指津》具有"口传"的性质。关于 maqāla 及其希伯来语对应词 ma'amar 的含义以及其与一般意义上的 kitāb(著作/书)的区别,参见:Leo Strauss, "Literary Character of *The Guide for the Perplexed*," in *Persecution and the Art of Writing* (Glencoe, Ill.: The Free Press, 1952), 47。中译本见施特劳斯 Leo Strauss,《迫害与写作艺术》[Persecution and the Art of Writing],刘锋 Liu Feng 译(北京[Beijing]:华夏出版社[Huaxia Publishing House],2012),40-41。

③ 参见:Ralph Lerner, *Maimonides' Empire of Light: Popular Enlightenment in an Age of Belief* (Chicago, London: University of Chicago Press, 2000), 141-153。中译本见摩西·迈蒙尼德 Moses Maimonides,《论知识》[The Book of Knowledge],董修元 Dong Xiuyuan 译(济南[Jinan]:山东大学出版社[Shandong University Press],2015),9—23。

science),而“神车论”则等于神的科学(divine science)。[①]《迷途指津》的英译者施洛莫·皮纳斯(Shlomo Pines)把 *ma 'aseh bereshith* 译作 the Account of the Beginning,把*ma 'aseh merkabah*译作 the Account of the Chariot。[②]显然,他是将有关“开端”和“神车”的《圣经》篇章理解为故事或寓言,因此,*ma 'aseh* 在这里就指某种“言述”或“记述”。[③]如果从语文学角度看,*ma 'aseh* 这个希伯来词的动词词根 *'asah* 意指“制作”“造就”,*ma 'aseh* 指“所做的事”,一般可以译作“行事”或“作为”。另一方面,*bereshith* 是《创世记》乃至整部《托拉》(*Torah*,犹太教《圣经》)开篇的第一个词,意为“在起初”(英文里一般作 in the beginning)。就其本义来说,一些学者的译法 the Work of the Beginning(开端/开端的作为)可能更接近 *ma 'aseh bereshith* 的**字面意思**,而另一些学者将其译作 the Work of Creation(创造的作为),则体现了他们对这个词的特定理解,亦即将 *ma 'aseh bereshith* 理解为上帝的“创造的作为”。[④]皮纳斯把 *ma 'aseh* 译作 account,表明他对迈蒙尼德所论述的 *ma 'aseh bereshith* 有不同于其他学者的看法。那么,究竟什么是迈蒙尼德所理解的“开端论”? 究竟又在什么意义上,迈蒙尼德将“开端论”与自然科学相等同?[⑤]

的确,从字面上看,“开端论”指与“起初”有关的《圣经》记述,在拉比传统中,

---

① 《迷途指津》的另一位英译者 Michael Friedländer 将 אלעלם אלאלאהי 即“(关于)神的科学”译作“形而上学”,这也是很多学者的译法,比如 Warren Zev Harvey, “Aggadah in Maimonides' *Mishneh Torah*,” *Diné Israel* 24 (2007): 197-207。

② *The Guide of the Perplexed*, 6。

③ 实际上,最初开始使用这种英译的是施特劳斯(Leo Strauss),早在其写于 1938 年的《〈迷途指津〉的文学特征》(Literary Character of *The Guide for the Perplexed*)里,施特劳斯就用 the Account of Creation 来译 *ma 'aseh bereshit* (按:bereshit 系 ברשת 的另一种转写),用 the Account of the Chariot 来译 *ma 'aseh merkabah*。见 Leo Strauss, *Persecution of the Art of Writing*, 41;施特劳斯,《迫害与写作艺术》,34—35。

④ 有意思的是,也有学者将该词译作 the Account of Creation。见 Moshe Halbertal, *Maimonides: Life and Thought*, trans. Joel Linsider (Princeton and Oxford: Princeton University Press, 2014), 205。即使施特劳斯本人在其写于 1938 年的《〈迷途指津〉的文学特征》里也将 *bereshith* 诠解为 creation(创世),见 Leo Strauss, *Persecution of the Art of Writing*, 41;施特劳斯,《迫害与写作艺术》,34—35。

⑤ 关于迈蒙尼德的断言“开端论等于自然科学”,见 Sara Klein-Braslavy, “On Maimonides' Interpretation of Genesis 1-5,” in *Maimonides as a Biblical Interpreter* (Boston: Academic Studies Press, 2011), 71-86。

这个“起初”就指《创世记》第 1 章[1]，正是在这个意义上，相当多学者将 *ma ‘aseh bereshith* 直接译作“创世论”(the Work / Account of Creation)。可是，仔细考察《迷途指津》会发现，情形很可能**不仅仅如此**。*ma ‘aseh bereshith* 在全书总共出现了 18 次。[2]其中有 4 次在迈蒙尼德引述的《塔木德》文本里；另外有 5 次，“开端论”与“神车论”一并被提及，迈蒙尼德总是在那些场合强调，解说这两个论题乃是他写作《迷途指津》的主要意图。在剩下的 9 次中，作者的确不断将它跟创世尤其是《创世记》第 1 章论述的创世相连[3]，也一再将之与“自然科学”并举。可是除此之外，有 3 次作者明确同时提到了“托拉”；另有 1 次迈蒙尼德直接将 *ma ‘aseh bereshith* 与“石板上所写的”(the writing on the tablet)[4]相提并论(卷一 66，152/161)。所谓“石板”，当然指摩西从西奈山上带给以色列民的写有“十诫”的那两块。正是迈蒙尼德将 *ma ‘aseh bereshith* 与“托拉”乃至写有“十诫”的石板一起讨论的做法，让我们疑心。在迈蒙尼德那里，“开端论”之“开端”，不仅仅局限于世界之“开端”，它还可能隐含了“律法”的“开端”，也就是说，它包含了**摩西在西奈山领受神启律法**这个“开端”。本文的任务，就是细致考察“开端论”的这两个维度，进而尝试回答迈蒙尼德在何种意义上说“开端论”等于自然科学。

“开端论”与创世

从迈蒙尼德所引述的拉比文献看，“开端论”的说法首先出自《密释纳 · 节日祭典》(Ḥagigah in *Mishnah*)：

> 被禁止的人际关系[这个论题]不能当着三个人的面加以阐释，“开端论”(*ma‘aseh bereshith*)不能当着两个人的面加以阐释，神车论(*ma‘aseh merkabah*)不能当着一个人的面加以阐释，除非这人是位智者[或贤人]，能靠自己来理解。

---

① 参见：Joseph Jacobs and A. Biram, “*MA ‘ASEH BERESHIT*; *MA ‘ASEH MERKABAH* (literary, ‘work of Creation’ and ‘work of the Chariot’),” in *Jewish Encyclopedia: A Descriptive Record of The History, Religion, Literature, and Customs of the Jewish People from the Earliest Times to the Present Day*, Volume 8, eds. Isaac K. Funk, Frank H. Vizatelly, Isidore Singer, et. al. (New York and London: Funk and Wagnalls Company, 1904), 235。

② 《迷途指津》提及 *ma ‘aseh bereshith* 之处有：卷首引言(4 次)，卷一 17 章、65 章、66 章(各 1 次)，卷二 2 章(2 次)，卷二 29 章(4 次)，卷二 30 章(2 次)，卷三引言、13 章、29 章(各 1 次)。

③ 尤可参见：迈蒙尼德，《迷途指津》卷二 29 章(319/345)、卷二 30 章(320—327/348—355)等。

④ 施洛莫 · 皮纳斯将“法版”译作“table”，见 *The Guide of the Perplexed*, 161。

谁要是推测这四种事——何者在上、何者在下、何者先在及何者后来——他最好不曾降世。

谁要是不为他的创造者的荣耀着想,他最好不曾降世。[①]

可以看到,与"开端论"及"神车论"相关的第一段话里有一种递进关系,讨论不正常的两性关系在任何社会都可谓一种禁忌,因而不该当着三个人的面议论,而"开端论"和"神车论"的保密性则更胜一筹。"开端论"被认为不可以同时向两个人传授,也就是说,只能一对一地口授。究竟是怎样的秘密需要如此来保守?后面的两段话或许可以给我们一点提示。"起初"是一个开端,可是总有好学好问的少年或青年可能会问:"起初"之前是什么?之后呢?我们死去之后会是什么?这个世界会恒久地持存吗?如果不会,之后会怎样?如此等等。拉比们说,这种问题,不能同时向两个人传授。

关于"开端论",迈蒙尼德在《迷途指津》里引述的另一段拉比文献是这样说的:

如先贤们(愿他们得平安)所说:不可能告诉凡人们开端论的力量。正因这个理由,经书上说得含含糊糊:起初,上帝创造,等等。[②]

这里,看上去非常明确,所谓开端就是我们这个世界的开端,就是上帝创造的开端。关于创世的开端,《创世记》是这样记载的:

起初,上帝创造天与地,地是混沌空虚、渊面黑暗。上帝的气息(*ruaḥ*)运行在水面上。上帝说,要有光,就有了光。上帝看光是好的,就把光与暗分开了。上帝称光为昼、称暗为夜,有晚上、有早上,[这是]头一日……[③]

对于这样的一个"开端",可以有很多种可能的解释,比如在上帝开始创造的时候,"地"是不是已经存在?再比如,"上帝的气息"(*ruaḥ elohim*,常常被译作"上帝的灵")跟上帝是什么关系?它独立于上帝还是内在于上帝?没有太阳这样的发光体,光从何来?这些以及其他一些,都可能成为难以回答的问题。对拉比们来说,真正的难题还在于,这些追问会跟犹太教内部已逐渐形成的上帝从无中创世的教义相冲突——正如迈蒙尼德指出的,是否信仰上帝从无中创世,对犹太教来说至关紧要[④],在这种情况下,先贤们立下禁令,要求不得向两个人同时传授

---

① 《密释纳·节日祭典》(*The Mishnah*), Ḥagigah 2.1.1, 见 *The Mishnah*, trans. Herbert Danby (Peabody, MA: Hendrickson Publishers, 1933), 212-213。另见《巴比伦塔木德·节日祭典》(*Balonian Talmud*), Ḥagigah 11b, https://www.sefaria.org/Chagigah.11b.16? lang=bi。

② Midrash, Shnei Ketubim, Batei Midrashot, Ⅳ,见迈蒙尼德,《迷途指津》,卷首引言,9/9。

③ 《创世记》1:1—5。本文中的《圣经》引文据迈蒙尼德引述的内容译出,译文参考和合本。

④ 参见:迈蒙尼德,《迷途指津》卷二23章,296/321。

有关创世的秘密。对迈蒙尼德来说，先贤的禁令当然要遵守，可是在他看来，由于犹太人长时间的离散，到他的时代，当年先贤们口口相传的那些关于“开端论”和“神车论”的答案已然失传，而他恰恰凭自己的才智和努力厘清这些秘密的答案，并认为自己有义不容辞的责任将这些答案传递给后人，他说，“就你和每一个像你那样感到困惑的人而言，**我会把那种行为当作极端怯懦之举。这就仿佛将真理从某个值得知晓真理的人那里夺走，或者剥夺某个继承人他的遗产**”（卷三引言，379—380/416）。事实上，在不止一个地方，迈蒙尼德提到《迷途指津》的“首要目的就是在尽可能的限度内，解释开端论和神车论”[①]。考虑到迈蒙尼德从一开始就表明“开端论等于自然科学，神车论等于神的科学”，可以说，《迷途指津》的首要目的是在尽可能的限度内解释自然科学和神的科学。

在《迷途指津》的卷首引言之后，迈蒙尼德第一次提及“开端论”是在卷一 17 章。该章起始迈蒙尼德就指出：

> 不要认为，不该向大众传授的只有神的科学。这一点在更大的程度上对自然科学同样适用。实际上，我们不断为你写下我们的断言：**开端论不应在两个人在场的情况下传授**。这一点不仅对律法的遵循者有效，在古代的各种共同体里，对哲学家和有学问的人一样有效。因为，他们将自己有关首要原理（the first principles）的言辞隐藏起来、呈现为谜语。因此，**柏拉图和他的前辈将质料（Matter）称为女性（female）、将形式称为男性**。你知道，**受制于生成和朽坏的存在物**的原理有三：质料、形式以及总是与质料相连的特定的匮乏（Particularized Privation）。因为，要不是有与匮乏的这种联结，质料就不能获得形式。正是在这个意义上，匮乏被当作[首要]原理之一。然而，一旦质料获得了某一种形式，相关的特定的匮乏——我指的是所获得的形式的匮乏——就消失了，而另一种匮乏就与质料相连；这种情形会始终持续下去，正如自然科学所显明的。**甚至那些就算清楚阐明事物也不会被指控腐蚀[青年]的人**，也采用比喻式措辞，乃至诉诸明喻来进行教导，那对**我们这些律法的遵循者**来说，就更有义务**不公开陈述这样的事**——不向没有理解力的大众或是那些对此事的想象跟我们的意图不符的人公开陈述这样的事。这一点你也要知道。[②]

特别有意思的是，迈蒙尼德在这一章列举的质料、形式、匮乏等概念出自亚里士多德的物理学（或曰自然学），可是他提到的哲学家却不是亚里士多德而是他的

---

① 参见迈蒙尼德，《迷途指津》卷二 29 章（319/346）及卷三引言（379/415）。

② 迈蒙尼德，《迷途指津》卷一 17 章，44—45/42—43。

老师柏拉图。[1]如《迷途指津》的英译者皮纳斯所言,迈蒙尼德这里对柏拉图的引述并不确切。[2]柏拉图在迈蒙尼德熟悉的《蒂迈欧》里说过,"可以把接受者(δέχομενον, recepient)比作母亲"(《蒂迈欧》50d),这个"接受者"出自《蒂迈欧》里一个非常重要的概念ὑποδοχή。ὑποδοχή的字面意思是"容器",通常被英译为receptacle,可以将之诠释为"承纳者"或"接收者"。关于这个"承纳者",柏拉图笔下的蒂迈欧这样说:

> 同样,那个经常以其整个范围很美地接受那些与所有永久存在者相一致的东西的东西,依据自然应该外在于所有形式。因此,让我们言说生成得可见的事物的**母亲和承纳者——它完全不被感受为土或气或火或水**,它也不是任何那些生成为这些东西的结合物或组成部分的东西。相反,如果我们说,它是某种不可见且无形状的形式,承纳所有东西,而且某种程度上以最令人困惑且最不好把握的方式分有可理知者,那么我们没在说谎。[3]

正是在这个地方,柏拉图将承纳者(ὑποδοχή)与"母亲"(μητέρα)相提并论。"承纳者"不同于土、气、火、水这些基本元素,也不同于这些元素的结合物,它无形而不可见,却分有可理知者。尽管对这个概念本身始终有争议,但后世学者多将柏拉图的这个"承纳者"对接于亚里士多德的"质料"(ὕλη),或许正因如此,迈蒙尼德在卷一17章说,"柏拉图和他的前辈将质料称为女性,将形式称为男性"。值得留意的是,蒂迈欧讨论他比喻为母亲的"承纳者"时,举的例子是水、火、土、气这四元素,而有关四元素的知识当然属于跟我们所见的生成世界相关的自然科学。可以说,柏拉图的《蒂迈欧》不仅论及这个可见的世界从哪里来这样的宇宙起源论,而且呈现了关于这个生成的世界如何运作的自然科学问题。柏拉图的《蒂迈欧》会不会是迈蒙尼德将"开端论"与自然科学相等同的一个范式?

在迈蒙尼德笔下,柏拉图就算清楚阐明"质料像女性、形式像男性"这个论题,也不用面对苏格拉底曾经面对的腐蚀青年的指控,即便如此,柏拉图还是用比喻方式解说质料与形式的关系。迈蒙尼德举这个关于形式、质料和匮乏的例

---

① 事实上,亚里士多德对质料与形式有过类似的比喻说法,见亚里士多德,《论动物的生成》,730ab1—12。参见:Jacob Klein, "Aristotle: An Introduction," in *Lectures and Essays*, eds. Robert B. Williamson and Elliott Zuckerman (Annapolis, MD: St. John's College Press, 1985), 182-183。

② Shlomo Pines, "Translator's Introduction," in Moses Maimonides, *The Guide of the Perplexed*, LXXVI.

③ 柏拉图,《蒂迈欧》,51a1—51b2。译文据叶然博士未出版译稿,略有改动,重点为笔者所加。中译本另参见:柏拉图 Plato,《蒂迈欧篇》[Timaeus],谢文郁 Xie Wenyu 译(上海[Shanghai]:上海人民出版社[Shanghai Renmin Publishing House],2005),35。

子，看上去好像就只是说明“自然科学不适合向大众公开传授”，其实读完《迷途指津》全书且细细琢磨之后会发现，这不是一个泛泛而言的例子——形式、质料、匮乏等概念恰恰与“开端论”有隐秘而密切的关联。一方面，质料——混沌的未被赋予形式的质料——恰恰位于“从无中创世”与“世界恒在”的对立的中心，这两者之间的对立在迈蒙尼德看来恰如哲学与律法的对立那样不可调和。[①]另一方面，表示“匮乏”的阿拉伯词‘*adam* 也可以指“无”（nothingness）或“不存在”（nonexistence）[②]，在迈蒙尼德有关上帝属性的论述中，“匮乏”恰恰跟上帝联系在一起：对迈蒙尼德来说，上帝是没有任何肯定意义上的属性的，也就是说，不能将“正义”“善”等属性归于上帝。就此而言，形式、质料、匮乏不仅与上帝创世的秘密相关，还与上帝究竟“是什么”（What）以及“如何是”（How）这样的问题相连。

从另一个角度看，比喻或寓言其实有一种双向的作用。一方面，比喻或寓言可以帮助理解力不足的人理解原本抽象的概念或理论，事实上，当柏拉图说“接受者像母亲”时，他很可能是在用一个常见的概念“母亲”解释一个抽象的概念“接受者”。另一方面，比喻或寓言也能将理解力不足的人阻挡在抽象理论之外。同样的比喻，到了迈蒙尼德这里，就变成一个隐藏“质料”“形式”尤其是它们与“匮乏”之间关系的谜。可以看到迈蒙尼德在卷一 17 章同时提到“开端论”与自然科学，意在呼应“卷首引言”里他做出的论断——“开端论等于自然科学”。可是除了“质料”“形式”“匮乏”等寥寥数个概念外，关于“开端论”涉及的自然科学，短短的卷一 17 章没有提及更多内容，尤其令人惊奇的是，这一章也没有提到任何跟创世有关的内容，它甚至是《迷途指津》里少数那些既未出现《圣经》引文也未出现拉比文献的卷章。

“开端论”再一次出现是在卷一 65 章。这一章一开始，迈蒙尼德就宣称我们的宗教共同体有一个共识，即《托拉》是被造的（created）。他认为这表明归于上帝的言辞亦是被造的：“上帝的言辞被归于他，仅仅因为摩西听到的那些话由上帝创造、上帝使之生成，正如上帝创造了所有他所创造并使之生成的事物。”（卷一 65 章，149/158）接下来，迈蒙尼德指出，该章的目的是说明，’*mirah*（讲话，*speaking*）和 *dibbur*（说话，*saying*）是多义词，既表示舌头发声吐出言辞，也表示无声的内心思想，比如“以扫在心里讲”（《创世记》27：41）等。与此同时，“讲”和“说”还表示愿望（wishing）。在迈蒙尼德看来，当《圣经》提及上帝“说话”或

---

① 参见：迈蒙尼德，《迷途指津》卷二 25 章，302/328。

② 见 Hans Wehr, *A Dictionary of Modern Written Arabic*, 4th edition (Ithaca, NY: Spoken Language Services, 1960), 698。参见：迈蒙尼德，《迷途指津》卷二 17 章，英译本第 296 页，英译者注 3。

"讲话"的时候,要么表示内在想法,要么表示愿望。他强调"说"和"讲"这种词用于上帝,是**把上帝比作人**,但事实上《圣经》提及"上帝说",绝非意指上帝真的用文字来发声。正是在同样的意义上,《圣经》把"**命令**"这样的词用于上帝,为的是表达上帝的**意愿**。随后,迈蒙尼德明确表示:

> 出现在开端论里的"他说","他说",在所有情形里都指"他意愿"或"他希望"……有关这一点的论证——我指的是有关[在创造世界时]他说的话(His *Sayings*)仅仅是意愿而非话语(speeches)——在于这样的事实,即话语只能诉诸一个可以接受相关命令的存在者。因此当圣经里说,"诸天借上主的言辞而造"[《诗篇》33:6]……其意图是指诸天由他的目的和意志而得以生成。①

在这一章里,迈蒙尼德的确将"开端论"与《圣经》记载的创世联系在一起。不过值得注意的是,在提到"诸天"(heavens)的创造时,他并没有引用《创世记》第1章,而是引用了《诗篇》,就此而言,英译者在上引段落里对迈蒙尼德文字所做的补充,未必切合他的本意。也就是说,当迈蒙尼德说,"我指的是有关他说的话仅仅是意愿而非话语"时,他未必仅针对上帝在创世时的"话语"。在这一章里,迈蒙尼德斩钉截铁地指出,上帝不会发声,不会像人类那样讲话。他的言下之意是,上帝并不像我们通常认为的那样,用言辞进行创造;相反,《圣经》里记载的"他说"都是比喻的说法,上帝的创造乃出于他的"目的和意志"。迈蒙尼德在讨论中还特地提到与"讲"和"说"相关的"命令",这绝非偶然。试想一下,如果律法中上帝的"命令"和"诫命"都不是由上帝所"讲",都不是摩西从上帝那里实实在在听到的,那么会有怎样"不得了的后果"?②要讲清楚上帝不会发声的原理,当然需要用到自然科学,需要解释人和动物如何发声、声音如何传播等。③在这里,我们再次看到"开端论"与自然科学的紧密关联。

"开端论"与西奈启示

《迷途指津》卷一65章虽然提到"开端论",但按迈蒙尼德自己的说法,此章的意图在于说明"说"和"讲"乃多义词,当这两个词用于上帝时,通常仅指上帝的

---

① 迈蒙尼德,《迷途指津》卷一65章,150/159,方括号中内容为英译者所加。

② 参见:Leo Strauss, "How To Begin to Study *The Guide of the Perplexed*," in *The Guide of the Perplexed*, XXXIX。

③ 关于如何理解将人的身体器官用于上帝的《圣经》篇章,见迈蒙尼德,《迷途指津》卷一46章,96—99/101—103。

意愿而绝非指上帝像人那样会发声讲话。所以看上去，“开端论”似乎并非此章重点。不过，卷一 66 章同样出现了 *ma ʻaseh bereshith*，这就值得我们细细思量两章之间的关联。

卷一 66 章始于一句《圣经》引文：“那[两块法]版是上帝的作品(*ma ʻaseh elohim*, Work of God)。”这句出自《出埃及记》第 32 章第 16 节的经文，恰恰用到了 *ma ʻaseh*(作为、作品，所记述的)这个词。[1] 之前提到 *ma ʻaseh bereshith*(开端论)传统上也被英译作 the Work of Beginning(开端的作为)或者 the Work of Creation(创造的作为)，实际上，这些译文无不体现了其作者将“开端”与“上帝创世的作为/作品”相等同的理解。让我们更完整地看一下这一章的开头：

> **那[两块法]版是上帝的作品**[《出埃及记》32:16]。他[指摩西]借此意在暗示，这个实存[世界]是自然的而非人工的(this existence is natural and not artificial)，因为所有自然事物都被称为“**上主的作品**(*the work of the Lord*)”：“这些人看见上主的作品[《诗篇》107:24]”。与此相应，在提及所有自然事物——诸如植物、动物、风、雨和同类的其他事物——之后，他[指大卫]说：“上主啊，你的作品[或“你所造的”]何其多！”[《诗篇》104:24] 他[大卫]不仅[把万物的创造]归因于他，甚至还说：“黎巴嫩的香柏树是他栽种的。”[《诗篇》104:16]正因为香柏树是自然的而非人工的，他才说，上帝栽种它们。[2]

在这段话里，出现了好几个“他”，只有熟悉迈蒙尼德所引《圣经》经文的出处，才能辨析这几个“他”是不是同一个人，如果不是的话，“他”们究竟分别是谁。第一个“他”很好认，“那版”指写着“十诫”的两块法版，章首的引文来自《出埃及记》，所以第一个“他”无疑是指摩西。接下来三句引文均出自《诗篇》，传统上，迈蒙尼德所引的两首诗均归于大卫名下，因此，后面的几个“他”指向以色列人的诗人王大卫。有意思的是，在这个段落里，迈蒙尼德借“上帝的作品”把**自然事物**与原本看上去绝非自然事物的“**法版**”糅合在一起——就仿佛对迈蒙尼德来说，**凡是“上帝的作品”都是自然而非人为的**。可是，“法版”上明明写了字，而且迈蒙尼德所引的那节《出埃及记》明确说：“那版是上帝的作品，所写的是上帝所写，刻在版上。”(《出埃及记》32:16)法版上上帝所“写”的难道不是最跟自然相对立的律

① 本节尽量将“the work of God (the Lord)”译作“上帝(上主)的作品”，仅在个别地方译成“上帝(上主)的作为”。

② 迈蒙尼德，《迷途指津》卷一 66 章，151/160；方括号中的文字为笔者所加。

法?何以在这儿迈蒙尼德要扯上自然事物呢?

迈蒙尼德接下来解释说,他已经在前面的章节阐明,要如何理解《圣经》里把“上帝所写的”描述为“用上帝的手指所写的”(《出埃及记》32:18)。在卷一46章,迈蒙尼德讨论了将人体器官与上帝相连的《圣经》措辞,如“上帝的脚”“上帝的手指”“上帝的右手”“上帝的声音”“上帝的眼睛”等。迈蒙尼德解释说,人的感觉器官和其他器官是人生存、繁衍、劳作的必需,但上帝的存在没有任何这类的需要,这些器官也不会增进上帝的行动。因此,“上帝没有器官……他不是一个身体,他的行动通过他的**本质**而非通过他的器官来实施”(卷一46章,98/102)。关于何为上帝的本质,迈蒙尼德在不同地方有不同的说法,大体而言无非两者——意志和理智。施特劳斯指出:“大体而言,根据所讨论的不同主题的要求,《迷途指津》游移在两种观点之间。一种观点认为[上帝之为]理智(Intellect)和[上帝之为]意志(Will)是不可分的;另一种观点认为,必须对两者做出区分(该观点由此必定**将上帝理解为理智**而非意志)。”①将上帝理解为理智与将上帝理解为意志可以对应亚里士多德的观点“世界恒在”与律法的观点“世界由上帝从无中创造”:“理智”的上帝自我沉思,是世界首要的动力因,而律法的上帝凭自己的意愿从无中创造世界。的确,我们看到,一方面,在《迷途指津》卷一68章,迈蒙尼德直接把不带任何肯定属性的上帝解释为亚里士多德意义上的“纯粹理智”。同时,迈蒙尼德也说,“以我们之见,**意志也是智慧的产物**,这些都是**同一件事——我指他的本质和他的智慧**——因为我们不相信[他有]属性”(《迷途指津》卷二18章,279/302)。由于“智慧”和“理智”用于上帝时在迈蒙尼德那里是同义词,故而迈蒙尼德在这里即使没有将智慧置于意志之上,也是将两者相等同。另一方面,在解释自己何以拒斥亚里士多德关于世界恒在的观点时,迈蒙尼德指出,亚氏意义上的世界恒在观会使所有奇迹不可能,从而使律法不可能。②

让我们回到卷一66章。迈蒙尼德说《出埃及记》第32章所言“用上帝的手指”可类比《诗篇》作者将“诸天”比作“你[指上帝]手指的作品”(the work [*ma 'aseh*] of Thy fingers)(《诗篇》8:9)。迈蒙尼德指出,“诸天凭上主的言辞而造”(《诗篇》33:6)这样的经文只是对“讲话”和“说话”的**比喻用法**,同样,“手指的作

① Leo Strauss, “How to Begin to Study *The Guide of the Perplexed*,” in *The Guide of the Perplexed*, LⅢ. 括号中文字为原文所有,方括号中文字为笔者所加。*Moshe Halbertal* 直接将“意志的上帝抑或智慧的上帝”(*Will or Wisdom*)当作理解《迷途指津》的钥匙。参见:Moshe Halbertal, *Maimonides*: *Life and Thought*, 312-353。

② 迈蒙尼德,《迷途指津》卷二25章,304/329。

品”也是一种比喻说法。与此相应，“凭上帝的言辞”就相当于“凭上帝的意志所写”。有心的读者会留意到，迈蒙尼德在提及创世时再次以上帝创造“诸天”为例，并且他论及上帝创造“诸天”时再次引述《诗篇》而非《创世记》，并最终将“上帝的手指”和“上帝的言辞”都解释为“上帝的意志”。这个细节让我们看到卷一65 章与 66 章之间的隐秘联系。

真正将这两章更直接联系起来的，是迈蒙尼德在卷一 66 章结尾处再度提到的 *ma ʻaseh bereshith*：

> 正如星辰的生成借助第一意志(the First Will)而非一种工具，因此，这凿刻的文字也是借第一意志而非一种工具而生成。你已经知晓《密释纳》所书“在黄昏所造的十件事”，其中就有“所写的”和“所刻的”。这就证明，在大众里有一种共识，即“法版上所写的”就像所有其他“开端的作品”(*ma ʻaseh bereshith*)一样，如我们在《〈密释纳〉义疏》(*Commentary on the Mishnah*)里表明的。[①]

这里的确很难将 *ma ʻaseh bereshith* 译成 the Account of the Beginning 或“开端论”，但皮纳斯将它译为 other *work in the beginning*，却使这个词与“开端论”的关联变得很难辨识。借着这句话——“‘法版上所写的’**就像所有其他‘开端的作品’一样”——迈蒙尼德绝无仅有地将“开端论”与“法版”“十诫”乃至西奈启示挂上了钩**。诚然，迈蒙尼德在这里将这样一种关联呈现为“大众的共识”，但我们可以体察到，这个“大众的共识”并不像他通常加以贬斥的大众的流俗意见，

---

① 迈蒙尼德，《迷途指津》卷一 66 章，152/161。关于“在安息日前的黄昏被造的十件事”，《密释纳》列出的是：

> [吞下可拉的]地的口(《民数记》16:32)、[在旷野里伴随以色列人的]井的口(《民数记》21:17)、[对巴兰讲话的]驴子的口(《民数记》22:28—30)、[上帝与亚伯拉罕立约指证的]彩虹(《创世记》9:13)、[上帝给以色列人在旷野吃的]吗哪(《出埃及记》16:4—21)、[摩西的]杖、[帮忙建造圣殿的]沙米尔虫(shamir)、文字(the letter)、所写的(the writing)，以及[摩西带下山的法]版。(《密释纳·祖辈训言》V，6)

迈蒙尼德在《〈密释纳〉义疏》里指出，这其中“文字”指“托拉”，“版”当然是指摩西从西奈山上带来写有“十诫”的“法版”，“所写的”就是在“法版”上“所写的”。迈蒙尼德说：“可能有人不理解，在六天的创造之后，所有奇迹已被纳入各种现象的自然中，为什么先贤还要挑出这十种事物来？”所谓的“所有奇迹已被纳入各种现象的自然中”是对《圣经》里发生的各种奇迹的一种解释性观点。这种观点认为，《圣经》记载的奇迹，诸如太阳停驻、红海分开、点水成血、天降吗哪等，看上去改变了自然进程，其实不然：所有这些奇迹的发生已经在上帝创世过程里得到考虑和安排，就此而言，创世过程一旦停止，世界就按万物的自然本性开始运行，上帝不再干预自然进程。可以说，迈蒙尼德本人就是这种观点的倡导者。对于先贤所说的“十件事”，他的解释是，这些事与其他奇迹的不同在于，其他奇迹是在上帝创造相关自然物时即已被纳入该自然物的本性中。比如，摩西会分开红海，这件事在上帝分开天上的水与地上的水的创世第二日就安排好了，而这十件事则是在创世第六日的黄昏得到安排的。见 Moses Maimonides, *The Commentary to Mishnah Aboth*, trans. Arthur David (New York: Bloch Publishing Company, 1968), 100。

因为他既没有用"广为接受的意见"(generally accepted opinion)这样与"真正的知识"相对的词,也没有说这共识乃出自**想象力**而非**理智**因而不可靠。毋宁说迈蒙尼德在这里是借先贤之口,坐实他心目中的另一维"开端论",即**作为律法之开端的西奈启示**。

可是,迈蒙尼德究竟在什么意义上把律法的开端与创世这个开端相提并论?要怎么理解"**'法版上所写的'就像所有其他'开端的作品'一样**"?他不太可能是为了强调石板上的律法乃出自上帝,因为这是所有人都知晓的。从卷一 65 章和 66 章的上下文看,把这两者联系在一起的,首先应该是迈蒙尼德对"所说的"(saying)与"所写的"(writing)两者的寓意式解读。如前文所表明的,在迈蒙尼德看来,"上帝讲""上帝说""上帝用手指写"等《圣经》说法都是比喻,都不能照字面理解。其次,在这两章里,他都指出,"讲""说""写"等词用于上帝都表示这些行动出自上帝的**目的**或**意愿**,也就是说,迈蒙尼德将创世与赐予摩西律法一并归于**上帝的意志**。

除此以外,还可以留意到,在这两章里迈蒙尼德提及创世引述的总是《诗篇》而非更"名正言顺"的《创世记》第 1 章,而且关于创世他举的例子总是跟"诸天"相关,这是为什么呢?从表面上看,出现在《迷途指津》卷一 66 章的《诗篇》第 8 章第 4 节"我观看你的**诸天——你手指的作品**"像一座桥梁,连接了卷一 65 章所引《诗篇》第 33 章第 6 节"诸天借上主的言辞(the word of the Lord)而造"以及 66 章所引《出埃及记》第 32 章第 16 节"那[两块法]版是**上帝的作品**(God's work)——[上面]所写的是上帝所写(the writing was the writing of God),刻在版上"。但往深里想一层,我们会认识到迈蒙尼德在这两章真正与众不同的想法是,"这个实存[世界]是自然的而非人工的,因为所有自然事物都被称为"**上主的作品**"[①]。这其实是一句非常令人费解的话,"作品"或曰"作为"(*ma 'aseh*)已然蕴含了"制作"(*'asah*)的行动,至少从人的角度,任何"制作"都是"人为的"而非"自然的",既然一切都是上帝"制造的",或者说,既然一切都是上帝的"作品",那么迈蒙尼德在何种意义上说,这个实存世界是自然的?如果照他所说,"'法版上所写的'就像所有其他'开端的作品'一样",那将意味着"法版上所写的"十诫乃至摩西律法,也是自然事物。尽管这个谜一样断言的真正意义还有待检审,但至少我们看到,在这个地方,"开端论"(开端的作品)不但与被造的自然世界密切相连,而且涉及西奈启示和摩西律法。

① 迈蒙尼德,《迷途指津》卷一 66 章,151/160。

“开端论”与预言

“开端论”再次出现在《迷途指津》里，已经是在卷二 2 章——在卷二 2 章短短的一篇“特殊导言”里[1]，“开端论”两度与我们相遇，两次它都跟“神车论”一并被提及。在解释自己写作《迷途指津》的意图时，迈蒙尼德指出：

> 你已经从本书的引言得知，这本书系于解释**开端论**和**神车论**中能得到理解的部分以及扫除涉及**预言和神的知识**的困难。与此相应，无论你在哪一章里发现，我的论述着眼于解释已经在自然科学或神的科学中得到论证的一件事，或是着眼于解释已经显现为最恰当地去相信的意见，或者着眼于解释已经在数学上得到解释的一件事——要知道，**那件特定的事必然成为一把钥匙**，[有助于]理解某个要在预言书里发现的东西，我指的是其中的某些寓言和秘密。我何以提到、解释、阐明那件事的理由，将会在为我们获取神车论或开端论的知识中被发现，或者，将会在为涉及**预言**概念的某种根基提供的解释中被发现。[2]

卷二 2 章的“特殊导言”可以说是《迷途指津》全书的点睛之笔。上引的这段话一方面以重复提及“开端论”和“神车论”的方式表明，《迷途指津》的首要目的是在“能得到理解的”范围内解释开端论和神车论；另一方面，这段话里迈蒙尼德两次论及“开端论”和“神车论”时都提到了“预言”，如果照迈蒙尼德在“卷首引言”所说，“神车论”等于神的科学从而对应“神的知识”，那这段话是否在暗示我们，等于自然科学的“开端论”对应《圣经》里的**预言**，尤其是《圣经》里**最独一无二的摩西预言**？当然，按犹太教传统，《创世记》所记载的创世也属于“摩西五经”，其因此在宽泛意义上也属于摩西预言。不过，我们从卷一 66 章和卷二 2 章看到的是，迈蒙尼德将最接近上帝的先知摩西接收到的西奈启示也列入了“开端论”。

“开端论”再次出现是在卷二 29 章。在这一章，“开端论”出现了 4 次，是所有章中出现次数最多的。这一章中迈蒙尼德讨论的主要论题是“每位先知都有独属于他的某种言说方式”[3]。他先以先知以赛亚为例来说明，以赛亚常常用比

---

① 参见：张缨 Zhang Ying，《〈迷途指津〉中的特殊导言》[Maimonides' Special Introductions in *The Guide of the Perplexed*]，收录于《犹太研究》(第 14 辑)[Jewish Studies(14)]，傅有德 Fu Youde 主编(济南[Jinan]：山东大学出版社 [Shandong University Press]，2016)，223—225。

② 迈蒙尼德，《迷途指津》卷二 2 章，237/254。

③ 迈蒙尼德，《迷途指津》卷二 29 章，310/337。

喻说明各王国面临毁灭时的景象，比如论及巴比伦的覆灭，以赛亚说“天上的众星群宿都不发光，日头一出，就变黑暗，月亮也不放光”（《以赛亚书》13:10）。迈蒙尼德指出，只有傻子才会认为星星、太阳、月亮真的会因为巴比伦末日的到来而改变本性，先知的话语只是表达巴比伦人逃跑时黯淡心情的一种修辞罢了。同样，在表达喜悦的时候，光也仿佛显得比往常更明亮些。论及以东的毁灭时，先知以赛亚预言道：“天上的诸军都要消亡，诸天被卷起，好像书卷，所有星星将下坠如葡萄藤的落叶，又如无花果从树上落下。”（《以赛亚书》34:3）迈蒙尼德在解释其比喻意义后，有些感慨地说：这些句子的意义明显得根本无需在《迷途指津》这样一本书里去解释，“可必然性要求”他做出解释，因为“普通人甚至理应属于精英的某些人，丝毫不考虑这一节的上下文，就拿它作为证据，仿佛其中蕴含着托拉里有关于诸天之消亡的信息给我们，就如其中有关于诸天之生成的信息给我们那样”①。

对迈蒙尼德来说，自然事物一经受造，就被赋予固定的本性——使某物是其所是的本性，没有什么力量能改变事物的本性。正因如此，先知的那类看上去有违事物本性的说法都要当作比喻来理解。即便以赛亚以上帝的名义说“看哪，我创造新天新地，从前的事不再被记起，也不再去追想”（《以赛亚书》65:17），但在迈蒙尼德看来这也只是表达一种“对地的祝福，以及对过往兴衰起落的忘却”，因为以赛亚接下来说“所以，你们要高兴，你们要永远喜悦，因为，看哪，我造耶路撒冷令人喜悦，造她的民令人高兴；我将为耶路撒冷喜悦，为我的民高兴，其中不必再听见哭泣的声音和哀号的声音”（《以赛亚书》65:18—19）。在迈蒙尼德看来，这显然是在表达信仰带来的喜悦的恒久状态，故而“新天新地”的“新”并非意味着取消天地之本性。

关于“新天新地”，以赛亚还说：“因为，正如我制造的新天新地会在我面前长存，上主说，你们的后裔和你们的名字亦会长存。”（《以赛亚书》66:20）对此，迈蒙尼德解释说：“这是律法之恒久性的一个迹象，正因如此我们有一个特殊的名字。”②《以赛亚书》的最后两章通常被视为有关弥赛亚的先知预言，因此，对照一下迈蒙尼德在《重述托拉》最后一卷最后一章借以赛亚的预言对弥赛亚时代所做的论述，会帮助我们理解迈蒙尼德对以赛亚所谓的“新天新地”的解读。

愿没人会认为，在弥赛亚时代，任何自然法则会被弃置，或者说，任何新事物

---

① 迈蒙尼德，《迷途指津》卷二29章，312/340。

② 迈蒙尼德，《迷途指津》卷二29章，314—315/342。

会被引入创造。世界将循着其正常的轨道。以赛亚的话——“豺狼会与绵羊羔同居，豹子会与山羊羔同卧”（《以赛亚书》11:6）——要以比喻的方式来理解，他的意思是，以色列将与被比作豺狼和豹子的凶恶的异教徒们安全地共处，[豺狼和豹子的凶狠]正如书上所言：“野地的豺狼必击杀他们，豹子要在城外窥视他们。”（《耶利米书》5:6）[在弥赛亚时代，]他们[异教徒们]都会接受真正的宗教，将不会劫掠也不会破坏，会和以色列一起以正当的方式赚取舒适的生活，如经上所言：“狮子必吃草如牛一般。”（《以赛亚书》11:7）所有与弥赛亚时代相关的类似表述都带着隐喻，在弥赛亚王的日子里，所有人都会清楚这些隐喻的完整含义及其暗示。[1]

在这段话里，迈蒙尼德向我们展现了一幅各民族、各宗教和平共处的弥赛亚时代景象。在迈蒙尼德看来，弥赛亚将是现世的君王，是将以色列人从异族统治下解救出来的那个王，弥赛亚时代不必是人类或世界的末日。这个解释完全契合先知以赛亚的预言。对我们来说更重要的是，他明确指出，**弥赛亚的到来不会改变自然的进程**。换言之，狮子和豺狼不会改变凶恶的本性，羔羊也不会变得凶狠，以赛亚描述的弥赛亚时代的“改变”是以动物们为比喻的强国与弱国的力量消长和各族各宗教共处的方式。当我们回到《迷途指津》卷二 29 章，会看到同样的思路：这样的概念——世界的消亡、世界改变其现有状态，或者一事物改变其本性并持久地改变其本性——在任何先知书里或任何先贤那里都没有得到过肯定。如迈蒙尼德引述的《传道书》中的智者所言，“太阳底下无新事”（《传道书》1:9）。[2]

迈蒙尼德指出，他之所以强调事物不会永久地改变本性，针对的是**《圣经》里有关奇迹的描述**。在他看来，的确没有什么自然原因可以解释摩西的杖何以变成了蛇、尼罗河水何以变成血，但这些变化都是暂时的，也没有使经受变化之物改变其本性(nature)。也就是说，杖在变为蛇后又变回为杖，尼罗河水变成血以后又恢复为水，故而杖与河水的本性或自然并未发生改变。正是在这里，迈蒙尼德第一次在卷二 29 章提及 *ma ʻaseh bereshith*：

[先贤]发现这是件极端困难的事——即承认在开端的作品(*ma ʻaseh bereshith*)之后[一事物的]本性会改变，或者说另一个意志会干预已经以明

① Moses Maimonides, “Treatise Five, Kings and Wars,” ch. 12, “The Messianic Age,” *The Code of Maimonides: Book Fourteen, The Book of Judges*, trans. Abraham M. Hershman (New Heaven: Yale University Press, 1949), 240. 方括号中内容乃笔者为顺通文意所加。

② 参见：迈蒙尼德，《迷途指津》卷二 29 章，317/344。

确方式确立起来的[该事物的]本性。①

这段话事实上呼应了卷一 66 章最后部分,迈蒙尼德在那里提及《密释纳·父辈训言》里有关"创世第六天黄昏所造的十件事",并提请读者参考他本人对此的注解。对迈蒙尼德来说,万事万物一经被造,就被刻上属于该事物的独有印记,这个"最初的印记"就是该事物的"自然"或曰"本性"。②在这里,"开端论"明确跟事物的本性(nature)之不易性相提并论:坚持事物本性的不易性,其实就是否认存在超自然的奇迹。迈蒙尼德断言:"**所有其他奇迹**都能以类比的方式得到解释。"③在《圣经》里,最大的奇迹无异于上帝创世的作为,而仅次于创世的,就是上帝启示摩西赐予他律法的作为。当迈蒙尼德将"开端论"与有关奇迹的讨论联系在一起,他应该已准备好面对解释这两个最大奇迹的任务。

在《迷途指津》卷二 29 章,*ma 'aseh bereshith* 连续出现了三次:

> 当我们的阐述最终到达这一点时,我们现在要专门用一章对涉及开端论的文本做几点提示(give several indications)。因为**本书的首要目的就是解释开端论和神车论里可以得到解释的内容**。在开始这一章之前,我们先要确立具有共同重要性的两个前提。这两者其中之一是:并非托拉里涉及开端论的一切都得像俗众所想象的那样要从其外在含义来理解。④

这段话是整部《迷途指津》里一共五次同时出现"开端论"和"神车论"中的第四次。可以看到,在这里,迈蒙尼德一方面预告他将于下章集中讨论与开端论相关的文本,另一方面,继卷二 2 章之后,他再次强调,解释"开端论"和"神车论"里可以解释的部分是《迷途指津》的"首要目的"。还可以留意到,在本章最后一次提及"开端论"时,迈蒙尼德同时提到了"托拉":究竟什么才是"托拉",这并非不言自明的一件事。在迈蒙尼德之前,犹太数学家、天文学家和哲学家亚伯拉罕·巴·希亚(Abraham bar Ḥiyya,1070—1136/1145,全名为 Abraham bar Ḥiyya ha-Nasi,拉丁名为 Abraham Savasorda)曾提出,按某种犹太传统的区分,"托拉"指《摩西五经》里第二部至第四部(《出埃及记》《利未记》《民数记》),而《申命记》应被称为"重述托拉"(*Mishneh Torah*)。⑤迈蒙尼德完全可能知道巴·希亚的这

① 迈蒙尼德,《迷途指津》卷二 29 章,317/345。

② 参见:迈蒙尼德,《迷途指津》卷二 29 章,317/345。

③ 迈蒙尼德,《迷途指津》卷二 29 章,318/346。

④ 迈蒙尼德,《迷途指津》卷二 29 章,318—319/346。

⑤ Abraham bar Ḥiyya, *Hegyon ha-Nefesch*, ed. E. Freimann (Leipzig: 1860), 38b. 英译本没有传递出文本里蕴含的 *Torah* 跟 *Mishneh Torah*(《申命记》)之间的区分,参见:Abraham bar Ḥiyya, *The Meditation of the Sad Soul*, trans. Geoffrey Wigoder (London: Routledge & K. Paul, 1969), 137。

个说法，因为他不仅将自己编写的犹太法典命名为 *Mishneh Torah*（重述托拉）[①]，而且在《迷途指津》里提到《申命记》时好几次称之为"*Mishneh Torah*"。[②]因此，当迈蒙尼德在这里提到"托拉里涉及开端论的一切"时，他未必仅指《创世记》第1章，而是很有可能兼指《出埃及记》里涉及**律法之开端**的"法版"及西奈启示。

结语

从以上论述中可以看到，迈蒙尼德在《迷途指津》里对"开端论"的论述紧紧围绕他对部分《圣经》章节的解释。然而，不同于传统的解经家，迈蒙尼德的《圣经》解释具有某种独特而鲜明的特征：他的《圣经》解释立足于他对整个犹太教信仰的理性重塑。这样的理性重构的一个最显著的例证就是他对上帝之无形体性(incorporeality of God)的强调。可以说，《迷途指津》卷一解释各种《圣经》用词的多义性的目的就是为了确立上帝是无形体的这个犹太教信仰的重要根基。正因为上帝没有形体，故而迈蒙尼德不断指出，"手" "脚""脸"等词用于上帝时，不能从字面上来理解；进而，《圣经》里的"上帝讲"和"上帝说"也并不意味着上帝像人那样用声带说话发声，《圣经》只是用形象的、普通人易于理解的方式表示上帝的意愿。否认上帝有形体当然与犹太教反对偶像崇拜的核心信仰要求紧密相关，可与此同时，迈蒙尼德对上帝之无形体性的坚持当然也可以说是他重塑犹太教的努力之一。

就"开端论"而言，当迈蒙尼德说"开端论等于自然科学"时，他理应排除了"开端论"与"**从无中创世**"相连的传统观点——难道还有比"从无中创世"更大的神迹从而可以产生更"非自然"地看待世界起源的视角吗？[③]就此而言，即便迈蒙尼德讨论的"开端论"包括了"世界的开端"，他关心的也是更理论性的"质料""形式""匮乏"这些哲学概念，以及(限于篇幅本文未及讨论的)四元素、天文、气象等更具体的自然科学内容。[④]

另一方面，迈蒙尼德在《迷途指津》里不断将"开端的作品"与带来摩西律法的"法版"以及西奈启示联系在一起，从而使传统上仅与创世相关的"开端论"兼

---

① 参见：Leo Strauss, "The Literary Character of *The Guide for the Perplexed*," in *Persecution and the Art of Writing*, 85-86；中译本见施特劳斯，《迫害与写作艺术》，77—79。

② 例如迈蒙尼德，《迷途指津》卷二31章(331/359)、卷二34章(337/366)等。

③ 参见：Leo Strauss, "How to Begin To Study *The Guide of the Perplexed*," in *The Guide of the Perplexed*, XXXIX。

④ 迈蒙尼德，《迷途指津》卷二30章，320—330/348—359。

容了“律法的开端”。这样一种“扩容”显然具有深远意义：不仅法版上“所写的”十诫像其他“开端的作品”一样是自然事物，而且在迈蒙尼德看来，“律法总是倾向于顺应自然”①，也就是说，**自然构成了律法的尺度**而非相反。正是在这样的意义上迈蒙尼德所说的“开端论等于自然科学”才能得到初步的理解。

① 迈蒙尼德，《迷途指津》卷三 43 章，523/571。

Maimonides' Examination of "The Account of the Beginning": A Preliminary Study of One of the Two Foci in *The Guide of the Perplexed*

ZHANG Ying

Abstract: In rabbinic tradition, ma'aseh bereshith (the Account of the Beginning; or, the Work of the Beginning) which is connected to Genesis 1, and ma'aseh merkabah (the Account of the Chariot), which is related to Ezekiel 1 and 10, are secret knowledge of God that are prohibited to teach. In *The Guide of the Perplexed*, Maimonides points out more than once that the first purpose of his Treatise is to explain what can be explained of the Account of the Beginning and of the Account of the Chariot. In this sense, these two Accounts can be seen as the two foci of the Guide. Since Maimonides also states that the Account of the Beginning is identical with natural science and the Account of the Chariot is with divine science, some scholars interpret his discussion of the Account of the Beginning in view of his exposition of Aristotelian natural science. By a detailed reading of the different contexts of Maimonides' use of ma'aseh bereshith, this article argues that Maimonides not only relates ma'aseh bereshith with the beginning of the world, as the generally accepted view, he also establishes a connection between ma'aseh bereshith and the beginning of the Torah, that is, the revelation at Mount Sinai or Mosaic prophecy. In addition, by associating the "work of the beginning" with the unchangeable nature of natural things, Maimonides insinuates that ma'aseh bereshith is not compatible with creatio ex nihilo.

Key Words: Maimonides, *The Guide of the Perplexed*, ma'aseh bereshith, the Beginning of the World, the Beginning of the Torah

JEWISH STUDIES
犹太研究
第18辑

中世纪犹太人的历史书写与认知活动*

曹坚**

【摘要】本文一方面通过归纳整理相关历史文献和当代犹太学者的考证，描述中世纪犹太人对于自身和世界历史的认知发展和相关著述，说明犹太人从约瑟夫斯时期至16世纪依然有不容忽略、相当活跃并富有时代特征的非常规历史书写活动。而从犹太人这一层面考察中世纪，也可为16世纪后出现的大量犹太人现代历史书写以及斯宾诺莎的圣经历史批判法提供内生的和自然的解释。另一方面，本文也讨论了中世纪犹太人生活中非书写性的历史记忆渠道及其对犹太人历史认知和族群认同的独特作用。

【关键词】中世纪犹太人；历史书写；历史；记忆

一般认为，犹太人在公元1—2世纪的约瑟夫斯之后一直到16世纪前夕的1000多年里似乎没有产生可观的历史著作。中世纪犹太人的宗教和知识渠道也仅限于哈拉卡、哲学和喀巴拉。他们相信这些渠道足以将他们引向终极真理和精神幸福，而不要求掌握历史知识。在他们眼里，掌握历史知识说得客气是避重就轻，说得不客气简直就是“糟蹋时间”。[①] 对于中世纪犹太人这种漠然的状

---

* 本文是教育部人文社科研究规划基金项目“关于现代犹太人历史意识的研究”(18YJA730001)和国家社科基金专项项目“关于以色列国新史学之构建的研究”(19VJX057)的阶段性成果。

** 曹坚，中山大学哲学系教授。

① Maimonides, *Commentary to Mishnah Sanhedrin*, ed. and trans. Fred Rosner (New York: Sepher-Hermon Press, 1981), 10:1. 在其《密释纳》注释书的介绍中，迈蒙尼德甚至对记录“律法传承”的重要性也不以为然，认为它“对于神的信仰的作用有限”，尽管它可以为那些“想提高密西纳学习的人”所用。参见：Y. Yerushalmi, *Zakhor: Jewish History and Jewish Memory* (Seatle: University of Washington Press, 1982), 114-115, n.5。然而，一方面，迈蒙尼德的《致也门书信》记录了犹太人的四次弥赛亚运动，反映出在这些传世文献之外，中世纪犹太人其实掌握更多的历史知识。参见：Maimonides, *Epistle to Yemen, Judeo-Arabic Text*, ed. A. Halkin, Eng. trans. B. Cohen (New York: American Academy for Jewish Research, 1952), XVIII-XX。另一方面，迈蒙尼德自有其对历史的兴趣和感悟，详见下文。

态，有说苦难和迫害使他们的历史意识变得麻木的，有说是因为他们没有通常被视为历史主题的国家和政权的，甚至有归咎于他们既无宫廷编年史也无投身于斯的僧侣的。①

然而常被忽略的一个重要事实是，在中世纪，犹太人中有持续、活跃的历史书写和认知活动。这些活动不仅有助于我们更加了解中世纪犹太人，且假如没有他们的这些历史书写和认识上的实践和积累，我们就无法充分理解为何从16世纪开始，即便上述因素同样存在，仍涌现了众多在规模上和质量上都十分独特的犹太历史著作。为此，本文将主要基于中世纪犹太人的历史书写活动，通过代表人物和作品分析这些活动背后犹太人对于历史的认知。同时，文章也将基于中世纪犹太群体的非历史书写类的记忆渠道，如宗教节期、仪式和读经等，分析其特殊历史认知方式。

中世纪犹太人遭遇的挑战和冲击既有内部的也有外部的，既有精神上的，也有物质和肉体上的。在犹太人内部出现了卡拉派对主流拉比犹太教的激烈攻击。卡拉派的核心立场是，拉比犹太教尊奉的口传律法传统掺杂了人的主观歪曲，加之时过境迁，因而偏离和丧失了摩西律法的原貌和真谛，而其唯有从成文律法中方可寻得，并借此秉持真正的犹太教。在外部，基督教和伊斯兰教对犹太人的威逼迫害不仅有对犹太教教义和信仰的攻击，还有经济上乃至肉体上的剥削、排挤、驱赶乃至屠杀。同时，在中世纪的数百年里，在夹缝中求存的大离散时期的犹太人也亲身经历了改变世界格局的重大历史事件，如十字军东征和穆斯林对基督教教会的重大军事胜利，由此不可避免地受到牵连。上述一切都迫使犹太人反省自身的民族认同、历史处境和未来发展，从而产生新的历史认知和历史书写动机。与此同时，宗教礼仪和节期作为传统的、主要的族群认同和凝聚手段，不仅得以延续甚至加强，而且与历史书写活动相契合，共同构建了中世纪犹太人的历史认知世界。

一

在针对内外威胁而出现的几类作品中，首先是“律法传承录”(shalshelet ba-qabbalah)。这类作品从拉比时期起就未曾间断。其传记信息常显不足，对于提到的历史事件也较随意，因为这类历史书写的动机大都不是记录或解释犹太民族历史，而是驳斥那些否定口传律法有效性的来自犹太人内部的异端并回

① Y. Yerushalmi, *Zakhor: Jewish History and Jewish Memory*, 52.

应外部的攻击。[①] 据卡斯蒂尔地区托雷多城的达乌德(Abraham Ibn Daud, 1110—1180年)的律法史《传统之书》(*Sefer Ha'Qabbalah*, *The Book of Tradition*,约1160年),神圣律法历经七个时代的导师而得以不间断地传承下来:《圣经》作者、第二圣殿时期的精神领袖、坦纳、阿莫拉、萨波拉、加昂和拉比。这类针对卡拉派的作品旨在说明,清晰确凿的律法传承史证实,作者所尊奉的拉比传统与《圣经》启示一脉相承、具有内在联系。[②]

其次是殉道录。这是大离散伊始就已存在的、有关犹太人殉道和受迫害的编年体书写体裁。相较于中世纪丰富的律法注释、神哲学著作、拉比问答集等,殉道录和哀祭、挽词等非常规历史书写占据了虽不起眼但实实在在的一席之地。[③]十字军对犹太人犯下的恶行激发阿什肯犹太人为后代记录下他们的悲惨遭遇和殉道事迹。这些记录反映了犹太群体与基督教世界关系的变化,如作于12世纪的四部十字军希伯来编年史;并且其内容的宗教意图明显——神拣选的殉道者使神的名得以洁净,也使他们的后代能借他们的德行蒙福,如巴尔·西蒙(Solomon bar Simeon)时序有误但生动丰富的十字军编年史。[④]

在殉道录中,一个明显的倾向是将重大的新发事件归为人们熟悉的《圣经》原型事件,因为当被放置在传统模式而非令人无所适从的具体性中省察时,即使是最可怕的事件也会让人觉得不那么恐怖了。如《以斯帖记》带给中世纪犹太人理解自身处境的启示。[⑤] "以撒被缚"(akedah, binding of Isaac)在整个编年史文献中也成为事件的原型和主题。对于众多犹太人宁可殉道也不改宗的场面,十字军编年史反复联系这一原型事件:

> 从亚当以来,曾发生过像这样的"以撒被缚"吗?一天之内发生一千一百桩"以撒被缚"!摩利押山上的"以撒被缚"仅一次便使世界为之震撼,"瞧!众天使哭泣而诸天暗淡。"而它们现在呢?为何诸天和星宿没有暗淡下来?……当一天之内有一千一百无辜的人被杀,包括婴儿和孤儿……?

① Y. Yerushalmi, *Zakhor*: *Jewish History and Jewish Memory*, 32. 律法传承录的写作也可能出于某个实际需要,如解答某一时期权威人物确定的律法疑难,或出于对拉比学术进展的探究。

② L. Kochan, *The Jew and His History* (New York: Schocken Books, 1977), 24-25. 坦纳(Tannaim)为1—2世纪密西拿时期的先贤。阿莫拉(Amoraim)是3—5世纪革马拉时期的学者。萨波拉(Savoraim)是6—7世纪《巴比伦塔木德》成书之后的巴比伦犹太先贤。加昂(Geonim)是7世纪末至11世纪中叶巴比伦犹太人的最高宗教权威。

③ E. Tcherikower, "Jewish Martyrology and Jewish Historiography," in *YIVO Annual of Jewish Social Science*, Ⅰ(New York: YIVO Institute for Jewish Research, 1946), 9-23.

④ M. Meyer, "Introduction to the Crusade Chronicle of Solomon bar Simeon," in *Ideas of Jewish History*, ed. M. Meyer (New York: Behrman House, 1988), 91-92.

⑤ Y. Yerushalmi, *Zakhor*: *Jewish History and Jewish Memory*, 36.

啊，主！你竟对此保持沉默！

这写的正是在缅因兹发生迫害犹太人事件时，编年史作者希姆匈(Shelomoh bar Shimshon)所发出的呐喊。[①] 莱茵地区的德国犹太人群体是虔敬的，灾难无法再简单地用罚罪来解释，他们与亚伯拉罕的相同点是二者的信仰都是完美的，都经受住了最大的考验。[②] 但这里也呈现了约伯式的义人：面对悲惨遭遇，没有沉默，而是主动向神发问和申诉。

最后是书信。其中许多是针对基督教和伊斯兰教威胁出现的、主要以弥赛亚为主题的作品。它们要么宣扬犹太教的优越，要么宣称末日临近。如迈蒙尼德(Moshe ben Maimon，1135—1204 年)在《致也门书信》(‘*Iggeret Teman*，*Epistle to Yemen*，1172 年)中认为，犹太教是唯一真正的宗教，基督教和伊斯兰教只不过是对它的拙劣模仿，而两教步入歧途则源于拜偶像。犹太教对拜偶像的胜利在《创世记》中即有见证。在以诺的时代(《创世记》第 5 章)就已存在星宿崇拜等现象，除以诺、玛土撒拉和诺亚等以外，“人类的嘴和心不再记念神的大名，他们已不认识他，男女老幼只知道木石造的偶像”。直到亚伯拉罕认识了独一真神，真理才开始战胜拜偶像。从吾珥到哈兰再到迦南，亚伯拉罕使成千上万的人认识了这一真理，成为“亚伯拉罕之家的人”。而当希伯来人在法老统治下拜偶像时，历史发生倒退，待到摩西开始发挥先知作用时，以色列民被拣选，神便赐予他们诫命，指明如何侍奉神并对拜偶像加以严惩。这一启蒙的过程包含了迈蒙尼德对历史的理解。[③]

可见，在迈蒙尼德独特的历史兴趣和理解中，他倾向于对一些《圣经》律法进行“历史化”处理，即神颁布律法是为了让古代以色列人远离当时流行的异教习俗。[④] 神选择在自然法范畴内行使他的计划，没有通过神迹突然去除幼年时期以色列的多神教思维习惯，而是逐渐改变他们的旧习。在此迈蒙尼德或许受到早期基督教和拉比文献的影响。奥古斯丁将通融性原则视为历史原则，而根据米德拉什对《利未记》第 17 章第 7 节的诠释：“既然以色列沉溺于埃及的偶像崇拜及其献祭……神说，且让他们在会幕前带着这些祭品，他们(迟早会)自行摈弃

---

① 转引自 A. Habermann, ed. *Sefer gezeret Ashkenaz ve-zarefat* (*The Book of the Persecutions of Germany and France*), (Jerusalem: Sifriyat haPo'alim, 1946), 32。该书汇编了全部四个十字军编年史作品。

② Y. Yerushalmi, *Zakhor*: *Jewish History and Jewish Memory*, 38.

③ Maimonides, *Mishneh Torah*, Book Ⅰ: knowledge, ch.1; *Guide of the Perplexed*, Ⅲ, 29. Cf. L. Kochan, *The Jew and His History*, 20-21.

④ Y. Yerushalmi, *Zakhor*: *Jewish History and Jewish Memory*, 114-115, n.5.

偶像崇拜而得救。"[①]这样,迈蒙尼德预示了一个在16世纪堪称"历史性"革命的基本方法,即在异化和重构中进行理解。[②]

在上述历史书写活动中,除了犹太历,中世纪犹太人有其他的时间参照系统:创世纪年(Era)、第二圣殿被毁纪年和塞琉西纪年(所谓 minyan shetarot,或"协议纪年"era of contracts,也称为"希腊纪年"minyan yevani)。迈蒙尼德曾一同使用这些不同的纪年。不同的纪年意味着不同的时间跨度、不同的历史共鸣和对历史时间的不同思考维度。创世纪年直到加昂时期才开始普及。三者之中只有第二圣殿被毁将人带回犹太历史中一个至关重要的时间点。塞琉西纪年以312年塞琉古尼卡特占领巴比伦为开端。犹太人起初是从协调和方便角度,与其他民族一道采纳它。埃及的奇姆拉大拉比(David Ibn Abi Zimra)1511年才将其加以废止,但也门犹太人一直沿用它直至20世纪。[③]

二

主要受西班牙或圣地的基督教和伊斯兰教之间激烈冲突的影响,塞法迪犹太人比阿什肯犹太人更关切弥赛亚主题,而这也成为塞法迪犹太人历史书写的显著特点。[④]其中一个重要方面就是历史对《圣经》注释持续的"激活"(activation)。塞法迪犹太人通常相信,先祖的行为预示了后代的境遇。[⑤] 加泰罗尼亚地区的纳曼尼德(M.Nachmanides,又称 Ramban)就认为以色列人战胜亚玛力人应许了弥赛亚的最终临到和胜利。[⑥] 这种诠释法很符合"历史—弥赛亚主义的"(historico-messianological)思维逻辑,等于宣告了历史结构的类型预表(typology),使《托拉》成为未来甚至当下历史的档案室。[⑦] 以下对几位塞法迪思想家的讨论旨在说明,在东西方列强争战之际和以色列的至暗时刻,历史书写体裁富有末世论色彩,弥赛亚成分与历史成分珠联璧合,无论是希亚、达乌德,还

① *Midrash Rabba*, eds. and trans. H. Freedman and M. Simon (London: Soncino, 1961), *Leviticus Rabba*, 22:6. 引文为笔者转译自该英译本。

② A. Funkenstein, *Perceptions of Jewish History* (Berkeley: University of California Press, 1993), 95-96.

③ Y. Yerushalmi, *Zakhor*: *Jewish History and Jewish Memory*, 41, 117, nos.23 and 25.

④ 关于塞法迪犹太人与阿什肯犹太人对该主题关注的不同及原因,可参见:G. Cohen, "Messianic Postures of Ashkenazim and Sephradim," in *Essential Papers on Messianic Movements and Personalities in Jewish History*, ed. Marc Saperstein (New York: New York University Press, 1992)。

⑤ L. Kochan, *The Jew and His History*, 20-21.

⑥ Nachmanides' Commentary to Exodus XVII, 9.

⑦ L. Kochan, *The Jew and His History*, 22.

是亚伯拉巴内都是如此。[①]

卡斯提利尔地区的占星家、几何学家和哲学家希亚(Abraham bar Hiyya, 1065—1143 年)的《启示者之卷》(*Megilat Ha'Megaleh*, *The Scroll of Revealer*, 约 1129 年)旨在“揭示拯救的秘密”。其观察主要依据《创世记》和星宿。关于《创世记》,如果希亚认可“世界及其一切仅为《托拉》而造”的传统观念,那么整个创世故事对他而言必定意味着以色列的命运。在十字军 1099 年从穆斯林手中收复圣地耶路撒冷后的 30 年里,希亚根据星象预测说,“战争与杀戮将连绵不绝,直到以东人开始失去对圣地的控制”[②]。在此基础上,他推算出世界的年岁,以及弥赛亚时代来临的最近和最远的具体时间。[③] 这无疑给人们带来拯救的希望,在一定程度上营造了当时在犹太—基督教世界的天启思想氛围。[④]

达乌德通过激活《圣经》中的应许向当代人发出安慰之光,其写作对于局势的分析也是弥赛亚性质的。帝国的更替在他笔下依次为波斯(包括巴比伦和米底亚)、希腊(包括罗马)、波斯—罗马、伊斯兰。达乌德聚焦西班牙,是这里让他看到了末日争战的临近。他从西班牙比从罗马看到了更真实的以东,他也因此称阿方索七世(Alfonso VII, 1105—1157 年)为古罗马真正的继承者。达乌德从历史中悟到:当罗马崛起,以色列就衰落;当波斯宽待以色列,自己也得繁荣,当它逼迫以色列,自己也会遭到神的惩罚。[⑤] 在《传统之书》的末尾,他驳斥撒都该人的观点,即《先知书》中所有安慰以色列的段落在第二圣殿时期已得应验。[⑥]他对《撒迦利亚书》第 14 章第 1 节预言的解释是,“耶和华的日子临近”,且“当在我们的时代”。[⑦] 这种信心来自他对 12 世纪局势的弥赛亚式分析和对犹太历史的程式化(schematological)理解。[⑧] 程式学不仅显示出对事件表面的兴趣,还表现出对事件意义及其在整个历史计划中地位的想法。[⑨]针对突麦尔特(Ibn Tumart,1078—1130 年)[⑩]事件,他引用《耶利米书》第 15 章第 2 节,感觉从中窥

---

① L. Kochan, *The Jew and His History*, 33-34.

② *Megilat Ha'Megaleh*, ed. by A. Poznanski, revised and introduced by J. Guttmann (Berlin: 1924), 1, 7, 11 and 144.

③ *Megilat Ha'Megaleh*, 20, 36.

④ L. Kochan, *The Jew and His History*, 23.

⑤ G. Cohen, “Messianic Postures of Ashkenazim and Sephardim,” 223-262.

⑥ G. Cohen, ed. *Sefer Ha-Qabbalah* (London: Routledge & Kegan, 1967), 74.

⑦ 转引自 G. Cohen, “Messianic Postures of Ashkenazim and Sephardim,” 214。

⑧ L. Kochan, *The Jew and His History*, 26.

⑨ G. Cohen, “Introduction,” in *Sefer Ha-Qabbalah*, 189-222.

⑩ 伊斯兰原教旨主义倡导人,北非姆瓦希德王朝奠基人,率队入侵达乌德的出生地安达卢斯,强迫犹太人改宗。

见了历史的方向:"我们神的安慰果然是信实的! ……因为(犹太人)离散的历史与得救的历史相对应。"[①]达乌德试图证明犹太人"历史的对称性"(symmetry in history):从亚伯拉罕到先知传言终止之间的阶段数与从先知传言终止到弥赛亚到来之间的阶段数是相同的。[②] 这种所谓的"历史对称性"是他理解未来模式的关键。[③]

生于里斯本、卒于威尼斯的《圣经》注释家亚伯拉巴内(Don Isaac Abrabanel,1437—1508年)亲身经历了15—16世纪基督教当局强迫犹太人改宗和驱逐犹太人等重大事件给犹太人带来的悲惨境遇和灾难。他的著作结合了末世拯救观和当下历史现实,并与他所处的政治和历史环境密切相关。1453年土耳其人占领君士坦丁堡后,亚伯拉巴内看到了土耳其对基督教世界取得的一系列重大胜利。与此同时,基督教列强内部分裂,特别是查理七世1494年率大军入侵意大利,攻取了罗马和那不勒斯。在亚伯拉巴内看来,以东人遭受的灾难,按照以赛亚、耶利米和俄巴底亚的预言,至此全部应验。但这并不代表伊斯兰世界的最终胜利,因为罗马灭亡之际,弥赛亚会自我彰显。而现在,以色列的物质和精神拯救完全展开,包括各代离散犹太人的复活。这一切都强化了亚伯拉巴内的弥赛亚思维,因为正是在这一时期,他写成了从历史和本地化角度探讨弥赛亚来临问题的三部曲,即《救恩的源泉》(*Ma'ayenei Ha'Yeshuah*, *The Wells of Salvation*)、《传救恩者》(*Announcer of Salvation*)和《他受膏者得救》(*Yeshuot Meshiho*, *Salvation to His Anointed*)。三部作品都是按照末日临近的思路来解释当代历史。[④]

亚伯拉巴内用弥赛亚理论解释离散是其弥赛亚理论的起点,他同样将历史信息纯粹用作预言末日降临的素材。[⑤] 一方面,亚伯拉巴内强调,希腊、罗马、亚述、波斯和巴比伦全都湮没在历史中,唯有以色列经受住了分解的力量存留下来。使以色列进而使全人类得救的是以色列与神的独特关系。借这一关系,以色列获得一种特有的历史,通常的历史因果律于此不再适用,因为神对世界的统治在以色列这儿是直接的、一对一的、不以任何其他影响(如星象)为媒介的。这就是赋予以色列永恒保证的力量,如《玛拉基书》第3章第6节所示。另一方面,他又强调,与神的独特关系和特有的历史带来的永恒保证本身并不

---

① G. Cohen, ed. *Sefer Ha-Qabbalah*, 66.

② M. Meyer, "Introduction to the Crusade Chronicle of Solomon bar Simeon," 79.

③ G. Cohen, "Introduction," in *Sefer Ha-Qabbalah*, 189-222.

④ L. Kochan, *The Jew and His History*, 28 and 33-34.

⑤ I. Baer, "Don Yitzhak Abrabanel Ve'Yahso el Baiyot Ha'Historiya Ve'Ha'Medina," in *Tarbitz*, Ⅷ, nos.3-4 (Jerusalem: 1937), 257.

能消除曲折。[①]

亚伯拉巴内需要驳斥两个流行说法：一是基督教关于耶稣作为弥赛亚曾经到来的说法，二是第二圣殿的重建表明以色列自身的拯救应许已部分实现的说法。他为此采用《圣经》和历史论证相结合的方法。对于前一种说法，基督教世界不是《但以理书》第2章第44节中可“灭绝”前面四个国度且“必存到永远”的第五个国度。[②]对于后一种说法或哈斯蒙尼王朝时期在犹太人中引发的弥赛亚时代的联想，亚伯拉巴内列举了10个从先知文献总结而来的条件，由于远没有满足它们，故重建第二圣殿就连部分实现神的应许都算不上。[③] 只有推翻以上两种说法，亚伯拉巴内才可能说明为何现在是“末日”。他毫不怀疑自己看到了《塔木德》提到的所有末日征兆。[④]它们暗示始祖的完美性至此已彻底消失，这是一个始于始祖第一次犯罪的毁灭过程，唯有神的拯救能扭转乾坤。出埃及事件就是这类拯救的原型，弥赛亚也因此好比摩西，但这一次拯救不单为以色列民，而是直接为了全人类。施特劳斯认为，在这个意义上，临近的弥赛亚时代对于亚伯拉巴内是非政治性的。[⑤] 但科罕提出，既然亚伯拉巴内是从当下政治着眼，就绝非没有政治性了。[⑥]

如何解释《但以理书》中的第四、第五国度对于亚伯拉巴内的弥赛亚学说十分关键。从犹太人的角度看，第五国度只能是以色列，从而表明神应许的实现。亚伯拉巴内通过历史激活了以赛亚、耶利米和俄巴底亚的话语并说明被传统指为第四国度的异教罗马和当今的罗马一脉相承[⑦]，因而第四国度依然在统治。对于《但以理书》没有预言的伊斯兰统治，亚伯拉巴内通过把它视为基督教世界内异变的部分而解决了这一难题。在亚伯拉巴内看来，世界分化成了两个交战的阵营。一方面，他用以东人指称基督徒和意大利本地人，他们是希腊和罗马的

---

① *Ateret Zekenim* (Warsaw: Lebenson, 1894), 106. 亚伯拉巴内特意把经文中的雅各换成了以色列。

② *Ma'ayenei Ha'Yeshuah* (Stettin:1860), Introduction, 17b.

③ *Yeshuot Meshiho* (Koenigsberg: 1861), 26a-b; 2nd ed., (Jerusalem: Sefrim benei Abrabanel, 1967). 这10个条件是：从大卫后裔中出现的弥赛亚王统治以色列、以色列的敌人遭惩罚、以色列地繁荣、以色列的智慧流行、以色列地圣洁、先知传言得恢复、神迹更新、离散结束、万民接受独一神的信仰、死者复活。

④ *Yeshuot Meshiho*, 33bff。这些征兆是：异端流行、家庭破裂、以色列地犹太人的集体生活瓦解、大离散、肉体折磨、饥荒、对学问和学者的藐视。

⑤ L. Strauss, “On Abrabanel's Philosophical Tendency and Political Teachings,” in *Isaac Abrabanel*, eds. J. Trend and H. Loewe (Cambridge: Cambridge University Press, 1937), 108-109.

⑥ L. Kochan, *The Jew and His History*, 31.

⑦ 具体参见：B. Netanyahu, *Don Isaac Abrabanel* (Philadelphia: Pennsyvanian University Press, 1968), 211f。

继承人;另一方面,他用以实玛利人指称伊斯兰世界的人或土耳其人,他们是巴比伦和波斯的继承人。[①] 这在《以西结书》第38章第21节已有预言:我必命我的诸山发刀剑来攻击歌革,人都要用刀剑杀害弟兄。亚伯拉巴内认为,这些"弟兄"指的正是以东人和以实玛利人。[②]

亚伯拉巴内了解希亚的弥赛亚—历史著作,并重拾其在圣地发生终结之战的观念,反对达乌德仅仅以西班牙为中心。[③] 亚伯拉巴内认为有两个主战场。一个在东地中海地区:在那儿,穆斯林统治的埃及会败于基督教列强的进攻,在以东人手中遭受《以赛亚书》曾预言的惩罚。接着,战争会转移到耶路撒冷附近,这样以色列失去的10个支派也会加入,因为犹太人的拯救不能没有犹太人自己的参与,即便这不会影响神掌控的战争结果。亚伯拉巴内实际预测的是以色列两大敌人的自相残杀和毁灭。[④] "君士坦丁堡败于波斯人(今天的土耳其人)之后,离散终告结束。"[⑤]

三

从以上历史激活《圣经》注释和历史弥赛亚主义的例证可知,虽然融通性(accommodation)释经原则是非历史的(ahistorical),但同样适用于历史思考。根据方肯斯坦的理论,历史书写方面,融通性原则首先为基督教所用。奥古斯丁将融通性原则视为历史原则。针对亚里士多德将时间定义为物体移动(motion)的某种度量,奥古斯丁提出这是一种主观但必然的对于持续性(duration)的度量,并暗示了其是一种持续的创造(*creatio continua*)。考虑到哲学家们不相信一个可以在历史中任意而为的神或一个特殊的天意,他提出历史进程并不是随意的,而是像宇宙一样呈现为一个美丽的整体。进程中的各阶段只适合当时,但"组合起来后的历史整体美得就像一段动听的乐曲"。神对此明了且据此行动。奥古斯丁区别了"适合"(*aptum*)和"美"(*pulchrum*):各部分本身虽不是"美"的,至多是"适合"的,但整体在各部分相"适合"的情况下却是"美"的。[⑥]

① *Yeshuot Meshiho*, 15a and 10a-b.

② *Ma'ayenei Ha'Yeshuah*, 50b.

③ L. Kochan, *The Jew and His History*, 32-33.

④ *Yeshuot Meshiho*, 35b and 34bff.

⑤ *Mashmia*, 77b.

⑥ 转引自 A. Funkenstein, *Perceptions of Jewish History*, 116 and 94-95。奥古斯丁也曾承认人生和世界历史各阶段"自身的美"(pulchritudo sua),因为各阶段的机制在相互作用下适合当时人类的禀赋。A. Funkenstein, *Perceptions of Jewish History*, 95。

进而在融通性原则下,基督教借助所谓"类型"(*typoi*)或"符号"(*figurae*)揭示历史的结构和意义。这些"内在的—历史的"符号是一些"象征性—预示性"类比,表示无论古今,无论人或事,都存在一方是另一方的"预表"(prefiguration),从而暗示一种同一、对应和整全的关系,合成一个内在的历史平行系统。这些符号不是语言学表达形式,而是具体的历史现实——物体、事件、人。对词和词的预表的明确区分使符号从天启论聚焦的暗喻转变为预表法聚焦的"真正的象征",即一种"现实事物里的先知传言"(a prophecy in things)。虽然基督教预表法思维的方法和许多意象源于天启主义,但教父们旨在明确新旧约之间的连续性和发展,而非为了测算世界末日,总之,要揭示的是历史的结构而非持续时间。基督教成为历史事件象征性解读沃土的原因首先在于,神圣意义的核心主要取决于基督的道成肉身及其一生不仅验证先知的话语,还再现和成全了古代以色列相关事件和人物。[①]

时至中世纪,12世纪的欧洲基督教世界兴起了"希伯来语真理"(*veritas hebraica*)探究、12世纪的象征主义或思辨圣经主义等思潮。《圣经》语文学与系统神学的预表法齐头并进。[②] 当下历史的神学意义被发现。这有赖于另一个发现,即当下历史与圣经历史同样具有预表法诠释价值。中世纪一众所谓的象征主义者以预表法处理人类全部的历史,通过揭示历史的结构明确自己所处的当下在神的拯救计划中的位置。这一方法至菲奥雷的乔吉姆(Joachim of Fiore)臻于完善。他分配给三位一体三个循序渐进的历史时期:旧约或圣父时期、新约或圣子时期、圣灵时期。这样,即将到来的千禧年结构就可以从历史进程中推断出来。[③]

此时人们普遍相信,神启适合人的禀赋,即"圣经说的是人的语言"[④];与之相应的历史哲学是,在历史进程中,神会随人的智力、道德和政治水准调整神启及其表达。可见,中世纪释经家已将拉比时期的律法诠释原则或早期基督教的《圣经》诠释原则扩展到哲学理解。根据神圣语言特性的理论,启示语言使用人类熟悉的成分以超越它们——而这一过程本身正是通过类比和暗喻完成的。最大化的方法认为,《圣经》说的是普遍意义上的人的语言,是科学与神学的集大成者,释经的任务就是解码其中的奥妙。而这成为中世纪犹太释经的主流。但最

① A. Funkenstein, *Perceptions of Jewish History*, 99-105.

② 阿奎那认为:只有圣经事件、制度和人物本身,而非指向它们的语言,才带有超越它们所处时代的意义。预表法的神秘释义必须以坚实的语文学为基础。*Summa Theologiae*, 1-1.9.

③ A. Funkenstein, *Perceptions of Jewish History*, 104.

④ 对应的拉丁文为 Sciptura humane loquitur,希伯来文为 dibra tora kileshon bene adam。

小化的方法认为,《圣经》说的是特殊意义上的人的语言,如埃兹拉(Ibn Ezra,1055—1139 年)不从经文的普通意义而从它们特指的物体或事件中寻找更深层面的含义(sod)。如《创世记》第 1 章第 1 节中带有定冠词的"天"(the Heavens)所指仅为那些可见的"天"或"月球下(sublunar)的天",因为这才是为人类而造的。埃兹拉这一方法打破了寓意解经的限制,比他的《圣经》诠释在更大程度上影响了斯宾诺沙的圣经批评法。[①]

在神六日创世叙事与世界历史时代对应这类论述中,奥古斯丁使类比的重要性从未知的世界时间转向可知的历史结构。到 12 世纪,最终借着希亚,这一转向也进入了犹太文献。[②] 融通性原则和预表法遂成为中世纪犹太—基督教的共同特征。虽然历史的预表法解释在犹太教中不比在基督教中丰富多彩且占据主流,但中世纪塞法迪犹太人接触到众多基督教预表法诠释作品并时加效仿。其中尤为值得一提的人物是纳曼尼德。

纳曼尼德是最先将哲学寓意解释整个地嵌入《圣经》普通含义的释经家。[③] 他相信《托拉》的事件和人物(非词语本身)都属于历史哲学象征,它们预示甚至预定了以色列未来的遭遇,并把这一思想贯彻到一切事物中。[④] 以扫预表罗马帝国的万民而非失去法定长子继承权的犹太人。雅各自保的策略(《创世记》32:8)预示了以色列在大离散中的命运:"雅各心想只要有一队能保存下来,他的子孙就不会都落入以扫之手。这也暗示了以扫的子孙将来也无法将我们的名抹除,而只能在一些国家逼迫我们当中的一部分……《大创世记》有言,'如果以扫灭掉一队',南面还会留有我们的兄弟,'这样,另一队就得以保存'。这些就是我们在离散中的兄弟。"正如此例所示,在纳曼尼德的预表法释经中,许多典故都出于米德拉什,但他显然是要对这些典故加以引申,且纳曼尼德的解释常有意无意地针对基督教的说法。[⑤] "无论三位先祖中的哪一位先知经历了什么,这都是在他子孙身上注定的。神的每一项决定,无论在哪儿从潜在的法令变为预表性的

① A. Funkenstein, *Perceptions of Jewish History*, 89-93.

② A. Funkenstein, *Perceptions of Jewish History*, 103。

③ A. Funkenstein, *Perceptions of Jewish History*, 105。纳曼尼德在四个层面进行《圣经》诠释,即所谓的"字面层、说教层、寓意层、神秘层"(*peshat*, *remez*, *derash*, *sod*)。索伦认为纳曼尼德显然受到基督教《圣经》解读的影响。G.Scholem, *Major Trends in Jewish Mysticism* (New York: Jewish Institute of Religion, 1941), 400, n.15.

④ A. Funkenstein, *Perceptions of Jewish History*, 110, 114. 方肯斯坦称之为"实践性象征主义"(praxis-symbolism)。

⑤ A. Funkenstein, *Perceptions of Jewish History*, 111。

实际,都将得以成全。”[①]

虽然在犹太教传统中,也是纳曼尼德首次意识到在预表化过程中可获得具体启示,但他并没有走很远,而是止步于族长的故事。其原因,据方肯斯坦分析,一是避免将基督教预表法普遍化。二是他没有完全将焦点从世界末日转向符号阐释的结构性意涵。犹太人从来没有必要证明两个或以上启示在多样性中的辩证统一。而纵观基督教预表法的历史,两约和合(concordia veteris ac novi testamenti)一直是主要的方法论范式。三是他和同代人的思辨主要集中在神的智慧而非历史智慧问题上。[②] 四是在基督教释经方式中,越是成熟的就越倾向于实践的而不是逻各斯的象征。而在犹太释经方式中,“道德义”(derash)和喀巴拉一样,与作为至高无上象征的《圣经》语言、文字甚至发音紧密相连。正如这在基督教世界没有真正的市场一样,预表法在犹太教世界也同样如此。五是包括预表法在内的基督教所有形式的历史推测都表达了在历史中有一种明显的稳步前进感;而犹太人没有类似感觉,因而也就没想要显示事情会往更高层次发生周期性重复。犹太人从未改变,他们总是带着相同的启示。[③]

四

尽管有前述不同类型的历史书写方式,但付诸印刷的屈指可数。[④] 中世纪犹太人秉持任何变化只有经过礼仪才能真正有机会得以长久保存的传统理念,因而宗教仪规和敬拜仪式依然是他们的重要记忆渠道。[⑤] 犹太人的这类“纪念性仪规具有某种不可思议的执重和无动于衷的特点,他们借此产生了自身的独

---

① Nachmanides, *Perush hatora*, ed. C. D. Chavel (Jerusalem: Mossad Harav Kook, 1960), Vol. Ⅰ, 77 to Gn.12:6.

② A. Funkenstein, *Perceptions of Jewish History*, 117-118. 即便早期的喀巴拉著作沉迷于历史思辨,它们也更多地脱离《圣经》的内容而攀附《圣经》的形式,即字母和专有名词的象征。A. Funkenstein, *Perceptions of Jewish History*, 118。

③ A. Funkenstein, *Perceptions of Jewish History*, 119-120。最早带有前进意味的犹太历史推测或许直到鲁里亚喀巴拉(the Lurianic kabbalah)时期才出现。前述迈蒙尼德在《致也门书信》中展示的历史图景,即世界时而是渐进的、时而是戏剧性的一神信仰化过程算是个例外。基督教通过历史和在历史中的得胜来证明自己。在自我理解中,其意义仍在展开。传统犹太教完全没有这样的自我认知。在科洛赫玛(Nachman Krochmal,1785—1840 年)之前,没有哪位犹太思想家能把犹太历史想象成一个隐藏内容的展开。A. Funkenstein, *Perceptions of Jewish History*, 120-121, 126.

④ 有几个例外如 *Seder'Olam Rabba*、*Seder'Olam Zuta*、*Iggeret R. Sherira*、*Sefer Ha-Qabbalah*、*Yosippon*。

⑤ Yerushalmi, *Zakhor: Jewish History and Jewish Memory*, 40.

特历史认知"[①]。然而,彻底探寻中世纪犹太人的记忆库,答案不仅在可以激发和规范我们集体记忆的现有形式之中,而且还在动态过程本身之中。非书写类记忆渠道如历史性节期和禁食以及相关的读经等活动,很好地体现了历史和仪式时间以及线性和循环的融合。虽然圣经时代的历史事件是一次性的、不会重复的,但它们可在心理上循环往复或至少是暂时地被体验。如安息日本源于创世和出埃及事件,后来却成为一个超越历史时间界限的日子,且最终成为每周对时间终末和对弥赛亚时代那种静止状态(messianic stasis)的期盼。"圣日、仪式和仪轨等都像音符一般,本身是无法传递实况演奏的微妙和神韵的。"[②]下文从逾越节、又一次普珥节(second Purims)和禁食日加以考察。

纪念性仪式仪规释放的记忆不是智识活动,而是再现和认同行为。那些突然从过去提取的不是需要考证的事实,而是一些能使人产生移情的状态。比如在逾越节晚餐,哈加大的仪式性诵读象征性地再现了一个"为奴之家—施救—最终得救"过程的历史剧。当无酵饼(matzah)在会众面前被举起,同时宣告:"这是我们祖先在埃及地吃的受苦之食(ha laḥma'anya)。"语言和手势激起的是结合过去与现在的记忆。这种记忆此时不再是仍有距离感的回忆往事,而是"再现实化"(reactualization)。[③] 逾越节哈加大旨在"使每一代的每一个人都感到他亲身经历着出埃及事件"[④]。

除了与第二圣殿被毁以及之前事件相连的古老记忆,另一个大的过往层面是由《塔木德》和《米德拉什》文献添加的,如拉比的生平故事。在这一层面,历史与传说的界限模糊。到了中世纪,犹太人承载这类记忆特有的渠道首先是大量对于灾难性历史事件的"悔罪祷告"(seliḥot)。其次是在阿什肯犹太人中很有市场的"记忆之书"(Memorbücher)。上面不仅印有著名拉比和领袖们的名字,还记录了供人们在会堂中定期大声诵读的犹太受害者和殉道者名单。[⑤]再次是在各地犹太社区被指定下来的、纪念本民族某次化险为夷经历的"又一次普珥节"。这类"普珥节"都是以《圣经》中的普珥节为原型、用来叙述事件的"书卷"

---

① G. Scholem, "Tradition and Creation in the Ritual of the Kabbalists," in G. Scholem, *On the Kabbalah and Its Symbolism* (New York: 1965), 121.

② G. Scholem, "Tradition and Creation in the Ritual of the Kabbalists," 42-43.

③ G. Scholem, "Tradition and Creation in the Ritual of the Kabbalists," 44.

④ *The Mishnah*, ed. and trans. H. Danby (Oxford: Oxford University Press, 1950), Pesahim 10:5.

⑤ G. Scholem, "Tradition and Creation in the Ritual of the Kabbalists," 45.祷告的诗歌形式本身在字面上并不拘泥于具体细节,对作者而言,读者理应了解相关"事实"。如今已难以确定某些"悔罪祷告"具体指哪些事件。大部分"记忆之书"的内容只限于当地社区的过去。著名的纽伦堡"记忆之书"的创作时间从 1296 年一直到 1392 年,当中的一段殉道史总结了从 1096 年第一次十字军东征到 1349 年黑死病英、德两地犹太人遭受的迫害。G. Scholem, "Tradition and Creation in the Ritual of the Kabbalists," 45-46.

(megillah),也都有意在风格、结构乃至语言上模仿《以斯帖记》。[①]例如,1524 年埃及统治者沙伊坦(Ahmed Shaitan)反叛土耳其苏丹苏莱曼一世,不但对开罗犹太人进行经济勒索还扬言要灭绝他们,最终却是他被苏丹的军队击败并斩首。因此产生了每年亚达月二十八日的埃及普珥节和被公开宣读的《埃及书卷》(*Megillat Mizrayim*)。其开篇是这样写的:"苏莱曼作王,从土耳其、黎凡特直到希腊,统管许多其他省,苏莱曼王在君士坦丁堡大城登基。"任何熟悉《以斯帖记》开篇的人都能一眼识别其中的刻意模仿。[②]

中世纪犹太社区还指定特别的禁食日,并诵读"悔罪祷告",使人牢记那些犹太人未能脱险的悲惨经历。如 1171 年 5 月发生在法国布卢瓦镇的屠犹事件中,有 32 位犹太教在火刑柱上殉道。当时犹太教的最高权威塔姆拉比(Jacob Tam,也称 Rabbenu Tam)规定将殉难日,即西湾(sivan)月第二十日,定为永久禁食日。在其后的几百年里,这一规定被广为接受和遵行。[③]

最后需要提醒,在本文涉及范围之外的中世纪犹太人主流文献,如《圣经》和律法诠释中,并非没有对历史与时俱进的思考。例如,加泰罗尼亚地区的格松尼德(Levi ben Gerson, Ralbag, 1288—1344 年)的《圣经》注释充实了占星术与集体命运或历史相关这样的简单又抽象的说法。一方面,格松尼德不仅只在月下世界认识偶然性领域,而且还把掌握着月下世界集体和个人命运的天文星座看作必然性的一个来源。[④] 另一方面,他把神的知识局限于普遍性(必然性)。人类面对世界,要么通过星座的知识,要么通过恪守正确的信仰和神圣的戒律。[⑤] 失去神的特殊眷顾,就等于任凭自然的必然性和偶然性摆布。[⑥] 在《出埃及记》第 17 章第 9 节的故事中,以色列只有通过对神的力量和大能信靠才可稳操胜券,因此摩西让约书亚具体指挥作战而自己站在全体以色列人能看到的高处做出必胜的标志,巩固以色列的信念。其道理是,神只帮助那些通过信靠神以自助的人。正是以色列对神的呼喊才使他们在"大限之前"(lifney heyot hazeman harauy),即在占星术可以推算的时间之前,摆脱了埃及的枷锁。这就是格松尼德对于格言"对以色列的眷顾"(eyn mazal leyisra'el)的理解,神的眷顾代表以

---

① G. Scholem, "Tradition and Creation in the Ritual of the Kabbalists," 46-47.

② 译本参见:G. Margoliouth, ed. "Megillat Miṣṣraim, or the Scroll of the Egyptian Purim," *Jewish Quarterly Review* (o.s.), 8(1896): 274-288。

③ Yerushalmi, *Zakhor*: *Jewish History and Jewish Memory*, 48-49.

④ A. Funkenstein, *Perceptions of Jewish History*, 126-127; Gersonides, *Milchamot*, Ⅱ, 6, 104-108.

⑤ Gersonides, *Commentary*, f.56b (*dvekut Moshe*) and f.71a.

⑥ 格松尼德谈自由意志对天体的干扰可参见其 *Milchamot Ha-Shem*, Ⅱ, 6, 111。他特别指出,从星座的征兆看,亚玛力人本可战胜以色列——倘若后者没有神的帮助(《出埃及记》17:9)。

色列可免于那些辖制万民的自然法。同时,这与自由意志并不矛盾:神甚至不知道当下和未来的偶发事件——正因为人有自由意志。人类的自由意志是唯一外在于一般星体法则和影响的。[①]

至此,一方面,中世纪犹太人对后塔木德时代事件的记忆至多是部分的和不规则的,有很强的选择性,因而没有在意更多的内容。他们的历史观往往从宏观意义上审视发生的事情,一代人甚至一个世纪的时段都可能无关紧要,因为演进的基本路径早已由古代以色列先知阐明了。若要理解当下,思索《圣经》话语比纠结于当下的经验有用得多。《圣经》和传统依然是人们理解历史的主要指南,因为它们本身就是历史演进的重要展现。[②] 12—15 世纪的一些历史著作基本遵循这一思维模式。[③] 另一方面,中世纪见证了针对宗教传统内部而非神圣领域展开的世俗化。在这一运动中,融通性原则在世俗与神圣之间架起了一座桥梁,帮助构建了理性的诠释和历史书写。[④] 这些历史书写和认知活动通过《托拉》,如对其中的《但以理书》的诠释和占星术等手段分析当代灾难性事件,特别是基督教和伊斯兰教之间的冲突,以及犹太人遭遇的至暗时刻,构建以色列即将得拯救的理论。这种世俗化运动和末日拯救理论构建在 12 世纪及之后的时期得到集中体现、历史书写和认知活跃,并与犹太人沿袭和发展的宗教仪轨和节期等其他记忆渠道发生深度和持续的融合,从而使犹太社群在艰难和挑战中走出中世纪。

---

① A. Funkenstein, *Perceptions of Jewish History*, 126-129; Gersonides, *Commentary*, f.54b.

② S. Baron, *A Social and Religious History of the Jews*, 2nd ed. (New York: Columbia University Press, 1974), Ⅵ, 234.

③ L. Kochan, *The Jew and His History*, 22.

④ A. Funkenstein, *Perceptions of Jewish History*, 97-98.

Historiography and Historical Memory of Medieval Jews

CAO Jian

Abstract: Based on historical documents and Jewish scholars' textual researches, this paper attempts to demonstrate how Medieval Jews understood and recorded their own as well as world history, thus arguing for unconventional but continuous and contextualized historiographic activities that should not be belittled from the time of Josephus up to the sixteenth century. That very fact about Medieval Jews offers a natural and inherent reason for the abundant modern Jewish historiography that suddenly appeared after the sixteenth century and even the historical criticism of the Holy Scriptures that Spinoza proposed shortly after. Besides historiography, other channels of historical memory among Medieval Jews are also covered, which prove equally if not more important to their historical consciousness and national identity.

Key Words: Medieval Jews, Historiography, History, Memory

B

思想、历史与社会

从犹太祭司到罗马史学家：论约瑟夫斯的神本史观*

何立波**

【摘要】约瑟夫斯是公元1世纪的犹太祭司，参加过犹太人大起义，归顺罗马人并获得罗马公民权，成为罗马史学家。他的《犹太战记》和《犹太古代史》成为关于公元1世纪犹太战争和早期犹太人最重要的史料之一。约瑟夫斯的著作总体来说做到了求真，他参考了《圣经》等宗教文献，其对早期犹太教的报道，对耶稣、彼拉多、雅各等基督教人物的记载等，提供了关于新约时代最重要的背景资料，成为新约时代的关键史料。约瑟夫斯的著作具有明显的致用特色，他把犹太人介绍给希腊罗马世界，也积极为罗马统治辩护。约瑟夫斯是第一位提出神本史观的罗马史学家，构建了犹太人的创世神话，这成为罗马时代第一个神本宣言，构建了一种线性时间观和历史发展观的雏形，为罗马历史书写提供了一种新的范式，成为基督教史学的源头。

【关键词】约瑟夫斯；祭司；新约；神本史观

在犹太史和古代基督教史上，约瑟夫斯都是一个无法忽略的名字。他是罗马帝国早期著名犹太史学家，其代表著作《犹太战记》(*The Jewish War*)和《犹太古代史》(*Jewish Antiguities*)以及两部文稿《驳阿皮翁》(*Against Apion*)和《自传》(*The Life*)，提供了一扇了解古代犹太人世界的窗口，具有重要的史学价值，在罗马史学史和犹太史学史乃至基督教史学中都具有特别重要的意义。本

* 本文是2021年广东哲学社会科学规划一般项目"罗马人王权意识演变与晚期罗马'多米那特'制形成研究"(GD21CWL01)和2016年国家社科基金一般项目"罗马帝国元首制研究"(16BSS011)的研究成果。

** 何立波，北京师范大学人文和社会科学高等研究院史学研究中心副教授。

文在前人研究[①]基础上，探讨约瑟夫斯的神本史观和宗教写作，抛砖引玉，以求教于方家。

① 约瑟夫斯研究大致始于20世纪20—30年代。从1927年起，约瑟夫斯著作的洛布（Loeb）版读本相继出版，为学者提供了文本。主持洛布本翻译工作的H.St.J.萨克雷（H. St. J. Thackeray），在译本导读中对约瑟夫斯进行了系统介绍和评析，更于1930年结集出版了其系列讲座的讲稿，但对约瑟夫斯生平的介绍并不多。目前看到最早研究约瑟夫斯的学者是理查德·拉克尔（Richard Laqueur），他在1920年出版的《犹太历史学家约瑟夫斯》（Richard Laqueur, *Der Jüdischer Historiker Flavius Josephus*, Giesen, 1920）中认为，约瑟夫斯应对犹太人毁灭负责，《犹太战记》本质上是罗马人的政治宣传。萨克雷在1929年出版的《约瑟夫斯：人和历史学家》（H.St.J, Thackeray, *Josephus: The Man and the Historian*, New York: Jewish Institute of Religion Press, 1929）一书中不赞成拉克尔的"黑色肖像"，认为约瑟夫斯用尽余生为犹太教辩护，赢得了爱国者的欢呼。在研究约瑟夫斯的学者中，威廉·法梅尔（William Reuben Farmer）在1956年出版的《马加比、狂热者与约瑟夫斯》（William Reuben Farmer, *Maccabees, Zealots, and Josephus*, New York: Columbia University Press, 1956）中认为，约瑟夫斯既要恭维讨好罗马弗拉维王朝同时又须维护犹太民族的双重目的，造成了其作品中的矛盾。到了20世纪80年代初期，学者科恩探讨了约瑟夫斯作品中的史学写作技巧，认为他可能在犹太战争之初即着手搜集资料，认为其创作《犹太战记》并非是为了背叛犹太人而恭维弗拉维王朝，而是为了表明其对自己犹太身份的清醒认识并笃定能够对自己亲历的犹太战争有客观而翔实的记述（Steve Mason, *Flavius Josephus on the Pharisees*, Leiden: Brill, 1997）。费尔德曼（Louis Feldman）提出，约瑟夫斯深受希腊文化的影响，在其创作中运用了大量希腊文化元素，同时重视犹太传统并将其与希腊文化相契合（Louis Feldman, *Josephus's Interpretation the Bible*, Berkeley: University of California Press, 1998）。S.J.D.克亨（S.J.D.Cohen）提出，约瑟夫斯既是一位罗马辩护者，也是一位犹太民主主义者（S.J.D.Cohen, *Josephus in Galilee and Rome*, Leiden: Brill Academic Publishers, 2002）。此外，泰萨·瑞洁克关注了罗马人与犹太人冲突中的宗教因素（泰萨·瑞洁克：《史学家约瑟夫斯及其世界》，周平译，商务印书馆，2014），约翰·萨克雷对约瑟夫斯与犹太教和基督教的关系进行了分析，强调其辩护家的身份超过了神学家（约翰·萨克雷：《约瑟夫斯评传》，陆路译，大象出版社，2019）。泰莎·拉雅克（Tessa Rajik）认为，现代学术研究证明了约瑟夫斯在犹太历史学家中的地位，他堪称罗马最伟大的希腊历史学家之一（Tessa Rajik, *Josephus: The Historian and Society*, London: Duckworth, 2002）。苏厄德叙对约瑟夫斯《犹太战记》进行了述评，其中涉及一些宗教因素（苏厄德叙：《约瑟夫斯与第一次犹太战争》，杨迎译，民主与建设出版社，2020）。唐纳德·R.凯利考察了约瑟夫斯为犹太人辩护的三重性（唐纳德·R.凯利：《多面的历史：从希罗多德到赫尔德的历史探询》，陈恒等译，生活·读书·新知三联书店，2006）。恩斯特·布赖萨德关注约瑟夫斯准世界史视野和神学史观（恩斯特·布赖萨德：《西方史学史》，黄艳红译，北京大学出版社，2019）。斯狄维·马逊（Steve Mason）关注了考古学对约瑟夫斯报道的证实（Steve Mason, *Josephus, Judea and Christian Origins: Methods and Categories*, Peabody, MA Hendrickson Publishers, 2009）。马德（Gottfried Mader）认为，综观《犹太战记》，约瑟夫斯未能恪守修昔底德的史学传统，其作品的主观性超过了他声称秉持的史学家的客观性（Gottfried Mader, *Josephus and the Politics of Historiography*, New York: Brill, 2000）。在中国学者中，约瑟夫斯也得到关注。吴晓群对约瑟夫斯进行了初步探讨，认为神意史观是约瑟夫斯历史书写的显著特征（吴晓群：《西方史学通史·古代时期》，复旦大学出版社，2011）。郭小凌认为约瑟夫斯神学史观是对古典史学历史观的突破和否定（郭小凌：《西方史学史》，北京师范大学出版社，2016）。吕厚量分析了约瑟夫斯的民族观及其形成背景，以及弗拉维王朝时期犹太问题的复杂性（吕厚量：《上帝选民与帝国子民间的两难抉择》，陈恒、洪庆明主编《叙述事实与历史事实（世界历史评论）》，上海人民出版社，2015）。就研究成果而言，对其神本史观和宗教写作的探讨还远远不够，有进一步研究的必要。

一、从犹太祭司到罗马史学家的身份转变

(一)作为犹太祭司的约瑟夫斯

约瑟夫斯·本·马提亚(Josephus Ben Matthias),生活在公元37—100年,出身犹太祭司家庭,是祭司马提亚的儿子。马提亚是犹太著名大祭司约书亚·本·迦马拉的密友,后来成为约瑟夫斯的盟友。[①] 他的母亲有犹太王族血统,享有“高贵的血统和长久以来显赫的家庭”[②]。约瑟夫斯很自豪地说:“我,马提亚的儿子约瑟夫斯,是耶路撒冷的一位祭司,曾在战争初期与罗马军队作战,后来并非情愿地见证了战争末期发生的事情。”[③]约瑟夫斯学识渊博,14岁时就与大祭司讨论犹太律法问题。他在《自传》中说:“14岁时,我就因为热爱知识而受到人们普遍的称赞,以至于为首的祭司和城里的领袖经常到我这里来询问一些有关我们律法细节的确切信息。”[④]约瑟夫斯《自传》中的这一段话反映出他的自负气质,这是当今人们难以忍受的,但是这在他之前的西塞罗和之后的文艺复兴人物身上都不鲜见。[⑤] 两年后,约瑟夫斯开始学习最主要的犹太教派——法利赛、撒都该和艾赛尼派。他一开始最喜欢艾赛尼派,在旷野中生活了三年,给一个名叫班努(Bannus)的隐士做门徒。约瑟夫斯19岁回到耶路撒冷,放弃苦修,加入了法利赛派。法利赛派在学说方面类似希腊斯多葛学派,主张彼此友爱,被认为是律法最有权威的解释者,将所有事情都归于命运或者主。[⑥] 他们认为罗马人的行为方式不干净,拒绝进入罗马人的建筑,宣称自己是唯一能解释律法的人。当时,法利赛教派成员属于犹太的精英阶层,包含许多王族及其追随者、祭司、地方市议会成员、大地主等,他们对犹太贵族与罗马统治之间的政治调和以及由此带来的利益相当关注,在政治上采取不抵抗主义,对罗马表示妥协,重律法胜于重圣殿。

---

① 斯德蒙德·苏厄德 Desmond Seward,《约瑟夫斯与第一次犹太战争》[Jerusalem' Traitor: Josephus, Masada, and the Fall of Judea],杨迎 Yang Ying 译(北京[Beijing]:民主与建设出版社[Democracy and Construction Press],2020),3。

② Josephus, *The Jewish War*, trans. Louis H. Feldman (Cambridge Mass: Harvard University Press, 1927), Ⅲ, 352. 本文使用的古希腊罗马史学家的古典著作,引自“洛布(loeb)古典丛书”(简称 LCL).

③ Josephus, *The Jewish War*, Ⅰ,3.

④ Josephus, *The Life*, trans. Louis H. Feldman (London: W. Heinemann; New York: G. P. Putnam's Sons, 1926, LCL), 9.

⑤ 保罗·梅尔 Paul Maier 编译,《约瑟夫著作精选》[A Selection of Joseph's Books],王志勇 Wang Zhiyong 译(北京[Beijing]:北京大学出版社[The Press of Peking University],2004),序言[preface],2.

⑥ Josephus, *The Life*, 11-12.

公元 64 年是约瑟夫斯与罗马关系史上的重要一年，他首次来到罗马，接触到了罗马皇室成员，对罗马统治阶层有了新的认识。他此行是为几位犹太祭司向罗马求情，他们是被犹太总督滕力斯送到尼禄那里去受审的。[①] 在罗马，犹太演员阿里图鲁斯把他介绍给尼禄的皇后波培娅（Poppaea）。罗马史学家塔西佗曾称波培娅是罗马最漂亮的女人，出身高贵，聪明有趣，但是生活淫乱，"除了品行之外拥有一切有利条件"[②]。约瑟夫斯称："波培娅，尼禄的妻子，是一位虔诚的女性……"[③]约瑟夫斯在《自传》中写道："我积极开展营救，设法获得波培娅的帮助，以求释放我们的祭司。"[④]波培娅可能是犹太教徒，接受了洗礼，任用犹太人作为随从，约瑟夫斯说她是"敬拜神的人"[⑤]。塔西佗曾记载波培娅无论作为情妇还是妻子，都控制了尼禄。[⑥] 波培娅很喜欢雄辩聪明的年轻犹太贵族约瑟夫斯，她通过尼禄，不但释放了犹太祭司，还送给他珍贵的礼物。针对古典作家对尼禄残害兄弟、弑父杀妻的描写，对尼禄充满感激之情的约瑟夫斯积极为其辩护："这些人用谎言描写尼禄的为人……对于不尊重事实的人来说，他们可以随心所欲地写作。"[⑦]

约瑟夫斯在罗马停留了两年到两年半的时间，这段经历对他此后亲罗马的立场和成为罗马人产生了重大影响。公元 64 年 7 月 18 日罗马城大火，约瑟夫斯目睹了这一事件。在这次罗马之行中，罗马城的繁华和权势给约瑟夫斯留下了深刻印象，这是他亲罗马倾向的开端。在旅居罗马期间，约瑟夫斯开始阅读希腊作家的作品，成为一名对希腊文学作品有浓厚兴趣的散居犹太人。他不仅阅读过荷马的作品，还涉猎过希罗多德、修昔底德、色诺芬、索福克勒斯、欧里庇得斯、德摩斯梯尼、伊壁鸠鲁等古希腊作家的著作，这奠定了他成为一名史学家的基础。而对罗马皇宫的访问，使得约瑟夫斯对罗马政治和如何对付罗马统治阶层有了直观了解。

（二）从犹太战俘到罗马人

在罗马犹太总督弗洛鲁斯的统治下，有暴动嫌疑的犹太人被处决，极端反抗

---

① Josephus, *The Life*, 13.

② Tacitus, *The Annals*, trans. Clifford H.Jackson (Cambridge Mass: Harvard University Press, 1931, LCL), XIII, 45-46.

③ Josephus, *Jewish Antiguities*, trans. Louis H. Feldman (Cambridge Mass: Harvard University Press, 1965, LCL), XX, 195.

④ Josephus, *The Life*, 16.

⑤ Josephus, *Jewish Antiguities*, XX, 195.

⑥ Tacitus, *The Annals*, XIV, 60.

⑦ Josephus, *Jewish Antiguities*, XX, 154-156.

组织“奋锐党”诉诸暴力。西卡里人(短刀党人)对罗马人实行白色恐怖且对不愿参加战斗的、温和的犹太居民的代表施加压力,导致了公元 66 年的犹太人起义,爆发了犹太战争。约瑟夫斯把弗洛鲁斯描绘得可恶至极,与他相比他的前任甚至都可以算作犹太民族的恩人。他慨叹道:“战火越烧越旺,直到最终演变为全面战争。”[①]犹太战争是犹太人历史上具有深远影响的重大劫难之一,战争中象征神权和王权的圣殿被毁,促使“上帝的选民”重新审视他们与上帝的关系,反思民族苦难在神学上的意义。

公元 66 年 9 月,约瑟夫斯写道:“我惊奇地发现革命运动在暗流涌动,许多人都在兴奋地盘算着反叛罗马。我试图抑制这种叛乱,劝说他们再深思熟虑一番”,“但是我的努力是徒劳的,因为这群亡命之徒已经彻底发狂了”。[②] 约瑟夫斯不认为发起叛乱的奋锐党人是爱国者。公元 66 年爆发的叛乱烧毁了犹太官方的档案记录,这是“为了销毁出借人的借款合同和阻止债务的重新偿还,也为了获得众多债务人的感激,使穷人毫无顾忌地反抗富人”[③]。他无力阻止愤怒的同胞,不得不加入了起义队伍,担任加利利城指挥官。基督教史学家保罗·奥罗西乌斯提到约瑟夫斯是犹太战争领导人。[④] 当罗马军队到来时,他训练部下,补充供给,加固城防。当罗马统帅苇伯芗的大军征服加利利城后,约瑟夫斯就以约他帕为据点固守。公元 67 年,在 47 天的围困之后,约他帕失守,约瑟夫斯等被迫藏身在一个山洞里。除约瑟夫斯和另一位幸存者之外,别的犹太人相继被杀。他们二人从山洞里出来投降。在记叙这段经历时,约瑟夫斯在《犹太战记》中为自己投降寻找到了宗教原因。“约瑟夫斯突然回想起来这些天夜里所做的梦,在梦中上帝向他预言了犹太人和罗马人的命运。他就默祷:‘既然你已经拣选我来宣告将要发生的事情,我愿意活下去。但我呼求你为我作证,我出去不是作为一个叛徒,而是作为你的仆人。’”[⑤]

约瑟夫斯被带到苇伯芗面前,他原本可能会受到刑罚,但他预言苇伯芗将成为元首:“你,苇伯芗,将成为恺撒,成为元首——你和你在这里的儿子。因为你不只是我的征服者,而且是大海和陆地的征服者,是整个人类的征服者。”[⑥]公元 69 年 7 月,苇伯芗被军队拥立为元首,同年 12 月进入罗马城,建立了罗马帝国

① Josephus, *The Jewish War*, Ⅱ, 265.

② Josephus, *The Life*, 17-19.

③ Josephus, *The Jewish War*, Ⅱ, 427.

④ Paulus Orosius, *The Seven Books of History Against the Pagans*, trans. A. T. Fear (New York: Columbria University Press, 1936), Ⅶ, 9.

⑤ Josephus, *The Jewish War*, Ⅲ, 340.

⑥ Josephus, *The Jewish War*, Ⅲ, 399.

历史上的第二个王朝——弗拉维王朝。保罗·奥罗西乌斯记载了苇伯芗称帝和约瑟夫斯预言的关系:“听到尼禄死讯后,他宣布自己为元首。无数国王和将军强烈敦促他称帝,但其中最主要是受约瑟夫斯——犹太领导人的话的影响。”[①] 苇伯芗想起约瑟夫斯还是他的阶下囚,于是下令释放他。提图斯建议砍断铁链,而不是打开铁链。这是对待蒙冤入狱之人的风俗,苇伯芗同意了。[②] 约瑟夫斯预言故事的成功,既说明了苇伯芗所谓的“天命所归”,也为约瑟夫斯投降罗马人找到了一个合理解释。公元 70 年,约瑟夫斯完成了从犹太祭司到罗马人的身份转变。这一年,苇伯芗长子提图斯率军围攻耶路撒冷,约瑟夫斯充当罗马人与犹太人的联系人。[③] 他作为罗马人的斡旋者和翻译,呼吁犹太同胞放下武器,拯救他们的城市和圣殿,不要继续对抗军事上明显占优势的罗马人。提图斯将他带到罗马,让他专事写作。苇伯芗破例授予他罗马公民权,赐其皇姓“弗拉维乌斯”,享受政府年俸,并在犹太省赏赐给他一块封地。[④] 约瑟夫斯所做的这些努力,以及他在约他帕投降罗马人的背景,使得很多犹太同胞骂他是懦夫和叛徒。约在公元 100 年,约瑟夫斯在罗马病死,著作被收藏到公共图书馆,基督教徒为他为树立了塑像。[⑤]

约瑟夫斯虽然成了罗马人,但这并未将他和罗马城的其他犹太人割裂开来。[⑥] 他始终保持着对于犹太文化的热爱和认同。他一直以犹太人自居,在《犹太战记》前言中自称“希伯来大祭司”和“土生土长的耶路撒冷人”,一个在罗马生活的“外邦人”[⑦],将犹太战争称作“我们犹太人与罗马人之间的战争”[⑧]。在《自传》中,他在一开始就向读者强调其家族在犹太社会的显赫地位,仅在文末提及自己获得罗马公民权。在《驳阿皮翁》中,约瑟夫斯毫不讳言犹太民族已经“像埃及人那样受到了罗马人的奴役”[⑨]。

---

① Paulus Orosius, *The Seven Books of History Against the Pagans*, Ⅶ, 9.

② Paulus Orosius, *The Seven Books of History Against the Pagans*, Ⅳ, 585.

③ Paulus Orosius, *The Seven Books of History Against the Pagans*, Ⅴ, 325.

④ Suetonius, *The Lives of the Caesars, the Deified Vespasian*, trans. T. C. Rolfe (London: W. Heinemann; New York: The Macmillan Company, 1926, LCL), XVII, 4.

⑤ Eusebius, *The Ecclesiastical History*, trans. Socrates Scholasticus (Cambridge Mass: Harvard University Press, 1964, LCL), Ⅲ, 9.

⑥ William Den Hollander, *Josephus, the Emperors and the City of Rome: From Hostage to Historian* (Leiden: Brill Academic Publishers, 2014), 126.

⑦ Josephus, *The Jewish War*, Ⅰ, 2-16.

⑧ Josephus, *Jewish Antiguities*, Ⅰ, 4.

⑨ Josephus, *Against Apion*, trans. Louis H. Feldman (London: W. Heinemann; New York: G. P.Putnam's Sons, 1926, LCL), Ⅱ, 125.

(三)约瑟夫斯对犹太史学传统和希腊史学的继承

约瑟夫斯告诉我们,在犹太人中,历史书写被视为只有先知和祭司才能从事的神圣事业,因而他对自己的犹太祭司身份引以为傲,对犹太史学充满了自豪。他曾嘲笑希腊罗马史学的"稚嫩",认为其无法与有悠久历史的犹太史学相媲美。他认为,在古希腊和罗马,撰史并非一项多么高尚的工作,史家在宫廷中的地位并不高,实际上与优伶无异。[①] 他在《驳阿皮翁》中指出,希腊罗马缺乏撰史的传统且不重视保存原始档案文献,造成希腊史家文风浮夸、记载多有错误和矛盾之处,由此断言希腊历史不可信。[②]

约瑟夫斯对犹太史学的自豪不是没有根据的。犹太史学是一部真正有关全人类的普遍的历史(普世史),它一直追溯到人类的起源,描述人类的不同种族是怎样出现并在大地上繁衍及分散于各个地区的。之后,上帝眷顾犹太人,在众多民族中唯独拣选了他们作为其子民。早在大卫王和所罗门统治时期,国家的繁荣昌盛就激发了古代以色列人强烈的爱国情怀,也激励早期的史家们要为犹太人写作。许多西方学者普遍认为,对于犹太民族来说,真正意义上的历史写作始于这一时期。因此,公元前 11 世纪末到公元前 8 世纪下半叶,被学者们视为犹太史学的真正开端,出现了《摩西五经》的雏形,《以色列诸王记》《犹太列王记》等第一批散篇史传和文集诞生。这一时期的作品尚未受到犹太祭司的加工,有较高的史料价值。从公元前 8 世纪末到公元前 6 世纪中期,犹太历史上出现了一场历时长久、影响深远的宗教改革,史称"申命运动",出现了一批按照新的宗教观念书写历史的"申命派史家"。他们将《约书亚记》《士师记》《撒母耳记》和《列王纪》编订完成,将所有材料按年代顺序重新排列,并做了重要加工,清除了"世俗之气",突出上帝和犹太民族的关系,使犹太历史写作从简单的材料收集、大事年表或宗族谱系制作进入更为自觉的历史书写。西方有学者认为写作《申命记》的作者及希伯来《圣经》最初六卷的作者都是真正的历史学家,也是最早为西方文明所了解的犹太历史学家。[③]在"巴比伦之囚"后,犹太人逐渐形成了以祭司为核心的神权国家,祭司史家实现了《摩西五经》的最后定型,编订了《历代志》《以斯拉—尼希米记》。祭司史家秉承神学史观,并进一步借助历史事件进行宗教说

① Zvi Yaveta, "Reflctions on Titus and Josephus," *Greek, Roman and Byzantine Studies*, 16 (1975):432.

② Josephus, *Against Apion*, Ⅰ,15-27.

③ 吴晓群 Wu Xiaoqun,《西方史学通史》[General History of Western Historiography]卷二[Vol. 2],(上海[Shanghai]:复旦大学出版社[Fudan University Press],2011), 269—269;约翰·萨克雷 John Thackeray,《约瑟夫斯评传》[The Review of Josephus] ,陆路 Lu Lu 译,(郑州[Zhengzhou]:大象出版社[Elephant Press],2019),58。

教。随着希腊化时代及罗马时期的到来，犹太史学进入最后阶段。一些犹太史家仍遵循犹太《圣经》史学的传统，以希伯来语或阿拉姆语（闪族语言）写作，代表作有《马厂比传一书》《以斯得拉一书》《圣经古代史》。而另一些犹太史家接受了希腊史学，用希腊语写作，代表作有《马卡比传二书》和约瑟夫斯的《犹太战记》《犹太古代史》等。[①]

约瑟夫斯的《犹太战记》遵循修昔底德《伯罗奔尼撒战争史》的写作模式，即当代人写当代史，且将尖锐的批评或赞美都蕴藏于史实中。不同的是，他发出了自己祖国陷落的哀叹。东部地中海世界盛行的希腊文化和希伯来《圣经》传统的影响，在约瑟夫斯作品中都有体现。与修昔底德一样，约瑟夫斯严厉批评那些在民众中煽动过激情绪的犹太人，认为正是他们误导了民众，最终引发了罗马人的镇压。这很容易让人联想到修昔底德笔下雅典的毁灭。约瑟夫斯在《犹太战记》中对罗马的态度，是修昔底德式的写实主义与传统犹太思想的结合。在《犹太古代史》中，约瑟夫斯对在希腊化时代已广为人知的亚伯拉罕的形象做了“希腊化式的”描绘。为迎合希腊化的读者，约瑟夫斯还把亚伯拉罕塑造成一个富有浪漫情怀的英雄，以此来反驳阿皮翁认为犹太人毫无艺术及技艺天分的言论。对亚伯拉罕政治才能的描写，则让人联想到修昔底德对伯里克利的描述。约瑟夫斯的读者中相当一部分是希腊人和接受了希腊文化的罗马人，因此他笔下的英雄必须是希腊式英雄。当然，这些品质对于犹太人而言也是同样重要的。与修昔底德一样，约瑟夫斯著作也采用了不少演说辞，包括他直接听来的以及文献记载的。约瑟夫斯与罗马帝国初期的希腊史学家——哈里卡那纳索斯的狄奥尼修斯之间也有许多相似之处，甚至他们著作的题目——《罗马古代史》和《犹太古代史》都很相近，著作的卷数也都是20卷。约瑟夫斯和狄奥尼修斯都描写了降临到其书中主人翁身上的种种幸运之事，描写手法也十分相近，比如约瑟夫斯笔下的摩西之死，实在可与狄奥尼修斯笔下的埃涅阿斯和罗慕洛斯之死相提并论。选择的写作题材均是他们想要为之辩护的对象，无论是罗马人还是犹太人，其预设的听众或读者都是希腊人，目的都是消除希腊人对于非希腊人的偏见。他们都强调虔诚、公正、悔改以及其他美德的重要性，批判权力腐败带来的恶劣影响等。这些希腊史学模式的影响，让约瑟夫斯成为希腊—罗马时代的一位著名史学家。实际上，在公元1世纪，已经有犹太知识分子把犹太人的传统和后期希腊文化调和起来，最著名的当属与耶稣同时代的亚历山大里亚城的斐洛（Philo of Alexandria），他甚至认为《圣经》和柏拉图的著作有相同之处，只不过《圣经》使

① 吴晓群，《西方史学通史》，271。约翰·萨克雷，《约瑟夫斯评传》，58。

用的是寓言,柏拉图学园派学说的精华是从《圣经》得来的。[①] 约瑟夫斯一生大部分时间都在竭力调适犹太、希腊和罗马这三种强大的文化传统,他作为一个学者致力于实现犹太主义和希腊主义的互相影响和互动。[②]

在罗马统治时期,犹太人几乎成为罗马治下唯一拥有自己漫长的历史记录,并将其继续保持、重新解释且不断实践的民族。到了公元1世纪晚期,犹太史写作变得更有挑战性。要写作当代史,也就是有关犹太战争的背景和过程,那就不可避免地要涉及犹太人的民族情感和罗马帝国统治的调适的主体,其中必然有冲突。这在约瑟夫斯的著作中都有反映,本文也将进行重点诠释。

二、约瑟夫斯史学著作的特点:求真和致用

古希腊罗马史学的根本特征是对历史真相的追求。还原事实、恢复真相、发现原因、探求因果,是评判史学著作的首要标准。约瑟夫斯的史学著作,总体来说是符合这一特征的。

(一)求真:"真实性自始至终就是我写作的目的",为新约时代提供了关键史料

作为一名历史学家,约瑟夫斯对历史的真实性问题是有自觉意识的,在用词特别是神学方面的用词上是非常谨慎的,尽力给读者留下一种客观公正的印象。在《犹太战记》序言中,约瑟夫斯声称他撰写此书是"为了爱好真理的人,而不是为了取悦读者" 。他在《犹太战记》中声称:"我可以大胆地毫不犹豫地说,真实性自始至终是我写作的目的。"[③]"我决定尊重史实,写一部历史。""这是为那些热爱真相而不是寻求消遣的人写的。"[④]他的写作重点是当代的历史:"在希腊史学家和我们的先知止笔的地方,我开始讲述我的故事,并将所目睹的战争事件详尽描述,而对于发生在我的时代之前的事件只做简要概述。"[⑤]在结束全书的时候,约瑟夫斯再次自信地写道:"这部历史到此结束。在这部书中,我们承诺要精确叙述罗马人对犹太人的战争史是如何发动的。我的读者可以评判我行文的风格,但是就事实的真实性而言,我可以大胆地毫不犹豫地说,真实性自始至终是

---

① Erwin R. Goodenough, *An Introduction to Philo Judaeus* (New York: Barnes & Noble, 1963), 75.

② J. Edmondson, S. Mason and J. Rives, *Flavius Josephus and Flavian Rome* (Leiden: Brill Academic Publishers, 2003), 13-14.

③ Josephus, *The Jewish War*, Ⅶ, 454.

④ Josephus, *The Jewish War*, Ⅰ, 3-4.

⑤ Josephus, *The Jewish War*, Ⅰ, 1.

我写作的目的。"[①]布朗特认为,约瑟夫斯给我们呈现的是一个相对公正的视角,既批评犹太权贵对穷人的压迫,也批评穷人对权贵的暴力报复。[②]

约瑟夫斯作品的史料来源基本是可靠的。《犹太战记》是约瑟夫斯奉命而写的一部作品,出版于公元75—79年,它起初是用阿拉米亚语写成的,后译成希腊文出版。作为一名犹太人,耶路撒冷圣殿被毁让他非常心痛。随着犹太人流散各地,由于宗教习俗等原因,犹太人备受歧视,受到了很多不公平的待遇。为了让那些深受希腊文化熏陶的人认可并欣赏犹太民族的历史,约瑟夫斯在出版商和赞助人艾巴诺蒂图斯的支持下,于公元93年出版了20卷的反映犹太人早期历史的《犹太古代史》。它是希伯来《圣经》的长篇摘录与改述,加以小幅的增删,增补巴勒斯坦随后的历史,也使用了罗马元首发布的一些公文。[③]《犹太古代史》第12—20卷记述了耶稣出生和基督教形成前的历史,成为犹太史研究的唯一资料来源。约瑟夫斯对历史事件发生的时间和地点做了清楚标记,引用了大量可证实或补充《圣经》原文的权威文献,进一步增加了该书的史料价值。在《犹太古代史》中,约瑟夫斯宣称:书中描写的所有内容都是依据文献而来的,并无任何添加或减损。[④]"在《犹太古代史》中,如同我一再说明的,我仅做了经文翻译的工作而已。"[⑤]"就我而言,我在此记载的每个细节都源自经书。"[⑥]"摩西所宣布的所有律法都在此,我没有增添任何内容。"[⑦]约瑟夫斯到罗马后住在苇伯芗的宫中,能看到国家档案,包括罗马官方记录的有关耶路撒冷围城等材料。他曾提到苇伯芗的"元首纪事",记载过提图斯的"恺撒记事本",称其为权威资料。[⑧]

在约瑟夫斯完成《犹太古代史》的公元93年,《马可福音》已完成并在罗马流传,《路加福音》也开始在罗马出现。约瑟夫斯与路加之间存在大量相似的地方,最明显的相似之处有,二人都提到了罗马人口普查(《犹太古代史》第18卷第1—2节和《路加福音》第2章第1—5节)和亚比利尼的分封王(the tetrarch of Abilene)里萨尼亚(Lysanias)(《犹太古代史》第15卷第92节和《路加福音》第3

① Josephus, *The Jewish War*, Ⅶ, 454.

② 布朗特 Peter A. Brunt,《约瑟夫斯论罗马犹太人的社会冲突》[Josephus on the Social Conflict of the Roman Jews],于《金陵神学志》[The Theology of Jinling],2015 第二期[2020, Issue 2],55。

③ Josephus, *Jewish Antiguities*, ⅪV, 190.

④ Josephus, *Jewish Antiguities*, Ⅰ, 17.

⑤ Josephus, *Jewish Antiguities*, Ⅰ, 54.

⑥ Josephus, *Jewish Antiguities*, Ⅱ, 347.

⑦ Josephus, *Jewish Antiguities*, Ⅳ, 196.

⑧ Josephus, *Jewish Antiguities*, Ⅰ, 56.

章第 1 节)。[①]

《犹太古代史》对耶稣生平的记载和解释,在基督教史上具有重大意义:

> 耶稣大概在此时出现,他是一位富有智慧的人——如果他可以被称为一个人的话。因为他是一位行动惊人的实干家,是一位乐于接受事实的人类导师,他为自己争取到许多犹太人和许多希腊人。他就是基督。在对我们中间一些重要人物的控告中,当彼拉多判决对他实施十字架绞刑的时候,那些最初热爱他的人之后并没有停下来。因为在他被钉死后的第三天,他又复活并现身在他们面前,神圣的先知们在此之前已预言了这些及其他千千万万件奇妙之事。甚至到今天,那些追随他而自称为基督徒的人,也并没有灭绝。[②]

这段文字表述非常清楚,但争议不断。从公元 4 世纪的基督教史学家尤西比乌斯开始到 16 世纪,人们一度对其完全认可,但此后出现了基督教徒对其进行了篡改的声音。目前有三种观点:其一,完全可信;其二,认为完全是基督教篡改的内容;其三,认为记载中包括了基督教徒篡改的内容。第一种观点赞成者寥寥,第二种观点在 19 世纪后期一度有市场,如今多数学者支持第三种观点。根据新发现的无任何篡改痕迹的亚基帕版本的《犹太古代史》,约瑟夫斯确实记叙了关于耶稣的基本史实。这一段落现存的是希腊文手稿,而且亚基帕版本和约瑟夫斯在别的地方叙述时所使用的词汇和语法非常一致。耶稣被描写为一个智者形象,而基督徒很少这样描绘。约瑟夫斯多次使用"智者"一词来指称大卫、所罗门等《旧约》人物。他曾提到耶稣有很多希腊门徒,但《新约》并未提及。在《犹太古代史》第 20 卷提及耶稣时,约瑟夫斯仅称他为"基督"而无进一步的解释,说明他在此之前已介绍过他。与约瑟夫斯同时代的罗马历史学家塔西佗也提到了基督:"群众则把这些人称作基督徒,他们的创始人基督,在提比略统治时期被元首提比略的总督彼拉多处决了。"[③]塔西佗极有可能看过约瑟夫斯的著作,因而并未特别解释"基督"一词。

在《犹太古代史》中,约瑟夫斯把耶稣与其同母异父兄弟雅各之死联系起来。《新约》没有告诉我们雅各是如何去世的,但约瑟夫斯进行了记载:"这些事情(罗马人对耶路撒冷的围城——笔者注)之所以降临到犹太人,是因为他们无视义者雅各的公义,杀害了他,他是那位被称为基督的耶稣的兄弟。""他(阿尔比努斯,

---

① 路易斯·H. 菲尔德曼 Louis H. Feldman,《约瑟夫斯论基督教的起源》[Josephus on the Origins of Christianity],于《金陵神学志》[The Theology of JinLing],2020 第 3 期[2020, Issue 3],121。

② Josephus, *Jewish Antiguities*, XVIII, 63.

③ Tacitus, *The Annals*, XV, 44.

尼禄派来的犹太总督——笔者注)把那位被称为基督的耶稣的兄弟雅各和其他人一起带到他们的面前,指控这些人违背了律法,应当用石头打死。"[①]约瑟夫斯的叙述非常流畅,并无任何篡改的痕迹。倘若被基督徒篡改过了,那么记载的资料会更为详细,而不会一笔带过。他们很可能会不吝辞藻来描写雅各,像《新约》中那样称呼他为"主的兄弟",而不是像约瑟夫斯所说的"耶稣的兄弟"。《新约》也不可能成为约瑟夫斯的资料来源,因为新约没有提供关于雅各之死的记录。约瑟夫斯进一步把耶稣定义为"被称为基督的那一位",因为他的作品中记录了20位耶稣。约瑟夫斯研究权威菲尔德曼在《犹太古代史》的注释中称:"几乎没有人怀疑关于雅各的这一段记述的真实性。"[②]

对于基督教徒来说,约瑟夫斯的《犹太古代史》第18—20卷是他们最关心的部分,因为其提供了整个新约时代的背景资料,其中对耶稣的记载是古典作家中最详细的,成为该书最具权威性的章节。对前面章节所述,约瑟夫斯既非亲眼看到,也非历史事件的当代人。约瑟夫斯对耶稣的先驱、施洗约翰,进行了栩栩如生的描写。据他记载,约翰告诉犹太人,"要操练德行,不仅要操练彼此间的公正,而且要操练对上帝的虔敬,只有这样做了,才能参加洗礼"[③]。约瑟夫斯对犹太总督彼拉多有较为详细的描述,有助于我们理解他在审判耶稣受到压力后的表现。就史料的丰富程度而言,约瑟夫斯对彼拉多的描写文字是《圣经》的10倍。[④] 约瑟夫斯对犹太人的城市、王宫、神庙、艺术、教派、圣殿仪式等进行了全景式的记载,成为关于公元1世纪犹太民族和历史的重要史料来源。他对巴勒斯坦地区人文地理的描述以及对罗马征服该地区的记载不仅准确可靠,而且有些还是《圣经》没有的。在耶路撒冷、希律堡垒、撒玛利亚-塞巴斯特、凯撒里亚、安提帕底、加马拉等地的考古发掘中,约瑟夫斯的记载被证实是真实的。《犹太战记》描述的马萨德要塞的巨大的岩石、8座罗马军队营房的石墙和山巅的王宫以及大型蓄水池,如今依然存在。斯提文·马逊指出:今天许多考古学家都认为约瑟夫斯是一位准确的记者。[⑤] 威廉姆森高度评价了约瑟夫斯作品的价值:"在那个动荡的岁月中,很难找出比约瑟夫斯更让我们感谢的一位历史学家。"[⑥]

---

① Josephus, *Jewish Antiguities*, XX, 197-203.

② Josephus, *Jewish Antiguities*, XX, 496.

③ Josephus, *Jewish Antiguities*, XVIII, 63.

④ 保罗·梅尔编译,《约瑟夫著作精选》,序言,1。

⑤ Steve Mason, *Josephus, Judea, and Christian Origins: Methods and Categories* (Peabody Mass: Hendrickson Publishers, 2009), 147.

⑥ 约瑟夫斯 Josephus,《犹太战记》[The Jewish War]王丽丽 Wang Lili 译(济南[Jinan]:山东大学出版社[Shandong University Press],2007),"威廉姆森导言"[Williamson' Introduction],8。

约瑟夫斯的著作有夸大数字的缺陷。《犹太战记》和《犹太古代史》同一事件的年代、次序、因果关系、动机、细节等方面的记载,也有不同或矛盾之处,其作品中存在夸张的倾向,尤其是在数字方面。实际上,上古史家普遍有夸大主题的倾向,他们总认为自己的主题是“最伟大的”。在《犹太战记》中,约瑟夫斯说耶路撒冷的他泊山(Tabor)高 48 千米(30 英里)[①],而它实际仅高 585 米(1920 英尺)。他在描写耶路撒冷城破的情景时称“许多地方的火都是被涌流成河的血水熄灭的”[②],并说被俘人数为 9.7 万人,围城期间死亡的人数为 110 万人,其中绝大多数是犹太血统。[③] 这个数字明显被夸大了,塔西佗记载被围在城中的犹太人是 60 万人。[④] 但看完约瑟夫斯战争故事的读者,几乎不曾质疑他的渲染:“上帝或人类造成的毁灭中,没有任何一件比得上这场战争的大屠杀。”[⑤]尽管存在这些缺点,但都无伤大雅。作为公元 1 世纪犹太史以及犹太人和希腊罗马世界关系史的最重要著作,约瑟夫斯的作品具有重要的宗教文献和史料价值,甚至可以说是不可替代的。正如美国学者汤普森所指出的:“如果没有约瑟夫斯,希腊—罗马时代的犹太史就不可能再现了。”[⑥]

(二)致用:向希腊—罗马世界宣传犹太人和犹太教,并为罗马统治辩护

古罗马著名学者琉善(Lucian,亦译作卢奇安)指出:“历史只有一个任务或目的,那就是实用。而实用只有一个根源,那就是真实。”[⑦]约瑟夫斯在做到写作基本真实的同时,注重史学的致用功能,最早向西方世界介绍犹太人,也接受了罗马人的统治并积极为之辩护。约瑟夫斯热爱犹太民族的文化,他撰史的一个重要目的就是宣传犹太文化,记载犹太人久远的历史,并为犹太人的不公正待遇正名。[⑧] 与《犹太战记》明显的亲罗马立场相比较,《犹太古代史》则有意淡化作者与罗马的政治联系,更注重自己所扮演的犹太历史学家和民族辩护人的角色,

---

① Josephus, *The Jewish War*, Ⅳ, 55.

② Josephus, *The Jewish War*, Ⅵ, 403.

③ Josephus, *The Jewish War*, Ⅵ, 414.

④ 保罗·奥罗西乌斯也不同意约瑟夫斯 110 万犹太人死亡的数据,倾向于 60 万人。见 Paulus Orosius, *The Seven Books of History Against the Pagans*, Ⅶ, 9。

⑤ Josephus, *The Jewish War*, Ⅳ, 423-430.

⑥ 汤普森 Thompson,《历史著作史》[A History of Historical Writing] 孙秉莹 Sun Bingying 译,上卷[Vol.1],第一分册[Book 1],(北京[Beijing]:商务印书馆 [The Commercial Press],1988),150。

⑦ 卢奇安 Lucian,《论撰史》[On History],收录于《缪灵珠美学译文集》[A Collection of Translated Versions of Miao Lingzhu's Aesthetics] 卷一[Vol.1],章安祺 Zhang Anqi 编订,(北京[Beijing]:中国人民大学出版社[China Renmin University Press],1998),191。

⑧ 约翰·萨克雷 John Thackeray,《约瑟夫斯评传》[The Review of Josephus], 陆路 Lu Lu 译(北京[Beijing]:大象出版社 [Elephant Press],2019),58。

希望恢复与犹太人的关系。约瑟夫斯认为希腊—罗马世界能够从犹太民族的历史中学到很多,会发现这种学习非常值得,这样的感情迫使他写了《犹太古代史》。约瑟夫斯最先把犹太人的历史介绍给外部世界,使犹太史知识成为一般人都可占有的文学财富。[①] 在《犹太古代史》的后半部分,他认为犹太人需要与周围的民族保持良好关系,希望"民族之间和平共处,摒弃前嫌"。[②] 约瑟夫斯的叙述出自犹太人的视角,关注到犹太人的与众不同,指出他们随时准备为捍卫本民族的律法而牺牲。《犹太古代史》记载了犹太分封王希律(Herod Antipas)将异教徒的娱乐项目引入犹太而引起部分犹太人的不满,有十名犹太人准备暗杀他,事泄后被处决。约瑟夫斯写道:"那些犹太人英勇无畏地向希律展示了准备用来刺杀他的短剑。"[③]这种爱国主义和宗教感情构成了约瑟夫斯描写圣殿被毁和犹太人被屠杀的基调。约瑟夫斯在《犹太战记》中宣布上帝如今住在罗马,将《犹太古代史》作为一种教育罗马帝国犹太人的工具,把自己战略性地摆在了犹太人和罗马人之间[④],成为他作为犹太人和罗马人的一种调适。

约瑟夫斯在《犹太战争》对犹太人的英勇表示敬意:"他们宁愿牺牲在疆场,也不愿意因为饥饿而死。"[⑤]他对耶路撒冷圣殿被毁和同胞被屠杀痛心疾首:"儿童和老人、俗人与祭司同遭屠戮。各阶层都在战火中身陷囹圄,无论他们是自卫还是哭泣求饶。"[⑥]约瑟夫斯以末日将近的笔调描述最后的巨变:"当圣殿起火,掠夺持续在四处进行,被捕的人死于剑下……小孩与老人、俗人与祭司同遭屠戮;各阶级都在战火中身陷图圈,无论他们是自卫还是哭泣求饶。在火焰无情横扫的呼吼声中,隐约传来崩坏的低鸣。高耸的山丘与熊熊燃烧的庞大建筑让整座城市陷入火海之中,至于嘈杂的声音,再没有比这类声响更具毁灭性与令人惊恐……然而,比嘈杂声更可怕的是触目可见的景象。圣殿山从顶端到底部都被火焰包裹着,仿佛从最底层沸腾起来。"[⑦]类似记载在约瑟夫斯著作中并不鲜见,凸显了他对犹太人身份的认同感和民族自豪感。

约瑟夫斯在战败后投降罗马并为之效力,他因此受到犹太人和希腊人的指

① 汤普森,《历史著作史》,155。

② Josephus, *Jewish Antiguities*, XVI, 75.

③ Josephus, *Jewish Antiguities*, XV, 267.

④ Zuleika Rodgers, *Making History: Josephus and Historical Method* (Leiden: Brill Academic Publishers, 2006), Introduction, 8.

⑤ Josephus, *The Jewish War*, III, 181.

⑥ Josephus, *The Jewish War*, VI, 270.

⑦ Josephus, *The Jewish War*, VI, 270-277.

责，被认为是叛徒，“想把我抓回去处死”[①]。在亚历山大里亚，犹太人和希腊人陷入了没完没了的争斗。双方都派遣三名代表到罗马元首盖乌斯·卡里古拉面前说明情况。希腊人的代表阿皮翁攻击犹太人，诋毁他们没有像罗马帝国的其他地方一样建造祭坛、雕像及神殿来尊崇罗马元首。阿皮翁指控犹太人蔑视元首的尊严，不崇拜元首为神，认为崇拜盖乌斯·卡里古拉并为其雕刻塑像是可耻的。亚历山大里亚的学者斐洛代表犹太人进行辩解，但是被盖乌斯·卡里古拉打断。[②] 保罗·奥罗西乌斯指出：“卡里古拉仇恨人类尤其是犹太人。”[③]阿皮翁也对约瑟夫斯进行了严厉的批评。约瑟夫斯为此撰写了《自传》和《驳阿皮翁》，这两部著作成为希腊语檄文的典范，为自己辩解也为犹太人正名。约瑟夫斯的《驳阿皮翁》是一部论战性作品，第一次详细地阐明并且捍卫了犹太教的教义。[④]约瑟夫斯自己在作品中以第三人称形式出现，反驳那些犹太控告者。阿皮翁对亚历山大里亚犹太人拒绝崇拜希腊神感到非常愤怒：“如果说犹太人属于公民团体，那么他们为何不敬亚历山大里亚人所敬的诸神呢？”[⑤]约瑟夫斯驳斥希腊人对犹太宗教信仰的诋毁，希望希腊人能够尊重犹太人。虽然用希腊语写作，但他认可犹太人的律法，坚信犹太民族的“悠久历史”和种族的“纯洁”，绝不希望自己“从灵魂深处成为希腊人”[⑥]。他认为希腊作家的信仰浅薄而糟糕，文笔流畅却缺乏历史感。[⑦] 他认为希腊人“不断地自我膨胀”，错误认为希腊人是拥有古代知识的唯一民族。“他们忽视我们民族的历史，不是出于无知就是装作无知。”[⑧]约瑟夫斯愤慨地指出：“简言之，他们故步自封的方法，就是历史方法的对立面。”[⑨]他把污蔑犹太人的埃及人称为犹太人的死敌，认为是他们煽动希腊人反对犹太人，并谴责没有善待犹太人的埃及女王克丽奥帕特拉。约瑟夫斯在罗马时期致力于向希腊世界，包括受过教育的罗马人宣传犹太世界，将恢复犹太民族

---

① Josephus, *The Life*, 416.

② Josephus, *Jewish Antiguities*, XVIII, 257-260. 在当今西方学界，人们依旧视斐洛为“希腊化时期犹太人中最为重要的一个人物”，并认为斐洛在西方学术上最具影响的成就，便是“他对‘隐喻解经法’的理论发展”。见 Elizabeth, ed. *The Concise Oxford Dictionary of the Christian Church* (Oxford: Oxford University Press, 1977), 400。

③ Paulus Orosius, *The Seven Books of History Against the Pagans*, VII, 5.

④ 阿巴·埃班 Abba Eban,《犹太史》[Jewish History] 阎瑞松 Yan Ruisong 译(北京[Beijing]：中国社会科学出版社[China Social Sciences Publishing House], 1986), 96。

⑤ Josephus, *Against Apion*, II, 165.

⑥ Josephus, *Against Apion*, I, 180.

⑦ Josephus, *Against Apion*, I, 1.

⑧ Josephus, *Against Apion*, I, 5.

⑨ Josephus, *Against Apion*, I, 1, 26.

的名誉作为自己的职责，这对东地中海的希腊语世界正确认识犹太人和犹太教是有帮助的。

对约瑟夫斯这样亲罗马的犹太人来说，神本史观也是他解释罗马人统治地位的有力武器。接受罗马人的统治和罗马文化，对犹太人来说是一件痛苦的事情。约瑟夫斯是第一批认同罗马统治的犹太人，实现了从耶路撒冷祭司到罗马犹太人的嬗变。他的《犹太战记》是经过弗拉维皇室批准的官方史书，提图斯亲自为它签名，批准出版。[①] 约瑟夫斯最早向希腊罗马世界介绍犹太人和犹太教，也用神本史观为罗马统治辩护。约瑟夫斯认为："命运已经从四面八方(罗马人)来到那里。上帝在周游列国之后，现在已经安居在意大利那里。"[②]约瑟夫斯认为，将权力转入罗马人一方是上帝的安排，上帝决定了罗马人必须是胜利者，罗马军队的胜利是罗马人的命运和美德的结果，呼吁犹太人接受罗马人的统治。约瑟夫斯在罗马战神广场看到过罗马军团的游行，非常钦佩罗马军队："他们的训练和实战是没有区别的，每位士兵都在平时的训练中非常卖力，就像在作战似的。这就是为什么一旦事态紧张，他们马上可以起来作战。他们不会因为障碍而丧失纪律，不会恐慌，也不会惧怕，没有他们吃不了的苦。战胜那些没有怎么经过训练的人是理所当然的事情。把他们的练兵说成没有献血的战场，把战争说成流血的训练，是毫不为过的。"[③]因而在犹太战争初期，约瑟夫斯竭力劝说犹太人开战要慎重。"我促使他们好好思考即将与之开展的罗马人，要他们牢记，不管是在军事方面还是在运气方面，他们都要逊于罗马人。""我真诚而又执着地劝说他们不要妄自行动，因为我已经预判这场战争肯定会以我们毁灭性的失败收场。"[④]

为了替罗马人的统治辩护，约瑟夫斯在《犹太战记》中表达了更深层次的信息：上帝抛弃了他的犹太选民，并借罗马人之手毁灭了圣殿，就像借巴比伦人之手毁灭第一圣殿一样。这就是犹太人永远不应该向罗马人开战的原因，因为他们注定失败。约瑟夫斯用罗马帝国不可征服的思想安抚那些被征服者，并阻止犹太同胞和其他人的进一步反抗。[⑤] 约瑟夫斯对犹太起义持悲观态度："那么多的泱泱大国都被征服了，犹太人又如何能有希望获胜呢?"[⑥]他将战争责任推到犹太强硬派身上。"宗教骗子与盗匪头子合力驱使民众反叛，以死亡威胁那些服

① Josephus, *The Life*, 363.

② Josephus, *The Jewish War*, Ⅴ, 9.

③ Josephus, *The Jewish War*, Ⅶ, 73-87.

④ Josephus, *The Life*, 17-19.

⑤ Josephus, *The Jewish War*, Ⅲ, 108.

⑥ Josephus, *The Jewish War*, Ⅱ, 342.

从罗马的人。”[①]在犹太民间记忆中，提图斯一直是邪恶的“毁灭者”的形象，正是他下令焚毁圣殿的。在塔西佗的笔下，也是提图斯下令摧毁圣殿的，因为在讨论中提图斯认为，只有这样才能彻底肃清犹太人和基督教徒的宗教。[②] 但在约瑟夫斯的笔下，提图斯是一位极具仁慈心的罗马统帅。“提图斯非常渴望保护耶路撒冷城免遭毁灭，就派约瑟夫斯去用犹太人的母语跟他们谈判。”[③]约瑟夫斯认为，提图斯是想让犹太人投降的，最终不得不烧掉大门，但又下令扑灭大火。[④]约瑟夫斯力图描写提图斯拯救圣殿的愿望，一方面表现了他想要维护提图斯声誉的心情，另一方面也表现了他对已经消失的圣殿的怀念。在他的眼中，故意毁灭圣殿的行为令人发指，因此他才竭力为提图斯辩白。这也反映了约瑟夫斯对犹太圣殿有一种深深的挥之不去的情愫。关于对圣殿的敬意和圣殿被毁后其悲痛心情的描述，在约瑟夫斯作品中随处可见。约瑟夫斯没有把圣殿被毁的主要责任归结于罗马人，而是认为这是上帝对犹太人罪行的惩罚，是由于犹太人的内争，也由于对律法的违背。内部斗争既是《犹太战记》的中心主题，也是《犹太古代史》的叙述重点之一。[⑤]

弗拉维皇族并非朱里亚-克劳狄皇族的延续，其统治的合法性一直受到当时一些罗马人的质疑。取得犹太战争的胜利，是苇伯芗和提图斯最大的战功，是事关弗拉维王朝立国根本的大事，也是犹太教和犹太民族的心理创伤。约瑟夫斯对自己的祭司身份很在意，他在后来向罗马投降时说，他有释梦的本领，能够解释头脑中出现的有关犹太人和罗马人前途的幻象。作为祭司的后代和祭司，约瑟夫斯能够解读《圣经》中的各种预言。[⑥] 约瑟夫斯记载了一系列神秘迹象，将其看作罗马人拥有天命的依据。他描写了公元 70 年及前几年发生在耶路撒冷圣殿里或天上的许多离奇现象，如天空出现了一颗恒星和一颗彗星，圣殿每扇门自动开启，人们看到天上出现战车和军队的战斗场面，圣殿区有一头牛生下了一只小羊羔，圣殿里传来了宣告离开的神秘声音。公元 66 年，一位名叫耶稣的农民不断警告犹太人，一场悲剧即将降临。约瑟夫斯认为，犹太人执迷不悟，没有领会这些不详的凶兆，反而当成鼓励他们揭竿而起的吉兆。之后，他还指出了两个被严重误解的预言。一个是古老的预言，说当圣殿变成方形的时候圣城将被

---

① Josephus, *The Jewish War*, Ⅱ, 264.

② Tacitus, *The Histories*, *Fragments*, 2.

③ Josephus, *The Jewish War*, Ⅱ, 348.

④ Josephus, *The Jewish War*, Ⅵ, 124-129.

⑤ Louis H. Feldman, *Josephus's Interpretation of the Bible* (Los Angeles: University of California Press, 1998), 140.

⑥ Louis H. Feldman, *Josephus's Interpretation of the Bible*, Ⅴ, 419.

毁灭。他认为，在安东尼亚城堡遭围攻被毁灭时它就已实现。另一个预言是关于统治者的神谕："但是最能鼓励他们参战的就是那一则隐晦的预言……到那时，他们国中的一人将统治整个世界。"[①]在约瑟夫斯看来，这个人就是罗马统帅苇伯芗，而非哪一位犹太人。他认为，苇伯芗是上帝选中的代理人，苇伯芗之子提图斯则受神的特别庇护。塔西佗进一步说："大多数人却坚信他们的古老的宗教文献曾预言，正是在这个时候，东方才能强大起来，而从犹太出发的人将占有世界。这一神秘预言实际上指的是苇伯芗和提图斯。"[②]这些关于圣殿的奇谈怪事，一方面是出于古代作家写作的需要，另一方面也为罗马镇压叛乱提供了政治和宗教理由。

尽管为罗马人的统治辩护，但约瑟夫斯并没有放弃对犹太教的热爱，在书写时不自觉地流露出这种感情。犹太人维护宗教信仰的感情是强烈的。在塞琉古王国统治时期，犹太贵族耶孙在安条克四世的支持下曾推行"希腊化改革"。"希腊化"不仅是指把希腊语作为人们交流的主要语言加以推广，也包括推行希腊的教育、竞技会、体操、戏剧等文化，反对派以影响了他们的宗教信仰和生活方式为由激烈反对，改革最终失败。公元前 168 年，安条克四世宣布禁止犹太教，抢夺了圣殿的财富，引发了犹太人的暴乱。对冲突的原因，《剑桥古代史》认为是犹太人主动挑起冲突，才导致后来的迫害和殉难，犹太人要承担部分责任。[③]

在之后的罗马统治时期，约瑟夫斯记录了公元前 50—前 40 年罗马政府颁布的许多保证犹太人特权的诏书，它们称犹太人为"朋友加盟友"，允许其保持风俗习惯。[④] 罗马统治者对犹太人的态度总体是友善而宽容的。进入帝国时期以后，元首崇拜日渐兴起，元首被臣民视为神，元首塑像受到臣民的膜拜。而犹太教禁止偶像崇拜，也不允许将任何偶像带入耶路撒冷圣城，元首崇拜与犹太宗教难免产生冲突。约瑟夫斯小心翼翼地记录了这种宗教矛盾的演变过程。为了尊重犹太人的宗教信仰，罗马军队一直没有在耶路撒冷城使用带有塑像的军旗。公元 6—26 年担任犹太总督的彼拉多，在夜间军队移防中使用了印有罗马元首提比略半身像的军旗。犹太民众要求他撤去军旗，彼拉多则认为这是对罗马元首的侮辱，双方产生冲突。彼拉多还将元首肖像带入耶路撒冷，在犹太人中间引发骚乱。此外，彼拉多在建造为圣殿提供水源的工程时，动用了圣殿的祭祀基

---

① Louis H. Feldman, *Josephus's Interpretation of the Bible*, Ⅲ, 242-404.

② Tacitus, *The Histories*, Ⅴ, 13.

③ A.E.阿斯汀 A.E. Astin 等编，《剑桥古代史》[The Cambridge Ancient History]卷八［Vol.8］，陈恒 Chen Heng 等译，(北京[Beijing]：中国社会科学出版社［The Press of Chinese Social Science］，2020)，382。

④ Josephus, *Jewish Antiguities*, ⅩⅣ, 10.

金，引发了犹太民众的骚乱。[①] 在描写冲突的时候，约瑟夫斯对犹太民众持同情态度，记录了民众宁可死亡也不愿意看到律法被冒犯的宗教感情。叙利亚行省总督维特里乌斯及时制止了彼拉多的行为，让犹太人独立处理宗教事务，并主动改变行军路线以避免罗马军旗出现在耶路撒冷，赢得了约瑟夫斯的赞扬。[②] 公元 37—41 年在位的盖乌斯·卡里古拉，要求臣民称自己为“主人和神”，把自己当作神来崇拜。[③] 他下令把自己的塑像放进耶路撒冷圣殿，这在公元 40 年引发了犹太人的骚乱。据约瑟夫斯记载：“他们（犹太人）说，自己宁可死去也不愿看到自己的律法被冒犯，即便当时他们准备让自己的土地荒芜。”[④]约瑟夫斯同时代的犹太人裴洛的记载，也证实了此事：“他极为痛恨犹太人，从亚历山大里亚开始，他霸占了一座座城市，在会堂里摆满了他的画像和雕塑……在圣城，他霸占了圣殿，企图把它改造为自己的神庙，并且称之为‘朱庇特显灵、小盖乌斯的神庙’。”[⑤]约瑟夫斯笔下的犹太总督彼特罗尼乌斯，对犹太人的呼声表示理解和同情，并向元首求情。“除非元首想毁灭这个国家以及其中的居民，否则就应该收回敕令。”[⑥]不久，盖乌斯·卡里古拉被杀，“元首的死亡结束了犹太人的暴动”[⑦]。

约瑟夫斯笔下的继任者克劳狄在一定程度上保护了犹太人的权益，他颁布敕令，维护犹太人的宗教信仰和特权：“我希望没有谁因盖乌斯·卡里古拉的缺乏理解而损害犹太民族的权利，他们也应保留原先拥有的特权，犹太人应当始终致力于自己的习俗……”[⑧]而尼禄时代的犹太总督弗洛鲁斯则劫掠犹太圣殿宝库，纵容军队闹事和杀害平民，约瑟夫斯认为是弗洛鲁斯迫使犹太人与罗马人宣战，对他进行了无情的鞭挞。他认可对罗马元首的个人崇拜，称“我们只向元首——不向其他任何人——表达一种特别的尊敬”[⑨]。在约瑟夫斯看来，最大的不幸是后来的部分罗马总督的无能，但是犹太人不能总揪住有些事情不放。他明确指出，罗马元首不会支持总督的错误行为，他们不应为总督的错误行为负责。约瑟夫斯没有批评任何一位罗马元首，就连被罗马元老院宣布为“公敌”的尼禄，他也认为与弗洛鲁斯的错误无关。尼禄那封引发犹太人起义的诏书，约瑟

① Josephus, *The Jewish War*, Ⅱ, 169-174.

② Josephus, *Jewish Antiguities*, ⅩⅧ, 93; ⅩⅧ,106.

③ Paulus Orosius, *The Seven Books of History Against the Pagans*, Ⅶ, 5.

④ Josephus, *The Jewish War*, Ⅱ,160-170.

⑤ Philo, *Embassy to Gaius*, trans. F. H. Colson and G. H. Whitaker (Cambridge Mass: Harvard University Press,1930), 43.

⑥ Josephus, *The Jewish War*, Ⅱ,160-170.

⑦ Tacitus, *The Histories*, Ⅴ, 10.

⑧ Josephus, *Jewish Antiguities*, ⅩⅨ, 280.

⑨ Josephus, *Against Apion*, Ⅵ,77.

夫斯声称是收受了希腊人贿赂的秘书所写，与尼禄本人无关。[①] 约瑟夫斯尽力以一种中立的态度来记录罗马人和犹太人的宗教矛盾，这与塔西佗等对犹太人的歧视性叙述形成了鲜明对比。

三、约瑟夫斯的史学地位：对世界史叙述的尝试和神本史观的构建

约瑟夫斯对自己的祭司经历和犹太宗教深以为傲，首次提出了神本史观，不仅成为《圣经》的解释者，也是犹太人的宗教信仰、实践及运动的记录者。他认可犹太人的神权政体，认为上帝能够预见人类发展的方向，赋予犹太人在地中海世界各民族中以特殊的地位，构建了一种以犹太人为中心的世界史。他提出的以上帝为中心的神本史观，也为罗马历史书写提供了一种新的范式，成为基督教史学的源头。

（一）古希腊罗马时期的第一个神本宣言，成为基督教史学的源头

希伯来《圣经》的核心思想主要是由一神论、契约论和末世论组成的，这些思想也贯穿于其史学思想之中。希伯来《圣经》主要是一部历史著作，在其39部书简中有17部与历史有关。5位大先知和12位小先知的著作，主旨虽不是编写历史，但也包含了大量的历史情况。[②] 顾晓鸣认为："一部犹太《圣经》，不啻是民族历史行程的记载，民族经历过的往昔事件成为整个民族存在的文化标记……从作为小文化形态的历史编纂学角度来说，犹太民族较之其他民族，保留了更多部落生活和活动的历史记载。"[③]进一步而言，对于历史写作，希伯来《圣经》提供了一个宏大的编年的、宇宙的构架和道德判断的基础，其主题是歌颂古代以色列民族摆脱埃及的控制，在上帝的指引和庇护下重获自由。这个压倒一切的主题并不只是具有宗教上的意义，同时也体现了犹太人对历史的理解有不同于其他古代民族的视角。

约瑟夫斯以自己的祭司身份为荣，强调犹太民族是一个由上帝统摄、由祭司领导的民族，"我们的律法是按照上帝的意志制定的，对于我们来说不遵守律法就意味着对上帝的不满"[④]。约瑟夫斯指出，犹太民族是一个实行"神权政治"的

---

① Josephus, *The Jewish War*, Ⅱ, 250.

② 吴晓群,《西方史学通史》,299。

③ 顾晓鸣 Gu Xiaoming,《犹太：充满"悖论"的文化》[Judea: A Culture Full of "Perversion"]（杭州[Hangzhou]：浙江人民出版社 [Zhejiang People's Publishing House], 1996），33。Josephus, *Jewish Antiguities*, XIV, 10.

④ Josephus, *Against Apion*, XXI, 184.

民族,“所有的权力和权威都来自上帝”,“还有比这更神圣的政体吗?”[①]他以这种神权政治为豪:“有什么体制能比上帝统治一切,将最重要的事务交到祭司的手中,让大祭司统领所有祭司的制度更好更公正呢?”[②]约瑟夫斯进一步表明上帝主宰人类历史的观点:“任何认真研读历史的人从中得出的主要教训就是:人们要遵从上帝的意志,不要妄图僭越已经完美制定的法律。万事皆能取得意想不到的成功,因为人们的成就都是拜上帝恩惠所赐。”“那些遵行上帝旨意的人必然兴盛,那些偏离上帝律法的人,最终必然遭殃。”[③]对于如何处理现世的罗马元首统治和对待上帝的态度产生的悖论,约瑟夫斯认为,“即使对罗马元首和罗马人民的致敬也不能超过上帝”[④]。约瑟夫斯提出的以上帝为中心的神本史观,为一些犹太教神学家所接受,成为古典史学世界中第一个神本宣言。约瑟夫斯通过与其生平紧密联系的自我撰史实践,在希腊罗马史学之外为日后的基督教史学提供了另一种在历史中阐释“自我”的路径。

约瑟夫斯在作品中多次用上帝的意志来解释犹太人的历史。据约瑟夫斯记载,当以色列大祭司以利爱自己的儿子超过上帝时,上帝就托梦给他,以色列人将遭受一场大灾难,他的两个儿子都将死去。[⑤] 处死施洗约翰的犹太王希律,于公元 44 年在凯撒里亚死去。《使徒行传》第 12 章第 19—23 节)记载上帝派天使降下惩罚,希律遭到蛇的咬噬而死去。而约瑟夫斯也记载此事,并认为这是上帝的惩罚:“犹太人相信,希律 · 安提帕全军覆没的灾难,乃是上帝对他处死约翰的一种报应,是上帝执意要惩罚他。”[⑥]“不久,他抬头观看,发现自己头顶上有一位天使。他马上意识到,这是一位降灾的天使,因为赐福的使者之前也同样降临过他。”[⑦]在诸如此类的事情上,约瑟夫斯的记载总是与《圣经》的记载互相印证。就约瑟夫斯自己的命运而言,尽管多次遭人陷害,但是“由于上帝的恩典,我常常化险为夷”[⑧],因而对上帝充满感激。特萨 · 瑞杰克认为,约瑟夫斯的作品都是在宣扬上帝的全能以及与上帝建立正确关系的重要性,而对律法的坚定则是不容改变的。[⑨]

---

① Josephus, *Against Apion*, XXII, 188.

② Josephus, *Jewish Antiguities*, II, 185.

③ Josephus, *Jewish Antiguities*, I, 1, 14.

④ Josephus, *Against Apion*, VI, 76.

⑤ Josephus, *Jewish Antiguities*, V, 352.

⑥ Josephus, *Jewish Antiguities*, XVIII, 106.

⑦ Josephus, *The Jewish War*, XIX, 343-351.

⑧ Josephus, *The Life*, 425.

⑨ Tesaa Rajak, *The Jewish Dialogue with Greece and Rome Studies in Cultural and Social Interaction* (Leiden: Brill, 2001), 215.

在古希腊罗马史学中，人本史观占主要地位，求真精神一直为史学家所孜孜以求。尽管有些史学家在精神上与神灵有一定的联系，在解释历史的时候把神灵意志作为要素之一，但他们并不认为自己完全是神的奴隶，并不把自己的一切献给神。他们虽然在作品中为神搭建庙堂，但仅在需要时才去请教神。从本质上说，人本、求真是和敬神是冲突和矛盾的。修昔底德和波里比乌斯取得了很高的史学成就，这是在突破了神的界限后才实现的。[①] 而在约瑟夫斯之前，从未有史学家把上帝提升到主宰一切的地步。约瑟夫斯的历史书写，始终强调历史性事件的神秘性因素、上帝对人类事务的干预，这表明了他想要创造一种智慧的历史。约瑟夫斯在《犹太战记》中认为，“最能够煽动犹太人起来与罗马人进行战争的是一条神谕，那就是他们国家中要有一个人未来成为统治全世界的王”[②]，将战争归结于宗教原因。对约瑟夫斯而言，最理想的政体就是以法律和神权治国的神权政体，而对浮躁的民众和煽动者则表现出一种蔑视。“神权政治”的概念没有出现在任何非约瑟夫斯作品的希腊文献中，约瑟夫斯正是凭借“神权政治”这个概念体现犹太民族政治体系的独特性。[③] 由于约瑟夫斯尚处于罗马古典史学鼎盛时期，优秀史学传统仍在史坛居主导地位，神本史观并未造成严重影响。但约瑟夫斯提出的这种新的解释历史的方向，后来被尤西比乌斯、奥古斯丁等基督教史学家发扬光大（正如尤西比乌斯所说的：“用历史纪录来证明神的判断”[④]），影响长达数个世纪。希腊罗马的古典史学以理性思维方式构建了一种循环往复的历史观念，成为古代世界历史的主流，成为古典史学繁荣兴盛的重要基础。由约瑟夫斯开始的神本史观则突破了古典史学的这种历史观念，将未来纳入其中，从而将过去、现在和未来贯穿在一起，构建了一种线性时间观和历史发展观的雏形。

基督教史学源于犹太史学。圣杰罗姆（Eusebius Sophronius Hieronymus）的《基督教著名作家列传》中，就收录了约瑟夫斯。作为基督教史学的开拓者，约瑟夫斯开创了许多后来为基督教史学家所遵循的传统。第一，他开创了世界纪年法。根据约瑟夫斯的推算，从创世到出版《犹太古代史》是 4977 年。第二，他历史写作的根本目的是引导读者礼拜上帝。约瑟夫斯在《犹太古代史》的开篇序言中说：“现在我将读者召回，让他们思考上帝，判断我们的上帝是否如其本性那

① 郭小凌 Guo Xiaoling，《西方史学史》[History of Western Historiography]（北京[Beijing]：北京师范大学出版社[The Press of Beijing Normal University]，2016），114—115。

② Josephus, *The Jewish War*, Ⅵ, 281.

③ Per Bilde, *Flavius Josephus, between Jerusalem and Rome: His Life, His works and Their Importance* (Sheffield: Sheffield Academic Press, 1988), 117.

④ Eusebius, *The Ecclesiastical History*, Ⅱ, 10.

样值得礼拜，将合适于他的归于他，而不要受到其他那些民族那些不得体的传说的玷污。”第三，他严格按照《圣经》的顺序来讲述历史，既不增加也不遗漏。第四，他认为摩西是“史学之祖”。约瑟夫斯将摩西视作最初的律法制定者，认为摩西那受神启示而颁布的神圣戒律，代表一种不同于梭伦、罗慕路斯等古典立法者的文化内容。由于摩西是立法者，依据上帝而立法，因此他所记载的历史既讲述法律和行为，也充满了对本质的思考，尤其是对上帝的本质的思考。这是历史写作和阅读的根基，不再有什么不可理解的事情了，因为真理已经被上帝启示。[①]

当被誉为“教会史之父”的基督教史家尤西比乌斯写《教会史》时，他进一步解释了约瑟夫斯的神谕：“不过，苇伯芗并没有统治全世界，他所统治的范围仅限于罗马版图之内。这项预言所指的对象更应该是基督，圣父曾对他说：‘你求我，我就将列国赐你为基业，将地极赐你为田产。’而且，基督圣使徒的‘声音通遍天下，言语传到地极’。”[②]这个统治全世界的“王”，在尤西比乌斯的笔下，由苇伯芗转变为了耶稣基督。而在这样的转变过程里，虽然对同一条神谕的具体阐释不同，但对借这条神谕来解读历史的阐释策略，犹太教史家约瑟夫斯与基督教史家尤西比乌斯却如出一辙。我们可以在这种历史阐释理论策略的传承与嬗变中，更为深入地理解约瑟夫斯及其对早期基督教史学的意义。

（二）构建犹太人的创世神话，撰写犹太人的通史

在世界民族之林中，犹太人是一个重视历史、强调反思的民族，其史观既包括通过预言展望未来，也包括对历史的回溯和反思。犹太一神教开启了以神学理论解释历史的先河，提出了一种奠定在犹太教义之上的新的历史理论。《犹太古代史》摒弃了传统的希腊—罗马写作模式和当时盛行的罗马中心论，决心成为一部犹太人通史。约瑟夫斯是按照犹太教对世界起源的学说来撰史的，《犹太古代史》在某种意义上是一部以犹太人为中心的世界史，其历史视野更开阔，将自然史和人类史都囊括其中。李维从罗马建城写起，约瑟夫斯则从世界诞生处着笔。《犹太古代史》上迄上帝创世，下至公元 66 年犹太人大起义。“起初，上帝创造了天地。大地还没有出现，而是隐藏在漆黑中。当上帝说要有光时，灵气就在大地上运行。”[③]“起初所有人都讲同一种语言，他们建了一座通天塔，以为可以到天国。但上帝吹一阵风，摧毁了塔，给每个人以一种特别的语言……从那时

① 王晴佳 Wang Qingjia，李隆国 Li Longguo，《外国史学史》[A History of Historiography Around the World]（北京[Beijing]：北京大学出版社[The Press of Peking University]，1996），69—70.

② 优西比乌 Eusebius：《教会史》[The Church History]，梅尔 Paul L. Maier 英译，瞿旭彤 Qu Xutong 译（北京[Beijing]：生活·读书·新知三联书店[SDX Joint Publishing Company]，2009），120。

③ Josephus, *Jewish Antiguities*, Ⅰ, 27.

起,他们因语言不同而分散了,到处建殖民地。每群人都占领了他们在上帝指引下发现的国家,在每一片大陆上定居,跨海到海岛上生活。"[①]这就是约瑟夫斯作品中世界历史的开端。

约瑟夫斯在写作《犹太古代史》时查阅了《圣经》,对《圣经》的记载给予一些补充或删减。这既是他学习犹太律法与传统的结果,同时也是为了不给予外人攻击犹太宗教和历史的机会。古希腊作家普鲁塔克记载,恶神提丰在一场战斗后骑驴逃了七天,生了两个儿子——耶路撒冷和犹太[②],即将犹太人视为恶神提丰的后裔。在自己的作品中,约瑟夫斯略去了耶路撒冷圣殿中供奉着驴像的事实,以避免给人造成在希腊—罗马世界已形成的犹太人崇拜动物的印象。罗马元首提比略曾打算将犹太人都驱逐出意大利,他后来改变了主意。元首克劳狄曾威胁说要将犹太人驱逐出意大利,因为他认为犹太人总是在制造麻烦。据亚历山大里亚的斐洛记载,当他(斐洛)将一个使团带到罗马元首盖乌斯·卡里古拉面前时,元首问犹太人为什么从来不接触猪肉时,整个宫廷哄堂大笑。[③] 盖乌斯·卡里古拉下令将自己的塑像放到犹太圣殿,只是他后来被杀因而这一命令未来得及得到执行。[④] 这反映出部分罗马统治者对犹太人的歧视和傲慢态度。在罗马共和末期和帝国初期的知识分子中,西塞罗认为犹太教是野蛮人的迷信[⑤],塔西佗认为圣殿供奉动物像是不可思议的,"我们认为神圣的一切在犹太人看来却都是渎神的,我们所憎恨的一切在他们那里却又是合法的"[⑥]。在地中海世界,普遍存在对犹太人的偏见,涌现了一股强大的反犹主义思潮。亚述人、米底人、波斯人视犹太人为最低贱的民族,塞琉古人认为犹太教是迷信,埃及人认为犹太人祖先摩西是麻风病人。在希腊人看来,犹太人不与其他人共餐,也不与他人共同享福、祷告、献祭,比东方的苏萨、巴克特里亚或印度离他们更遥远。

但是我们对罗马共和末年和帝国初年罗马政府对犹太人的敌意不应过分夸大。恺撒颁布法律来保障犹太人宗教自由,因而在公元前 43 年恺撒被杀后,犹

① Josephus, *Jewish Antiguities*, Ⅰ, 118-120.

② Plutarch, *Plutarch's Lives*, *on Isis and Osiris*, trans. Bernadotte Perrin (Cambridge Mass.: Harvard University Press, 1959, LCL), XXXI, 1.

③ Martin Goodman, *Rome and Jerusalem* (London: Penguin Books Ltd, 2008), 285.

④ Tacitus, *The Annals*, Ⅻ, 54.

⑤ Cicero, *Pro Flacco*, trans. Clifford H. Jackson (Cambridge Mass.: Harvard University Press, 1964, LCL), 28, 67.

⑥ Tacitus, *The Histories*, trans. Clifford H. Moore (Cambridge Mass.: Harvard University Press, 1930, LCL), Ⅴ, 4.

太人非常悲恸。公元1世纪末的罗马作家苏维托尼乌斯写道:“在公共哀悼的高潮中,许多外籍人也按照各自的习俗成群围着他痛哭流涕。尤其是犹太人,他们甚至连续几夜集合起来在焚尸场哀悼。”①奥古斯都继续确认了恺撒颁布的保障犹太人宗教自由的法律,还免除了犹太人的兵役。奥古斯都还分封希律为以大、以买土和撒玛利亚的分封王。② 塔西佗写道,在提比略统治时期,犹太局势平静无事。③ 保罗·奥罗西乌斯还提到提比略向元老院建议将基督视为神,但是元老院拒绝神化基督。④ 在克劳狄统治时期,犹太成为罗马的一个行省,到任的总督想取消大祭司的圣服,但是克劳狄下令恢复犹太大祭司的圣服。⑤ 在一个人口众多、移民不断涌入的特大城市罗马,对犹太人的反感并不普遍,他们在融入罗马生活方面并不困难。虽然犹太人不用向罗马的神祇献祭,但是他们并不反对在会堂里为政府的福祉祈祷。这是其他任何一个团体都不具有的特权。

约瑟夫斯对犹太人的历史充满了自豪。他坚持认为犹太人的祖先比希腊人和罗马人的历史更悠久,“犹太人已拥有五千年的历史”⑥。在他看来,犹太人在地中海各民族中占有特殊的地位和历史,能够超越希腊人的“神话帝国主义”。约瑟夫斯认为摩西早于荷马,他骄傲地指出:“作为将军,几乎无人能与他比肩;作为先知,他是独一无二的。他所有的宣告,使人仿佛听见上帝自己的声音。”⑦ 约瑟夫斯对法老宫殿中的摩西英俊的相貌、成人后卓越才能的描写,出埃及期间在西奈半岛的经历以及此前此后犹太人对他的各种称呼,都是《旧约》中没有的。上帝为了帮助摩西带领犹太人出逃埃及,给予埃及法老和埃及人很多惩罚。《犹太古代史》不仅为基督徒也为犹太人证明了“神授启示”的真理,同时进一步证实了业经考据证实的与《圣经》有关的诸多历史事实,对犹太人“特选子民”的历史研究有重大价值。

四、结语

约瑟夫斯非常喜欢历史写作,他认为自己正在跟随修昔底德、李维等人的脚步。他无疑与那个时代的希腊罗马史家有密不可分的关系,他用希腊文写作,有

---

① Suetonius, *The Lives of the Caesars, the Deified Caesar*, LXXXIV, 5.
② Josephus, *Jewish Antiguities*, XVII, 324.
③ Tacitus, *The Histories*, V, 9.
④ Paulus Orosius, *The Seven Books of History Against the Pagans*, VII, 4.
⑤ Josephus, *Jewish Antiguities*, XX, 1.
⑥ Josephus, *Jewish Antiguities*, I, 13.
⑦ Josephus, *Jewish Antiguities*, IV, 329.

学者将他称为"希腊史学家"。[①] 约瑟夫斯引述或重复希伯来《圣经》中的明显的"非希腊"特征。同时,他仍处于希腊史学传统之中,"以希腊式的武器来对抗非希腊"[②]。约瑟夫斯的著作正是这两种特征的奇妙结合。从公元 69 年始,约瑟夫斯成为罗马公民,有 30 余年的时间在罗马度过。正是在罗马,他写作并完成了他所有的作品,《犹太古代史》最后三卷(第 18—20 卷,公元 6—66 年)描述的都是有关罗马的历史,因而有学者将其称为"罗马史学家"。公元 1 世纪,犹太人、希腊人、罗马人及基督教徒等在许多问题上都是相互影响的。与其他作家相比,约瑟夫斯有意识地将犹太人有关上帝在历史进程中的作用的观点引入历史写作。在记叙《圣经》故事时,约瑟夫斯既没有肯定它,也未否定它。[③] 对犹太人而言,理想不仅与一神教相联系,也与普世主义的欲望相联系,约瑟夫斯的历史写作试图把其他民族的历史包括在《圣经》叙述和年代记中。在罗马时期,约瑟夫斯的犹太身份在寓居罗马期间非但没有削弱反而有所加强。因此,约瑟夫斯的著作始终不同于罗马统治时期以希腊文写作的其他非罗马本土的史家,如狄奥尼修斯、阿庇安等人。约瑟夫斯由此被誉为犹太历史中的希罗多德或者李维,或是哈里卡纳苏斯的狄奥尼修斯。[④] 他的著作体现了公元 1 世纪罗马历史书写的潮流,尤其是《犹太战记》代表了当时的主流历史写作风格,成为那个时代历史写作的方向。

约瑟夫斯生活在公元 1 世纪的东地中海世界,这是一个充满矛盾的时代和地域。约瑟夫斯获得罗马公民权前后的个人生涯,以独特的方式反映了这一时期巴勒斯坦等东部地中海地区的政治冲突和时代主题:地方行省和地方本土主义、民族情结与维护罗马帝国统治之间的矛盾,本土文化、民族主义和占主体地位的希腊—罗马文明之间的矛盾,"灵活的实用主义与忠实的宗派主义之间的矛盾以及忠于阶级利益与忠于小集团之间的冲突"[⑤]。约瑟夫斯的史学世界属于犹太史和希腊—罗马史研究范畴,犹太人、希腊人、罗马人以及基督徒等群体在许多问题上都是相互作用和影响的。与其他作家相比,约瑟夫斯有意识地将犹

---

① Mireille Hadas-Lebel, "Flavius Josephus, Historian of Rome," in *Josephus and the History of the Greco-Roman Period Fausto*, eds. Parente and Joseph Sievers (Leiden: Brill, 1994), 99-106.

② Shaye Cohen, "History and Historgrahpy in the Against Apion of Josephus," in *Essays in Jewish Historygraphy, History and Theroy*, ed. A. Papoport Albert (Middletown: Wesleyan University Press, 1988), 1-11.

③ Shaye Cohen, "History and Historgrahpy in the Against Apion of Josephus," Ⅲ, 81.

④ 唐纳德·R. 凯利 Donald R. Kighley,《多面的历史:从希罗多德到赫尔德的历史探询》[Multifaceted History: A Historical Inquiry from Herodotus to Herder] 陈恒 Chen Heng 译(北京[Beijing]:生活·读书·新知三联书店[SDX Joint Publishing Company],2006),141。

⑤ 泰萨·瑞洁克 Tessa Rajak,《史学家约瑟夫斯及其世界》[Josephus: The Historian and His Society] 周平 Zhou Ping 译(北京[Beijing]:商务印书馆[The Commercial Press],2014),绪论(Preface),1—5。

太人有关上帝在历史进程中的作用的观点引入他的历史写作。在约瑟夫斯写作的时期，作为弗拉维皇室的座上宾，他已从帝国政治的边缘转向了帝国的中心。约瑟夫斯希望犹太世界与非犹太世界尤其是与罗马统治者和谐共存，这从侧面展现了行省与罗马政府之间的依从关系，他的信念和尝试也反映了罗马统治下地方精英们的期望。约瑟夫斯从犹太祭司成为罗马史学家，为传统的希腊罗马历史叙述尤其是那个历史叙述主体的“自我”，提供了极富原创性与冲击力的范式，缔造了一种新颖的阐释策略。

参考文献

(一)中文参考文献

1.A. E.阿斯廷等编:《剑桥古代史》第八卷，陈恒等译，北京:中国社会科学出版社，2020 年。

2.保罗·梅尔编译:《约瑟夫著作精选》，王志勇译，北京:北京大学出版社，2004 年。

3.郭小凌:《西方史学史》，北京:北京师范大学出版社，2016 年。

4.斯德蒙德·苏厄德:《约瑟夫斯与第一次犹太战争》，王迎译，北京:民主与建设出版社，2020 年。

5.汤普森:《历史著作史》(上卷，第一分册)，孙秉莹译，北京:商务印书馆，1988 年。

6.唐纳德·R.凯利:《多面的历史:从希罗多德到赫尔德的历史探询》，陈恒译，北京:生活·读书·新知三联书店，2006 年。

7.王晴佳、李隆国:《外国史学史》，北京:北京大学出版社，1996 年。

8.吴晓群:《西方史学通史》第二卷，上海:复旦大学出版社，2011 年。

9.优西比乌:《教会史》，梅尔英译、评注，瞿旭彤译，北京:生活·读书·新知三联书店，2009 年。

10.约翰·萨克雷:《约瑟夫斯评传》，陆路译，郑州:大象出版社，2019 年。

11.约瑟夫斯:《犹太战记》，王丽丽译，济南:山东大学出版社，2007 年。

12.章安祺编订:《缪灵珠美学译文集》第一卷，北京:中国人民大学出版社，1998 年。

13.布朗特:《约瑟夫斯论罗马犹太人的社会冲突》，《金陵神学志》，2015 年第 2 期。

14.路易斯·H.菲尔德曼:《约瑟夫斯论基督教的起源》，《金陵神学志》，2020 年第 3 期。

（二）英文参考文献

1. A. Papoport Albert ed., *Essays in Jewish Historygraphy, History and Theory*, Middletown: Wesleyan University Press, 1988.

2. Cicero, *Pro Flacco*, Cambridge Mass.: Harvard University Press, 1964.

3. Elizabeth ed, *The Concise Oxford Dictionary of the Christian Church*, Oxford: Oxford University Press, 1977.

4. Erwin R. Goodenough, *An Introduction to Philo Judaeus*, New York: Barnes & Noble, 1963.

5. Eusebius, *The Ecclesiastical History*, Cambridge Mass.: Harvard University Press, 1964.

6. Fausto Parente and Joseph Sievers eds., *Josephus and the History of the Greco-Roman Period*, Leiden: Brill, 1994.

7. J. Edmondson, S. Mason and J. Rives, *Flavius Josephus and Flavian Rome*, Leiden: Brill Academic Publishers, 2003.

8. Josephus, *Against Apion*, London: W. Heinemann; New York: G. P. Putnam's Sons, 1926.

9. Josephus, *The Life*, London: W. Heinemann; New York: G. P. Putnam's Sons, 1926.

10. Josephus, *The Jewish War*, Cambridge Mass.: Harvard University Press, 1927.

11. Josephus, *Jewish Antiguities*, Cambridge Mass.: Harvard University Press, 1965.

12. Louis H. Feldman, *Josephus's Interpretation of the Bible*, Los Angeles: University of California Press, 1998.

13. Paulus Orosius, *The Seven Books of History Against the Pagans*, trans. A.T. Fear, New York: Columbia University Press, 1936.

14. Per Bilde, *Flavius Josephus, between Jerusalem and Rome: His Life, His Works and Their Importance*, Sheffield: Sheffield Academic Press, 1988.

15. Plutarch, *Plutarch's Lives*, Cambridge Mass.: Harvard University Press, 1959.

16. Steve Mason, *Josephus, Judea, and Christian Origins*, Peabody Mass.: Hendrickson Publishers, 2009.

17. Suetonius, *The Lives of the Caesars*, London: W. Heinemann; New York: The Macmillan Company, 1926.

18. Tacitus, *The Annals*, Cambridge Mass.: Harvard University Press, 1937.

19. Tacitus, *The Histories*, Cambridge Mass.: Harvard University Press, 1930.

20. Tesaa Rajak, *The Jewish Dialogue with Greece and Rome Studies in Cultural and Social Interaction*, Leiden: Brill, 2001.

21. William Den Hollander, *Josephus, the Emperors and the City of Rome: From Hostage to Historian*, Leiden: Brill Academic Publishers, 2014.

22. Zuleika Rodgers, *Making History: Josephus and Historical Method*, Leiden: Brill Academic Publishers, 2006.

23. Zvi Yaveta, "Reflctions on Titus and Josephus," *Greek, Roman and Byzantine Studies*, 16 (1975).

From Jewish Priest to Roman Historian: On Josephus' s God-Historical Viewpoint

HE Libo

Abstract: Josephus was a 1st century Jewish priest who took part in the great Jewish revolt and became a Roman historian in deference to the Romans and the Roman citizenship. The Jewish War and Jewish Antiguities became one of the most important sources of information about the Jewish war and the early Jews in the first century AD. Josephus' s work was generally truth seeking, with references to religious texts such as the Bible, reported on early Judaism, and accounts of Christian figures such as Jesus, Pilate, and James, provided the most important background information about the New Testament era and became the key historical data of the New Testament era. Josephus's work was characteristically utilitarian in that he introduced the Jews to the Greco Roman world and actively defended Roman rule. Josephus was the first Roman historian to put forward a theosophical view of history, constructed the Jewish creation myth, became the first theosophical declaration in Roman Times, and constructed a linear concept of time and the embryonic form of historical development, it provided a new paradigm for the writing of Roman history and became the source of Christian historiography.

Key Words: Josephus, the Priests, the New Testament, Theosophical View of History

先知传统的复兴:以色列《独立宣言》中的政教博弈

高书顺*

【摘要】以色列于 1948 年 5 月 14 日建国,大卫·本-古里安在建国典礼上宣读了以色列《独立宣言》。由于时间紧促,在这份《独立宣言》制定的过程中,全国委员会关于宣言内容的讨论机会较少。这份宣言主要由以色列工人党的部分成员以及两位犹太拉比共同参与制定。与会成员针对宣言的框架结构以及其中带有神学意涵的字句是否应该删改存在不同意见,并为此对宣言进行了多次修订。尽管最终版本的以色列《独立宣言》神学色彩较为稀薄,然而从宣言制定过程以及最终文本的部分字句,仍然可以透视以色列建国之时世俗的复国主义者与宗教人士的分歧与博弈。

【关键词】《独立宣言》;以色列;先知传统;复国主义;犹太拉比

1947 年 11 月 29 日,联合国大会通过了第 181 号决议①。决议规定:“巴勒斯坦之委任统治应尽快终止,无论如何至迟当于 1948 年 8 月 1 日以前结束。”此外,决议还规定受委任统治的国家在撤军两个月后,应在巴勒斯坦的土地上建立起阿拉伯国和犹太国,并详细划定了两个国家的地域及两国人民的政治经济权利。然而,联合国的分治决议对于犹太人的建国进程并没有直接助益:阿拉伯国家联盟拒绝这一决议,受委任统治巴勒斯坦地区的英国政府也未曾表示支持犹太人建国。这一决议还引起了阿拉伯人与犹太人之间持续五个多月的暴力冲突升级。在这种情况下,犹太国家事务委员会于 1948 年 5 月 12 日紧急通过了建国的决议。以色列的《独立宣言》(*The Declaration of the Establishment of*

---

* 高书顺,复旦大学哲学学院博士研究生。

① 该决议标题为《关于巴勒斯坦问题专设委员会报告书所通过之决议案》(*Resolution Adopted on the Report of the Ad Hoc Committee on the Palestinian Question*)。这项决议的具体内容可以在联合国文献中心网站查看,网址为 https://www.un.org/zh/documents/view_doc.asp? symbol=A/RES/181(II)。

the State of Israel)①也正是在这十万火急的形势下撰写而成的。从5月9日兹维·贝伦森(Zvi Berenson)写成初稿,到1948年5月14日下午全国委员会召开会议通过,宣言制定过程不足一周。而这份文件却成了以色列独立和拥有主权的标志②。

遗憾的是,国内外学者几乎未曾撰写专文对这份文件进行分析,只能在以色列通史类的专著中略见一星半点的描述。究其原因,可能是由于从美利坚合众国发布《独立宣言》至今,已经有上百个国家陆续发表了自己的《独立宣言》。正如大卫·阿米蒂奇(David Armitage)所言:"有许多(宣言)直接受美国《独立宣言》的启发。③ 有的直接抄录《宣言》的原词句,有时稍做调整,更多的是借鉴《宣言》的叙事框架……所有宣言都有明显的类似之处。"④因此,除了美国《独立宣言》以外,学者对其他国家的《独立宣言》关注甚少。此外,以色列的《独立宣言》发表于二战后民族国家建立的高峰期,因此这份文件也往往被人们忽视。

但是对于研究以色列史的学者而言,这份文件的重要程度无须赘言,其中丰富的历史、法律等内涵,更是值得我们一一挖掘。本文也将试图探究以色列《独立宣言》中包含的圣经时代的先知传统及其精神。并在此基础上讨论在《独立宣言》制定过程中,世俗的犹太复国主义者与宗教人士之间的博弈。

一、以色列《独立宣言》制定的背景

由于以色列《独立宣言》的制定时间较短,故而为此召开的会议、参与讨论的

① 以色列官方所译的《独立宣言》的标题名为"*The Declaration of the Establishment of the State of Israel*",中文直译为《以色列建国宣言》,但是中文研究文献指称这份文件时通常将其翻译成"以色列《独立宣言》",因此笔者仍然按照现行的习惯在文中使用"以色列《独立宣言》"这一标题名。笔者在本文中引用参考的《独立宣言》版本,皆源于以色列外交部提供的英文版的独立宣言。网址:http://mfa.gov.il/MFA/ForeignPolicy/Peace/Guide/Pages/Declaration% 20of% 20Establishment% 20of% 20State% 20of%20Israel.aspx。

② 以色列国至今尚未制定宪法。因此,对于以色列国而言,这份独立宣言成了具备宪法性质的文件。关于这份文件法律性质的讨论,参见:E. Rubinstein, "The Declaration of Independence as a Basic Document of the State of Israel," *Israel Studies* (1998): 195-210。

③ 关于美国《独立宣言》与以色列《独立宣言》的比较研究,参见:S. I. Troen, "The Hebrew Translation of the Declaration of Independence," *The Journal of American History* (1999): 1380-1384。

④ 大卫·阿米蒂奇 David Armitage,《独立宣言:一种全球史》[The Declaration of Independence: A Global History],孙岳 Sun Yue 译,(北京[Beijing]:商务印书馆[The Commercial Press],2014),2—3。

人数都较少。根据雪莱·克雷曼(Shelley Kleiman)描述的以色列建国的过程[①],《独立宣言》在制定过程中总共有五个版本。前两版分别是由犹太总工会的法律顾问兹维·贝伦森撰写的初稿,三位律师贝哈姆(A. Beham)、欣茨海默(A. Hintzheimer)以及贝克(Z. E. Baker)修订完成的第二稿。1948 年 5 月 12 日,在讨论了边界问题及国家命名问题之后,摩西·谢尔拓克(Moshe Shertok)于 5 月 13 日提交了一份有 22 项条款的修改稿,这个版本的内容已经接近于最终版本的《独立宣言》。针对这份修改稿,大卫·本-古里安(David Ben Gurion)提出一些非希伯来语化的措辞表达问题。此外,还专门针对宣言中"God 的名字"的存留问题成立了四人小组进行讨论。5 月 14 日,本-古里安提交了他深夜修订的稿子,这份稿子是在摩西·谢尔拓克的稿子基础上修改而成的。除了措辞以外,本-古里安的版本在框架上也进行了一定的调整。在建国典礼召开前的全国委员会最后一次会议上,参会成员再次针对宣言中的"God 的名字"问题进行了讨论,这一讨论结束后递交的稿子即为本-古里安在建国典礼上所宣读的以色列《独立宣言》。

除了三位核查法理的律师以外,其余参与讨论及撰稿的成员皆有较浓厚的政治或宗教背景。其中,属于世俗的复国主义的成员共有六位,分别是以色列工人党领袖本·古里安、以色列工人党法律顾问兹维·贝伦森、以色列工人党成员大卫·雷梅斯(David Remez)和摩西·谢尔拓克、进步党领袖费利克斯·罗斯嫩布卢特(Felix Rosnenbluth)以及极端世俗主义分子阿哈龙·齐斯林(Aharon Zisling),其中工人党在政治团体中占据主流地位。[②] 其中的宗教人士有两位,分别是拉比摩西·夏皮罗(Moshe Shapiro)和拉比耶胡达·莱布·菲什曼(Yehuda Leib Fishman)。

这是一场犹太复国主义者与宗教人士之间的较量。并且在宣言制定过程中,政治势力要远胜于宗教势力。难怪丹尼尔·戈迪斯会认为:"以色列《独立宣

① 雪莱·克雷曼撰写了一篇名为"The State of Israel Declares Independence"的文章,这篇文章叙述了以色列《独立宣言》的撰写过程,刊载在以色列外交部的网站上,网址:www.mfa.gov.il/mfa/mfa-archive/1999/pages/shelley% 20kleiman% 20-% 20the% 20state% 20of% 20israel% 20declares% 20ind.aspx。关于以色列《独立宣言》制定过程的记录,也可参见:Z. Sharef, *Three Days*, trans. Julian Louis Meltzer (London: Doubleday & Company, 1962), 124-137, 217-230, 256-290。

② 关于以色列建国之前的工人党的发展史,可参见:李志芬 Li Zhifen,《以色列民族构建研究——意识形态、族群、宗教因素的探讨》[The Research of Israel Nation-Building],西北大学博士学位论文[Doctoral Dissertation of Northwest University],2009,38—45。简而言之,工人党是以劳工犹太复国主义为主要意识形态的派别。劳工犹太复国主义则是将社会主义和犹太民族主义结合在一起的学说。

言》不是一份神学文件,而是一份历史文件。”[①]不过,细心的读者仍然可以从这份文件中发现零星点缀的宗教痕迹。譬如以色列《独立宣言》在开篇中,就用两个词将以色列国的宗教性质表达得淋漓尽致——代表应许之地的 ERETZ-ISRAEL[②] 和代表《圣经》的“永恒的书中之书”(the eternal Book of Books)。在回顾以色列历史的过程中,该宣言着意使用了《圣经》中的 ma'apilim[③] 来描述被逼反抗回归的非法移民,并运用了犹太历法来表达时间概念。在正文部分之后,它更将国家的前景建构在犹太先知们提出的设想之上。比起末尾模糊不清的“以色列的磐石”(the rock of israel),这里提及的先知群体给以色列《独立宣言》加添了更多宗教色彩。

二、以色列《独立宣言》中与先知传统相关的政教博弈

希伯来先知是古代犹太社会中的一个重要群体,他们被看作耶和华上帝讯息的传达者。因此在早期犹太人的社会中,先知居于一个崇高的地位。可是在犹太人被迫流散时期,以拉比教导和会堂崇拜为核心的拉比犹太教兴起,希伯来先知在这个过程中被拉比群体边缘化。这一转变的重要原因之一,是先知群体积极面向世界的观念与拉比群体重视个人内化提升的思想之间存在冲突。[④]

犹太人的第二圣殿被毁之后,一直是这群恪守律法、重视《妥拉》(*Torah*)的犹太拉比带领犹太人进行宗教领域的活动。他们在犹太会堂中年复一年地诵读《妥拉》,但是对记载着先知言论的《先知书》(*Prophets*)甚少提及。甚至在犹太拉比的重要经典《密释纳》(*Mishnah*)以及《革马拉》(*Gemara*)中,对《塔纳赫》的引用也多为《妥拉》部分。根据费尔迪南(Ferdinand)的统计,以《密释纳》为例,

---

① 丹尼尔·戈迪斯 Daniel Gordis,《以色列:一个民族的重生》[Israel: A Concise History of a Nation Reborn],王戎 Wang Rong 译,(杭州[Hangzhou]:浙江人民出版社[Zhejiang Renmin Publishing House],2018),155。

② ERETZ-ISRAEL 指 the land of Israel,即以色列地,这个词特指希伯来《圣经》中上帝应允给亚伯拉罕、以撒和雅各的应许之地。该宣言借此表达犹太人拥有这片土地的所有权,因为这片土地是犹太先祖的家园。

③ ma'apilim 是希伯来《圣经》中特有的词,在希伯来《圣经》中共使用了两次。在《民数记》第 14 章第 44 节,וַיַּעְפִּלוּ 指“以色列百姓贸然进攻应许之地迦南”,在“哈巴谷书”第 2 章第 4 节中 עֻפְּלָה 指“迦勒底人自高自大”,而在《独立宣言》中用此指 20 世纪 30—40 年代,在英国委任统治下非法移民巴勒斯坦的犹太人。使用这个词是为了强调非法移民的犹太人的目的是返回家园,这是对古代神圣历史的延续。

④ 关于先知群体被边缘化的背景及原因,可参见:王强伟 Wang Qiangwei,《犹太传统中的“先知”》[The Prophets of the Jewish Tradition],于《宗教学研究》[Religious Studies],2017 第四期[2017, Issue 4],253—258。

这部经典对《塔纳赫》中《妥拉》的引用为67%,对《先知书》的引用为16%,对《圣著》(*Ketuvim*)的引用为17%。[①] 而实际上《先知书》的篇幅是《妥拉》的两倍,是《圣著》的1.48倍。由此可见犹太拉比对先知群体的重视程度之低。

在犹太复国主义思潮兴起之后,先知传统重新获得重视。犹太复国主义者在复国计划中借用先知传统中的普世面向,寻求融入欧美各国的主流社会。此外,犹太复国主义者否定流散时代的耻辱,他们认为流散生活使犹太人成为屈服、脆弱与胆怯的民族,并由此养成了对外力强加的迫害与杀戮不加反抗的性格。[②] 犹太复国主义者反对大流散时期拉比犹太教的历史,圣经时代希伯来先知的思想与精神则在这一背景下重获新生。然而先知群体已经不复存在,拉比群体仍是主导现当代犹太教的中流砥柱。因此复国主义者与宗教人士在交流过程中必然产生分歧。由这两个群体共同参与制定的以色列《独立宣言》就明显展现出这一张力。

(一)传给普世永恒的"书中之书"

以色列《独立宣言》的起始段先指明了巴勒斯坦是犹太人的发源地,且犹太人在这片土地上创造了具有普遍意义的文化价值,并给世界带来了具有永恒价值的"书中之书"。尽管该宣言没有明确说明,但是犹太教徒不难揣测,这本"书中之书"是指犹太经典——希伯来《圣经》。值得推敲的是,在序言中陈述以色列建国的历史原因时,除了表明以色列人对这片土地的所有权以外,以色列《独立宣言》的撰写者还着重强调犹太人带给整个世界的价值。而这种普世面向正是政治犹太复国主义者乐于传达给整个世界的讯息。

然而,对于统管犹太人宗教事务的拉比群体而言,这本"书中之书"的产生,真的是为了赠予世界吗?换句话说,在拉比犹太教传统中,《圣经》被传播至其他民族中真的是他们期待的事情吗?对于犹太宗教应该保持内在化还是应该持有普世面向,犹太学者历来有不同的观点[③]。而犹太群体从大流散开始至今仍然严苛地强调宗教的内在特性,这与大流散时期兴起的拉比传统不无关系。作为

---

① 参见:Ferdinand E. Deist, "The Prophets: Are We Heading for a Paradigm Switch?," in *The Place is Too Small for Us: The Israelite Prophets in Recent Scholarship*, ed. Robert P. Gordon, (Pennsylvania: Eisenbrauns, 1995), 584。

② 张倩红 Zhang Qianhong,艾仁贵 Ai Rengui,《犹太史研究入门》[An Introduction to Jewish History](北京[Beijing]:北京大学出版社[Peking University Press],2017),238。

③ 比如 Heinrich Graetz 在历史书写中重视撰写犹太集体灵魂的历史,重视自我教化的经典内涵。而 Georg G. Iggers 则追求融入主流社会,期待成为世界公民的一部分。可参见:宋立宏 Song Lihong,《格奥尔格·伊格尔斯的德国—犹太遗产》[The German-Jewish Heritage of Georg G. Iggers],于《文汇报》[Wenhui Daily]2018年10月19日,第W11版。

犹太人中的宗教导师，拉比群体用小而精的聚集形式和繁杂的行为条例保持了犹太社群的独特性。因此拉比群体对于这本“书中之书”的归属并没有政治家的广阔视野。

在针对以色列《独立宣言》的讨论中，不同学者对于“书中之书”的给予对象持有不同的观点。比如，在谈及以色列开国典礼上那群熙熙攘攘的西欧和美国记者时，泽夫・沙伊夫(Zeev Sharef)就指出：“这些人的文化就是由书中之书构成的，对他们而言，这个时刻也是《圣经》文本的重现和先知愿景的实现。”[①]可见，对于泽夫・沙伊夫等犹太复国主义者而言，这本“书中之书”是以色列与西欧、美国人民所共同拥有的。而美国学者伊兰・特龙(S. Ilan Troen)则认为：“以色列《独立宣言》的首段就是他们背离传统信仰的明证……他们不接受《妥拉》是上帝所写，且在西奈山上传给摩西和以色列百姓，他们认为《圣经》的作者是人类而非上帝。”[②]在伊兰・特龙看来，这本“书中之书”本该是以色列所独享的，是上帝借着摩西传给犹太民族的礼物。因此，认为希伯来《圣经》是犹太人创造又传递给世界的东西并赋予它普世价值，是以色列人背离信仰的表现。

在针对摩西・谢尔拓克提交的第三个版本的稿子进行讨论时，贝霍尔・施特里特(Behor S. Shitreet)率先提出应该把“书中之书”置于宣言首段。他认为，“比起驱逐和大流散的历史，将犹太人在这片土地上长久居住时赖以为生的宗教、传统和书中之书放在首段更为合适”[③]。针对这一框架修改的提议，阿哈龙・齐斯林提出了反对意见。不过由最终版本的以色列《独立宣言》以及之后的讨论可以看出，阿哈龙・齐斯林并未过分关注这一问题，而本-古里安在修改稿子时显然也采纳了贝霍尔・施特里特的建议。

关于“书中之书”的使用及安放位置没有引起参会成员过多的争执，这是制定以色列《独立宣言》时政教博弈达至平衡的第一个体现。笔者认为有如下原因。首先，犹太复国主义者借用犹太历史中的经典希伯来《圣经》来传递先知的精神，一方面贴合了欧美基督教徒的思想，为这份《独立宣言》能够被欧美更好地接纳提供思想背景，满足了复国主义者争取政治平和与国际支持的目的；另一方面大部分世俗的复国主义者并不反对希伯来《圣经》，甚至从中提炼形塑当代以色列的元素。比如工人党领袖本-古里安就强调组成犹太“三位一体”的元素是

① Z. Sharef, *Three Days*, 282.

② S. I. Troen, “The Hebrew Translation of the Declaration of Independence,” *The Journal of American History* (1999): 1383.

③ Z. Sharef, *Three Days*, 226.

犹太人、土地和《圣经》。[①] 其次，拉比群体也可借这一模糊的措辞传递以色列立国的宗教指向，因为希伯来《圣经》无疑是犹太教最为重要的经典之一。对于拉比群体而言，借用“书中之书”来隐喻希伯来《圣经》或许给他们带来更多解释上的便利，模糊的措辞似乎也能够指称《密释纳》《革马拉》等拉比群体撰写的经典。

(二)在安息日前夕，5708 年以珥月 5 日

在以色列《独立宣言》全文中，总共有六处具体的时间。其中三处使用公历纪年，三处使用犹太历纪年。在使用公历纪年的三处中，一处涉及《贝尔福宣言》，两处引用联合国决议。使用犹太历纪年的三次分别涉及西奥多·赫茨尔召开的第一届犹太复国主义者代表大会、委任统治结束以及宣告独立。不难看出，关涉国际事务的部分，《独立宣言》的撰稿者都使用了国际通用的纪年法；而涉及以色列建国的部分，该宣言都以犹太历法来呈现。

具有浓烈宗教色彩的词是该宣言两次提及的“安息日前夕”(the sabbath eve)。根据犹太历法，完整的计日是从日落时分开始，到第二天的日落结束。安息日前夕按公历计时是指周五晚上，对于犹太人而言已经进入安息日。犹太人自古以来恪守安息日，以此为圣日，因为这是耶和华颁布的十诫之一。[②] 关于安息日，拉比群体在《密释纳·节期》的安息日卷中提出了详细的规定，要求犹太教徒在安息日期间遵守各类禁令。其中有一条安息日的禁令为“书写两个字母”[③]。若是按这些规定，在宣言上签名的人都触犯了安息日的禁令。在《革马拉》中关于安息日的禁令与诠释则更为繁复，若是一一查考，建国典礼过程中可能干犯的条例不止有书写这一项。

不过，犹太人在整个建国典礼中并没有干犯安息日的禁忌。原因在于，以色列建国典礼开始的时间为 1948 年 5 月 14 日，周五下午 4 点整。整个典礼持续了 32 分钟，典礼结束时太阳还未下山。将建国典礼时间定在这个时候，并非最稳妥的安排。只要稍有意外发生，就可能导致典礼推迟至日落。况且犹太人守安息日的习惯是 25 小时，即提早半小时进入安息日，在次日推迟半小时结束。一旦在这时候签名，就干犯了前文提到的安息日条例。雪莱·克雷曼对此做出的解释是：“在 5 月 12 日的会议上决议建国后，就只剩 48 小时来完成典礼的预备。将时间定在周五下午 4 点，是为了在委任统治结束前建国，且不会与安息日

① 参见：A. Shapira, “The Bible and Israeli Identity,” *AJS Review*, (2004): 11-12。

② 《出埃及记》20:8—11。

③ 张平 Zhang Ping 译注，《密释纳·节期》[The Mishnah: Seder Moed](济南[Jinan]:山东大学出版社[Shandong University Press],2017),141,155—156。

冲突。”[①]

可见,民族执行委员会选在这个时间段进行典礼并非没有考虑过安息日的问题。但是,在仅有两天的紧急情况下,他们分明没有考虑周到。因为典礼结束的第二天即安息日,以色列同阿拉伯国家的战火熊熊燃起。本-古里安在与西蒙·佩雷斯对话时说道:“今天每个人都高兴。明天就有流血。”[②]本-古里安早已预知安息日会发生战争,却仍旧将建国之日安排在安息日前夕。

笔者认为在《独立宣言》中提及安息日,并在安息日前夕举行开国典礼,仍是政教双方博弈的结果。对于世俗的以色列工人党而言,在以色列《独立宣言》中提及安息日,会增加宣言的宗教意味。全国一半以上的人口可能被宣言中看似轻描淡写的时间陈述吸引。这一做法或许能够提升犹太教徒对以色列《独立宣言》的认可程度,从而为随之而来的独立战争增加军力与士气。正如安东尼·史密斯(Anthony D. Smith)所言,民族主义常常以宗教神话为基础建构国家。[③]而对于渴望在巴勒斯坦重新恢复弥赛亚信仰的宗教犹太复国主义者而言,安息日一词或许是整篇宣言中最突出的具有犹太教色彩的词。

(三)以色列先知的愿景

在《独立宣言》的序言、正文之后,是对未来的展望。在这一部分中,撰稿者着重提出:以色列国将建基于自由、公平与和平。宣言详述了自由、公平与和平的内涵:这种公平是确保所有宗教、民族和性别的居民都享有社会和政治权利;这种自由是保证宗教自由、道德自由、语言自由、教育自由和文化自由;这种和平是保护所有宗教的圣地[④],且遵守联合国宪章。而且它进一步指出,这些思想正是以色列的先知所设想的愿景。

将自由、公平等思想归拢到先知笔下,这个说法从初稿到终稿都未曾被删除。古特曼(P. E. Gutmann)教授提出:“将自由、公平与和平定为以色列的先知所设想的,只是为了展现以色列作为一个犹太民族的特性。”[⑤]且不论这些愿景

---

① Shelley Kleiman,“The State of Israel Declares Independence”.

② A. Lam, “Peres Recalls Declaration: We Didn't Have Time to Celebrate,” Ynet News, (December 21, 2014), http://www.ynetnews.com/articles/0,7340,L-4606090,00.html. 转引自丹尼尔·戈迪斯 Daniel Gordis,《以色列:一个民族的重生》[Israel: A Concise History of a Nation Reborn],王戎 Wang Rong 译,(杭州[Hangzhou]:浙江人民出版社[Zhejiang Renmin Publishing House],2018),155。

③ Anthony D. Smith, *Nationalism and Modernism: A Critical Survey of Recent Theories of Nations and Nationalism* (London: Routledge, 1998), 6-7.

④ 虽然没有明言,但是显然圣地(Holy Place)指的是三教圣地耶路撒冷。

⑤ P. E. Gutmann, “The Declaration of the Establishment of the State of Israel,”以色列外交部网站, http://www. mfa. gov. il/mfa/aboutisrael/israelat50/pages/the% 20declaration% 20of% 20the% 20establishment%20of%20the%20state.aspx.

是否真为犹太的先知所构想，单论这份由政治复国主义者与宗教复国主义者共同讨论完成的以色列《独立宣言》，没有提及拉比群体最为重视的《妥拉》，没有提及拉比群体共同完成的旷世著作《塔木德》，反而将拉比们着意冰封雪藏1000多年的先知群体呈于纸上，这一做法无疑是劳工犹太复国主义者在建国之时对犹太传统的选择。

首先，对于犹太复国主义者而言，圣经时代的先祖建立过统一强盛的国家，其是即将重建的以色列国的典范。而他们对待大流散时期的犹太传统的态度是：正如宋立宏所言，"这一时期形成的犹太教经典比如《塔木德》——统统是需要抛弃的糟粕"[①]。因而他们在形塑新犹太人时，是以圣经时代的开拓者、征战者为标准，而非以饱读经书的犹太拉比为标准。

其次，自由、公平、和平等概念很容易使人联想到18世纪欧洲启蒙运动宣扬的思想。这些思想在18世纪风靡欧美，还深刻影响了美国的《独立宣言》、法国的《人权宣言》等。以色列《独立宣言》将其重新提起，还列举了多个例子来表达以色列的决心，这明显是犹太复国主义者欲求面向世界、靠拢世界的做法。

最后，若直言这些思想源于普世价值本也无妨，可是撰稿者偏偏为其添上了"正如以色列先知所提出的"这一定语。这种做法原本无可厚非，因为《先知书》中确实包含了诸多与自由、公义等概念相关的内容。只是被宗教人士有意隐藏的先知群体，现今却被世俗主义者重新提起，而拉比犹太教近2000年的历史却被忽视，这可能都是为掩盖犹太复国主义者不愿面对的大流散的历史。

拉比群体意欲涂写的宗教色彩在这一段落中仅留下"先知"一词。甚至祖先建造圣殿的"圣地"都要为"自由"的缘故而白白与"所有宗教"共同分享。[②] 对于宗教人士而言，能否坦然接纳所有宗教、语言、文化、种族的人群尚未可知，而以色列《独立宣言》已经帮他们做好了决定。拉比群体在这一段落中做出了极大的妥协。

（四）将我们的信仰建立在以色列的磐石上

就以色列《独立宣言》最后一段的首句"将我们的信仰建立在以色列的磐石

① 可参见宋立宏教授为《以色列：一个民族的重生》所做的序言。譬如，《圣经·耶利米书》第34章第15节记载："如今你们回转，行我眼中看为正的事，各人向邻舍宣告自由，并且在称为我名下的殿中、在我面前立约。"又如，《圣经·以赛亚书》第16章第5节记载："必有一位诚诚实实坐在其上，在大卫帐幕中施行审判，寻求公平，速行公义。"

② 参见以色列《独立宣言》：THE STATE OF ISRAEL ... will guarantee freedom of religion, conscience, language, education and culture; it will safeguard the Holy Places of all religions; and it will be faithful to the principles of the Charter of the United Nations。

上”,制定宣言的委员会召开了多次会议进行讨论。这个问题同“边界问题”[1]并列为制定宣言过程中的两大难题。

“Placing our trust in the rock of Israel”在初稿中是“把我们的信仰建立在万能的上帝之上(Placing our trust in the Almighty)”。极端世俗主义者阿哈龙·齐斯林认为,人们不应该被强制违背自己的意愿宣称自己相信上帝。拉比摩西·夏皮罗和耶胡达·莱布·菲什曼则提出:要代表全世界犹太人签署的《独立宣言》上不应该遗漏掉上帝的名字。他们的意思是在这个世界上,有大量的犹太人相信这位上帝,而这份《独立宣言》也是代表他们签署的,应该传递出他们的声音。摩西·夏皮罗随后还提出,应该使用“把我们的信仰建立在以色列万能的上帝之上(Placing our trust in the Almighty God of Israel)”或者至少使用“把我们的信仰建立在万能的上帝以色列的救赎者之上(Placing our trust in the Almighty and Redeemer of Israel)”。总之,上帝之名在这份宣告以色列独立的文件中是不应该被省略的。

在双方互不相让的情况下,本-古里安于 5 月 13 日成立了一个四人小组委员会解决这一问题。除了本-古里安以外,其余三人分别为阿哈龙·齐斯林和摩西·谢尔拓克以及拉比耶胡达·莱布·菲什曼。政教成员人数仍以 3∶1 的压倒性比例倾向世俗主义者。四人小组委员会最终商定的结果是删除“救赎者(Redeemer)”,使用“万能的上帝(Almighty God)”。[2]

然而在典礼开始前的最后一次全国委员会会议上,阿哈龙·齐斯林再次对“万能的上帝(Almighty God)”这个说法提出质疑。他的提法得到了迈尔·格拉博夫斯基(Meir Grabowsky)的支持。然而平克斯(D. Z. Pinks)却回应道:“这种表达只是为了团结大多数的犹太人。”他甚至还提出应该在宣言开头加上“以色列地是《妥拉》和《先知书》应许给犹太人的土地,也是犹太人的诞生地”[3]。

面对双方的矛盾,本-古里安最后提出使用“以色列的磐石(Rock of Israel)”一词作为替代。本-古里安说道:“我们每个人都可以按自己的方式来构思‘以色列的磐石’的意思。”他甚至提出“不要让我把这句话付诸投票表决”。因而,尽管阿哈龙·齐斯林仍然不同意将这句话放在宣言中,但这句话最终还是未经过投票就通过了。这个短语有一定的合理性,因为有一个可以表达“万能的上帝

① 边界问题是指是否要在以色列《独立宣言》中明确说明以色列和巴勒斯坦的边界。为解决这一问题,民族执行委员会也多次召开会议,最终以本-古里安决定不在该宣言中加入边界划分为结果。

② Z. Sharef, *Three Days*, 227.

③ Z. Sharef, *Three Days*, 278.

(Almighty)”的希伯来文短语“Tsur Yisrael”[①],它在字面上也可以翻译为“以色列的磐石(Rock of Israel)”。因此把“以色列的磐石”翻译成“Tsur Yisrael”,就可以将其解释为上帝,也可以解释为应许之地。

虽然“以色列的磐石”在信奉犹太教的群体中明显指向上帝[②],但是许多宗教人士,甚至宗教复活主义者都对这一做法表示强烈不满。极端正统派的成员代表在典礼结束后甚至对宣言表示反对,提出这种措辞大大冒犯了他们的敏感性。在宣言上签名的迈尔·大卫·洛温斯坦(Meir David Loewenstein)后来也提到“这个措辞忽视了我们所拥有的应许之地的唯一权利。这是基于上主与亚伯拉罕的约定,这个约定在《塔纳赫》中也一再被允诺”[③]。

前三项关涉宗教的措辞,在政教双方都没有激荡起太大的波浪。唯独是否要将上帝的名字添加至宣言中这件事,从第一次会议讨论到最后一次会议,甚至在典礼结束后仍有人心存芥蒂。关于以色列《独立宣言》的政教博弈,在这一分歧上达致白热化。可见双方对待此事的慎重态度。因为这句话或许就决定了以色列国之后的走向。

在同样面对争执的情况下,处理“边界问题”时,本-古里安以美国《独立宣言》为例一锤定音;而处理“God”问题时,本-古里安却抛开这一例子不谈。这种前后不一致的做法并未引起拉比群体的反对。伊兰·特龙认为,美国《独立宣言》的作者谨慎地避开提及他们所信仰的神的名字,而以色列《独立宣言》的制定者也同样绕开了这一主题。他还提出这两种做法采用的词在意义上是相同的。[④] 笔者认为,尽管他们都没有直呼“God”之名,但是这两部《独立宣言》的制定者对于在宣言中隐晦提及上帝之名的态度却是不同的。美国《独立宣言》的作者在宣言的开头和结尾都明确提出“创造主(Creator)”及“神的旨意(Divine Providence)”的概念,他们深信美国《独立宣言》依据的“天赋人权”来源于他们所信赖的上帝。[⑤] 以色列《独立宣言》的制定者中世俗主义的犹太复国主义者居多,他们中甚至有人公然宣称自己是无宗教信仰的。因而他们最终选用了这样

---

① 其希伯来文为 צוּר יִשְׂרָאֵל。

② 根据戈迪斯书中的注释,选用 Rock of Israel 是源于《撒母耳记下》第 23 章第 3 节。而在希伯来文《圣经》中,还有更多指向上帝的“磐石意象”的经文。

③ “Wallish and the Declaration of Independence,” *The Jerusalem Post*, 1998 (republished on Eretz Israel Forever), http://www.eretzisraelforever.net/Articles/Articles_ViewArticle.asp?sAction=view&iArticleId=1825010290&bSearchOn=True&sKeyWord=Meir+David+Loewenstein.

④ S. I. Troen, “The Hebrew Translation of the Declaration of Independence,” 1383.

⑤ 美国《独立宣言》(*The Declaration of Independence, 1776*),提及“with a firm reliance on the Protection of Divine Providence”。

一个有分歧的、模糊的词来解决这一难题。

笔者更愿意相信，双方在这一句话上的妥协是迫于时间的缺乏。在这历史性的关键时刻，双方都暂且放下成见。事实也证明，对于宗教人士而言，"以色列的磐石"指的都是《圣经》中的那位至高无上的耶和华。而对于世俗主义者而言，这个短语指的就是犹太人的历史、文化以及这片思念千年的土地。

三、小结

由上文对涉及宗教思想表达的四个关键讯息所做的考察可知，以色列《独立宣言》的宗教色彩较为稀薄且措辞含糊。尽管措辞含糊，该宣言却能够从侧面反映出以色列建国时的政治与宗教分歧。这种模糊的表达究竟是犹太复国主义者对宗教人士的妥协，还是犹太复国主义者出于自己的目的进行的选择？笔者倾向于后者。在这场政教博弈中，倾向世俗主义的犹太复国主义者是最大的赢家。

首先，以色列《独立宣言》提及的宗教措辞的严谨程度和宗教化表达都远没有达到虔诚的标准，所以才在典礼之后引起宗教人士的强烈不满。"书中之书""以色列的磐石"这些模糊不清的概念，无法完全展现犹太教的根本特征。此外，以色列《独立宣言》中传递的宗教思想也并不是拉比犹太教固守了 2000 年的思想。诸如面向世界等先知思想，大多是世俗分子强行用以替代拉比犹太教历史的工具。

其次，参与以色列《独立宣言》制定的成员在政治派别的比例上存在极大的不协调。整个制定过程中，有六个具有强烈世俗主义倾向的犹太复国主义者和两个拉比参与，即使在讨论是否要将上帝之名纳入以色列《独立宣言》时，也是三个世俗主义者和一个拉比参与。这种压倒性的优势使得拉比群体的呼声被压制。

最后，以色列工人党的领袖大卫·本-古里安在宣言制定过程中起了主导作用，这不可避免地导致了宣言的政治化及世俗化特征。在讨论国家命名、边界问题以及上帝之名等问题时，都是由本-古里安一人做出最终的决定。为尽可能多地获得所有人的支持，他使用模棱两可的宗教用语讨得双方的欢心，并最终实现塑造"新犹太人"的梦想，这一手段在以色列《独立宣言》中可谓表达得淋漓尽致。不过，将时钟往后拨几个小时，当拉比耶胡达·莱布·菲什曼念完"你赐予我们生命(shehecheyanu)"的祈祷之后，人们热烈地回应"阿们(Amen)"[①]。民众的欢呼声证明，本-古里安的做法是正确的。

① 希伯来语为 אמן，意指"是的，这正如我所想的"。

参考文献①

(一)中文参考文献

1.大卫·阿米蒂奇:《独立宣言:一种全球史》,孙岳译,北京:商务印书馆,2014 年。

2.丹尼尔·戈迪斯:《以色列:一个民族的重生》,王戎译,杭州:浙江人民出版社,2018。

3.张平译注:《密释纳·节期》,济南:山东大学出版社,2017 年。

4.张倩红、艾仁贵:《犹太史研究入门》,北京:北京大学出版社,2017 年。

5.李志芬:《以色列民族构建研究——意识形态、族群、宗教因素的探讨》,西北大学博士学位论文,2009 年。

6.王强伟:《犹太传统中的"先知"》,《宗教学研究》,2017 年第 4 期。

7. 宋立宏:《格奥尔格·伊格尔斯的德国—犹太遗产》,《文汇报》2018 年 10 月 19 日,第 W11 版。

8.《关于巴勒斯坦问题专设委员会报告书所通过之决议案》,https://www.un.org/zh/documents/view_doc.asp? symbol=A/RES/181(II)。

(二)外文参考文献

1. Anthony D. Smith, *Nationalism and Modernism: A Critical Survey of Recent Theories of Nations and Nationalism*, London: Routledge, 1998.

2.Robert P. Gordon, ed., *The Place is Too Small for Us: The Israelite Prophets in Recent Scholarship*, Pennsylvania: Eisenbrauns, 1995.

3. Z. Sharef, *Three Days*, trans. by Julian Louis Meltzer, London: Doubleday & Company, 1962.

4.A. Shapira, "The Bible and Israeli Identity," *AJS Review* (2004).

5.E. Rubinstein, "The Declaration of Independence as a Basic Document of the State of Israel," *Israel Studies* (1998).

6.S. I. Troen, "The Hebrew Translation of the Declaration of Independence," *The Journal of American History* (1999).

7."Wallish and the Declaration of Independence," *The Jerusalem Post*, 1998 (republished on Eretz Israel Forever), http://www.eretzisraelforever.net/Articles/Articles_ViewArticle.asp? sAction = view&iArticleId = 1825010290&bSearchOn = True&sKeyWord = Meir +

① 这篇论文中有不少原始材料都源自报纸、以色列外交部官网、联合国文献中心网上刊登的文件,因此笔者在参考文献中也一并将这些文献的网址附在其后。

David+Loewenstein.

8.A. Lam, "Peres Recalls Declaration: We Didn't Have Time to Celebrate," Ynet News, (December 21, 2014), http://www.ynetnews.com/articles/0,7340,L-4606090,00.html.

9.P. E. Gutmann, "The Declaration of the Establishment of the State of Israel,"http://www.mfa.gov.il/mfa/aboutisrael/israelat50/pages/the%20declaration%20of%20the%20establishment%20of%20the%20state.aspx.

10.Shelley Kleiman, "The State of Israel Declares Independence,"http://www.mfa.gov.il/mfa/mfa-archive/1999/pages/shelley%20kleiman%20-%20the%20state%20of%20israel%20declares%20ind.aspx.

11."The Declaration of the Establishment of the State of Israel," http://mfa.gov.il/MFA/ForeignPolicy/Peace/Guide/Pages/Declaration%20of%20Establishment%20of%20State%20of%20Israel.aspx.

The Revival of the Prophetic Tradition: An Interplay between Politics and Religion in *The Declaration of the Establishment of the State of Israel*

Gao Shushun

Abstract: The State of Israel was founded on May 14, 1948. David Ben-Gurion read The Declaration of the Establishment of the State of Israel at the founding ceremony. During the formulation of this declaration, the Israel National Foundation Committee had few opportunities to discuss the detail of the declaration, for the time is too short. This declaration was mainly formulated by some members of the Israeli Workers' Party and two Jewish rabbis. They disputed the framework structure of the declaration, and whether the words which contains theological meaning should be deleted. For this reason, they revised the declaration many times. The final version of the declaration did not show strong religious elements, but from the process of formulating the declaration and some phrases in the final text, we can still see the divergence and interplay between Zionist and rabbis when Israel was founded.

Key Words: *The Declaration of Independence*, Israel, Prophetic Tradition, Zionism, Rabbi

佛教的“神通”观念及其历史演化[*]

王萌[**]

【摘要】“神通”现象是佛教文化体系不可分割的组成部分。对于“神通”现象的性质，佛教通过“自内证”的方式做出评判，即它们属于佛教修行悟道过程中的随附性现象，与通向终极解脱的圆满智慧相比，是属于第二位的东西。在佛教发展史中，“神通”实践与不同社会的文化传统相适应，成为佛教文化脉络中一个富有活力的内在因素，同时它们的影响力也受到具体文化环境的制约。作为宗教经验的特殊表现，佛教的“神通”实践将实践者导向了更为超越的人生目标，即人的升华和觉悟。佛教对“神通”现象的理解，反映了人类自我认知的高度智慧，在当代仍然具有发人深省的启发意义和不可磨灭的认识价值。

【关键词】佛教“神通”；历史分衍；自内证；宗教经验

任何宗教都包含了与“超自然”有关的内容，这是与宗教文化本身的性质密切相关的。宗教之所以能够为人提供关于“彼岸”的讯息，建立诸多关于“来世”的精致教义，正是因为宗教通过其特有的途径打开了一条通向这个陌生世界的通道。这一通道就是宗教学研究所称的“宗教经验”①。宗教学研究已经表明，通过宗教实践，宗教修行者会进入“出神”状态，产生诸如“人神际遇”“神我合一”等神秘体验。佛教是一种长期存在于历史时空中的宗教文化现象，它有自身生

* 本文是国家社科基金项目“以宗教神秘主义问题为核心的宗教与科学关系研究”(14BZJ002)的阶段性成果。

** 王萌，中南民族大学民族学与社会学学院教授。

① “宗教经验”是宗教信仰者在信仰和修行过程中产生的一系列特别的感受和体验，它对经验者的身心世界会产生重要的影响。在宗教学发展史中，美国学者威廉·詹姆士最早对宗教经验做出了全面的研究。参见：威廉·詹姆士 William James，《宗教经验之种种：人性之研究》[Varieties of Religious Experience: A Study in Human Nature]，唐钺 Tang Yue 译，(北京[Beijing]：商务印书馆[The Commercial Press]，2002)。

存和演化的历史，也发展出了一套具有丰富内容的宗教实践体系，而且它在适应社会发展的过程中，对于宗教实践中产生“神通”现象提出了其独有的评判标准。这一特殊的认识方式，保证了佛教避免走入“着魔”的歧途，也使得佛教在人类文明史上做出了独树一帜的贡献。对佛教“神通”现象的梳理和分析，有助于深化我们对宗教经验问题的认识。

一、佛教的“神通”实践及其自我定位

（一）“神通”与佛教修行的究竟目标

佛教以庞大而精致的哲学思维著称于世，其教义被称为“最为宏大的神学唯心主义体系”[1]；同时，作为“一种寻求神秘结合的宗教”[2]，它又是具有丰富神秘主义内容的东方宗教文化的代表。作为当时印度社会中的沙门思潮之一，佛教是在对婆罗门教的反拨、批判中诞生的，它否定了“自我”（ātman）或者“神我”（purusa）的实在性，提出了不同于其他“外道”（tīrthika）的解脱之路，即“八正道”（āryāṣṭāṅgika-mārga）。但是，在宗教修行的目标上，佛教仍然是追求解脱与觉悟，在宗教修行的方式上，佛教也继承了印度传统的宗教修行方式，即经由“神秘知识”（jnāna, vidyā）消除“无明”（avidyā）或者揭开“摩耶”（māyā）之幕而获得解脱。[3] 释迦牟尼在获得觉悟的过程中，采取了印度传统的瑜伽修习方式，佛陀进入“涅槃”（nirvāṇa）的方法也有瑜伽的结构，这一系列冥想和禅定的方法经过佛陀新的解释，成为佛教基本的修行内容。

佛典记载，释迦牟尼的悟道过程就伴随各种不同寻常的心理体验。这一过程实际上也典型地反映了宗教导师“悟道”或领受“启示”的过程。[4] 佛典记载，

---

① 方立天 Fang Litian,《佛教哲学》（增订本）[Buddhist Philosophy]（updated edition),（北京[Beijing]：中国人民大学出版社[China Renmin University Press], 1997)。

② 杰弗里・帕林德尔 Geoffrey Parrinder,《世界宗教中的神秘主义》[Mysticism in the World's Religions]，舒晓炜 Shu Xiaowei，徐钧尧 Xu Junyao 译，（北京[Beijing]：今日中国出版社[China Today Press],1992),72。

③ 对于佛教而言，觉悟就是获得真正的知识，佛陀因此成为一个“觉者”。参见：米尔恰・伊利亚德 Mircea Eliade,《宗教思想史》[Histoire des croyances et des idées religieuses]，宴可佳 Yan Kejia，吴晓群 Wu Xiaoqun，姚蓓琴 Yao Beiqin 译，（上海[Shanghai]：上海社会科学院出版社[Shanghai Academy of Social Sciences Press],2005),491。

④ 在早期的巴利语三藏中并无关于释迦牟尼生平的完整记录，在小乘佛教向大乘佛教的演变过程中，顺应对教主崇拜和宗教感情的需要，才开始出现佛陀的传记，包括用梵语写成的《大事》《佛所行赞》《神通游戏》。参见：郭良鋆 Guo Liangjun,《佛陀和原始佛教思想》[Buddha and Primitive Buddhist Thought],（北京[Beijing]：中国社会科学出版社[China Social Sciences Press],1997),19—24。

太子乔达摩·悉达多进入甚深的禅观后,引起了魔宫的极大震动。魔王通过美色的引诱、恐怖的侵扰等都没有让菩萨(修行中的释迦牟尼)退失坚定的信心。菩萨通过观察离欲之道,远离欲界欲望,生起初禅的神足通,变化出种种相对应的境界:

> 尔时菩萨住于正定,其心清白光明无染,离随烦恼,柔软调和无有摇动,至初夜分得智得明,摄持一心获天眼通。菩萨即以天眼观察一切众生死此生彼、好色恶色、胜劣贵贱、随业而往,皆悉了知。……于中夜分摄持一心,证得忆念过去宿命智。通观过去自他所受生事,皆悉了知一生二生乃至十生,百生千生万生亿生,百亿生千亿生,乃至照过无量百千那由他拘胝数生,乃至成劫坏劫,无量无边成劫坏劫,皆悉忆知。[①]

这些描述,可以作为释迦牟尼在修行中的宗教经验来理解,即伴随着他的修道和悟道,他获得了超越性的感知、领悟和控制能力。在世界宗教史上,佛教对释迦牟尼所经由的超常能力的描述和渲染是超过了任何其他宗教的创始人的。当然,这是由释迦牟尼在佛教中的地位决定的,因为依据佛教的义理,他不是任何神的代表,而是超越了任何神灵的究竟觉悟者,这些神通是作为成就无上正等正觉者所理应具备的。[②]

在佛教中,对"神通"最典型的描述是所谓的"五眼""六通"[③]。如佛典所述,佛是成就"五眼"、具足"六通"的,在佛教看来这也反映了佛的圆满功德。根据佛教的义理,"五眼""六通"是佛教信仰者通过修行都可以具备的,其中的某些"神通"如天眼通、天耳通、他心通、宿命通等神通力是其他宗教("外道")的修行者,甚至包括"六道"中的其他众生都可以具有的,但是慧眼、法眼、佛眼与漏尽通是

---

① 《方广大庄严经》,CBETA, T3, No. 187, 595b。

② 对于佛教典籍中的此类描述,当然不可能全部是对释迦牟尼悟道过程中心理体验的实际记载。在佛教传播过程中,其必然会依据民族的文化习俗和自身的宗教教义将一些神话传说编织进去,这一倾向在大乘佛教的经典中表现得更为突出。参见:郭良鋆,《佛陀和原始佛教思想》,30—33。

③ 佛教中所说的"五眼"是指五种代表功能福德的眼力。一是肉眼,为凡夫肉身所具之眼。二是天眼,为色界天人因修禅定所得之眼,世界之远近、前后、内外悉皆能见。三是慧眼,为二乘人(阿罗汉、辟支佛)所得之眼,能洞察一切现象皆为空相。四是法眼,是菩萨所得之眼,能彻了一切法门。五是佛眼,是诸佛具足觉了诸法实相的眼力。"六神通"是佛教描述的六种神妙自在的能力。一是天眼通,能见六道众生的生死苦乐之相和一切世间种种形色,无有障碍。二是天耳通,能闻六道众生关于苦乐忧喜的语言和世间的种种音声。三是他心通,能知六道众生心中所念之事。四是宿命通,能知自身和六道众生三世宿命和所作之事。五是身如意通,身能飞天入地,出入三界,随意变现。六是漏尽通,谓断尽一切烦恼惑业,脱离生死轮回。关于"五眼""六通"的描述,见于《长阿含经》《集异门足论》《俱舍论》《大品般若经》《大智度论》等佛教典籍。这些资料表明,佛教所说的"神通"是有经验基础的,但它们是在经过佛教义理的阐释后才被纳入佛教经典体系的。

佛教的圣者才具备的。[①] 这从一个方面显示了佛教的宗教理想和修行旨趣，即超常的“神通”能力是宗教修行过程中的产物，它们在一定程度上代表了修行者的成就与功德。但是佛教所追求的根本目标，在于通过宗教实践证悟宇宙人生的真理。正如佛学家木村泰贤先生所论述的，佛教修行的特征，在于基于事实对事物进行如实观察，契于“法性”（Dhammatā）而获得“如实智见”（Yathabhuūtanandassana）。[②] 真实的佛陀并非“无所不知”的全智者，他只是提出了基于对世界的如实观察而觉悟的解脱之道。虽然佛陀继承、实践了印度传统的修行方式，然而其根本目的不在于获得禅定功夫，而在于通过自己的身体力行实现“自知、自觉、自作证”，所以原始佛教戒绝鬼魅、奇异之行法，从根本上以精神、道德为中心。[③]

（二）“神通”与禅定的关系

在佛教的修行理论中，“神通”（abhijñā，siddhi，ṛddhi）的获得与禅定有密切的关系。虽然佛教根本的宗教理想并不是获得超常的神异能力，但是禅定修习对于修行者改变惯常的“俗知俗见”、获得对于身心微妙变化的觉知，从而达到所谓的“由定发慧”“定慧等持”，具有不可替代的重要作用。因此，不论是小乘佛教还是大乘佛教的修行体系，禅定的修习都占据了一个不可或缺的地位。如佛陀宣讲的“八正道”就包括了“正定”的内容，在大乘佛教中“禅定”也属于菩萨道“六波罗蜜”（六度）的六种行持之一。实际上，全部佛教的义理就被概括为戒、定、慧三学，“三学”在实践中以禅定为中心，禅定贯彻了“三学”中最重要的定、慧二学，大乘“六度”中的禅那、般若二度。[④]《俱舍论·分别定品》云：“一切功德多依静虑。”[⑤]佛教天台宗的创始人智者（智顗）在《释禅波罗蜜次第法门》中也谈到了修习禅定的“功德”：

> 一切自在变现，诸神通力，皆借禅发。……因禅具足智波罗蜜者，若一切智道种智，一切种智，非定不发，其义可见。行者善修禅故，即便成就十波

---

① 《阿毘达磨俱舍论》：“通有六种。一、神境智证通。二、天眼智证通。三、天耳智证通。四、他心智证通。五、宿住随念智证通。六、漏尽智证通。虽六通中第六唯圣，然其前五，异生亦得。依总相说，亦共异生。如是六通，解脱道摄，慧为自性。如沙门果。解脱道言，显出障义。神境等四，唯俗智摄。他心通五智摄。谓法类道世俗他心。漏尽通如力说。谓或六或十智。”CBETA, T29, No. 1558, 142c-143a.

② 参见：木村泰贤，《原始佛教思想论》［原始仏教思想］，欧阳翰存 Ouyang Hancun 译，（台北［Taipei］：台湾商务印书馆［Taiwan Commercial Press］，1999），61。

③ 木村泰贤，《原始佛教思想论》，228—229。

④ 陈兵 Chen Bing，《佛教禅学与东方文明》［Buddhist Zen and Eastern Civilization］，（上海［Shanghai］：上海人民出版社［Shanghai People's Publishing House］，1997），25。

⑤ 《阿毘达磨俱舍论》，CBETA, T29, No. 1558, 145a。

罗蜜,满足万行一切法门。是故菩萨,欲具一切愿行诸波罗蜜,要修禅定。[①]

在《释禅波罗蜜次第法门》中,智顗还谈到了在禅定中获得的"神通":

> 上根行人福德智慧利故,证初禅时有二因缘得五神通:一者自发;二者修得。一自发者,是人入初禅时,深观根本世间三事,即能通达义世间相,觉义世谛时,三昧智慧转更深利,神通即发。更得色界四大清净造色眼成就,以此净色之心眼彻见十方一切之色事相分明,分别不乱,名天眼通。所余天耳、他心、宿命、身通亦复如是。[②]

这说明"神通"的获得,与特殊的禅定状态或"三昧智慧"存在某种因果关系。结合色界四禅的修习,还要进一步修行慈、悲、喜、舍四无量心,止观双修,方可引发无漏智慧,征得"圣果"。

定、慧二学在实践中被天台宗概括为止观法门。《解深密经》说:"一切声闻及如来等,所有世间及出世间一切善法,当知皆是此奢摩他(止)、毗婆舍那(观)所得之果。"[③]智顗提出:"泥洹之法,入乃多途,论其急要,不出止观二法。""此之二法,如车之双轮,鸟之双翼,若偏修习,即堕邪倒。"[④]在天台宗的修学体系中,"止"(śamatha)是止息散心,属修定;"观"(vipaśyana)是观想简择,属修慧,即通过对现象作如实的观察,获得般若智慧。通过"止观"获得佛智,把握"实相"(dharmatā),被智顗论证为佛教解脱的根本途径。大乘佛教最重要的典籍之一《瑜伽师地论》也讲道,依大乘经论得闻思智慧,修学止观,即是菩萨禅的基本特性。[⑤] 由此可见,修止是入观的基础,通过修观最终获得出世间的智慧,从而断灭烦恼彻底解脱,才是佛教宗教修行的根本目标。

(三)"神通"与"智慧"的关系

依佛教典籍的论述,禅定的修习是引发"神通"的基本条件,实际上,有些佛典也论述了某些"神通"与"智慧"("明",vidyā)一体不二的关系。这突出体现了佛教"神通"的特质,说明佛教的"神通"与"智慧"存在更为密切,也更为根本的关系。佛教经典中有"三明"之说。"三明"(tri-vidyā),是指除尽愚暗所获得的

---

① 智顗,《释禅波罗蜜次第法门》,CBETA, T46, No. 1916, 477a。

② 智顗,《释禅波罗蜜次第法门》,CBETA, T46, No. 1916, 533c。

③ 《解深密经》,CBETA, T16, No. 676, 701b。

④ 智顗,《修习止观坐禅法要》,CBETA, T46, No. 1915, 462b。

⑤ 《瑜伽师地论》:"若有获得九相心住中第九相心住,谓三摩呬多,彼用如是圆满三摩地为所依止,于法观中修增上慧。彼于尔时由法观故,任运转道无功用转,不由加行。毗钵舍那清净鲜白,随奢摩他调柔摄受,如奢摩他道摄受而转,齐此名为奢摩他、毗钵舍那二种和合平等俱转。由此名为奢摩他、毗钵舍那双运转道。"CBETA, T30, No. 1579, 458b。

三方面的智慧：一是宿命智证明，即明白了知众生过去世各种经历的智慧；二是生死智证明，即了知众生随业趣于生、死的因缘及其相状的智慧；三是漏尽智证明，即如实了知谛义，而断尽三界有漏烦恼，远离生死系缚的智慧。[①] 若与六神通相配，则此三明依次以六通之第五（宿命通）、第二（天眼通）、第六（漏尽通）作为自己的功用。这三类“神通”之所以又被称为“明”，是因为它们不但可以知晓众生过去、未来世生命流转的相状，而且还能明了这些现象之所以产生的种种因缘，通达了知涅槃寂灭的实相。它们“皆能随顺厌舍生死，皆能引发殊胜功德，皆能趣向毕竟涅槃”。其中“第四通能除常见，第五通能除断见，第六通既离二边安住中道”。由于这样的“胜用”，“故六通内偏立为明”[②]。这种“神通”与“智慧”的统一，是获得解脱的阿罗汉、辟支佛所具有的特征。但是他们的能力与智慧与佛相比仍然是有限的，只有圆满智慧的获得者（佛），才会得到完全的“明行具足”[③]。实际上，佛教最高的“神通”漏尽通体现的就是智慧的圆满无碍。作为法界实相的彻悟者，由于如来对于宇宙万象的体性，都能了悟其空性实相，乃至彻底超出“三界”生死，这是任何其他的“有漏”神通不可同日而语的。[④] 所以，佛教修行实践的本质，是对宇宙“实相”的契悟，这也是佛教提出的超越生命有限性的根本途径。

（四）“神通”的有限性

“神通”虽然看起来十分神奇，但还是受到各种因缘条件的限制，无法改变众生的“业力”，故佛教有“神通不敌业力”之说。[⑤] 利用“神通”有时会达到某种目的，但只是暂时改变了业力、果报的顺序而已，并不能从根本上改变一个人的命运。在佛陀的弟子中，就有以神通著称的目犍连尊者，他虽然号称“神通第一”，但是他也要承受过去所造业而果报，“终不可避”[⑥]。这一事例实际上说明了神通现象也不能改变因果律。在《增一阿含经 · 卷三八》之《马血天子问八政品》中，佛陀这样告诉比丘：

> 戒律之法者，世俗常数；三昧成就者，亦是世俗常数；神足飞行者，亦是

---

① 《佛地经论》，CBETA，T26，No. 1530，299a—299b。

② 《阿毘达磨大毘婆沙论》，CBETA，T27，No. 1545，530a—530b。

③ 《大智度论》：“云何名明行具足？宿命、天眼、漏尽。名为三明。……行名身、口、业，唯佛身、口、业具足。余皆有失，是名明行具足。”CBETA，T25，No. 1509，71c—72a。

④ 因此而论，佛教“神通”的获得途径与其批评的“外道”有根本的差别，所以佛教是反对依靠扶乩、咒术、药物等获得超自然力量的。

⑤ 《阿毘达磨大毘婆沙论》：“问：神境通力与中有位诸有，所行何者为疾？有作是言：中有行疾。所以者何？经说‘业力胜神通’故。”CBETA，T27，No. 1545，364a。

⑥ 参见：《增一阿含经》，CBETA，T2，No. 125，639b。

世俗常数；智慧成就者，此是第一之义。

随后，佛陀说偈曰：

由禅得神足，至上不究竟，不获无为际，还随五欲中，智慧最为上，无忧无所虑，久毕获等见，断于生死有。①

在这里佛陀说明，神通力也属于一类“世俗常数”，它也是因缘和合而起，也是一种“有漏法”（sāsravadharma），是不可能不受因果律的支配的。② 基于这样的认识，佛教在特定的情况下才会使用“神通”这一不同寻常的手段。在佛教中，显示“神通”一般是用来启发、调伏一类“骄慢”众生，使他们了解佛法不可思议的殊胜之处，以此成为引导他们入道的方便法门。

在特殊的因缘条件下，菩萨也会运用“神通”的力量，让某些众生脱离面临的灾难。当然，根据佛教的义理，其前提是这些众生先前所做的恶业已经报尽，或者他们因为自己的善行应该得到这样的拯救，菩萨只是在满足特定的因缘条件下才会示现。由于“神通”的产生与实现，是在行者的禅定功夫、智慧的境界达到一定的程度之后才会发起的，这些条件的丧失，如因欲望的生起而丧失定境，也会导致失去已得的“神通”。③ 这都说明“神通”效用是有限的，它乃是对某种宇宙法则的认知和利用，一切有限的“神通”，与究竟的觉悟是不能相提并论的。④

（五）佛教“神通”的性质与地位

佛教典籍保留了大量有关“神通”“异能”的记载，出于宗教信仰的热情，其中不可避免地存在诸多夸张的想象甚至虚构之处，但是如果把这一切记载全部归

---

① 《增一阿含经》，CBETA，T2，No. 125，759c。

② 佛教所讲的因果观不同于现代自然科学的因果观，它不但认为在物质现象之间存在因果关系，更突出强调了心理和精神现象方面的因果关系，即因果的道德属性，这种道德的法则即是业（karma）的表现。参见：Stcherbatsky 舍尔巴茨基，《小乘佛学：佛教的中心概念和法的意义》[The Central Conception of Buddhism]，立人 Li Ren 译，（北京[Beijing]：中国社会科学出版社[China Social Sciences Press]，1995），63—64；木村泰贤，《原始佛教思想论》，91。

③ 参见：《阿毘达磨大毘婆沙论》：“昔有王号坞陀衍那，将诸宫室诣水迹山，除去男子，纯与女人奏五妓乐，纵意嬉戏，乐音清妙，香气馚馥，命诸女人露形而舞。时有五百离欲仙人，乘神境通经此上过，有见妙色，有闻妙声，有嗅妙香，皆退神通。”CBETA，T27，No. 1545，314b—314c。

④ 禅宗通过一则“公案”（嵩岳元珪禅师对岳神的示导）表达了对“神通”的有限性的认识：“佛能空一切相，成万法智，而不能即灭定业。佛能知群有性，穷亿劫事，而不能化导无缘。佛能度无量有情，而不能尽众生界，是谓三不能也。定业亦不牢久，无缘亦谓一期。众生界本无增减，亘无一人能主其法。有法无主，是谓无法。无法无主，是谓无心。如我解，佛亦无神通也。但能以无心通达一切法尔。”参见：普济 Puji，《五灯会元》[Five-lantern Festival]，苏渊雷 Su Yuanlei 点校，（北京[Beijing]：中华书局[Zhonghua Book Company]，2008），79。

于人为的造作，那么就会忽视宗教史的一些基本史实。[①] 根据佛典，“神通”大致属于佛教徒修行悟道过程中产生的随附性产物，它与佛教徒的宗教实践构成了一种奇妙的“依附”关系。佛教承认“神通”现象存在并肯定其“超常”的性质，但是这种力量的产生和发挥作用都要取决于各种因缘条件，它与通向终极自由的智慧力相比，是属于第二性的东西，这就是佛教通过“自内证”(pratyātmādhigama)的方式对其所做的判断。对此问题，宗教学家伊利亚德(Mircea Eliade)给出的解说是：“在修炼瑜伽的过程中不可避免会获得‘神通’，正因为如此，神通就构成了比丘精神发展的标志：它们能够证明比丘处于‘无缚’的过程，挣脱正在无情挤压他的自然规律。但是另一方面，‘神通’无疑也是危险的，因为它们诱惑比丘们以无用的‘神奇奥秘支配世界’。”[②]哲学家雅斯贝尔斯将产生了孔子(中国)、佛陀(印度)、琐罗亚斯德(伊朗)、赫拉克里特(希腊)等第一批哲学家的时代称为人类的“轴心时代”，这是一个奠定人类精神基础的时代。在这个时代，“当神话被毁灭的同时，过去的那些神话都被改变了形式，并被赋予深刻的意义”[③]。在人类理性思想的光华喷薄而出之际，神话被“转写”与“重构”，异乎寻常的“神通”也被置于次要的、随附性的地位。

二、“神通”问题在佛教史中的分衍

作为当时印度社会的一种新兴的思想运动，佛教对婆罗门教的教义做出了很多的甚至是根本的改造。它反对自我与世界皆是从唯一的大梵流出、转变而成的“转变说”(Parināma-vāda)的观点，也不认为大梵是唯一的绝对者。梵天(Brahmadeva)、天道(deva)等神灵不但不能决定人的命运，而且也像人一样处于尚未解脱的轮回之中。因此，人的自主性在佛教中得到了充分的肯定，表现出了显著的理性特征，这与婆罗门教等“神教”思想存在很大的不同。正如英国学者查尔斯·埃利奥特所说的，佛陀与中国儒家思想的创始人孔子在思想上存在

---

① 现代宗教学的基本观点是将宗教实践中获得的身心体验作为“宗教经验”来认识，并“企图作出心理学的分析和社会学的解释”。参见吕大吉 Lü Daji，《宗教学通论新编》[A New Edition of General Religious Studies](北京[Beijing]：中国社会科学出版社[China Social Sciences Press]，1998)，262。

② 米尔恰·伊利亚德，《宗教思想史》，530。

③ 卡尔·雅斯贝尔斯 Karl Jaspers，《智慧之路》[An Introduction to Philosophy]，柯锦华 Ke Jinhua，范进 Fan Jin 译，(北京[Beijing]：中国国际广播出版社[China International Broadcasting Press]，1988)，69—71。

某些奇妙的暗合之处。[①] 但是佛教与儒家思想毕竟还是存在很大的不同。佛教否定了神灵具有创造和控制世界的能力,然而根据流传至今的佛教经典可知,虽然理性特征在原始佛教中体现得最为突出,但是在原始佛教的经典中也不乏对"神通"的修习与运用的内容,因此可以肯定地说,佛教从根本上是承认所谓"超自然"现象的存在的。[②] 从佛教的发展史来看,产生于不同历史时期和不同文化环境中的各佛教派别对"神通"问题的态度存在很大差别。

(一)"神通"在印度佛教中的表现与发展

由于原始佛教就对"超自然"的"神通"现象持肯定的态度,如何看待"神通"以及各类"超自然"存在者的性质与作用,在以后佛教的发展演化过程中产生了很大分化。佛陀灭度后百年左右,佛教僧团就发生了分裂,这次分裂的直接原因就是僧团内部对戒律与教义的理解产生了难以弥合的矛盾,其中很重要的就有对佛和阿罗汉的看法出现了根本分歧。由于这次分裂,佛教进入了部派佛教时期。《异部宗轮论》记载,大众部对佛陀的认识与上座部出现了明显的差别,在他们的眼中,佛陀"出世"的超自然倾向得到了明显强化,佛陀越来越拥有了异于常人的"法力":

> 诸佛世尊皆是出世,一切如来无有漏法。诸如来语皆转法轮,佛以一音说一切法,世尊所说无不如义。如来色身实无边际,如来威力亦无边际,诸佛寿量亦无边际。[③]

从大众部与上座部的分歧中,我们就可以发现佛教在各种地域文化因素的影响下出现的融合趋势。佛陀在大众系的案达罗(Andhra)各部中被神化,也是佛教为适应该地区的固有文化所做出的发展。这里本来就是婆罗门教盛传的地区,婆罗门教的湿婆派即是此地的产物,对佛陀的神化就是大众部用一种新方式

---

① 查尔斯·埃利奥特 Charles Eliot,《印度教与佛教史纲》(第一卷)[Hinduism and Buddhism: An Historical Sketch](Volume One),李荣熙 Li Rongxi 译,(北京[Beijing]:商务印书馆[The Commercial Press],1982),281。

② 佛教史一般将释迦牟尼在世至佛教僧伽集团分裂这段时期称为原始佛教时期(大致为公元前530—前370年),原始佛教以四圣谛、八正道、十二因缘、无常、无我等理论为核心,具有显著的理性精神。但不论是汉译的《阿含经》还是南传巴利语的《尼柯耶》等早期佛典,都包含了关于"神通"现象的描述。现代佛教研究者,也肯定了"神通"在佛教实践体系中的地位。参见:Conse 孔滋,《佛教的本质及其发展》[Buddhism, Its Essence and Development],胡国坚 Hu Guojian 译,(贵阳[Guiyang]:贵州大学出版社[Guizhou University Press],2013),86—90。

③ 《异部宗轮论》,CBETA, T49, No.2031, 15b。

发展的“超验主义思想”。[①] 通过各部派对不同的民族文化的适应与融合，佛教的文化适应力和创造力得到了新的发展。

大众部出现之后，就“开始改造佛陀和他的学说理论，这就一步步地引向大乘(Mahāyāna)，从原始三藏的人道主义走向大多数大乘经典的超自然主义”[②]。随着第一批大乘经典的产生，佛教史发展到了一个新的阶段——大乘佛教时期。佛教的这种变化，当代佛学家释印顺将其归结为“佛涅槃所引起的，对佛的永恒怀念”[③]。实际情况就是为了适应和满足人们的宗教热情，佛教融合进了更多神话式的想象，逐渐与原始佛教那种朴素的特点拉开了距离。[④] 但是佛法的真正特色仍然在于其不用“神通”“神变”，而以“教诫神变”度化众生(观察有情何种烦恼最盛，为说正法以行对治)。因此，从根本上说，为适应某些信众的信仰心理而增添到佛陀身上的神话故事只是佛教一种方便说法的方式。这些描述固然可以认为是来自一些佛教信仰者的具有直觉性质的“通感”，但是也显然带有了一般宗教情感所产生的更浓厚的主观色彩。

大乘佛教的出现，一方面更显著地体现出佛教普度众生的入世宗教精神，另一方面，一些佛教思想家也以更为深湛、圆融的哲学思维弥合、超越了原始佛教和部派佛教中的遗留下来的问题和分歧，开显了甚深难言的“内自证圣智境界”。当然，大乘佛教的典籍有自己的演说方式，如果不能结合作者立论的针对性、叙述的“善巧方便”和佛教史的发展逻辑加以理解，将很难把握领会作者的真意而落入思维的“边见”。不论是对于中观学派，还是瑜伽行派，都是如此。《大智度论》《大乘义章》《宗镜录》等大乘佛教的典籍，对各类“神通”“神变”都有集中的描述，这些“神通”境界的不同表现，从不同侧面反映了具备“神通”的佛教圣者所成就的定境、智慧、福德等。宣说如来由于成就无上智慧，具足圆满悲心，能够自觉觉他，可以靠不可思议的神通力量度化众生，这成为最能凸显大乘佛教特色的内容之一。根据佛教义理，《华严经》描述的各种世界亦是唯心所现，喻示了菩萨永无止境的修学境界；同时，它也是华严哲学“相即相入”“圆融无碍”思想的最形象化的表述，可以看作用隐喻的、象征的语言“来烘托一种精神的意境”[⑤]。以《华

---

① 渥德尔 Warder，《印度佛教史》[Indian Buddhism]，王世安 Wang Shi'an 译，(北京[Beijing]：商务印书馆[The Commercial Press]，2000)，303。

② 渥德尔，《印度佛教史》，198。

③ 释印顺 Shi Yinshun，《初期大乘佛教之起源与开展》(上)[The Origin and Development of Early Mahayana Buddhism](Volume One)，(北京[Beijing]：中华书局[Zhonghua Book Company]，2011)，16。

④ 释印顺，《初期大乘佛教之起源与开展》(上)，93。

⑤ 方东美 Fang Dongmei，《华严宗哲学》[Huayan School Philosophy]，(北京[Beijing]：中华书局[Zhonghua Book Company]，2012)，191。

严经》为根本经典形成的华严宗,通过对真如"法界"(Dharmadhātu)的直观和领悟,得以进入显现佛果庄严的"华严三昧"。[①]

大乘佛教中一些具有神秘色彩的描述也可以从宗教经验的角度进行理解。大乘佛教中的净土信仰,就是适应慧根弱而信根强的众生产生的修行"法门"(dharma-paryāya)。净土类经典对"极乐世界"(Sukhāvatī)和佛的形象之庄严殊胜做出了无以复加的描述,这适应了净土信仰者特殊的宗教修行方式。《十住毗婆沙论》讲初修者应念佛色身,修行深入之后则是念佛的法身,最根本的则"应以实相念佛而不贪着"[②]。即要求在对佛国净土的观想中进入"念佛三昧",从而融于佛的"法身",达到与"实相"契合。[③] 净土经典中对佛的光明身相的描绘,是光明崇拜、太阳崇拜心理在佛教中的体现,实际上也反映了佛教对"异教"文化的融合。[④] 在佛教史中,对于瑜伽行派的根本论典《瑜伽师地论》的作者存在不同的说法。根据《婆薮槃豆法师传》的记载,弥勒每天晚上从天上来到人间,为大众诵出《十七地经》,只有无著能亲见弥勒的圣容。[⑤] 类似说法在佛教历史中也不乏其例,根据现代宗教学的理论,这可以理解为无著论师在佛教的修持中出现的心灵通感。释印顺认为,这种情况出现在瑜伽行者的定境中,类似于"秘密大乘"悉地成就的本尊现前,修行者可以向其请教自己的疑问。[⑥] 联系世界各大宗教经典出现于世的情况,我们可以肯定地认为,虽然这些经典的出现伴随一些神秘的传说,但是在宗教修持中其作者进入了一种特殊的"入神"或"出神"状态,创作灵感得到了高度的激发,则是见诸历史的客观事实。[⑦]

---

① 追根溯源,《华严经》对佛国世界的描述也可以在印度传统文化中找到原型。参见:魏道儒 Wei Daoru,《中国华严宗通史》[A General History of Huayan School in China],(南京[Nanjing]:江苏古籍出版社[Jiangsu Ancient Books Publishing House],2001),29。

② 《十住毗婆沙论》:"应以法身念佛心转深入得上势力,应以实相念佛而不贪着。"CBETA, T26, No. 1521, 86a。

③ 《菩萨念佛三昧经》:"正念诸法真实之相,是名念佛。"CBETA, T13, No. 414, 828a。

④ 参见:释印顺 Shi Yinshun,《初期大乘佛教之起源与开展》(中)[The Origin and Development of Early Mahayana Buddhism](Volume Two),(北京[Beijing]:中华书局[Zhonghua Book Company],2011),686—687。

⑤ 参见:《婆薮槃豆法师传》,CBETA, T50, No. 2049。

⑥ 参见:释印顺 Shi Yinshun,《印度佛教思想史》[A History of Indian Buddhist Thought],(北京[Beijing]:中华书局[Zhonghua Book Company],2010),215—216。

⑦ 宗教史的研究表明,不只是佛教,道教、基督教、伊斯兰教等宗教经典的形成都是在某种特殊的灵感思维中完成的。参见:王亚平 Wang Yaping,《基督教的神秘主义》[The Mysticism of Christianity],(北京[Beijing]:东方出版社[The Eastern Publishing Co., Ltd.],2001),第一、二章;菲利浦·希提 Philip K.Hitti,《阿拉伯通史》[History of the Arabs],马坚 Ma Jian 译,(北京[Beijing]:新世界出版社[New World Press],2016),第八章。

佛教具有的神秘特征,在佛教的密教化时期有了最为突出的体现。从佛教自身的特点来看,佛教圣者证悟的过程本来就具有神秘的性质。正如佛教研究家平川彰先生所言,原始佛教所讲的“觉悟之智”“虽然是理性的,充满光明的智慧,但是并非所谓合理的、逻辑的知识”①。在释迦牟尼的时代,由于否定神权的需要,一切方技之术与咒语术数之学均为世尊所斥责,然而即使是在原始佛教时期,密咒的使用也没有被完全禁绝,原因就是密咒在佛教中被认为的确具有一定的“效验”。② 随着印度教(革新后的婆罗门教)的复兴,受到挤压的佛教吸收了印度教的神灵与教义、仪轨,开始走向印度佛教最后的形态“秘密佛教”(Tāntric Buddhism)。密乘佛教具有很多不同于以往佛教的特征,它不是以理论建树著称,而是以特重瑜伽实践为特色,在修行方式方面有了很多的发展。密乘佛教的瑜伽修行,即通过行者的身、口、意三方面的修持,与佛菩萨等本尊的“三密”③得以相应,从而为真如之力所加持,进入“三摩地”境界,成办多种多样的所谓“悉地”(siddhi),“神通”的力量和表现得到更进一步的推崇和宣扬。④ 实际上,密乘佛教结合了印度深厚的神秘文化传统,是佛陀的启示与瑜伽冥想技术更紧密结合后产生的新的佛教文化形态。⑤

(二)“神通”在中国佛教中的地位及评价

佛教在印度消亡后,密乘佛教在中国西藏地区得到了保留和发展,产生了融合西藏原始宗教、大乘显教与密乘佛教于一身的藏传佛教。它与早期的佛教具有不同的面貌,这可理解为佛教在传播过程中进一步融合与嬗变的结果。藏传佛教不但传承了印度金刚乘的密法,还融合了西藏传统文化中苯教、萨满教的信仰和技术,有些宗派还受到了内地禅宗的影响。藏传佛教虽然吸收、融合了各种不同的文化因素,但其根本的宗教理想和哲学仍然属于佛教的范畴。正如伊利亚德所说,修行者的观想方式虽然“在结构上是萨满的”,但是其宗教实践的“精

① 平川彰,《印度佛教史》[インド仏教の歴史],庄昆木 Zhuang Kunmu 译,(台北[Taipei]:商周出版社[Business Weekly Publications, Inc.],2009),449—450。

② 释圣严 Shi Shengyan,《印度佛教史》[A History of Indian Buddhism],(苏州[Suzhou]:弘化社[Honghua Society]),228—229。

③ 密法认为身、口、意在众生为“三业”,于佛菩萨为“三密”,因其具有不可思议之力用。

④ 相对于前期的大乘佛教,密乘的“悉地”表现出更加依赖禅定的倾向。参见:释印顺 Shi Yinshun,《华雨集》(三)[Hua Yu Collection(3)],(北京[Beijing]:中华书局[Zhonghua Book Company],2011),128—137。

⑤ 对密乘佛教的认识,经常受到特定伦理意识的影响,但从历史的角度看,它的产生是多种文化传统相互作用的结果。参见:以利亚德 Mircea Eliade,《死与自由:瑜伽实践的西方阐释》[Yoga: Essai ser l'origine de la mystique Indienne],武锡申 Wu Xishen 译,(北京[Beijing]:中国致公出版社[China Zhigong Publishing Housc],2001),第五、六章。

神意义和价值"却是与萨满教全然不同的。① 苯教藏传佛教中产生了很多著名的修行"成就者",他们表现出了很多超越常人的神功异能,有些记载甚至说他们可以转化人的色身为光明虹霓之身。② 这些修行的成就,常令很多与传统的宗教文化日渐疏远的现代人感到不可思议,但是佛教自己的理论系统很好地容纳并解释了这些现象。据说著名的密教修行者、噶举派的上师米拉日巴在修行中就产生了不可思议的境界,但这同样是"殊胜心道所引起的缘起",所以才会让他超出轮回,得到最终的解脱。③ 因为瑜伽修法是属于方便道,它可以使人的主观精神和客观事物都发生变化,但是要获得彻底的解脱,还需要显、密结合的"明空双运",这也是佛教与"外道"的根本差别之处。④

佛教在中国的传播,是与中国的固有文化相互影响、相互作用的过程,其结果就是产生了具有鲜明中国文化特色的汉传佛教。汉传佛教作为一种新的文化产物,在教义教理、价值观念、修行方式等方面都与印度佛教有了显著的区别,它既不像印度佛教那样长于构造鸿篇大论,也不像藏传佛教那样遵循次第严格的瑜伽修持,而是将修行与日常生活融为一体,追求在生活中悟道。关于佛教徒神异事迹的记载,自佛教传入之后便不绝于史籍与僧传,但是最能体现中国文化特色的是禅宗行者的悟道行状。禅宗的出现,将佛教的修证悟道与中国传统的哲学思想、人文传统、生活方式有机结合起来,是佛教在中国文化土壤中的新发展。从历史的角度看,这也是印度佛教传入中国之后,被中国人消化吸收,创造性地重构之后再次流布的结果。从东汉魏晋至隋唐,佛教与中国文化经过了几百年的碰撞与磨合,一种新的文化降生于世的因缘已经成熟。菩提达摩传来的"南天竺一乘宗",历经东山法门的演化,至六祖惠能大师终于形成了中国佛教"教外别传"的禅宗风貌。禅宗的史传记载,在禅宗行者参禅悟道的过程中,并不是没有

---

① 米尔恰·伊利亚德,《宗教思想史》,1174。

② 藏传佛教将这类现象视为"即身成佛"的实际例证。如果这类现象被认定实际存在,心理学等学科将从科学的视角做出研究和说明,这将不同于佛教从教义层面做出的解读。

③ Sanjay Gyaltsen 桑杰坚赞,《米拉日巴传》[The Biography of Mira Raba],刘立千 Liu Liqian 译,(北京[Beijing]:民族出版社[The Ethnic Publishing House],2000),134。

④ 刘立千 Liu Liqian,《刘立千藏学著译文集·杂集》[Liu Liqian Tibetan Learning Translation Collection · Miscellaneous Collections],(北京[Beijing]:民族出版社[The Ethnic Publishing House],2000),34。相对于汉传佛教而言,藏传佛教更重视"神通"的作用,鼓励弟子要修神通,但是前提也是要先修福德智慧,圆满修行的资粮。如11世纪到西藏传法的阿底峡在《菩提道灯论》中云:"福智为自性,资粮圆满因,一切佛共许,为引发神通。如鸟未生翼,不能腾虚空,若离神通力,不能利有情。具通者日夜,所修诸福德,诸离神通者,百生不能集。若欲速圆满,大菩提资粮,要勤修神通,方成非懈怠。"参见:阿底峡,《菩提道灯论》,收录于宗喀巴大师 Master Tsongkhapa,《菩提道次第广论》[lamrimchenmo],法尊 Fazun 译,(莆田[Putian]:广化寺佛经流通处[Guanghua Temple Buddhist Circulation Office],1997),589。

神异情况出现，实际上他们很多人的禅修过程都伴随身心方面的奇妙变化，只不过他们多将其看作所谓的“门头光影”不予理睬。[①] 因为在禅宗看来，在修证过程中出现的诸多“神通妙境”只是走向终极解脱过程中的沿途风光，如果为这些现象所迷惑，那么就会丧失真心，偏离悟道的正途。因为“现前种种境界，都是幻妄不实，唯是真心中所现影子”。“以八识根本未破，纵有作为，皆是识神边事。若以此为真，大似认贼为子。”[②]在此时只有打破迷障，才可能觑见终极的“本来面目”，归家稳坐。[③]

在人类文化史上，禅宗的出现具有重要的启示意义，它说明了文化发展的过程是一种前行与回归的统一过程。《五灯会元》中有这样一个公案：

> 世尊在灵山会上，拈花示众，是时众皆默然，唯迦叶尊者破颜微笑。世尊云：“吾有正法眼藏，涅槃妙心，实相无相，微妙法门，不立文字，教外别传，付嘱摩诃迦叶。”[④]

这一公案的意义在于说明，释迦牟尼以正法眼藏付与大弟子迦叶，象征了佛教“以心传心”授法的开始。因此，我们可以说禅宗虽然出现在7世纪的唐朝，但它实际上是佛陀所证悟境界的重现，是佛教在中国文化时空中的本真回归。这一点还可以在藏传佛教中得到印证，藏传佛教宁玛派的最高密法“大圆满”，噶举派传法的心髓“大手印”，其法要都在于指示如来所证“涅槃妙心”，故堪称藏传佛教一系的正法眼藏。禅宗传承了佛陀所证境界的真髓，舍弃了作为一种文化现象在历史时空中产生的赘积，的确具有返璞归真、直彻心源的意义。

如前所述，佛教典籍中存在大量关于“神通”现象的记载，除去其中神话性质的构造和文学的夸张，很多都可以作为一类“宗教经验”来看待。佛教不但以丰富的禅修实践活动展示了形形色色的“神通”现象，为我们认识这种现象积淀了

---

① 由于担心扰乱世道人心，在大众面前显示“神通”在禅宗中是一项受到戒绝的行为，只允许在特殊情况下偶尔使用。这种典型的态度可以在下面一则“公案”中得到说明：唐代的邓隐峰禅师路过淮西时，遇到官军与吴元济叛军交战。为了平息战事，他利用“神通”在两军前“掷锡空中，飞身而过。两军将士仰观，事符预梦，斗心顿息”，于是一场兵祸消于无形。邓隐峰禅师显示“神通”后，担心造成“惑众”的后果，就往五台山“倒立而化”。参见：普济，《五灯会元》，169—170。

② 《憨山老人梦游集》，CBETA，X73，No. 1456，468b—469b。

③ 虽然禅宗对“神通”现象采取正文所述的基本态度，但是“神通”仍然是禅宗乃至汉传佛教历史中一个不可忽视的因素，很多禅宗和尚如普庵(1115—1169年)、济公(1148—1209年)等人在民间的影响与他们的“神异”风范有很大关系。

④ 普济，《五灯会元》，10。《大梵天王问佛决疑经》的记载是：“尔时如来，坐此宝座，受此莲华，无说无言。但拈莲华，入大会中。八万四千人天时大众，皆止默然。于时长老摩诃迦叶，见佛拈华示众佛事，即今廓然，破颜微笑。佛即告言：‘是也，我有正法眼藏涅槃妙心，实相无相微妙法门。不立文字，教外别传。总持任持，凡夫成佛第一义谛，今方付嘱摩诃迦叶。’言已默然。”CBETA，X01，No. 27，442a。

丰厚的经验基础,而且也发展出了评价种类现象的理论原则,即佛教在其宗教实践中通过“自内证”的方式,形成的对于人类心识问题特有的认知和判断。回顾佛教的历史可知,“神通”是佛教自身宗教实践的产物,它在不同社会文化环境中的影响及其评价是不尽一致的,但是它们都构成了佛教文化不可分割的组成部分,是佛教连绵不断的文化脉络中一个富有活力的内在因素。它们与不同的文化传统相适应,不断以新的文化形态在不同的历史时空中衍化与发展。也就是说,在不同的社会文化环境中,“神通”都是构成佛教超越性的一个内在因素,但是对它的价值评价以及对它们的理解受到特定的社会文化环境的制约和影响。

三、余论

“宗教经验”这一概念源自对宗教现象的研究,但是它作为一种人性的表现形式不止见诸传统的宗教文化中。随着人类文化形式的发展与分化,曾经以宗教文化的形式表现出来的人类的潜能及其释放和升华,也表现在哲学沉思、文学艺术创作、科学探索等活动中。对此,威廉·詹姆士在《宗教经验之种种》中已经有所论述。他认为“神圣的”(divine)经验的对象不一定表现在对某个人格神的虔敬中,也表现在对自然之美的感知、对现实生活的经历中。人本主义心理学家马斯洛则排除了宗教经验的“超自然”性质,并将“神秘体验”转换为一个新的概念“高峰体验”(peak-experiences),从而把宗教拉到科学研究的领域中。他认为“从高峰体验所具有的最美好、最深刻、最普遍和最人道的意义上看”,这类体验可以被看成“真正的宗教体验”①。马斯洛对神秘体验的看法说明不论是宗教现象还是其他领域,人们都会遇到一些令人惊异的“奥秘”,但是它们并非产生于“超自然”的原因。对宗教文化的跨学科研究进一步表明,宗教经验包含了特殊的“意识变更状态”(altered states of consciousness, ASC),宗教经验的种种表现与人的社会历史的存在方式之间存在密切的关系,它是人的自然属性和社会属性的集中表现。②

如英国学者杰弗里·帕林德尔所言,“许多宗教中都有神秘的表征,这被视作内在精神生活的普遍性的证明,也被当作所有宗教之间的真实的联系——宗

① 马斯洛 Maslow,《谈谈高峰体验》,陈维正 Chen Weizheng 译,收录于《人的潜能和价值》[Human Potential and Value],林方 Lin Fang 主编,(北京[Beijing]:华夏出版社[Huaxia Publishing House],1987),368。“体验”与“经验”在英语的表述中,都是“experience”一词。

② 研究表明,“意识变更状态”可以由大脑的动力学变化以及神经化学和代谢过程引起,此外,环境刺激、心理活动和自我控制也可以改变大脑的功能和意识体验。参见:D. Vaitl, et al., “Psychobiology of Altered States of Consciousness,” *Psychological Bulletin*, 131. 1(2005): 98, 99。

教可以因教条而区分为许多种，但它们在寻求普遍的整体性时，实质上是统一的"[①]。也就是说，各种宗教的神秘主义体验除去宗教教条和教义方面的差异，在实质上都具有共同的经验基础。但是，对宗教经验的不同领悟，则赋予了该经验不同的价值和意义，并将实践者导向不同的人生追求目标。通过对佛教"神通"实践的分析，我们会进一步理解佛教宗教修持的本质特征，即佛教实践的根本宗旨和目的是人的升华和觉悟。以此而言，佛教对"神通"现象的理解，反映了人类自我认知的高度智慧，即使在当代的历史时空中，仍然具有发人深省的启发意义和不可磨灭的认识价值。

① 杰弗里·帕林德尔，《世界宗教中的神秘主义》，2。

The "abhijñā" Concept of Buddhism and Its Historical Evolution

WANG Meng

Abstract: The phenomenon of "abhijñā"(supernatural power)constitutes an integral part of the Buddhist cultural system. For the nature and status of the phenomenon of "abhijñā", Buddhism has made the judgment by the way of pratyātmādhigama(internal self-proving), that they belong to the accompanying phenomenon in the process of Buddhist practice, which is the second thing compared with the perfect wisdom to ultimate nirvana. In the history of the development of Buddhism, the practice of "abhijñā" adapt to the cultural traditions of different societies and become a dynamic intrinsic factor in the Buddhist cultural context, but their influence will be limited by the specific cultural environment. As a special manifestation of religious experience, the practice of "abhijñā" in Buddhism leads practitioners to a more transcendent life goal, that is, human sublimation and enlightenment. Buddhism's understanding of the phenomenon of "abhijñā" reflects the high wisdom of human self-cognition, and it still has thought-provoking significance and indelible cognitive value in the contemporary era.

Key Words: Buddhist "abhijñā", Historical Evolution, Self-introduction, Religious Experience

明弘治正德时期犹太教与伊斯兰教汉文碑刻对比研究*

马保全**

【摘要】明弘治正德时期，犹太教留有两通汉文碑刻，伊斯兰教则留有六通汉文碑刻。通过研读、比较，可总结出两教在经书名称翻译与儒家祭祖观念借鉴方面有相异之处；另可总结出两教对崇拜对象、宗教职业者称呼是相同的，同时两教修建宗教场所的经费来源、忠君观念、与中国传统文化的关系等方面也多有相通之处。笔者通过两教碑文互证认为：两教碑刻翔实地展现了当时犹太人与穆斯林的状况；这些碑刻是两教中国化的历史思想资源，是两教文化与中国思想文化比较、对话的重要史料，在丰富了两教思想的同时，对中国文化有一定贡献。

【关键词】弘治；正德；犹太教；伊斯兰教；汉文碑刻

一、问题的提出

在宗教学研究视域中，犹太教、基督教与伊斯兰教，皆属亚伯拉罕宗教体系。这三种宗教在具有很大共通性的同时，也因内在教义与外在环境不同等，产生了多种不同面貌。犹太教与伊斯兰教同样发源于中东，有大量共通的宗教记忆，有共同承认的不少先知事迹。在历史上，诸如迈蒙尼德等犹太贤哲均曾与当时的穆斯林社会有融洽的关系与频繁的往来。近代以来，随着二战之后世界格局的形成，犹太教与伊斯兰教的关系更加引人瞩目。两教的对比研究，可谓不可胜数。笔者关注两教汉文碑刻有年，并注意到学界对明弘治正德时期两教汉文碑刻的对比研究尚显缺乏，故以之为题进行研究。

---

* 本文是国家社科基金青年项目“中国近代学者海外出版阿拉伯文译著搜集、整理与研究”(17CTQ019)和教育部人文社会科学重点研究基地重大项目“犹太教与伊斯兰教关系的历史与现实研究”(18JJD730001)的成果。

** 马保全，山东大学犹太教与跨宗教研究中心博士研究生、山东师范大学外国语学院阿拉伯语系讲师。

两教的中文文献，有教内文献(以碑刻与谱牒为代表，伊斯兰教还有明清汉文回儒译著)，另有中国各类正史、方志、文人笔记等文献中的记载。就中文文献而言，以两教寺碑的宗教性最强。有关两教的外文文献，欧洲方面，在元代有鲁布鲁克(Guillaume de Rubruquis)、马可波罗(Marco Polo)、孟高维诺(Giovanni di Monte Corvino)、鄂多立克(Odoric de Pordenone)、海屯一世(Hethum Ⅰ)等人的记载；其时间明显早于本文研究的明弘治正德(1488—1521 年)时期，而明清来华的利玛窦(Matteo Ricci)、钟鸣礼(Jean Fernandes)、骆保禄(Gozane Giampaolo)、孟正气(Jean Domenge)等欧洲人，则晚于明代弘治正德时期半个世纪或更久。中亚与西亚方面，唐代有苏莱曼(Sulayman Altājir)与艾布·载德('abū Zayd)，元末有伊本·白图泰(Ibn Baṭūṭah)，明永乐时期有盖耶速丁(Ghiyāthu Aldin)等对两教的记载，但距弘治正德时期也是半个世纪或更久。正德时期，有阿里·阿克巴尔(Sayyid 'aliy'akbar Khatāy)来华，他以波斯文著成《中国纪行》，介绍了明正德时期的一些情况，但与本文关注的汉文碑刻几无关联。[①] 可见这一时期有关中国犹太教与伊斯兰教的记录不足，故本文研究的汉文碑刻有补阙之功。

现存最早的两通犹太教汉文碑刻，为河南开封明弘治二年(1489 年)《重建清真寺记》[②]与正德七年(1512 年)《尊崇道经寺记》[③]——这也是犹太教留下的仅有的两方明代碑刻。现存最早的伊斯兰教汉文碑刻是元代的，凡三通，分别位

---

① 阿里·阿克巴尔 Ali Akbar,《中国纪行》[khiṭāya nāmah]，张至善 Zhang Zhishan，张铁伟 Zhang Tiewei，岳家明 Yue Jiaming 译，(北京[Beijing]：生活·读书·新知三联书店[SDX Joint Publishing Company]，1988)。

② 碑存开封博物馆，拓片有多种流传。陈垣先生曾据当时可见的一个拓本与"康熙间拓本"整理出碑文，载《开封一赐乐业教考》中，此为一权威整理本。见陈垣 Chen Yuan:《陈垣学术论文集》(第一集)[Chen Yuan Academic Essay Collection Episode One]，(北京[Beijing]：中华书局[Zhonghua Book Company]，1980)，256—259。在此整理本的基础上，笔者又根据国家图书馆所藏拓片——载北京图书馆金石组 Inscriptions Compilation Group of Beijing Library 编，《北京图书馆藏中国历代石刻拓本汇编》[Compilation of Chinese Inscriptions Collected in Beijing Library]，(郑州[Zhongzhou]：中州古籍出版社[Ancient Books Publishing House]，1997)，第 53 册，2——逐字核对，发现国图拓本缺字很多，远不及陈垣先生使用的康熙拓本。陈所用康熙拓本或照片，笔者未查到。笔者曾于 2018 年 5 月去开封市博物馆访此碑并拍照，碑残泐甚，效果不及北图拓片。本文使用陈整理本。下文将简称之为开封碑一。

③ 碑存开封博物馆，陈垣先生曾整理出此碑碑文，载《开封一赐乐业教考》，此为一权威整理本。见陈垣，《陈垣学术论文集》(第一集)，260—262。在此整理本的基础上。笔者又根据国家图书馆所藏拓片(载北京图书馆金石组编，《北京图书馆藏中国历代石刻拓本汇编》，第 53 册，177)逐字核对，本文使用陈整理本。下文将简称之为开封碑二。笔者曾于 2018 年 5 月去开封市博物馆访此碑并拍照，效果不及北图拓片。

于泉州、广州与河北定州。伊斯兰教在明代留下的汉文寺碑约40种[①]，其中立于明弘治正德时期的碑刻凡六，分别为弘治五年(1492年)南京《敕建净觉礼拜二寺碑记》[②]，弘治八年(1495年)济南《济南府历城县礼拜寺重修记》[③]、弘治九年(1496年)北京《敕赐礼拜寺碑记》[④]、弘治九年北京《敕赐礼拜寺增修碑记》[⑤]、正德十四年(1519年)大名《礼拜寺碑记》[⑥]、正德十六年(1521年)定州《重修清真礼拜寺记》[⑦]。

两教汉文碑刻是否具有可对比性，是本文须解决的首要问题。从大的方面

---

① 杨晓春 Yang Xiaochun,《元明时期汉文伊斯兰教文献研究》[A Study on Chinese Islamic Documents in Yuan and Ming Dynasties],(北京[Beijing]:中华书局[Zhonghua Book Company],2012),253—327。

② 碑佚，亦无拓本传世。碑文见《清真教考群书汇辑》[A Collection of Books Related with Islam],影印件收录于吴海英 Wu Haiying 主编,《回族典藏全书》[The Book Collection of Hui Nationality],(兰州[Lanzhou]:甘肃文化出版社[Gansu Culture Press];银川[Yinchuan]:宁夏人民出版社[Ningxia People's Press],2008),第63册,222—225;刘智 Liu Zhi 撰,《天方至圣实录》[The Record of Prophet Mohamed],(成都[Chengdu]:锦城宝真堂[Baozhen Press of Jincheng],1872,10—12),影印件见吴海英主编,《回族典藏全书》,第23册,531—535。此碑文亦为山东临清仁寿堂《马氏族谱》所收录，文字略有出入，见伊牧之 Yi Muzhi 主编,《山东回族谱序集注》[Annotation of Muslim Pedigrees in Shandong Province],(济南[Jinan]:《济南穆斯林》编辑部[*Muslims in Jinan* Editorial Department],2013),92—93。经比较,《马氏族谱》中录文误多。此外,《马氏族谱》中，将可马鲁丁写作马鲁坤丁，这究竟是同一个人的字号之别，还是其他原因，待考。有杨晓春先生据《清真教考群书汇辑》所录整理本(杨晓春,《元明时期汉文伊斯兰教文献研究》,270—271)。核原书后，本文使用杨整理本。下文简称之为南京碑。

③ 碑存济南清真南大寺。据载曾有人作拓，然笔者未找到收藏该拓片之所。碑文收录于伊牧之 Yi Muzhi,《济南伊斯兰教碑刻笺注》[Annotation of Jinan Islamic Inscriptions],(济南[Jinan]:济南伊斯兰教协会[Jinan Islamic Association],2004),3—7。笔者据此对照原碑逐字核对，本文使用伊整理本。下文简称之为济南碑。

④ 碑存北京牛街礼拜寺南碑亭。见北京市宣武区伊斯兰教协会 Islamic Association of Xuanwu District, Beijing 编著,《清真古韵——北京牛街礼拜寺》[Ancient Muslim Charm—Beijing Niujie Mosque],(北京[Beijing]:文物出版社[Cultural Relics Press],2009)。该书第195页有是碑汉文内容拓片照片，第196页有整理本。另有杨晓春先生整理本(杨晓春,《元明时期汉文伊斯兰教文献研究》,272—274),核拓片照片后，本文使用杨整理本。下文将简称之为北京碑一。又及：同书第197页有该碑碑阴波斯文内容拓片，价值亦很大，因本文是对两教汉文碑刻的对比研究，故对波斯文内容，笔者拟另做研究。

⑤ 碑存北京牛街礼拜寺北碑亭，见北京市宣武区伊斯兰教协会编著,《清真古韵——北京牛街礼拜寺》。第198、200页有是碑内容拓片照片，第199、201页有整理本。另有杨晓春先生整理本(杨晓春,《元明时期汉文伊斯兰教文献研究》,274—276),核拓片照片后，本文使用杨整理本。下文将简称之为北京碑二。

⑥ 碑佚，亦无拓片传世。碑文收录于程廷恒 Cheng Tingheng 等纂,《大名县志》[Daming County Chronicles],第二十五卷，宗教，民国二十三年(1934年)铅印本,14—15。另有杨晓春先生整理本(杨晓春,《元明时期汉文伊斯兰教文献研究》,284—285)。核县志后，本文使用杨整理本。下文将简称之为大名碑。

⑦ 碑存定州清真寺内。有杨晓春先生整理本(杨晓春,《元明时期汉文伊斯兰教文献研究》,279—282),本文使用杨整理本。下文将简称之为定州碑。

来看，两者皆属一神教，在万有根源、世界缘由、列圣事迹等方面，有大量共享的传统资源。就小的方面来说，有以下五点对比基础：就文种与载体而言，都是汉文碑刻；就时间而言，均产生于明弘治与正德这两个前后相接的时期；从文献来源来看，都在宗教场所内；就存世数量而言，犹太教碑二块，伊斯兰教碑六块，虽有一定差距，但都是个位数，尚不悬殊，且犹太教碑字数略多于其他伊斯兰教碑，此外两教在明代留下的碑刻与同时期儒释道碑刻相比，数量差距悬殊；就地点而言，本文碑刻涉及北京、南京、开封、济南、定州、大名等地，均属当时具有一定规模的重要汉地城市。当然，通过对碑文内容的具体研究，将发现更多可供对比的内容，请允许笔者在后文中详谈。因之不难看出，弘治正德时期两教汉文碑刻的对比研究，是有充足逻辑依据的。

两教碑刻撰写者在具有宗教属性的同时，也有不同程度的官方属性，这是本文要说明的另一重要问题。宗教学的知识告诉我们，世界上各宗教的信徒（自然包括犹太人与穆斯林），都将其宗教场所视为神圣之地，此神圣之地碑刻的宗教属性自不必多言。本文涉及的寺碑，都与宗教场所的兴建、翻修有关，而且建修过程中有非本教的官方赞助，比如开封碑一记载“奉周府定王传令，赐香重修清真寺”，南京碑记载寺是明太祖“敕建”，北京碑一“蒙宪宗皇帝敕赐曰礼拜寺”。再比如南京碑撰者是汉族知识分子“赐进士、奉训大夫、右春坊右谕德吴郡王鏊”，济南碑“知府蔡公晟，暨知县盛公敬，请于藩司，荐玺于礼部”。定州碑提到曾经设想得到皇帝敕额，最终得到的是礼部侍郎张昱所写的匾额。这些碑文所载都直接表现了寺与皇帝、宗室和各级官员有不同程度的关系，在当时的环境下，涉及这些内容的记载必然是重要的，撰写者体现出一定的官方属性也是毋庸讳言。

同时我们发现，碑文记载了各种教内人士对清真寺建修的帮助，包括官员、宗教人士、信教群众等。就官员而言，开封碑一的撰写者金钟是犹太人，他也是“开封府儒学增广生员”；开封碑二撰写者犹太人左唐是“四川布政司右参议”这样的在职官员；济南碑的撰写者刘瓒是穆斯林，是“赐进士、中顺大夫”并从“陕西按察司副使”职位退休；北京碑二有杨永，他“崇信本教，喜舍金帛”，也是“内府酒醋局右□使”；此外还有刘昇，为“尚衣监太监”；大名碑作者金贤是穆斯林，曾任大名府知府等职；定州寺的修建则有武平伯陈勋、陈熹这样的世袭官员参与。就宗教人士而言，下列三碑的记载比较详尽：开封碑一记载了“列微五思达”“李诚、李实、俺平徒、艾端、李贵、李节、李昇、李纲、艾敬、周安、李荣、李良、李智、张浩”等满剌，这些或是该寺历代的拉比；南京碑记载可马鲁丁、亦卜剌金后代九户各姓“习学本教……奉礼部札付事理”，即他们是一直学习伊斯兰教经典、持明廷礼部颁发的许可证从事法律许可宗教活动的阿訇，他们参与修寺，并希望立碑以为

记录；济南碑详尽记载了元代的满剌艾迪，明朝的木铎、陈礼等该寺历史上的阿訇，以及本次修建的主要倡议者阿訇陈玺。就信教群众而言，各碑中均有记载，且人数更多，比如开封碑一"诸氏"犹太人，济南碑中的"教中趋义者"等，信教群众参加宗教场所修建的筹资是常见的情形，兹不多举例。据此不难看出，石碑能长期保存在宗教场所中，无论其撰写者是否为本教人，其内容必然符合宗教教义，起码是基本合理的，而且在立碑时受到本教文武官员，寺中犹太教拉比、伊斯兰教阿訇（两者当时的称呼都是满剌），以及人数众多的一般教众的认可。由此，我们有充分的理由相信，如此严肃且受到教内外认可的碑文，必然是撰写者以理性态度进行的表达，是可信的。我们也很难想象：在本教人心中神圣的宗教场所内，有一种荒诞或饱受争议的观点能够铭诸金石，矗立几百年而未被毁掉。

二、相异之处

犹太教与伊斯兰教是两种宗教，两教汉文碑刻中出现不同之处，是正常且合理的。例如就教义而言，两者有根本性的不同——犹太教碑刻中没有也不会出现关于《古兰经》、穆罕默德等内容；伊斯兰教碑刻中，没有也不会出现自称一赐乐业（以色列）等内容。就宗教活动而言，开封碑一记载，犹太人当时有"礼拜"，以及"斋"——"每月之际四日斋"现通称为"安息日"和"戒"——"一日大戒"，现通称为"赎罪日"等活动。[①] 关于伊斯兰教的基本功修则，济南碑记载为"诚礼斋济游"[②]，现多称为念礼斋课朝，为伊斯兰教五大功修。对于礼拜这一重要的宗教仪式，犹太人"寅午戌而三次礼拜"，这与伊斯兰教每日五次礼拜也是不同的。碑中此类例子尚多，不赘。这些不同是域外犹太人与穆斯林固有的不同之处，换言之，在当时的西亚或中亚、南亚任何一处，如果当地有犹太人且有穆斯林，这些基本的教义、宗教功修都会不同，不能混为一谈。本文更多的是关注犹太教与伊斯兰教在域外趋同，但到达中国后表现不同的地方。

（一）对经书的译法不同

犹太教《圣经》包括直接来自神启的《托拉》《先知书》与人在圣灵感动下写作的《圣著》。其中，犹太人认为《托拉》是神对先知摩西的启示。开封碑一曾记载《托拉》（*Torah*）为"《正经》一部，五十三卷"此处将《托拉》翻译为《正经》[③]，同碑

---

① 解释见：刘百陆 Liu Bailu，《开封犹太人碑文研究》[Research on the Kaifeng Jewish Inscriptions]，河南大学 2006 年硕士论文[2006 Master Thesis of Henan University]，25—26。

② 济南碑。

③ 开封碑一。

又载“恭敬进于《道经》之前”，此处又将《托拉》译为了《道经》。开封碑二亦称其为《道经》，指出“《道经》四部，五十三卷”并反复强调《道经》在犹太人生活中发挥了重要作用，并以此入碑额。由此可见，当时对《托拉》的翻译虽不稳定，但整体而言，是以《道经》这一译法为使用最多者。伊斯兰教的核心经典为《古兰经》(القرآن\Qurān)，穆斯林相信这是由真主通过天使启示给先知穆罕默德的。弘治正德时期伊斯兰教碑刻中，南京碑将伊斯兰教经典称为《真经》，据前后文看，这应是对包括《古兰经》在内的伊斯兰教各类经书的笼统称呼。北京碑二记载“经则曰《天之经》”，此处将《古兰经》译为《天之经》。其他略早明碑如杭州景泰四年(1453年)《杭郡重修礼拜寺记》载：“杭郡礼拜寺……中间不设形象，惟庋《天经》一函。”[①]此处将《古兰经》译为《天经》。万历七年(1579年)的著名碑刻《清真法明百字圣号》里面，也有“正烈衍政《天经》”，同碑中，在“本教经中译述圣赞”中又有“接受《天经》，三十部册”的记载。同碑最后另有“道传万代，教授《真经》”[②]。其余明碑中此类记载尚不少。结合上述几则碑文记载，可见在明代，对《古兰经》的翻译虽也不稳定，但整体而言，以《天经》这一译法为使用最多者。

对来自同一个崇拜对象的经书，有两种不同的翻译，所为何因？或可试从意译与音译两方面进行分析。在意译层面，不难看出开封碑一中有大量从犹太文化与中国传统文化的角度解释“道”的内容，例如“道无形像，俨然天道之在上”“鞠躬敬道，道在鞠躬也”“中立不倚敬道，道在中立也”“静而存养，默赞敬道”等；开封碑二指出“经以载道”，认为“圣贤之道，垂六经”，即圣贤之道，记载于《诗》《书》《礼》《易》《乐》《春秋》六经中。两碑认为，犹太教是符合道的，而且此教是敬道的，则其经书为《道经》，在意译层面自然是非常合理了。同时，这一译法与中国固有的老子《道经》(《道经》与《德经》组成《道德经》)一致，显得更有中国文化内涵。但为何翻译成固定的《道经》而非其他？本文认为：这个道字，很可能也有音译的成分，即对应《托拉》的“托”(To)这个发音，并脱落或未译《托拉》的“拉”(rah)，故《道经》很可能是兼顾意译与音译的一种精妙翻译，由此广受欢迎。然此音译之说仅为蠡测，暂无更多证据。弘治正德前后伊斯兰教碑刻把《古兰经》翻译为《天之经》或《天经》，碑文中不乏关于天的记载：“唐初开元年，有圣人者出，代天传道”[③]“面西礼拜，告天祝圣”[④]“上天至尊至大，无比无对”[⑤]“以敬天为

① 杨晓春，《元明时期汉文伊斯兰教文献研究》，264。

② 此碑现存北京东四清真寺，笔者2009年亲访此碑并拍照。

③ 济南碑。

④ 景泰四年1453年《杭郡重修礼拜寺记》[The Reconstruction of the Mosque in Hangzhou]碑。

⑤ 北京碑一。

主"[①]。既然此教的崇拜对象用汉语表达为天,其经书译为《天经》,就是一种合理的意译了。《天经》这一译法看不出音译的存在。这与之后形成的《古兰经》这样一个兼顾意译与音译的译法是不同的。

(二)对中国文化中的敬祖观念,两教有不同维度的吸收与融通

以儒家为代表的中国传统文化,强调尊敬祖先,并由此衍生出维护祖先荣誉、保持宗族秩序、祭祖等观念,并产生了涉及各种仪式与用品(包括三牲和冥纸等)的官方与民间祭祀活动等。如何面对中国文化这一传统,是两教需要解决的一个问题。通过考察碑文等文献,大概可知两教自身文化背景有异,对这一重要传统,双方进行了不同方式的吸收借鉴与融会贯通。

开封碑一中,追溯了人类始祖盘古阿耽(亚当)以及阿无罗汉(亚伯拉罕)、乜摄(摩西)等先知,由于犹太教是民族性宗教,这部分先知自然也是整个犹太民族的祖先,进而碑文指出以斯拉"系出祖师,道承祖统",这里的"祖师"与"祖统",是对祖先的尊重,也是对其宗教正统性的表达。接下来碑文又说:"敬天而不尊祖,非所以祀先也。春秋祭其祖先,事死如事生,事亡如事存,维牛维羊,荐其时食,不以祖先之既往而不敬也。"这一段提出了"祀先"这一中国文化高度重视的概念。"事死如事生,事亡如事存""荐其时食"语出《礼记·中庸》;"维牛维羊"语出《诗经·我将》。此碑中未就"祀"的仪式做出进一步明确说明,给人的印象似为接近儒家那样使用牛羊,按照时令来祭祀祖先。但隔了几句,碑文又说:"四季之时七日戒,众祖苦难,祀先报本,亡绝饮食。"此处表达则更接近于通过犹太教的斋戒,也就是"亡绝饮食"来"祀先报本",即通过不吃不喝来祭祀祖先——这与儒家的传统祭祀方式是不同的。稍晚的开封碑二,也提到了阿耽(亚当)、女娲(诺亚)、阿无罗汉(亚伯拉罕)等先知;还提到了阿无罗汉(亚伯拉罕)是"立是教者",是"教祖";乜摄(摩西)是"师法"。碑中关于祭祖,提及了"道行于祭祖,必孝必诚",指出要有孝心、真诚地祭祀,然此碑并未详细提及他们祭祖的方式。晚200年的天主教牧师骆保禄于1704年记载:"他们在那里[②]怀着极大的尊重和崇拜的心情,在四周的案子上摆设了……十三套(正如他们自己所说的那样,指册或本)摩西的《五经》,其中有十二卷是为了纪念一赐乐业(以色列)十二部族的,纪念摩西的只有一卷。"[③]这似乎是犹太人表达对祖先纪念的另外一种方式。根据

---

① 大名碑。

② 笔者按:当指犹太会堂内。

③ 荣振华 S.J. Joseph Dehergne,李渡南 Dr. Donald Daniel Leslie 等编著,《中国的犹太人》[Juifs de Chine]耿昇 Geng Sheng 译,(郑州[Zhengzhou]:大象出版社[Elephant Press],2005),82。此处蒙倪爱霞女士提示,特致谢。

这不太多的记载，虽然我们无法确知其祀先的具体方式，但能明显看出弘治碑展现了当时犹太人对敬祖观念的高度重视，而且在保持固有犹太文化的基础上，主动吸收了儒家祭祖的观念，但祭祖的方式与儒家不同。

观伊斯兰教碑刻，南京碑未述及伊斯兰教的先知穆罕默德，只是记载了明初可马鲁丁、亦卜剌金内附并受到照顾的情况，这可大概算作对当地本教早期名人的追溯；济南碑追溯了历代与清真寺有关的穆斯林名人，主要有官员、阿訇，例如木八剌沙、艾迪、陈英、木铎、陈礼、陈玺、唐世杰，之后更加着重介绍了伊斯兰教先知穆罕默德是"唐初开元年，有圣人者出，代天传道。始自西域"，足可见作者对本教先知的推崇；北京碑一中残损甚，可见内容中没有关于伊斯兰教先知穆罕默德或其他先知的记载，只提及"金吾卫指挥□□□"等人，其应为该寺建设的有功之人；北京碑二则记载了"列圣巍巍，莫及光□"以及杨永等人捐款修寺等，同时背阴记载了为修寺捐款的大量官员（包括宦官）；大名碑提到了穆罕默德、当地"主其教者"即阿訇杨济民。定州碑提到了元代建寺的"普公"——普颜帖睦儿，明代的陈勋、张昱、陈熹等为建寺做出贡献的人物。读弘治正德时期伊斯兰教六碑，可以看出其中有些关于先知穆罕默德的介绍，但为数不多，没有见到对穆罕默德先知之外其他先知的介绍；对于教内先辈祖先，名碑留下了姓名并记载了其贡献，碑文中未见关于祭祀先知和本教祖先的记载。①

通过比较，不难看出，对于以儒家为代表的中国传统文化中浓重的敬祖观念，两教都进行了积极的借鉴吸收，且都非常巧妙地找到了自然的契合点。但在处理方式上，是有所差别的：犹太人更强调祭祀祖先。这一不同的出现，除受中

---

① 笔者未能发现同时同地相关穆斯林家谱。但明弘治正德略早或略晚的时期，中国穆斯林的家谱中不乏对敬祖方面的记载。笔者仅以手头能找到的几份明代谱序为例进行说明。山东临清仁寿堂《马氏族谱》，萨琦在明正统十年（1445年）序文中说："良以当代士大夫，家必有谱，念惟先世虽出遐裔，实有德名，乃作《马氏世谱》。""立氏则自其祖，以见分派之所由始。盖本古人宗法之意也。"（伊牧之主编，《山东回族谱序集注》，95—96）这体现出修谱深受儒家敬祖以及宗法制度的影响。安徽怀宁敦悦堂《马氏族谱》中，成化七年（1471年）马奉廷记载："圣人制礼莫重于宗族……日后任其子孙迁居异地而猝然相遇各述其班次尊卑之辨，斯不亦百代如一家，千世若同堂者乎！且望尊戒卑长谕少，若有不孝不悌辱及先祖者，则相与惩治之。砺行立名，光耀前烈者，则相与奖励之。"见马文清 Ma Wenqing 编著，《回族谱序与宗源考略》[The Preface of the Hui Nationality's Pedigrees and the Research of Their Origin]，（鞍山[Anshan]：辽宁省鞍山市档案局、辽宁省鞍山市社会科学联合会[Archives Bureau of Anshan City, Liaoning Province Anshan City Federation of Social Sciences, Liaoning Province]编印，2009），88—89。这不但提到了宗族中的尊卑观念，而且制定了一定的奖惩方案。再如嘉靖庚子年（1540年）杨应奎在《益都杨氏世谱》的序文中写道："自周衰五宗九两废而族不聚，比庐井田坏而民不生，学士大夫不忘其先者，于是有氏族谱焉。"（马文清编著，《回族谱序与宗源考略》，252。）萨琦、马奉廷、杨应奎都是教内人，也都是有一定地位的官员、知识分子。各家立谱追溯祖先功绩、强调宗族秩序并邀请上述人物作序，体现出当时穆斯林对儒家祖先观念、宗族观念的重视，这多表现在修谱上，没有过多强调儒家的祭祖等内容。

国文化环境影响外，也与两教固有的信仰体系有关：犹太教是民族宗教，犹太教先知均为其祖先；而伊斯兰教并非民族宗教，就一般穆斯林而言，先知穆罕默德并不是其血统的祖先①。

三、相同或相通之处

如上文所述，弘治正德时期的两教碑刻有诸多不同。笔者对比阅读两教碑文后，发现其中相同或相通之处，亦复不少。这些相同或相通之处多是在域外不曾面临的问题，同样值得注意。兹列出五条，并尝试进行分析解读。

一是对于崇拜对象的表述一致。众所周知，犹太教、伊斯兰教的崇拜对象都是神（The God），犹太教称为雅威，伊斯兰教称安拉或真主。弘治正德时期，两教碑刻中，作者都将这一崇拜对象称为“天”。开封碑一记载：“天者轻清在上，至尊无对，天道不言。”开封碑二提到了“尊崇如天”“天命”等。济南碑记载：先知穆罕默德是“代天传道”，去麦加朝觐是“格享上天”。北京碑一记载：“上天至尊至大，无比无对。”大名碑指出伊斯兰教“敬天为主”。据此可见，“天”是犹太教与伊斯兰教在弘治正德时期对崇拜对象的普遍称呼。当时两教尚未形成对崇拜对象专用的、固定的汉文表述。② 伊斯兰教在明末清初，最终形成了使用“真主”来称呼崇拜对象的传统并延续至今。虽如此，至今伊斯兰教在很多术语中仍使用天这一概念，比如“天课”“天房”，而没有使用“主课”“主房”。

二是对宗教职业者的称呼近同。现今，在汉语语境中，犹太教的宗教职业者称拉比，伊斯兰教宗教职业者称阿訇。当时，犹太教的宗教职业者是“满剌”——开封碑一记载“惟李诚、李实……张浩等，正经熟晓，劝人为善，呼为满剌”；开封碑二、南京碑中均未出现相关表述；济南碑也明确写明“至我朝宣德丙午，满喇缺人”。北京碑一、北京碑二与大名碑中未见相关表述，或有，后因残泐缺失了。定州碑阴有“住持满喇马昂 陈俊”。满剌或满喇是阿拉伯文—波斯文（مولي\ملا\mulā）的不同音译，是阿拉伯语—波斯语中对宗教人员、教师的称呼，现通译为毛拉。开封碑一中另有两处阿拉伯文—波斯文职务与人名，现一并解读。是碑载：“……宋孝隆兴元年癸未，列微五思达领掌其教，俺都剌始建寺焉。元至元十六年已卯，五思达重建古刹清真寺……”“五思达”（أستاد\'ustād）一词系波斯语—阿拉伯语中对尊长、老师、先生的称呼，阿拉伯语作（أستاذ\'ustādh）。现存弘治正

① 当然，也有反例，世界各地穆斯林中都有先知穆罕默德圣裔的分布。但就数量而言，他们只占整个穆斯林群体中很少的一部分。

② 犹太教在康熙碑刻中仍然使用天，此外还有关于帝的表达。

德伊斯兰教碑刻中，无“五思达”相关记载。明代官方波斯语—汉语分类词典——《回回馆译语》人物门中有之，作（أستاد\'ustād），将该词翻译为“师”，读音为“五思他得”①。而建寺者“俺都剌”则是阿拉伯语、波斯语中常见的穆斯林人名'abdu llah\عبد الله一词，意为“真主的仆人”或“天仆”。在元朝，常译为谙都剌，《元史》第192卷有传的一位名臣，即为此名。明代官方文献，多将其译为阿都剌②。现通译为阿卜杜拉。当代犹太学者 Tiberiu Weisz 先生，认为此似职位，而非人名，误。③ 满剌、五思达、俺都剌三处记载，表明这些犹太人与内地穆斯林一样有波斯地区的母语习惯，显示出他们中大多数人的来源地很可能与元明穆斯林的主要来源地一致。

三是修建宗教场所的经费来源状况近同。宗教场所的修建，除需要信众的虔诚之心外，还需要购置土地，面临建材、人工等系列经济问题。关于宗教场所重修的费用来源，开封碑一中，虽有“永乐十九年奉周府定王传令，赐香重修清真寺”的记载，但也仅仅出现了一次，更多的是“李荣复备资财，起盖深邃，明金五彩妆成，焕然一新。成化年高鉴、高锐、高鋐，自备资财”之类教人出资建寺的记录；开封碑二中未见官方出资，是教内人员“请道经”“立二门”等；南京碑记载的情况比较特殊，可马鲁丁、亦卜剌金两人因故入附，大概是在军事或技术领域有突出贡献，故受到朱元璋的特殊关照，故而“钦蒙高帝……敕建二寺安扎”，尽管寺是敕建，到了弘治时期，明廷也不再十分关注，以至于有了“市廛之处，易侵易越”，即随时面临周围商家住户侵占土地的问题。济南碑则有“其费资皆教中趋义者助焉”与“又课凡助之者并列其姓氏于碑阴”的记载；北京碑一中修寺人情况内容多残泐，但观全文推测还是以教内官员之类为主，碑文记载：“奏请寺额，蒙宪宗皇帝敕赐曰礼拜寺”，虽然明宪宗朱见深给写了寺名，但也是“奏请”之后才给的，孰先孰后，非常明确。北京碑二记载了以杨永为代表的大量穆斯林官员、宦官修寺的行为；大名碑未载经费来源；定州碑记载修寺的经费是陈勋与“教之缙绅士大夫”的捐款，后陈熹尝试获得皇帝敕额，却被告知“敕命未易倅得”，但得到了负责全国各宗教管理的礼部侍郎张昱所写的匾额。综上不难看出：弘治正德时期

---

① 刘迎胜 Liu Yingsheng，《〈回回馆杂字〉与〈回回馆译语〉研究》[Research on "Huihuiguan Miscellaneous Characters" and "Huihuiguan Translated Language"]，（北京[Beijing]：中国人民大学出版社[China Renmin University Press]，2008），92。

② 张鸿翔 Zhang Hongxiang，《明代各民族人士入仕中原考》[A Study of People of Various Nationalities Entering Officials into China in Ming Dynasty]，（北京[Beijing]：中央民族大学出版社[Central University for Nationalities Press]，1999），178。

③ Tiberiu Weisz, *The Kaifeng Stone Inscriptions: The Legacy of the Jewish Community in Ancient China* (New York, Lincoln; Shanghai: iUniverse, Inc, 2006), 12.

两教寺院建修的主要经费，是教内人士出资解决的，当然因种种缘故，会有皇帝敕建、赐名、王府出资、官员帮助等，但都不是主流。与当时的儒释道三教寺院庙堂相较，两教更有民间性。

四是劄付内容、使用万岁牌、祝延圣寿反映出两教的忠君观念一致。忠君是事关封建王朝统治的重要问题，两教面对这一问题的处理方式是相同的。开封碑一记载："寺中奉大明皇帝万万岁牌""祝圣寿于万年"。这类"万岁牌"也见于一些清真寺中，至今仍有实物留存。南京碑记载可马鲁丁、亦卜剌金的后代在清真寺内"习学真经，焚修香火，祝延圣寿"；济南碑指出礼拜寺"颂祷天子万寿者，在是"。北京碑一记载清真寺："上则祝延圣寿，下则永济斯民。"北京碑二记载："祝延圣寿于无疆……"开封碑二、大名碑、定州碑未述及此类事。两教碑刻一致体现出的忠君观念或表现为万岁牌的使用，或表现为祝延圣寿成为寺的一大普遍功能。其圣，乃圣天子，即当时的皇帝，而非各教圣人，这是两教在域外时，不可能出现的思想，为中国皇帝祝寿的内容，实际上集中反映了两教人对中国作为祖国的高度认同并表现出对中国的真挚热爱之情。这一方面是因为中国给予了两教教人好的待遇，忠君是"受君之恩，食君之禄"而"报国忠君"(均自开封碑一)的表现；另一方面，也体现出两教人积极与中国的忠君文化相适应。

五是碑文体现出两教文化与以儒释道为代表的中国传统文化的关系一致。弘治正德时期，犹太教、伊斯兰教文明与以儒释道为代表的中华文明相遇时，其状态如何？从碑文中不难找到答案。第一种是直接引用儒释道的表述，比如开封碑一中的古刹(佛教、道教)，清真(道教，之后伊斯兰教普遍使用清真一词)，《道经》(道家)；开封碑二中的女娲、《道经》；南京碑中的焚修(道教，佛教也有使用)；济南碑中的焚修、慎终具(慎终，儒家)；北京碑一中的焚修；定州碑中的住持(佛教、道教)等。

第二种是用儒释道的概念，来解释两教信仰、功修等内容。例如开封碑一记载："今日积一善，明日积一善，善始积累。至斋，诸恶不作，众善奉行。七日善终，周而复始，是《易》有云。'吉人为善，维日不足'之意也。"其中"七日善终，周而复始"源自《周易·复》的"反复其道，七日来复"，而"吉人为善，维日不足"则是《尚书·泰誓中》的内容。这样本来属于犹太教的七天一次的安息日，就在中国传统文化古老的两部书中找到了合理贴切的解释，也丰富了当时犹太人的文化。伊斯兰教其他明代文献也对《易经》多有引用，例如明嘉靖七年(1528 年)《来复铭》等。开封碑二指出犹太教，"虽与儒书字异"，但"其理……以其同也"，进而强调犹太教在父子、君臣、兄弟、夫妇、朋友这些儒家强调的家庭与社会关系中与儒家相仿佛。大名碑的作者金贤是穆斯林，他通《周易》，著有《春秋纪愚》《春秋或问》。碑文用中国文化中的种种概念深入阐释了伊斯兰教，充分体现出儒家文化与伊斯兰教文化的汇通。例如碑载:"《尧典》首钦若之文,虞廷谨敕天之戒,恐惧著于大《易》,休咎衍于箕畴,自古圣贤未有不以敬天为急者。"金贤通过古代圣贤尧、舜、文、武的例子,指出《尚书·尧典》开端就有"钦若昊天"即尊重伟大的上天这样的文字记载;《尚书·益稷》记载舜曾重申要遵守"敕天之戒"即奉正天命;《周易》中的《震卦·彖传》有"君子以恐惧修省",即君子通过恐惧来修身、自省的记载;《尚书·洪范》记载箕子给周武王所论"九畴"中有"休咎"即善与恶、吉与凶的内容,并总结"自古圣贤未有不以敬天为急者"。这些内容,粗略看来,似除"敬天"与伊斯兰教对真主的尊崇有关之外,其他与伊斯兰教没什么关系。若进一步从伊斯兰教传统的视角审视上文,不难发现其行文亦是在阐释伊斯兰教信仰体系,且逻辑性较强。就其所阐释内容而言,在伊斯兰教的传统中,有大量经典、文献与之对应,限于篇幅,本文仅做最为简单的列举。"钦若昊天",可以理解为对唯一崇拜对象真主的尊重,也即认主独一,这是《古兰经》多次强调的伊斯兰教基础信仰之一。例如《古兰经·开端章》:"一切赞颂全归真主,众世界的主"(《古兰经》1:2)[①],"真主是独一的主宰"(《古兰经》4:171)。"敕天之戒",可以理解为人们作为代治者充分发挥智慧并按照真主的命令在人世间进行工作。《古兰经》记载:"我必定在大地上设置一个代理人"(《古兰经》2:30)。对代治者人类而言,他们首先是被真主赋予了独特的智慧,是有能力的,但是行事过程中,要遵按照真主的意志,遵守天命,实现"敕天之戒",此处可理解为对伊斯兰教的社会公德的表达。"恐惧修省",可理解为因为畏惧真主而内心不断反省更新。《古兰经》记载:"你们应当只畏惧我"(《古兰经》2:40)。"真主是接受他的仆人的忏悔的"(《古兰经》9:104)。此处可以理解为对伊斯兰教个人美德的表述。休咎,在伊斯兰教中,可做两个层面的理解。其一,伊斯兰教是入世的宗教,而非出世的宗教,既然入世就要考虑到今世(人类可见的社会)中行善与作恶会得到不同的结果。在今世中,应当劝善戒恶,日积月累,才能有更好的未来。"凡培养自己的性灵者,必定成功;凡戕害自己的性灵者,必定失败"(《古兰经》91:9—10)。其二,伊斯兰教是具有今世、后世两世观的宗教。该宗教认为在后世中,每个人都要为自己今世的所作所为负责,并受到真主相应的奖惩。《古兰经》描述在后世中:"行一个小蚂蚁重的善事者,将见其善报;作一个小蚂蚁重的恶事者,将见其恶报"(《古兰经》99:8)。碑文中的这四句话,表达了首先要知道真主独一,尊重真主,按照真主的意愿行事,不断反省忏悔,最后是做事要真正负责任,要知道还有后

① 本文所用《古兰经》,均使用马坚先生译本。马坚 Mohamed Makin 译,《古兰经》[The Chinese Translation of Holy Quran],(北京[Beijing]:中国社会科学出版社[China Social Sciences Press],1985)。引用时仅注明章节序号,不再标注所在页码。

世的奖赏与惩罚。以上是笔者尝试从《古兰经》经文角度对大名碑几句碑文进行的解读,此外当然还可从圣训学、伊斯兰教认主学、苏菲学等维度解读。故而笔者所述,肯定不是对这些内容的唯一解读方式。但这不妨碍表明这样一个意思:这些碑文引用《尚书》《易经》的概念,在说明了儒家思想的同时,也表达了清晰的伊斯兰教义理,表明了两者相通、趋同的关系。南京碑中,其作者认为伊斯兰教"精微韫奥,宏博广衍,自君臣、父子、夫妇、昆弟、朋友之伦,以至天文、医卜、农圃小道之术,靡不该存,靡不与中国情俗相仿佛",强调伊斯兰教重视君臣、父子、夫妇等儒家社会秩序的内容。同样,济南碑把伊斯兰教的五功做了儒家文化样式的解读:"谓诚、礼、斋、济、游是已。诚者,物之终始,君子诚之为贵;礼者,天理之节文,人事之仪则;斋者,斋戒沐浴,迁善改过;济者,补其不足,助其不给;又有游焉,游诸西域,以格享上天。"比如把礼拜,丰富为"天理之节文,人事之仪则",谈到了宋明理学中的天理,赋予礼拜这一伊斯兰教宗教功修以理学与人关系层面的内涵。

第三种,是以完全中国化的观念、思想、审美去写作。这类例子在碑文中较多,恕不举例。其中尤为有趣的是,弘治正德各碑都在努力追溯宗教场所久远的历史,这是中国尊古思想的表现,也是教人努力表达该教在中国的时间久远,并非新兴事物。笔者认为,两教碑刻中上述内容显示了碑文撰写者在两教传统的宗教文化和中国传统文化之间,找到了好的衔接点(比如第一种)、找到了文化深层的同源性(比如第二种)。尽管这种尝试,也许并未得到中国主流文化的确认,但并不妨碍他们在发展丰富了本教文化的同时,在客观上也发展了主流文化。当然,我们也要承认,两教碑刻透露出的内容,也同样体现出撰写人对两教文化的精熟、认同与自信。

四、结语

以上是笔者不揣鄙陋,对两教碑刻的异同之处进行的初步对比。由于水平有限,行文不免挂一漏万,但仅就所列举的方面来看,其中的确蕴含一定的意义,兹分述如下。

一是两教文献互证,更加确切地展现了明弘治正德时期犹太人与穆斯林的状况。正如文章开始所述,现可见到的弘治正德时期的两教文献是很少的,除却上述碑记外,几无其他。两教碑记中的很多记载,如果仅从一教角度去研究,似不免有"孤证"之虞。对两教碑刻进行比较研究,可发现其中的相异、相同与相通之处,从而获得更加确切的答案。比如两教碑刻均将宗教职业者称为"满剌",而这一称呼又是元明时期中亚、西亚对宗教职业者的普遍称呼,可知就整体而言,明代这批犹太人与穆斯林的来源是一致的。比如体现忠君观念的万岁牌、祝延圣寿等,两教碑刻对其都有记载,这就能充分说明两教对忠君观念的重视是当时的一种普遍状态,而非个例。再比如,两教碑刻显示的当时两教人积极同以儒释道为代表的中国文化相融通的状态,也可以互为参照,进行某种复原。

二是两教中国化的历史思想资源,亦是两教文化与中国思想文化比较、对话的重要史料。犹太教与伊斯兰教作为外来宗教,弘治正德时期两教碑文无论是形式、内容乃至行文逻辑,甚至小到装饰等(比如开封碑一、开封碑二碑额使用了仙鹤、祥云作为装饰)都有重要的中国文化印记。而且两教都在想方设法强调自身的"古",也就是在中国时间久远,实为强调其所奉宗教是中国文化的一部分,与儒释道同源且可互有裨益。碑文展现出的,是中国化了的犹太教、伊斯兰教,而不是犹太教、伊斯兰教在中国。当然,我们也应该承认,弘治正德时期两教碑刻也展现出了碑文撰写者对两教文化的自信,其中对本教的精熟、热爱之情也是洋溢其中的。两教碑文撰写者固然没有当代意义上的文明对话概念,但碑文中处处都是本教文明与儒释道等中国传统文明对话的内容,这充分展现了以撰写者为代表的两教教人包容、吸收的精神状态与开放、宏阔的文化视野,同时也为我们留下了文明对话的珍贵历史思想资源。对于伊斯兰教而言,这部分珍贵的历史思想资源值得重视,在当代也很有进一步继承与使用的价值。

三是上述资源在丰富了两教思想的同时,丰富了中国文化思想,乃至人类文明的宝库。两教都是沿着海陆丝绸之路传入中国的,二者的中国化过程、与以儒释道为代表的中国文明交融的过程,充分体现了不同文明间的交流互鉴,丰富了两教的思想与精神内涵。从另一个层面看,实事求是地讲,这些碑刻中的思想对博大精深的中国文化乃至人类文明的不断繁荣与多元化发展做出了一定贡献。这种贡献,固然不会像佛教、道教对中国文化的影响那样深刻,固然是影响力较小而非全局性的,固然不会受到很多人的关注,但这种经验对中国文化的均衡发展有不可或缺的补足价值,也在不断引起关注。

A Contrastive Study on the Chinese Inscriptions of Judaism and Islam during the Hongzhi Zhengde Period (1488-1521)

MA Baoquan

Abstract: During the Hongzhi Zhengde period of the Ming Dynasty, Judaism left two Chinese inscriptions, while Islam left six. Through study and comparison, it can be concluded that the two religions have differences in the translation of scripture names and the Confucian concept of ancestor worship. It can also be concluded that the two religions have the same Chinese name for worship object and religious professionals. At the same time, the two religions have many similarities: The economic sources for building religions sites, the concept of loyalty to the monarch, and the relationship with traditional Chinese culture. The author believes that: the comparative study of the inscriptions of the two religions showed the conditions of the Jews and Muslims at that time more accurately; these inscriptions are the historical thought resources of the sinicization of the two religions, and are important historical materials for the comparison and dialogue between the cultures of the two religions and the Chinese thought and culture; These inscriptions are products of the exchange and mutual learning of civilizations along the Belt and Road has enriched the ideas of the two religions while also contributing to Chinese culture.

Key Words: Hongzhi, Zhengde, Judaism, Islam, Chinese Inscriptions

论以色列基布兹社会主义的理念危机及其当代批判*

李勇　薛丽**

【摘要】以色列的基布兹运动是指犹太移民从1909年开始在巴勒斯坦地区建立一个个具体的集体农庄的社会主义运动。基布兹在共有、劳动、平等、共产主义教育等理念体系的指导下得以建立与发展，并取得了举世瞩目的成绩。但从20世纪80年代中期开始，基布兹陷入了危机；与基布兹危机相伴随的是基布兹理念体系也遭到质疑与攻击。面对危机，基布兹在展开经济改革的同时，也展开了以重塑传统理念为核心的针对理念危机的改革；但这种重塑是一种被动性的重塑，本质上是对断裂的现实与传统进行连接与妥协的尝试，而非着眼于现实与未来发展的先导性的理念重塑。从目前的效果看，这种重塑取得的成就也是喜忧参半。

【关键字】基布兹；公共理念；劳动理念；现代批判

"基布兹"又被称为社会主义农庄，是以色列特有的一种社区组织模式，至今已有110年的历史。早期的基布兹具有公有制性质和社会主义特色，主要表现在社区成员在平等与自愿的原则下共同参与义务性劳动，实行财产和生产资料公有制以及按需分配制度等。基布兹运动的初衷旨在建立一个社会主义的以色列国。基布兹为以色列国的建立与建国后国家经济发展做出了巨大贡献。基布兹也被誉为资本主义世界中的社会主义细胞①、人类历史上一场尚未

* 本文是2021年教育部人文社会科学研究青年项目"以色列基布兹社会主义的实践与理论研究"(21YJC710014)的阶段性成果。

** 李勇，山东大学犹太教与跨宗教研究中心暨哲学与社会发展学院副研究员；薛丽，重庆大学公共管理学院社会工作系硕士研究生。

① 林建 Lin Jian,《资本主义中的"社会主义细胞"》[The Socialist Cells in Capitalism],于《科学社会主义》[Scientific Socialism],2006第5期[2006,Issue 5],121。

失败的共产主义实验[①]。

一、基布兹社会主义的早期成就

1910年初，几名接受了社会主义思想的欧洲犹太青年在约旦河谷南部建立了世界上第一个基布兹，名为德加尼亚，希伯来语意为“粮食产地”。该基布兹最初只有7名成员，内部实行生产资料完全公有制、按需分配、直接民主制度等。他们集体劳动、集体生活、集体拥有财产并保卫自己的安全，一起描绘他们的社会蓝图[②]。这些人坚信自己的实践正在为一个基于合作、平等和共有生活的，崭新的犹太社会奠定基础。1910年后，陆续有上百个基布兹在巴勒斯坦地区建立，史称“基布兹运动”。德加尼亚基布兹的基本原则被后来的基布兹继承并发展。基布兹的发展并非一帆风顺，经历了第二次世界大战、以色列独立战争、20世纪80年代以色列的经济危机、2008年的世界金融危机等诸多挑战，但基布兹在这些挑战面前表现出顽强的生命力和社会主义实践的优越性。目前，以色列有274个基布兹，总人口约14万。根据基布兹在规模、组织模式等方面的特征，大致可以将110多年的基布兹发展历史划分为四个阶段。第一阶段为初步探索时期(1909—1920年)，主要表现为小型基布兹的建立。自1910年第一个基布兹建成后的4年间，犹太移民在巴勒斯坦地区很快建立了6个小型基布兹。第二阶段为大型基布兹建设时期(1920—1947年)。随着《贝尔福宣言》的发表，大批犹太移民涌入巴勒斯坦，形成了第三次犹太移民高潮。在此期间，第一个大型基布兹得以建立。截至1947年，巴勒斯坦地区已建立基布兹147个。第三阶段为从分散到联合时期(1948—1985年)。1948年以色列建国后百废待兴，需要集中力量发展政治、经济、文化，基布兹在其中发挥了重要的作用，并从分散逐渐走向联合。1963年，全国性的基布兹运动联盟得以成立。第四阶段为改革时期(20世纪80年代中期至今)。20世纪80年代，在以色列国内经济危机以及基布兹原有体制弊端的双重影响下，基布兹陷入了严重的发展危机。1985年，全国性的基布兹运动联盟分裂为三个基布兹联盟，基布兹自此进入了漫长的改革期。[③] 时至今日，基布兹依然享有“国之基石”的美誉。

---

① Martin Buber, *Paths in Utopia*, trans. R. F. C. Hull (Boston: Beacon Press, 1958), 139.

② Stephen Charles Mott, “The Kibbutz's Adjustment to Industrialization and Ideological Decline: Alternatives for Economic Organization,” *The Journal of Religious Ethics*, 19.1(1991):86.

③ 李勇 Li Yong,《论以色列基布兹运动的兴起与当代改革》[On the Rise and Modern Reform of Israeli Kibbutz Movement]，收录于《犹太研究》(第15辑)[Jewish Studies(15)]，傅有德 Fu Youde 主编，(济南[Jinan]:山东大学出版社[Shandong University Press],2018),128—130。

在经济上，基布兹在十分贫瘠的土地上创造了“奇迹”。现今，基布兹以占以色列3%的人口和36%的耕地，创造了产值占全国工业总产值42%的工业产值，为国家提供了50%的小麦、56%的牛肉、82%的棉花、98.8%的鱼类、51.3%牛奶；农产品出口占全国的43%，工业出口总值占以色列工业出口总值的9%；基布兹经营的行业包括农业、工业、手工制造业、珠宝业、教育行业、电子行业等。基布兹农业创造了“滴灌”技术，历史性地解决了以色列的节水与浇灌难题。基布兹的经济地位在以色列举足轻重。

在政治上，基布兹为以色列国的建立奠定了基础。基布兹为以色列建国提供了必要的经济资源和人力资源。基布兹运动使犹太复国主义的实现成为可能。早期基布兹的建立吸引了世界各地犹太人到巴勒斯坦地区定居，使其成为最大的犹太人聚集地。由于战争和压迫，犹太人分散在世界各地，没有统一的组织和明确的目标。基布兹开拓者赤手空拳地到荒芜之地进行土地开垦。在经过不断的努力和尝试后，建立了基布兹——犹太人的新家园，使犹太人的大规模聚集成为可能。基布兹的建立使得犹太复国主义不再是空中楼阁，而变成了一种现实可能。

在文化上，基布兹社会主义的实践历史成了以色列文化的有机组成部分。基布兹是艺术创造的源泉。基布兹艺术家以社区生活为主题，创造了一系列作品，涉及文学、艺术、民族歌舞等领域。基布兹文化的最典型体现是成员的日常对话，甚至他们的新床单、墙、报纸上印的都是希伯来语，居民的日常对话成为璀璨的文学作品素材。基布兹文化的另一体现是民族节日，传统的犹太年会、节假日和周年庆典等活动成为基布兹独特的文化特征。另外，基布兹的独特价值观和组织原则也是以色列对外文化传播的一大亮点。

此外，以色列政治、教育、国防等领域中的许多精英人物都出身基布兹。自1948年建国以来至少有4位总理来自基布兹，如本-古里安、摩西·夏里特、莱维·艾希科尔和果尔达·梅厄。以色列精英人物中有相当多的人要么出生于基布兹，要么生活在基布兹。在工党执政的29年中，其内阁成员约有1/3来自基布兹。以色列国防军中有许多高级将领原本也是基布兹成员，如曾任国防军总参谋长和国防部长的摩西·达扬就出生于以色列的第一个基布兹。在1967年的“六五战争”中，以色列有30%的空军驾驶员和近1/4的陆军军官是基布兹成员。在这场战争中，以军阵亡778人，其中200人也都来自基布兹。基布兹培育出的优秀人才为以色列建国、国家的稳定与发展做出了不可磨灭的贡献。

基布兹社会主义实践在当时表现出来的生命力与优越性是显而易见的。这种优越性来源于基布兹的社会主义生产模式、分配原则、民主制度、技术创新等多个层面，而贯穿于所有这些层面的是其社会主义基本原则与理念。一个显而

易见的事实是,基布兹的理念先于基布兹的产生,并且犹太先驱正是依据其系统化或半体系化的社会主义复国主义理念来建立与发展基布兹的。

二、基布兹社会主义的基本理念

基布兹是实体化的社会经济政治组织,它的建立与发展必须在某种系统化的理念、愿望或原则的指导下进行。由于基布兹社区的分散性、具体实践的差异性、单个基布兹的规模限制等因素的影响,基布兹并没有形成统一的社会主义理论体系。但是,纵观基布兹的发展史,几乎所有基布兹都遵循下述社会主义理念。

(一)共有理念

共有理念由如下三个方面组成。首先,自愿原则是共有理念的基础。[①] 基布兹首先是一个自愿性组织,有明确的组织形式,有共同目标和任务,成员有明确的权利和义务。相应地,基布兹为其成员的生存与发展提供保障,包括健康、安全、教育、住房、休闲和福利等所有领域。其次是,集体主义共有理念的本质诉求。[②] 作为基布兹最高利益的集体主义主要表现为两个方面。一是集体生活制度。由于早期基布兹存在资源不足的问题,集体生活的方式在一定程度上有利于资源的有效集中和使用。基布兹成员白天在公共食堂吃饭,晚上则自愿待在一起分享一天的收获和情感,这种情感的分享被认为是集体生活非常重要的一环。成员劳动所得的大部分用于公共生活和开销。二是为了提高劳动生产率,男女成员都要从事直接劳作。出于对男女性别差异的考虑,组织安排大部分男性从事体力劳动,多数女性则从事儿童照顾、卫生医疗等服务性工作。最后,民主集中原则是共有理念的现实表现。基布兹采用少数服从多数的民主决策制,每个人都有权利参与公共事务。基布兹通常每周召开全体成员大会,基布兹的日常事务由全体大会选出的管理委员会负责。管理委员会下辖生产计划、文教、劳动、财务、卫生体育、住房等若干专门委员会。如果遇到问题,先由专门委员会进行初步表决,然后将讨论决定交由成员代表大会最终表决。遇到比较重大的事务,简单多数票还不够,须有 2/3 或 4/5 的通过率才行。

---

① Constance Smith and Anne Freedman, *Voluntary Associations: Perspective on the Literature* (Harvard University Press, 1972), 133.

② 陈艳艳 Chen Yanyan,薛丽 Xue Li,《以色列的基布兹社会主义实验》[Israeli Kibbutz Socialist Experiment],于《中国社会科学报》[Social Sciences in China],2018 年 1 月 23 日[23rd January,2018]。

(二)劳动理念[①]

在基布兹里,劳动不仅为社区未来提供可持续的物质条件,更重要的在于它是一种共同价值的表述,“一个有共同信念的集体只能在集体劳动中才能真正存在”[②]。“劳动”不仅是基布兹集体主义教育的关键载体,更是基布兹社会认可的核心价值。[③] 基布兹在某种意义上就是各种协作的、创造性的具体劳动的集合。“劳动”作为一个中心概念,包含了各种形式的体力劳动与脑力劳动。基布兹中公社式的生活并非共产主义的目的与终点,它只是为达到共同目的所做的努力,是一种最为有效的方式。在基布兹中,劳动是“生活的真实,所有的逻辑,所有的绝对公正,所有美好与崇高的东西;所有这些才能使每个人享有平等。为了创造而共同使用人力,这并非出于饥饿与奴役,乃是出于自由意志;它是人内心深处的呼唤,是一首灵魂之歌”[④]。正如早期基布兹创始人所表达的那样:我们“每日的各项劳动是社区成员生活的中心,也是个人灵性的表达。我们将我们的灵魂投入这些事情,就像作家与艺术家将他们的灵魂投在他们的作品中一样。我们没有别种生活,我们也不想要其他的生活”[⑤]。不难看出,在基布兹中,劳动不仅被看作一项社会必须性行为,也被视为道德崇高的行为;它是精神生活的一部分,也是情感价值的表达[⑥];它连接社区中的“你”和“我”,既是社区的一种理念,也是实现其他理念的手段。

(三)平等理念

基布兹的平等理念既是社会主义实践的内在要求,也是犹太民族大流散历史的必然要求。首先,基布兹反对一切形式化的“机械式的平等”或“数字上的平等”。用本-古利安的话来说“(基布兹里的)平等是根据每个人的需要给予,又根据每个人的能力索取”[⑦]。这种平等观的内核在于其“双向性”与“整体性”。“双

① 黄福武 Huang Fuwu,《现实中的神话——以色列基布兹现象浅析》[Myths in Reality: An Analysis of the Israeli Kibbutz Phenomenon],于《当代世界社会主义问题》[Modern Global Socialist Problems],2006 第 3 期[2006, Issue 3],71。

② Martin Buber, *Paths in Utopia*, 135.

③ 王太文 Wang Taiwen,《以色列基布兹:乡村集体经济合作组织的极致演绎》[Israeli Kibbutz: The Ultimate Interpretation of a Rural Collective Economic Cooperative],于《浙江农业科学》[Journal of Zhejiang Agricultural Sciences], 2020 第 7 期, [2020, Issue 7], 1277。

④ Shlomo Lavi, *Four Years* (Mibifnim 17, 1925), 336.

⑤ Shmuel Dayan, *Degania at Its Half Jubilee* (Tel Aviv: Stiebel, 1935), 100.

⑥ Muki Tsur, "The Intimate Kibbutz," in *Kibbutz: An Alternative Lifestyle*, eds. Divid Leichman and Idit Paz (Ramat Efal: Yad Tabenkin, 1997), 12.

⑦ 1960 年,本-古利安在以色列第一个基布兹德加尼亚成立 50 周年纪念会上发表了一段讲话,其中对基布兹的存在与发展的根本原则进行了界定。1961 年 3 月,那次讲话得到扩充整理后出版。

向性”指集体与个人、个人与个人之间的“真正相遇”，相互关系与责任上的平等；“整体性”则表现为个人与集体作为统一的“一”而存在，同时集体的“一”融入个人中，个人的“一”也融入集体之中。[①] 基布兹倡导的这种平等观成了基布兹理论与意识形态中的核心概念[②]，得到社区成员的普遍赞同和接受，并真正内含于“各尽所能，按需分配”的分配制度之中。其次，大流散的历史让犹太人饱受歧视、驱逐和屠杀的苦难。社会主义复国主义的犹太先驱认为，犹太复国的一个核心目标就是实行全部犹太人的平等。这种理念作为最基本的建设理念被带到了基布兹的建设与发展中。平等是每个基布兹人的心声，也是他们的行为准则；他们需要在集体中平等地使用权利，平等地履行义务。这种极强的平等原则让基布兹在以色列建国前表现出强大的凝聚力，也让基布兹成为犹太移民最为向往的定居点。

（四）共产主义的养育理念[③]

基布兹创立不久，下一代子女的养育就成了最紧要的问题。经过全面考量，基布兹人决定用共产主义方式来养育后代。共产主义的养育理念与方式主要体现为以下两个方面。一方面，基布兹强调家庭的功能。家庭是“小堡垒”，它是应对逆境的盔甲，被几个世纪以来犹太人的生活方式锤炼成型，其功能是增加儿童数量，保证犹太血缘传统和文化的延续。从功能上来说，家庭的存在能源源不断地提供劳动力。另一方面，发挥集体主义养育方式在儿童成长过程中的重要作用。集体照顾指由基布兹组织负责建立统一的儿童照顾中心，负责社区内儿童的生活照顾、学习、性格培养等多种任务。基布兹成立初期采用家庭照顾理念，但随着现实状况的改变，逐渐从家庭照顾过渡到集体照顾。基布兹人选择共产主义教养方式主要基于两个原因：一是出于现实的考量，把孩子集中在一起养育比单独照顾更具可行性。基布兹的共同劳动理念要求妇女也要参加生产活动，这样养育下一代的任务只能由集体来负责。另外，基布兹建设初期，敌视他们的阿拉伯“邻居”让基布兹不得不将每一位成年劳动力投入生产与防御。二是出于意识形态的考量。基布兹社会主义的实践与理念需要后代来传承与发展，集体教养更利于社会主义实践与理念的传递。

基布兹社会主义实践的四大理念体系涵盖了其组织与生产原则、分配方式

---

① Shalom Lilker, “Martin Buber and the Kibbutz,” in *Kibbutz: An Alternative Lifestyle*, 76-78.

② Shimon Shur, “The Evolution of the Idea of Equality in the Kibbutz Movement,” *Hakibbutz* 9-10(1983/4): 162.

③ Stanley Diamond, *Kibbutz and Shtetl: The History of an Idea* (Oxford University Press, 2017), 87-89.

与社会主义实践接班人的培养等领域。[①] 每一个理念体系又包括其他具体理念，如劳动理念体系下有创新与生态理念。20 世纪 80 年代的经济与社会危机以及新技术革命的到来，让基布兹遭遇了前所未有的大危机，这些理念体系在新形势下的具体实践过程中，也无一例外地遭到了不同程度的挑战与质疑。

三、基布兹社会主义的理念危机

20 世纪 80 年代，在以色列国内经济危机与生产转型滞后等多重因素的打击下，基布兹遭遇了一场空前的发展危机，具体表现为劳动力流失、生产效率下降、债台高筑、组织成员生活水平下降等。这场经济危机也是一场基布兹理念危机，并且理念危机的持续时间要长于经济危机，某些理念危机早于经济危机爆发，有些理念危机则伴随改革的开展而产生。“传统基布兹模式高扬集体主义旗帜、抑制个性发展、消除劳动分工、追求绝对平等和社团和谐的原则，在长期历史实践的检验中，越来越与复杂的社会现实、人性自利的动机和追求个性表现自由的时代趋势相悖。”[②]相较于数据上显示的经济危机，基布兹理念上的危机更为复杂、持续时间也更长，改革的难度和效果也更难掌握。

（一）共有理念的衰落

在基布兹建立初期，共有理念是基布兹最重要的基础理念。这一理念在保证资源的有效利用以及充分调动成员的积极性等方面产生了重要影响。但是随着社会经济的发展以及西方个人主义思潮的传入，共有理念陷入前所未有的困境。

首先，自愿原则衰落。基布兹建立初期，基布兹人在自愿原则指导下，自愿

① 有学者从社会学角度进行考察，认为以色列基布兹实际得以运行，依靠的是七大原则或手段。一是自愿原则：加入基布兹的劳动或离开都出自一种自我意识选择。二是财产共有原则：所有财产由社区组织统一管理，所有财产的法定拥有者是集体，而非个人，个人无财产拥有权。三是强制劳作原则：每个人都必须参与体力劳动，尤其是农业生产劳动。四是劳动独享原则：劳动只能由社区成员来完成，禁止社区外界人士参与社区劳动活动。五是自我管理原则：社区的所有管理组织活动都由社区成员自己完成。六是直接民主原则：每个成员都参与的投票，是社区的最高立法与执行权威。七是公有制教育与孩子抚养原则：社区负担下一代的教育与抚养责任，而社区教育的一个责任在于培育下一代集体主义生活方式。这些原则大部分延续到了 20 世纪 80 年代中叶。随着 80 年代的经济与社会危机以及新技术革命的到来，这七大原则都得到相应的调整与修改。参见：Michael Harris，“*The Kibbutz：Uncovering the Utopian Dimension*，” *Utopian Studies* 10.1(1999)：122。

② 从日云 Cong Riyun，马涛 Ma Tao，《对以色列基布兹模式的历史考察及思考》[A Historical Examination of the Israeli Kibbutz Model and Reflections]，于《当代世界与社会主义》[Modern World and Socialism]，2020 年第 2 期[2020，Issue 2]，75。

加入组织,接受规定的责任和义务,共同劳动,共享成果。基布兹为成员提供生活所需的一切物品,个人自愿接受组织的分配。[①] 第二代成员出生在基布兹又有极大可能会自愿留在这里,因为个人从出生到去世的一切都由基布兹满足,而且他们从小接受的就是基布兹共产主义教育。如果离开基布兹,他们对外面的世界充满恐惧和未知。20 世纪 70—80 年代西方个人主义在以色列盛行,加之 80 年代开始的基布兹改革,导致了自愿原则的危机。一方面,个人需求由早期的依赖集体组织,转变为通过自身来满足。这种改变影响了自愿原则的继续存在,影响了成员维护基布兹和为组织做贡献的意愿。曾经由坚持自愿原则的人负责的岗位,现在只能由给薪工作者来承担。曾经部门经理的位置都是成员自愿承担,但是现在必须基于经济奖励才能实现。这意味着成员对组织的认同感和归属感降低。另一方面,成员的需求和选择意愿越来越多,很多年轻成员倾向于其他生活方式,反对基布兹的自愿原则。21 世纪初期,一部分基布兹成员陆续定居国外,他们把基布兹看作高压社会,过时的、没有公众声望和地位的社会等。自愿原则的衰落使基布兹出现人员流失,并且对外界的吸引力下降,这给基布兹的改革与发展带来了不确定因素。

其次,财产集体所有制及其价值观衰落。财产集体所有制的衰落表现在以下三个方面。第一,集体共担责任价值观的衰退。基布兹免费为其成员提供家电、食物、教育、医疗等各方面的服务,但是在 20 世纪 80 年代国内经济不景气的情况下,基布兹的财政压力加大。个体对这种集体分配方式产生了质疑,认为在这种体系中,共担责任是体制化的,消费较少资源的成员实际上补贴了消费较多的成员。这种质疑代表集体价值观的衰退。第二,由于共担责任价值观的衰落,大约有 1/4 的基布兹决定把房屋所有权从基布兹转到个人名下,使之成为可继承的财产,以此满足成员的个人需求。第三,这种改变使得企业在用人与分配方面产生了重大变革,这些变革又加剧了集体价值观的衰退。70%的基布兹工厂和 40%的农业部门都由受薪董事会经营,而董事会成员部分是非基布兹成员。40%的基布兹雇用私营团体来管理工厂,60%的基布兹雇用非基布兹成员作为企业管理者。一些基布兹开始雇用基布兹成员作为管理者,这些基布兹成员已经终止了他们的强制性轮换制度,开始依据个人能力说话。基布兹曾经遵循“一切劳动价值同等”的原则,即不管成员的职业是什么,他们所得的工资和个人消费津贴都是一样的。然而,由于市场经济的发展和个人意识的增强,基布兹开始奉行“按贡献比例补偿”原则,很多基布兹开始实行“有差别的奖励”工资机制。根据这些原则,成员的消费津贴是根据他们在自由劳动市场获得的工资而定,而

① Nir Tsuk, *The Rise and Fall of The Kibbutz* (University of Copenhagen, 2000), 22.

不是所有人享有平均收入。

最后,集体主义道德观衰落。集体主义道德观是基布兹文化的重要价值观,简单来说,就是个体之间、集体与个体之间的“友爱”,也是基布兹的主要意识形态。[①] 在危机与改革时代,集体主义作为一种意识形态和生活方式与日益个体化的现代社会发展趋势之间的矛盾激化[②];继而集体主义道德观遭到了全方位的冲击。这种道德观主要基于四条原则,在基布兹改革过程中,这四条原则都遭到了不同程度的质疑与抛弃。一是“共同责任”原则。例如:如果某个成员有很多孩子,那么该成员的消费津贴就比其他人多;如果该成员要求特殊的食物,公共食堂也需要满足这种需求等。简单来说,基于这个原则,基布兹的资源将根据“从依靠个人能力,到依靠个人需求”的原则进行分配。在财政危机与改革背景下,“共同责任”遭到了事实性的抛弃。二是集体利益优先原则,即当集体利益与个人利益发生冲突的时候,集体利益应该居于首位。例如在 1960 年,如果某个基布兹成员无法完成农业收割任务,那么其他基布兹成员当根据计划优先帮助其完成这项收割工作。但是在改革后的基布兹中,个体价值观盛行,个人利益得到更多保护的同时,集体利益被进一步弱化。三是集体的决定是合理的决定原则。传统基布兹中,由全体会议所做的决定不仅影响整个基布兹,而且对每个成员都产生影响。改革后的基布兹将一些原先由基布兹承担的责任下放到个人或家庭,以此调动个人积极性。于是,集体所做的决定不再能影响每个人,成员需要自己对所负担的责任做出决定。四是情感共享原则。在传统基布兹中,基布兹通过鼓励成员自由地表达情感体验来提高集体凝聚力,强调集体情绪体验的表达。但是,现代基布兹成员更倾向于自己支配娱乐时间,注重隐私与自我保护,没有人愿意和一群人待在一起分享自己的情感和经历。这在基布兹年轻一代中更为明显,年轻成员不愿意被集体限制,渴望支配自己的时间和空间。

(二)完全平等理念遭到质疑

在传统基布兹文化中,平等是最重要的价值。这种平等主要体现在两个方面。首先是经济上的平等。集体所有制经济下的个人不仅在土地、房屋等生产资料上享有平等权利,甚至在牙刷、梳子等私人物品之外的消费物品上也享有平等权。生活消费品依靠平均分配制度进行分发,基布兹的所有成员,不管其工作

---

① Melford E. Spiro, “Utopia and Its Discontents: The Kibbutz and Its Historical Vicissitudes,” *American Anthropologist* 106 (2004): 558.

② 从日云 Cong Riyun,马涛 Ma Tao,《对以色列基布兹模式的历史考察及思考》[A Historical Examination of the Israeli Kibbutz Model and Reflections],于《当代世界与社会主义》[Modern World and Socialism],2020 年第 2 期[2020, Issue 2],73。

领域，也不管他们的工作在技能、责任、生产效率上存在什么差异，每个人所得的消费津贴都是相同的。这种制度曾令经济学家感到十分困惑，因为在经济学家看来，经济奖励是工作的主要动机。其能够在基布兹中得以施行，是因为彼时基布兹成员把集体利益置于个人利益之上，他们坚持集体利益取决于每个成员的努力。[①] 到了 20 世纪 80 年代中期，越来越多的基布兹成员不愿为了集体利益忽视自身需求，对组织的无私奉献只存在于第一代和部分第二代基布兹成员身上。年轻基布兹成员更加重视自身发展需求，追求经济奖励。

其次，基布兹强调每个个体社会地位平等的价值观。基布兹如果不能完全阻止社会分层，这个团体就会消亡。因此，在基布兹理论和实践中，所有成员的社会地位都是平等的。但随着危机的爆发与改革的推进，基布兹外的社会阶层分化越来越明显，个人社会地位开始影响别人对自己的评价。外界的现实与看法对基布兹成员的影响不断加深，越来越多的成员开始关注社会地位对自己以及下一代发展的影响。

（三）养育理念的转变

在基布兹发展早期，为了增加劳动力数量与传递基布兹理念，对于儿童必须采用集体教养的方式，即设立儿童教养中心，由基布兹培育的专业人员来照顾。父母白天将儿童送往儿童照顾中心，等到晚上再把孩子接回家。有些基布兹规定父母每天只被允许和自己的孩子相处一至两个小时。这种集体教养方式对早期基布兹的发展发挥了不可估量的作用。

随着基布兹以及以色列社会的发展，集体教养儿童的必要性丧失了。一方面，基布兹的生产资料不断增加，这已经彻底改变了过去基布兹成员为了工作而无法照顾儿童的状况。另一方面，基布兹的劳动制度越来越规范，劳动时间设置更加合理，父母可以有更多的时间陪伴和照顾儿童。对基布兹儿童的养育方式出现由集体照顾向家庭照顾转变的趋势。此外，父母的观念也发生了改变。在过去集体生活时代，为了集体利益，基布兹成员可以无条件地接受集体的安排和号召。随着基布兹改革的不断推进、现代儿童教育学与心理学的兴起，越来越多的父母坚持家庭照顾理念，开始强调家庭在儿童成长过程中的至关重要性，认为家庭是儿童社会化的开端，是人格培育和发展的起源。在现代的基布兹中，已经基本找不到传统的集体教养模式了。

① Melford E. Spiro, "Utopia and Its Discontents: The Kibbutz and Its Historical Vicissitudes," 557-558.

四、理念危机的改革与批判

在出现20世纪80年代中期的发展危机后，基布兹随即在职业结构、所有制结构、个人分配制度、管理模式、雇佣结构等多方面进行了改革，多元化的基布兹发展成为现实。基布兹的经济改革让濒临破产的基布兹重获生机。需要指出的是，这种危机的度过只是经济和政治上的，即作为整体的基布兹经济再次实现正增长，并且以色列政府也无法取消作为社会主义特殊存在的基布兹，从而将其变为一个个普通的公民社区，虽然这种呼声在以色列政府官员和普通市民那里时有出现。虽然经济与政治上的危机已经解除，但是改革引入的侵蚀其传统的基本价值的举措所带来的理念与文化危机依然存在，并且成了21世纪以来基布兹发展的最主要矛盾之一。从某种意义上来讲，经济与政治改革进一步加剧了基布兹原有的理念危机。截至2010年，大约有2/3的基布兹参与了私有化或者私营化的改革行动，通过给自己贴上“差异化”或“新型”基布兹的标签，使自己的改革合法化；另外1/3则是“集体主义”或传统类型的基布兹。[①] 一些基布兹甚至将房屋的所有权转让给他们的成员，一些人现在正在考虑将基布兹的财产分割给成员。人们往往把这种非同寻常的变化称为基布兹理念的消亡。“基布兹已死”在20世纪末21世纪初的以色列社会成了一种普遍认识，这种“死亡”并非经济或者社会存在方面的死亡，而是指原有的集体主义理念的死亡。

面对原有的理念危机以及改革进一步加剧的理念危机，基布兹对此进行了有针对性的改革。第一，针对自愿原则的衰落，基布兹进行了改革。首先，调动和发挥老一辈成员对年轻成员的影响，增强年轻成员对组织的认同感和归属感。其次，提高对成员的服务质量和水平，放宽定居标准，在自愿原则下吸引更多移民。第二，针对集体观念的衰落，基布兹的改革措施主要有：首先，将部分资产划归个人，但大部分财产依然由集体掌控，个人的生产与分配依然在集体中进行；其次，在实施“按贡献比例补偿”分配的同时，实施新的社会保障制度来控制“有差别的奖励”工资结构造成的社会与成员“分层”。第三，基布兹还主动改革绝对平等制度，承认绝对平等理念的衰落是时代的新要求：一方面，承认个人经济上的需求，不再坚持所有资产和分配完全平等的理念；另一方面，强调劳动的重要性，坚决维护成员社会地位的绝对平等。但是“很多以色列人认为，新型基布兹允许成员收入存在差异，已经失去了维护社会平等的职能，与其他社区没有区

---

① Michal Palgi and Shulamit Reinharz, eds. *One Hundred Years of Kibbutz Life: A Century of Crises and Reinvention* (London: Transaction Publishers, 2014), 7.

别，不应该再享受与其相关的优待，尤其是廉价土地”①。第四，随着时代发展，基布兹儿童教养理念发生了很大转变，集体照顾不再被视为儿童教养的唯一方式，成员强调家庭照顾在儿童成长和人格塑造过程中的重要作用，同时强调集体教育对儿童社会化成长的影响。第五，随着强意识形态教育的日益受阻，基布兹的教育系统开始以价值认同教育替代原有的强意识形态教育。第六，基布兹的文化重塑。20 世纪 90 年代以来，基布兹经历了重大变革，基布兹人需要寻找基布兹社会主义新的意义，即对基布兹的重新定义，给予历史与现实合理的有效解释。面对这种现实的迫切需要，21 世纪以来的基布兹展开了一项系统性的文化转向工程。需要指出的是，与西方其他社会主义思想的文化转向相比，基布兹的文化转向既是一种研究和理论的转向，更是一种生产与社会实践维度的文化转向。总的来说，基布兹的文化转向走了一条从社会主义实践与历史的文化阐释到社会主义文化遗产的保护，再到基布兹社会主义文化旅游产业的开发的道路。

但是，理念或意识形态上的改革要比经济层面的改革困难得多，改革效果也不如经济改革那么“立竿见影”。改革取得了一定的积极效果，巩固了经济和政治改革在当下取得的成果，但是这次针对理念危机进行的改革及其采取的措施并未从根本上扭转这场危机，并且为基布兹社会主义未来的发展埋下了隐患。首先，多元化与个性化已经成了今日基布兹最显在的特质，多种意识形态在基布兹内存在，人们很难发现一种社会主义的意识形态在所有基布兹中处于统治地位。其次，经过 21 世纪文化转型，以色列性与犹太性成了基布兹人最重要的特征，但是集体主义与社会主义文化一直未能取得应有的位置。以色列海法大学基布兹与合作理念研究中心主持过一项研究，其成员将基布兹受访者在资本主义—社会主义连续统一体中的自我定位与向以色列有代表性的犹太人口提出的相同问题的答案进行了比较，结果显示：55%的受访基布兹成员将自己定义为社会主义者，而一般样本为 25%；13%的基布兹成员将自己定义为资本主义者，而一般样本为 31%。② 造成这种喜忧参半的改革效果的原因主要有以下两点。

首先是先导性理念缺失。这种缺失体现在先导性发展理念与改革理念的缺失上。正如习近平总书记所说，发展理念是发展行动的先导，是管全局、管根本、管方向、管长远的东西，是发展思路、发展方向、发展着力点的集中体现。换言

---

① 刘铁柱 Liu Tiezhu，苑鹏 Yuan Peng，《以色列集体村社制度基布兹的“私有化”改革及其启示》[The “Privatization” Reform of Kibbutzim in the Israeli Collective Village System and Its Implications]，于《农业现代化研究》[Agricultural Modernization Research]，2021 第一期[2020, No. 1]，7。

② Menahem Rosner and Shlomo Getz, “Undergoing Change Recent Publications on the Israeli Kibbutz,” *International Sociology* 21.6 (2006): 810.

之,先导性理念是一种对现实与未来的连接,是现实分析基础上对未来的总规划与总布局。但是综观基布兹应对理念危机的改革以及 21 世纪的文化转向,它们都属于一种被动式的理念重塑:前者是面对危机被动做出的应对之举,后者则更多地发挥了一种对改变了的现实的解释功能。因此,当代基布兹被动式的理念重塑可以看作基布兹成员在断裂的传统与现实之间进行的一种连接尝试,也可以说是对现实环境的一种妥协。这种先导性理念与被动性理念的差异也造成了以色列基布兹社会主义实践在 20 世纪上半叶与 21 世纪所取得的成就有较大差异。从基布兹理念与基布兹发展的关系史来看,早期的基布兹理念是先导性的,它为基布兹的建立与发展提供了有力的思想与理论支持,并取得了举世瞩目的成绩。但是,进入 20 世纪 80 年代的危机期后,基布兹不得不进行经济改革,并且在改革的基础上被动地对传统理念进行了重塑。从其取得的效果来看,这种理念的重塑是失败的,今天基布兹的模式多元化已经成为既定事实。改革后的基布兹大致有三种模式,即集体主义基布兹(占总基布兹数量的 25%)、改革派基布兹(占总基布兹数量的 72%)和城市基布兹(占总基布兹数量的 3%)。大多数基布兹开始减少对其成员的"责任",并制定相应的策略来"削弱平等"、鼓励与制造差异等。如今,已经很难发现有某种或者某几种统一理念存在于所有的基布兹实践中,反倒是"个性化"成了基布兹的总体特性,甚至有些城市基布兹表现为城市居民仅仅在某种生态生活理念下组成的松散的联合体。

其次,基布兹的社会主义理念没有转化成系统性的社会主义理论,一种缺乏系统理论支撑的实践很难在政治、经济、文化等方面竞争日益激烈与多样的以色列国中脱颖而出。社会主义系统理论的缺乏将在未来很长一段时间成为以色列基布兹社会主义实现其最终目标的掣肘因素。21 世纪以来,有关基布兹社会主义理论的研究虽然屡屡提及本·勃洛霍夫(Ber Borokhov, 1881—1917 年)和马丁·布伯(Martin Buber,1878—1965 年)等人关于基布兹社会主义的思想和理论,但一直未能引起基布兹管理者和成员的共鸣。究其原因,首先,刚走出危机的基布兹尚处于被动性的文化和理论辩护阶段,对一种先导性的文化与理论的研究与建构还未进入其视野。另外,纵观基布兹的百年历史,基布兹内部一直有重实践、轻理论的传统。恩格斯评论德国、法国、英国等国家如何进入现代社会时说道,德国是通过"哲学革命",法国是通过"政治革命",而英国是通过实践。[①] 套用恩格斯的话可以说,以色列的基布兹是通过实践进入社会主义的,实践性是以色列基布兹社会主义最显著的特征。基布兹在筹建之初并没有相关的理论体

① 参见:《马克思恩格斯文集》[The Collected Works of Marx and Engels],第一卷[Volume 1],(北京[Beijing]:人民出版社[People's Publishing House],2009),87。

系。第一个基布兹就是由几名年轻的犹太青年于 1910 年在加利利沿岸建立的;从那时起,273 个基布兹(其中一半是在以色列建国之前)逐渐遍布全国,并在一定程度上确定了以色列国的边界。[①] 这些犹太青年怀揣着犹太复国主义和社会主义理想试图通过放弃私有财产、个人主义和"资产阶级"家庭单位来实现平等、自由和社会正义,并且自愿尝试完全平等的社区生活模式,从而直接投入基布兹社会主义社区建设。正是这种凸显的"实践性"映射出基布兹系统理论的缺乏,基布兹建立之前的社会主义复国主义理想从一开始就处于一种系统化或者半系统化的理念阶段,而基布兹在其 100 多年的发展历程中从未产生过一种真正意义上的系统性的社会主义理论。这种理论的缺乏是基布兹在面对 20 世纪 80 年代晚期开始的基布兹大危机时表现得力不从心的原因之一,同时也使得基布兹社会主义在 21 世纪的理念重塑过程中捉襟见肘。

参考文献

(一)中文参考文献

1. 林建:《资本主义中的"社会主义细胞"》,《科学社会主义》,2006 年第 5 期。

2. 傅有德主编:《犹太研究》第 15 辑,济南:山东大学出版社,2018 年。

3. 陈艳艳、薛丽:《以色列的基布兹社会主义实验》,《中国社会科学报》2018 年 1 月 23 日。

4. 黄福武:《现实中的神话——以色列基布兹现象浅析》,《当代世界社会主义问题》,2006 年第 3 期。

5. 王太文:《以色列基布兹: 乡村集体经济合作组织的极致演绎》,《浙江农业科学》,2020 年第 7 期。

6. 丛日云、马涛:《对以色列基布兹模式的历史考察及思考》,《当代世界与社会主义》,2020 年第 2 期。

7. 刘铁柱、苑鹏:《以色列集体村社制度基布兹的"私有化"改革及其启示》,《农业现代化研究》, 2021 年第 1 期。

8.《马克思恩格斯文集》,第一卷,北京:人民出版社,2009 年。

(二)外文参考文献

1. Martin Buber, *Paths in Utopia*, trans. by R. F. C. Hull, Boston: Beacon Press, 1958.

2. Stephen Charles Mott, *The Kibbutz's Adjustment to Industrialization and*

① 资料来源于以色列基布兹工业协会:http://www.kia.co.il/infoeng/kibbutz.htm。

Ideological Decline: *Alternatives for Economic Organization*, *The Journal of Religious Ethics* 19.1 (1991).

3. Constance Smith and Anne Freedman, *Voluntary Associations*: *Perspective on the Literature*, Harvard University Press, 1972.

4. Shlomo Lavi, *Four Years*, Mibifnim 17, 1925.

5. Shmuel Dayan, *Degania at Its Half Jubilee*, Tel Aviv: Stiebel, 1935.

6. Divid Leichman and Idit Paz, eds. *Kibbutz*: *An Alternative Lifestyle*. Ramat Efal: Yad Tabenkin, 1997.

7. Shimon Shur, "The Evolution of the Idea of Equality in the Kibbutz Movement," *Hakibbutz* 9-10 (1983/4).

8. Stanley Diamond, *Kibbutz and Shtetl*: *The History of an Idea*, Oxford University Press, 2017.

9. Michael Harris, "The Kibbutz: Uncovering the Utopian Dimension," *Utopian Studies*, 10.1 (1999).

11. Nir Tsuk, *The Rise and Fall of the Kibbutz*, University of Copenhagen, 2000.

12. Melford E. Spiro, "Utopia and Its Discontents: The Kibbutz and Its Historical Vicissitudes," *American Anthropologist* 106 (2004).

13. Michal Palgi and Shulamit Reinharz, eds. *One Hundred Years of Kibbutz Life*: *A Century of Crises and Reinvention*, London: Transaction Publishers, 2014.

14. Menahem Rosner and Shlomo Getz, "Undergoing Change Recent Publications on the Israeli Kibbutz," *International Sociology*, 21.6 (2006).

On the Ideas Crisis of Israeli Kibbutz Socialism and Its Modern Criticism

LI Yong, XUE Li

Abstract: Israel Kibbutz movement refers to the socialist movement that the Jewish immigrants established the individual collective farms one by one in Palestine since 1909. Kibbutzim are built on the educational system which adheres to the idea of common property, labor, egalitarianism, and communism. Therefore, it had made the remarkable achievements in the global scope. But since the mid-1980s, Kibbutzim were in crisis; and the core ideas for establishing Kibbutzim were challenged and attacked. To deal with the crisis, Kibbutz implement economic reform, and launched a reform to address the idea crisis by rebuilding the traditional concept as the core at the same time. But this rebuilt is a passive one, it is an attempt to connect and compromise the fractured reality and tradition essentially, rather than making a plan for the future development according to the current position. The results so far have been mixed in terms of what this rebuilt has accomplished.

Key Words: Kibbutz, Public Idea, Labor Idea, Modern Criticism